Curriculum and Methods of Teaching

Curriculum and Methods of Teaching

[Second Revised Edition]

H.S. Srivastava
Former, Dean NCERT, New Delhi
Head Research, Development & Consultancy Division, CISCE, New Delhi
Adviser, International Cell, CBSE, Delhi

SHIPRA

(2014, 2010 Revised Ed., First Published 2006)

Rs. 1500; US$ 30

ISBN: 978-81-7541-556-0

2022 Impression

Curriculum and Methods of Teaching

Published by:
SHIPRA PUBLICATIONS
LG 18-19, Pankaj Central Market
I.P. Ext., Patparganj, Delhi 110092, India
+91 11 2223 5152/6152; 96500 28065
info@shiprapublication.com
www.shiprapublication.com

Perface to the Second Edition

It is the aspiration of every author to see his book appreciated and accepted. Curriculum and Methods of Teaching has most certainly yielded such a gratification. I therefore cannot but be grateful to the teacher trainees, practising teachers, teacher educators and educational administrators for their patronage to this humble work.

Since it was the first published in 2006 valuable suggestion for further improving the book have been received. These have been duly incorporated in this second edition by adding new chapters and the reorganization and reinforcement of the content of some of the existing chapters. This, it is hoped will further enhance the value of the book to the readers.

The most encouraging thing about the book has been a demand for its Hindi translation. I am happy that the publishers have promptly and positively responded to this felt need by roping in a scholar of the eminence of Dr. M.G. Chaturvedi for accomplishing this task and bringing out a Hindi version as well, in 2009.

It is my confident hope, that the book in its new "avatar" will better serve the needs of the users and the cause of education as such.

March 20, 2010

Prof. H. S. Srivastava
The Humanity House
143, Dayanand Vihar
Delhi-110092

Preface to the First Edition

The book 'Curriculum and Methods of Teaching' marks a valuable addition to pedagogic literature. It is unique in so far as it supplements theories with their practical applications, presents difficult concepts in simple language and provides positive directions for their use in day-to-day work.

The book stands divided into three sections: Section I covers the Fundamental Themes in Curriculum and Evaluation, Section II deals with Conventional and Unconventional Methodologies for Teaching and Learning and Section III with Methods of Teaching Specific Subjects.

The comprehensive coverage of the book and the intensive treatment of themes, makes it a textbook for the students of education, a treasure trove for the pedagogues and a ready reckoner for the schools and practising teachers.

A cursory look at the table of contents will easily reveal that the book has not missed any theme of importance in the area of curriculum — objectives, content material, methodology, aids and evaluation.

All this makes the author confident about the immediate relevance and functional utility of the book he is placing in the hands of all those with a stake in education and growth of children.

The references easily give out the wide range of publications consulted for enriching the book.

Suggestions for further improving the book are earnestly solicited and will be thankfully received.

The Humanity House
143, Dayanad Vihar
Delhi–110 092.

Dr. H.S. Srivastava

Contents

PART II
SOME CONVENTIONAL TECHNIQUES OF TEACHING

PART III
SOME UNCONVENTIONAL TECHNIQUES OF TEACHING

PART V
TEACHING OF SPECIFIC SUBJECTS

PART I

FOUNDATIONS OF TEACHING AND LEARNING

1

Education for the Twenty First Century
(*UNESCO Report—Learning the Treasure Within*)

No educational document can and should in the present century start without a reference of the UNESCO report 'Learning the Treasure Within'—Education in the 21st Century. The pointers and recommendation of its different chapters are, therefore, presented as an introduction to the present book.

1.1 From the Local Community to A World Society

Worldwide interdependence and globalisation are major forces in contemporary life. They are already at work and will leave a deep imprint on the twenty-first century. They require that overall consideration, extending well beyond the fields of education and culture, be given, as of now, to the roles and structures of international organisations.

The major danger is that of a gulf opening up between a *minority* of people who are capable of finding their way successfully about this new world that is coming into being and the *majority* who feel that they are at the mercy of events and have no say in the future of society, with the dangers that entails a setback to democracy and widespread revolt.

We must be guided by the Utopian aim of steering the world towards greater mutual understanding, a greater sense of responsibility and greater solidarity, through acceptance of our spiritual and cultural differences. Education, by providing access to knowledge for all, has precisely this universal task of helping people to understand the world and to understand others.

1.2 From Social Cohesion to Democratic Participation

Education policy must be sufficiency diversified and must be so designed as not to become another contributory cause of social exclusion.

The socialisation of individuals must not conflict with personal development. It is, therefore, necessary to work towards a system that strives to combine the virtues of integration with respect for individual rights.

Education cannot, on its own, solve the problems raised by the severance (when this happens) of social ties. It can, however, be expected to help to foster the desire to live together, which is a basic component of social cohesion and national identity.

Schools cannot succeed in this task unless they make their own contribution to the advancement and integration of minority groups by mobilising those concerned while showing due regard for their personality.

Democracy appears to be progressing taking different forms and passing through stages that fit the situation in each country. Its vitality is nevertheless constantly threatened. Education for conscious and active citizenship must begin at school.

Democratic participation is, so to say, a matter of good citizenship, but it can be encouraged or stimulated by instruction and practices adapted to a media and information society. What is needed is to provide reference points and aids to interpretation, so as to strengthen the faculties of understanding and judgement.

It is the role of education to provide children and adults with the cultural background that will enable them, as far as possible, to make sense of the changes taking place. This presupposes that they are capable of sorting out the mass of information so as to interpret it more effectively and place events in a historical perspective.

1.3 From Economic Growth to Human Development

Further reflection on the theme of a new model of development, showing more respect for nature and the structuring of people's time.

A future-oriented study of the place of work in society, taking into account the effects of technical progress and change on both private and community life.

A fuller assessment of development, taking all its aspects into account, along the lines of the work done by UNDP.

The establishment of new links between educational policy and development policy, with a view to strengthening the bases of knowledge and skills in the countries concerned: encouragement of initiative, teamwork, realistic synergies taking local resources into account, self-employment and the spirit of enterprise.

The necessary improvement and general availability of basic education (importance of the Jomtien Declaration).

1.4 The Four Cornerstones of Education

Education throughout life is based on four pillars: *learning to know, learning to do, learning to live together and learning to be.*

Learning to know, by combining a sufficiently broad general knowledge with the opportunity to work in depth on a small number of subjects. This also means learning to learn, so as to benefit from the opportunities education provides throughout life.

Learning to do, in order to acquire not only an occupational skill but also, more broadly, the competence to deal with many situations and work in teams. It also means learning to do in the context of young peoples various social and work experiences which may be informal, as a result of the local or national context, or formal, involving courses, alternating study and work.

Learning to live together, by developing an understanding of other people an appreciation of other people and an appreciation of interdependence—carrying out joint projects and learning to manage conflicts—in a spirit of respect for the values of pluralism, mutual understanding and peace.

Learning to be, so as to better develop one's personality and be able to act with ever greater autonomy, judgement and personal responsibility. In that connection, education must not disregard any aspect of a person's potential: memory, reasoning, aesthetic sense, physical capacities and communication skills.

Formal education systems tend to emphasise the acquisition of knowledge to the detriment of other types of learning: but it is vital now to conceive education in a more encompassing fashion. Such a vision should inform and guide future educational reforms and policy, in relation both to contents and to methods.

1.5 Life-long Education

The concept of learning throughout life is the key that gives access to the twenty-first century. It goes beyond the traditional distinction between initial and continuing education. It links up with another concept often put forward, that of the learning society, in which everything affords an opportunity of learning and fulfilling one's potential.

In its new guise, continuing education is seen as going far beyond what is already practiced, particularly in the developed countries, i.e., upgrading, with refresher training, retraining and conversion or promotion courses for adults. It should open up opportunities for learning for all, for many different purposes—offering them a second or third chance, satisfying their desire for knowledge and beauty or their desire to surpass themselves or making it possible to broaden and deepen strictly vocational forms of training, including practical training.

In short, 'learning throughout life' must take advantage of all the opportunities offered by society.

1.6 From Basic Education to University

A requirement valid for all countries, albeit in various forms and with different types of content—the strengthening of basic education: hence the emphasis on primary education and its traditional basic programmes—reading, writing, arithmetic—but also on the ability to express oneself in a language that lends itself to dialogue and understanding.

The need, which will be still greater tomorrow, for receptivity to science and the world of science, which opens the door to the twenty-first century and its scientific and technological upheavals.

The adaptation of basic education to specific contexts, the most deprived countries as well as the most deprived sections of the population, starting out with the facts of everyday life, which affords opportunities for understanding natural phenomena and for different forms of socialisation.

The pressing needs of literacy work and basic education for adults are to be kept in mind.

In all cases, emphasis is to be placed on pupil-teacher relations, since the most advanced technologies can be no more than a back-up to the relationship (transmission, dialogue and confrontation) between teacher and pupil.

Secondary education must be rethought in this general context learning throughout life. The key principle is to arrange for a variety to individual paths through schooling, without ever closing the door on the possibility of a subsequent return to the education system.

Debates on selection and guidance would be greatly clarified if this principle were fully applied. Everyone would then feel that whatever the choices made or the courses followed in adolescence, no doors would ever be closed in the future, including the doors of the school itself. Equality of opportunity would then mean what it says.

Universities should be central to the higher level of the system, even if, as is the case in many countries, there are other, non-university establishments of higher education.

Universities would have vested in them four key functions:

1. To prepare students for research and teaching.
2. To provide highly specialised training courses adapted to the needs of economic and social life.
3. To be open to all, so as to cater for the many aspects of lifelong education in the widest sense.
4. International co-operation.

The universities should also be able to speak out on ethical and social problems as entirely independent and fully responsible institutions exercising a kind of intellectual authority that society needs to help it to reflect, understand and act.

The diversity of secondary schooling and the possibilities afforded by universitics should provide a valid answer to the challenges of mass education by dispelling the obsession with a one-and-only educational 'king's highway'. Combined with more widespread application of the practice of alternating periods of education with periods of work, these approaches can provide effective tools for fighting against school failure. The extension of learning throughout life will require consideration of new procedures for certification that take account of acquired competencies.

1.7 Teachers in Search of New Perspectives

- While the psychological and material situation of teachers differs greatly from country to country, an upgrading of their status is essential if 'learning throughout life' is to fulfil the central function assigned to it by the Commission in the advancement of our societies and the strengthening of mutual understanding among peoples. Their position should be recognised by society and they should be given the necessary authority and suitable resources.
- The concept of learning throughout life leads straight on to that of a learning society, a society that offers many and varied opportunities of learning, both at school and in economic, social and cultural life, which need more collaboration and partnerships, with families, industry and business, voluntary associations, people in active cultural life, etc.
- Teachers are also concerned about the imperative requirement to update knowledge and skills. Their professional lives should be so arranged as to accommodate the opportunity, or even the obligation, for them to become more proficient in their art and to benefit from periods of experience in various spheres of economic, social and cultural life. Such possibilities are usually provided for in the many forms of study-leave or sabbatical leave. Those formulae, suitably adapted, should be extended to all teachers.
- Even though teaching is essentially a solitary activity, in the sense that each teacher is faced with his or her own responsibilities and professional duties, teamwork is essential, particularly at the secondary level, in order to improve the quality of education and adapt it more closely to the special characteristics of classes or groups of pupils.
- The commission stresses the importance of exchanges of teachers and partnerships between institutions in different countries. As is confirmed by current activities, such exchanges and partnerships provide an essential added value not only for the quality of education but also for a greater receptivity to other cultures, civilisations and experiences.
- All these lines of emphasis should be the subject of a dialogue, or even contracts, with teacher's organisations which go beyond the purely

corporatist nature of such forms of collaboration: over and above their aims of defending the moral and material interests of their members, teacher's organisations have built up a fund of experience which they are willing to make available to policy-makers.

1.8 Choices for Education: The Political Factor

Choosing a type of education means choosing a type of society. In all countries, such choices call for extensive public debate, based on an accurate evaluation of education systems. The Commission invites the political authorities to encourage such debate, in order to reach a democratic consensus, this being the best route to success for educational reform strategies.

The Commission advocates the implementation of measures for involving the different persons and institutions active in society in educational decision-making: administrative decentralisation and the autonomy of educational establishments are conducive in most cases, it believes, to the development and generation of innovation.

In view of the foregoing, the Commission wishes to reaffirm the role of the political authority, which has the duty clearly to define options and ensure overall regulation, making the required adjustment: education is a community asset which cannot be regulated by market forces alone.

The Commission nonetheless does not underrate the force of financial constraints and it advocates the bringing into operation of public/private partnership. In developing countries, the public funding of basic education remains a priority, but the choices made must not imperil the coherence of the system as a whole, nor lead to other levels of education being sacrificed.

It is essential that funding structures be reviewed in the light of the principle that learning should continue throughout individual's lives. The Commission hence feels that the proposed study-time entitlement, as briefly outlined in the report, deserves to be discussed and explored.

The progress of the new information and communication technologies should give rise to a general deliberation on access to knowledge in the world of tomorrow. The Commission recommends:

- the diversification and improvement of distance education through the use of the new technologies;
- greater use of those technologies in adult education and especially in the in-service training of teachers;
- the strengthening of developing countries infrastructures and capabilities in this field and the dissemination of such technologies throughout society; these are in any case prerequisites to their use in formal education systems; and
- the launching of programmes for the dissemination of the new technologies under the auspices of UNESCO.

2

The Perspectives of Indian Education

2.1 The Change

In education no barriers have to be broken but only its advancing horizon are to be chased. In this perspective one comes across the situation where 'change' has remained the only 'constant'. But, when one thinks of the realities of this phenomenon of change one usually stops just at changes only in the fields of Science and Technology. We do not stretch our thinking and imagination to other fields to discover that even HISTORY has changed. With the recent excavations in Haryana and Kutch even our ancient civilisations have got pre-dated. GEOGRAPHY too has undergone a change with so many new countries having come into existence, POLITICS has witnessed another phenomenon of change with so many erstwhile colonies and dictatorships having become democracies. Such a dawn of democracy has also in many cases brought about corruption and criminalisation in its wake in the initial stages of their emergence in the new garb. SOCIOLOGY too has undergone change with rural communities having got dismembered with onslaughts of urbanisation and migration. At the micro-level too the joint families have yielded place to nuclear families breaking away from the age-old bonds and affiliations with the cultural heritages. ECONOMICS too has changed with materialistic pragmatism replacing philosophic idealism, globalisation taking over protective consumerism, trampling the valued concept of thrift where even students have come to be treated as consumers and education a business enterprise and so on.

So, it could be safely concluded that knowledge in all fields is growing fast but to our astonishment is also becoming redundant faster. Acquisition of knowledge, therefore, has become a risky dissolvable and drainable temporary asset which cannot any more be depended upon as ones wealth. Educational ventures in this context have but aim at not being content with just imparting '*temporary knowledge*' but work towards imbibing in the students *permanent multi-use competencies*' which are abiding assets, usable in different situations.

2.2 The Changed Purposes of Education

Education for education sake, is no more an acceptable proposition. It has to be purposeful and demonstrate usefulness not just to the individual and the community but to the nation and the world at large. In the context of the present situation it has to be:

- a *literacy enhancement programme* for attaining cent per cent literacy in course of time with particular reference to girls.
- a *poverty eradication programme* through the imparting vocational skills for making a living.
- an *employment creation programme* by opening up professional possibilities in unexplored fields and avenues for self-employment.
- a *wealth generation programme* which will be a natural off-shoot of the above ventures, through economic elevation of individuals and communities in both rural and urban areas.
- a *health promotion programme* through awareness about keeping healthy and thus improving efficiency in both quantitative and qualitative terms. Reduction in child and female mortality and increasing functional longevity of all.
- a *social regeneration programme* through participative and cooperative initiatives.
- a *cultural enrichment programme* for taking advantage of our ancient wisdom and heritage.
- a *religious enlightenment programme* incorporating and advocating a concept of religion as a flowing stream and not a stagnant pool incorporating values of peaceful co-existence through tolerance and non-violence preached by all of them.
- a *human emancipation programme* heralding freedom from conservatism rigidity, and dispelling blind-faith, superstition and narrow-mindedness.
- a *visionary futuristic programme* offering opportunities for inculcation of abilities and proficiencies for meeting the challenges of the future with confidence and success. Entrepreneurship will be an essential component in this regard.

Education must aim at training individuals to be innovative, capable of evolving, adapting to the rapidly changing world and assimilating change.

Education for the future too deserves a more elaborate analysis. Future as we perceive it, is no more just *unknown* but has become *unpredictable.* Yesterday's education has no more remained relevant today and today's education will become even more irrelevant tomorrow. With reference to this phenomenon *one time education has remained completely inadequate for life-time employability.* Continuous upgradation of skills has therefore become imperative, further reinforcing the concept of '*life-long-education*'. Thus the old concept of the life-cycle of individuals as consisting of education-work-retirement', has become redundant, having been replaced by that of education-work and no retirement. *Education thus has to have only commas and no full-stops*.

In the words of Dr. R.H. Dave, "*Education in the life-long perspective, is a process of human transformation, human enlightenment and human empowerment for the attainment of a better and a higher quality of life.*"

Objectives, aims and goals have also to be conceived stated and defined comprehensively yet specifically in all the three domain of development. Cognitive (thinking), Affective (feeling) and Psycho-motor (doing). Focus of attention here, has to be not just on acquisition knowledge but application of knowledge in life situations. In addition, aesthetic sense, values and reflection about what is acquired, have also to be incorporated in the programmes of education, which would need to cover the development of total personality of the students in both scholastic and non co-scholastic aspects for becoming enabling, empowering and enriching.

2.3 New Directions in the Content of Education

A shift of focus in regard to the content of education is also be called for and this will have to imply change in spirit and not just in name like the overnight change of name of Primary Schools into Basic Education Schools, just by the change of the sign boards.

Collaboration with business and industry in the development and transaction of educational content than just lip-serviced *consultation* too is needed. This will be necessary for developing industry and business related skills and thus strengthening the relationship of education with the clients/ consumers of our products (the educated work-force).

A shift from the concept of *Syllabus* to that of *curriculum,* will also be called for, by moving beyond course content to the enunciation of objectives, of course content, of methodology of teaching and learning, of aids to instruction and of evaluation.

Change in the enunciation of content with a *disciplinary* approach to an *integrated* one, will also have to be a part of this process.

From discipline-based *fundamentals to applications* of the basic elements of content will also be needed. Thus from the teaching of say the history of Physics (Newton did this Einstine did this) to Applications of Physics will need to be focussed upon.

A shift from only vertical treatment of subjects (Like Babar, Humayun, Akbar, Jahangir…..) to both vertical and horizontal treatment of content (like who ruled France when Shajahan ruled India) will be called for. Japan it may be mentioned has introduced a new subject '*Contemporary Society*' in its new curriculum in this context.

A move from *abstract to concrete* entities and examples of realities will also be necessary for consolidating the elements of content in the minds of students.

In addition to the *immediate* use of the contents in life, to their *long range implications* will also be needed to be incorporated in the courses of study for inculcating in students not just insight but also foresight in their decision-making abilities.

Besides facts, generalisations in terms of *basic understandings* would also need to be incorporated as part of content. This would imply moving beyond the statements like Aryan civilisation flourished on the banks of the rivers of the Indo gangetic plain. Persian Civilisation on the banks of Euphrates and Tigris, Egyptian civilisation of the banks of the Nile. Basic understanding based on these facts would be "Early civilisations grew in river beds."

The fast growing changes in content would also need to be taken care of through the incorporation of the concepts of *Frontline Curriculum,* where the major part of the prescribed contents (say 90%) may be changed after four or five years, but a 10% part of it, listing new developments called the Frontline Curriculum may change say every two years.

There has to be yet another change in content. Instead of defining parameters an attempt should be made to explain them so as to bring them within the effortless comprehension of the students. Pictorial or diagrammatic or graphical representations prove to be valuable instruments in such a consolidation of content. This not just leads to self-growth but influences the *total overall perceptions and growth* as such.

2.4 Curriculum Transaction

With different institutions following the same prescribed courses, the marked differences in the quality of education imparted by them occur mainly because of methodology of teaching and learning they advocate and practice. Transaction of curriculum thus becomes one of the key foundations of education chiefly responsible for the degree of realisation of the goals set.

The first thing that needs to be mentioned in this regard is the need for an immediate shift form the traditional *tongue and ear method* to a variety of unconventional approaches of teaching and learning. (An independent chapter is being devoted to these methods in the book.)

With the enormous advances in the different subjects of study the prescribed content too has swelled up. Thus an individual learner finds it difficult to cover it. *Group and participatory learning practices* have, therefore to be encouraged and adopted. Apart from this, group and participatory learning becomes more illuminative, leading to better internalisation. It also generates team spirit which turns out to be a great asset in the live realities of professional situations.

Learning only from the *print media to internet surfacing,* CD-ROMs etc. have also to be fully explored for enrichment of learning. Approaches to effective utilisation of these sources has also to be imparted to the students.

This will also make the teacher conversant with the new techniques and enable him to assume his real role of being a *guide rather than just a dispenser of information.* With knowledge growing fast the teacher too will need to become a *co-learner with the students* particularly so in regard to the content of the Frontline Curriculum.

Students will thus naturally become '*Subjects*' of education and not remain only '*objects*' of education. They will *not only learn but learn how to learn* and finally voluntarily assume the responsibility of moving ahead in their crusade through *self-directed learning* and later to the needed initiatives in this regard.

The locale of teaching and learning will in this situation move *beyond the classroom* to laboratories, environmental observations, different life and work settings. With these situations emerging as the new locations of learning there will naturally be another great transformation. The students would thus be better prepared to meet and tackle live *natural challenges and instead of testing imaginary concocted hypothesis (and these too) in simulated situations.* Such experimental learning will find immediate assimilation uprooting the need for memorisation.

Field Surveys and library research will also, in this context, become everyday pursuits of learning, when things like Engel's law of consumption will not need to be memorised for reproduction at examination time, but a self-deduced conclusion which would be impossible to forget.

These new approaches will, quite naturally and not just incidentally improve the *pace* of learning, the *quality* of learning beside enhancing the *quantum of learning.*

Interactions of different kinds, with the teachers, with peers and with ones own self, will also then take place with increased levels of motivation and concentration as one moves from one stage to another.

The *marriage of technology and pedagogy* will also enable transversing longer distances and digging deeper into the treasures of knowledge through all possible delivery modes, be they instructor led, or of distance learning or of on-line learning or learning through CD-ROMs.

Curriculum Transaction will also need to acquire and demonstrate flexibility for being adaptable the needs of different times, different content, different individuals and become relevant and accountable to all settings. The *bright children* will only need to be introduced to the learning material and learning processes and they would then move on, on their own. The *mediocre children* with initial exposure will also need reinforcement. The *weaker students* would need repeated teaching and repeated reinforcement for consolidation and internalisation of learning.

2.5 Learning Materials

The emergent realities will as mentioned earlier expect and require the learning materials to *move beyond the print media to technological aids* (the CD-ROMs the internet etc.). These could be used both for teacher-directed learning as also self-learning. Both teachers and students would, therefore, need to acquire the needed proficiencies for effectively and profitably using them. In this context *they would all, not just need to be computer literate but computer savvy.*

2.6 Evaluation of Student Growth

With education as a process of human enablement, human empowerment and human enlightenment, growth among students, will also be recorded in different facets of personality. Thus evaluation would need to:

- be a process spread over the total span of education.
- consist of exercises related to the collection of evidences about the kind and degree of growth occurring among the students in the context of the inputs provided.
- be designed to cover all the three domains of development Cognitive, Affective and Psycho-motor—and related growth in both scholastic and non co-scholastic areas.
- press into service a variety of conventional and unconventional techniques and tools of evaluation.
- be in both qualitative and quantitative terms.
- not just assess growth but help to improve its pace and quantum.
- result in meaningful declaration of results and become useful in taking a variety of decisions about individuals and/or groups evaluated.

The above descriptive definition of evaluation assumes greater importance particularly because customarily *we teach what we test and not so much test what we teach.*

With shortcomings in our external/public examinations and with institution-based evaluation too becoming their replica, only academic aspects by-and-large come under the purview of our testing programmes with almost complete neglect of the non-academic areas, which are considered to be more important for success in life.

The exigencies and emergencies, the inherent defects and operational shortfalls go to greatly erode the sanctity and credibility of our external examinations. Furthermore the irreversibility of the results of such unfair examinations, do call for the emancipation of our helpless students from them.

Selective teaching and selective learning too have become common features, because of the short-falls in our traditional question papers which had few questions to be attempted out of those given and provided options.

In these traditional external/public examinations the inter-examiner variability, variations in the ranges of scores and patterns of their distribution from subject to subject, year to year and examination to examination led to the non-equivalence of a particular score in different subjects. The use of sacrosanct cut-off scores (33%, 45%, 60% and 75%) for classifying the levels of achievement of students in all subjects in all examinations and in all years thus became atrociously unscientific propositions. It has been to overcome these shortcomings that the National Policy on Education 1986/92 has suggested the use of *grades in place of marks.* When grades are used, the cut-off scores for grades are *determined and declared subject-wise for each examination* and in relative grading on the basis of the obtained scores of the students and not in advance of examination for being used perpetually. The concept of Pass and Fail is also alien and not admissible when grades are awarded. The aggregation of these non-equivalent entities (marks) for obtaining an overall indicator of performance in terms of divisions and distinctions is *like adding temperature (in celcius), humidity (in percentage) and rainfall (in centimetres) for obtaining an index of weather.*

The prescription of year long courses in different subjects, and with all subjects required to be cleared simultaneously in a single attempt for obtaining a certificate of qualification, are provisions which have all along been the cause of undue pressure and stress on the students. It has been to eliminate this that the NPE has also recommended a change over to the *semester system,* where credits could be earned and accumulated by clearing examinations in parts, finally encashing them into certificates of qualification when the requisite number of credits have been earned.

The traditional examinations also mainly attempted to test *memorisation* and not so much other higher abilities. *Certificates of qualification* for having cleared the examination did not also effectively assess and testify to the possession of specific competencies by the students. They were, therefore, wallets without any money in them.

Yet another thing which needs a special mention is that with a perpetually used 33% score in all the prescribed subjects as the qualifying level, the all India pass percentage of class X examinations is around 50%. Such a dubbing as failure is disqualification for entering a course of higher education or a job for which these are eligibility examinations. Does that therefore mean that this half of the total number of candidates who are declared as failure are good for nothing. Even otherwise the faith in the results of external examination is continuously on the ebb with employers and institution of higher education instituting their own selection tests. The institution of external examination by itself displays a mistrust of the teacher who teaches. What is really required is the introduction of Continuous and Comprehensive School-based Evaluation with an independent certificate issued by the school covering both scholastic and non co-scholastic aspects of pupil growth *as a supplement to the certificate of external* examinations.

Meaningful certification of abilities, proficiencies, achievements, skills etc. is another important aspect to be realised. Thus instead of being a certificate of having crossed the minimum required level of attainment, the examinations should certify the possession of specific competencies by the concerned students.

2.7 Globalisation of Indian Education

The education ventures of our country in their aspiration of reaching out to the skies should not get their feet uprooted from the soil. We must appreciate that *everything that is western is not essentially modern.* Our conceptual starting point in India is *idealistic* whereas that of the west is *realistic* from beginning to the end. We conceive things idealistically and practice realistically. The west aims mainly at *physical fulfilment. Spiritual fulfilment* too is one of the main targets of Indian Education beside other things.

Indians unlike the west do not discard and reject the past, they assimilate. If the west explores life the orientalists celebrate it.

These are things, which our education should also take into consideration for enabling us to live our lives nationally and think globally.

It is with the above in mind that we should proceed towards globalisation appreciating and releasing that :

- There is no escape from globalisation now.
- Globalisation has to be perceived as a holistic concept and not just a truncated one focussing on economic issues alone.
- Globalisation ventures have so far touched only macro-economics and not other facets of life and that the road map for its percolation on to the micro-level has yet to be charted.
- Globalisation has to be perceived as a reciprocative, concept involving give and take and should not be taken only as a one way traffic under any conditions.
- Globalisation of Indian education presents both prospects and dangers. The pros and cons of the issues and their implications, therefore, need to be critically examined for evolving an Indian point of view.
- India should not succumb to pressures and formally guard against onslaughts on the soul of Indian culture, in the name of liberalisation and globalisation.
- Regulations for negotiating globalisation deals in education so arrived at, need to be strictly enforced for saving the country from foreign

educational invasions imbued with commercialisation with a hidden agenda of economic exploitation.

2.8 Let Us Continue To Be Givers

Althrough the history of civilisations, India has all along been contributing to growth and progress of the world we live in. We have given to the world.

- the concept of *zero* which has revolutionised mathematics.
- the concept of *decimals* which has helped in re-inventing calculation.
- the concept of the *wheel* which became the basis of Industrial Revolution in Europe.
- the *numerals* which are the basic foundations of life and living.

Let us continue this process by further expanding such an export presently in areas like information technology and aspire to become world leaders in as many fields as possible, for which we have an inherent capacity and potential.

Our strengths and export oriented initiatives are not just ancient relies but a modern reality. We are indisputably accepted as the second largest supplier of technical manpower in the world and are also exporting it. The expertise we possess is largely an outcome of our indigenous education.

However we have not been good salesmen because of not being outgoing. Let us now realise that *modesty is no doubt a great virtue but the introvert behaviour which often generates, invariably proves to self-defeating, as it invariably inhibits even due publicity to our strengths and achievements.*

In this context while educational philosophies and ideologies which originated in other countries, have been extensively researched upon and documented (through modern methods) those that evolved in our own country have comparatively remained less noticed by the worlds community.

Let us come out of this shell with sturdier determination, even though important breakthroughs in this regard have already occurred.

Some safeguards too are necessary. We cannot afford to glorify the accomplishments made in the past and even the present, without a futuristic perspective for making further advances by empowering ourselves for successfully competing with other advanced nations in all fields, through an assimilation of international developments. This, however, should not be done without critically analysing these for their compatibility with our culture and needs.

In this context, it will also be necessary to first establish a balanced alignment between our national goals and educational aims which is being attempted hereunder in a broad manner.

2.9 National Goals

In regard to India the National Goals derived mainly from our constitution and the cultural heritage could be listed broadly as under:

- Promotion of the principles of democracy.
- Respect for the individual.

- Equality of opportunity for all regardless of race, sex, language and religion and in all other aspects.
- Respect for the Constitution and the law.
- National integrity, unity and security.
- Social and economic justice, and development.
- Preservation and promotion of the diverse cultures of the country and the world.
- International co-operation and peace on the basis of tolerance, reciprocity, mutual respect and trust.
- Support to UN and other international bodies and contribution to their activities for international understanding and peace.

2.10 Aims of Education

In the context of the above National Goals, the Aims of Indian Education could be spelt out as under :

- To develop a human person with desirable abilities, proficiencies, attitudes, values and qualities of self-confidence and creativity.
- To develop culturally conscious individuals with pride in the country and a desire to contribute to its development as good citizens of the country and the world.
- To kindle a desire for preserving and promoting democracy, secularism, unity, social justice and ethics with accountability in pursuing life situations.
- To prepare for entering the world of work easily and effectively through the development of appropriate, flexible, adaptable and multi-use competencies and a requisite mind set (This aim is best actualised by developing and transaction of courses of study not just in consultation but involvement of business, industry and the larger job market).
- To develop sound physical health and fitness among students for undertaking physical activities, demanding dexterity, diligence and hardwork.
- To develop the innate abilities, talents and potentials to the optimum level and to further enrich the same through appropriate inputs.
- To acquire the ability of critical thinking, problem-solving, decision making and of squarely facing unforeseen situations, while pursuing education or at the work places.
- To develop abilities for meeting the social, cultural, economic, technological needs and aspirations of the country through an appropriate design of the curriculum and its transaction.
- To develop a sense of international brotherhood, through an understanding of contemporary society in different parts of the world and mutual gestures of goodwill.

3

The Theory and Principles of Learning

3.1 A Macro Overview

Teaching becomes successful only when learning takes place. It is, therefore, necessary for teachers to be conversant with the manner in which learning comes to occur.

As learning is the undisputed goal of teaching, it is desirable to understand the phenomenon of learning—the factors that accelerate it and those that retard it, the conditions which make it easy and those that put road blacks, in its way, the situations which promote its success and those that don't.

Education is supposed to create:

— enablement
— empowerment and
— enrichment

and learning for inculcation of competencies is the most important means for attaining these goals through the modification it injects in the individuals, which result in enhancement of his capacities as reflected through his behaviour.

Three main types of interactions take place in schools as a part of the teaching-learning process.

Teacher-Learner Interaction where the teacher normally plays a dominant role and the student usually a passive one. In these situations *the concentration of students is minimal.*

Learner – Learner Interaction, where the students work in situations of participatory learning or group work or project work. In these situations *the level of concentration rises/increases.*

Self-Self interaction or self-learning or auto-instruction which marks the beginning of self-directed learning, where the challenges increase and *the level of concentration is the highest.*

It, therefore, becomes an important function or responsibility of the teachers to make the students independent of him by making them the '*subjects*' rather than '*objects*' of education.

Technology too has come to play an important role in the teaching learning process. Technological aids, working models, video films are now being increasingly used, not just for augmenting knowledge but more so for providing insight into varied facts and phenomenon of the environment. *The television has added a new curriculum, on the educational scene, as an important supplement to the curriculum of the home, of the immediate environment, of the peer group and that of the school. The internet is the new source of enrichment curriculum.* It has, however, to be simultaneously appreciated that *technology can only at best be an enabler and not the answer.* It can never replace the teacher though it can surely provide valuable reinforcements to his plans and designed programmes of instruction. Technology has surely to be adjusted and adapted to the maturity level of the students and the curriculum they are learning from. The technological resources have also to take care of the pre-requisites *of availability* and *accessibility.* Technological aids because of their versatile and universal applications have but to admit adaptation, as they can be used at any time, at any place and by any individual. These aids to instruction, therefore, have to be relevant, efficient and utilised with accountability.

The delivery modes in education have of late undergone a dramatic change and these changes have but to be taken cognisance of, for being relevant to the environmental transformations and transactions. The methodologies pressed into service, therefore, have to cater to these demands and be open to other changes that may get ushered in, in course of time. The main of these according to present day demands are:

- Instructor-led Learning
- Distance learning
- Learning through CD-ROMs/DISCS
- On line self-learning

The extensions and diversifications of techniques have not just become desirable but necessary, as education cannot survive in its present form and students have to take over the responsibility of learning from the teachers. In this context it will be *undesirable to take students as customers and consumers of education by converting the philanthropic activity that education should be into commercial and a business enterprise.* The concept of 'Education for All' has therefore to receive our focussed attention.

There has also to be a *marriage of technology and pedagogy* for self-growth for influencing the process of growth in its wider context.

Irrespective of the variations in the methods of teaching, some of the common purposes to be served and challenges to be met by them are those of:

- Modernisation
- Globalisation
- Liberalisation

- Technologisation
- Professionalisation and
- Indianisation

The last of these, is the most important because education cannot succeed if it is alien to the social and cultural ethos as also the heritage.

The salient aspects of theory and practice of learning have been vary explicity and yet briefly enunciated by *Rajamal P. Devadas* in her book Methods of Teaching Home Science which is given below:

"How does Learning take place? What are the conditions which favour learning? Learning is change or modification that occurs in performance as a result of training and experience, (*McConnell*). Learning in school means, modifying or changing the behaviour of the pupils, in terms of achieving the goals. It is the process by which the pupil profits from past experience. According to *Skinner* learning "is a process of progressive behaviour adaptation." When learning takes place, new technique or ability, based on past experience, develops.

Learning leads to establishing relationships between the stimuli and the responses, through a mental connection. Learning is thus implies connecting idea, events phenomenon and so on. Man is the greatest of all learners, because he is capable of forming many connections. Good teaching based on the psychology of learning and adequate preparation, leads to numerous connections born out of effective thinking, planning and execution. Understanding the factors involved in the learning process is, therefore, important for the teacher. Pupils respond to knowledge in different ways. When the teacher recognises the factors which favour learning, she will make the teaching-learning process efficient accelarated and economical leading to deeper learning, by discarding the wrong steps and establishing the correct connections.

3.2 Principles of Learning

Hullfish and Smith have expounded five principles of learning. According to these authors, learning is:

1. Motivated when the learner has some stake in the activity.
2. Geared to the learner's level and compatible with his physical and intellectual ability.
3. Patterned when the learner can see meaningful relationships between the activity and the goal.
4. Evaluated when the learner has some way of knowing the progress he is making, and
5. Integrated with personal and social development, when the learner experiences satisfactory growth and adjustments.

3.3 Motivation in Learning

Motivation is the most powerful director of learning. In learning and living motivation is indispensable for success. Achievement in learning depends largely on how much the pupil really wants to study and succeed and how far he is willing to put forth the cost in terms of human effort and energy to reach the goal.

Teachers use many approaches for motivating children to learn. *Compulsion, coercion, tempting with reward or praise and rousing their interest and eagerness to acquire knowledge are some of the common methods used.* Wherever all-round development of character and personality through voluntary self-activities, self-direction and self-expression are emphasised coercion and tempting will have no place. Pupils learn and develop best when they exert their utmost, when they energise their responses and behaviour and when they have dynamic relationship with their environment.

Teachers must learn the *art of stimulating and sustaining pupils' interest in learning.* A high degree of motivation helps in impelling pupils into action and ensures their active participation in learning activities. Mere repetition does not lead to learning. The repetition must be purposive and active; it must enlist the involvement of the pupil. The teacher needs to direct the learning process through such a positive motivation.

Richardson has formulated the following principles linking teaching and learning.

Learning

1. results from the active involvement of the learner,
2. begins with the learner's present achievement,
3. increases its effectiveness with motivation,
4. occurs through various channels,
5. bases meanings of words and other symbols on experience,
6. takes place in the total organism in response to the total situation, and
7. varies with individual differences in respect of needs and abilities.

In *Thorndike's* view, the laws which operate in the learning process are those of *readiness, effect and exercise including frequency and recency.* If the pupil has been prepared to learn through meaningful suggestions, he is ready to learn. The *law of readiness* then operates. If an effort brings success, reward or satisfaction, it is likely to be repeated. If the size of the incentive or reward increases, the efficiency of learning may also increase, provided the motivation continues. This illustrates the *law of effect.* The speed of performance depends on the satisfaction-value of the reward. 'Adaptation', 'adjustment', 'regulative change' and similar terms describe successful learning, indicating effect. Repeated effort gathers strength making repetition easier. This is the *law of frequency*. The act that has been performed recently has an advantage of being easy to repeat. This is the *law of recency*. The laws of frequency and recency together constitute the *law of exercise*. However, as learning ability depends upon the stages of growth reached by the nervous and muscular systems, mere exercise or drill alone cannot effect learning.

3.4 Maturation and Learning

Maturity has an important bearing on the learning process, particularly the maturity reached by the central nervous system and the muscular system. As the organism matures, the innate potentialities unfold themselves. In the development and functioning of brain, adequate nutrition during pregnancy and early childhood plays a dominant role. The degree of maturation necessary for a particular training to be effective, is usually called 'learning readiness'.

Thyne points out four features of learning in terms of behavioural outcomes:

(1) In each learning situation the learner learns to do something. This is the feature of behaviour;
(2) Also previously he did something differently—hence there is change of behaviour;
(3) The change of behaviour occurs in a particular kind of situation and
(4) Finally the old and new behaviour do not merely happen in the situation—each is occasioned by, or is a response to it. To learn is to adopt a new response to a situation.

There are four requirements for learning to take place; cue, force, promptness and reinforcement. Cue means, "In any instance of learning, there must be a series of situations showing the 'cue' of that instance. The teacher has to ensure a series of situations containing the cue. For example giving the page numbers in the references assigned to the pupil. Behaviour has two aspects: form and time of beginning. The learner must make his response in terms of these two which constitute the situation, which must have '*force*' for learning to take place. The situation must make the learner react and elicit a response." In any instance of learning, the 'cue' must have 'force'. '*Promptness*' ensures that the response which the cue evokes has the specified form. In any instance of learning, a 'prompt' must appear in one or more of the successive situations. In the school, the 'prompt' is usually in the form of instruction form the teacher. '*Reinforcement*' implies that the specified form of 'response' must be tied to the 'cue'. Learning will occur only when all these four functions are fulfilled.

3.5 Conditioned Learning

Conditioning is a form of learning in which the capacity to elicit a response is transferred from one stimulus to another. Conditioning means the establishment of a connection between a response and a stimulus which may not have a known natural connection with it. Conditioning represents learning at a simple level. The principles of conditioning in learning were first established by *Pavlov*. He was conducing some experiments on dogs. Food is a natural stimulus to the salivary reflex. Pavlov demonstrated that the dog can be made to salivate to any stimulus associated with food, such as resonating a tuning fork. Since the secretion of saliva, which is a reflex action, resulted from the dog's response to the stimulus of the tuning fork, Pavlov designated such reflexes as 'Conditioned reflexes'.

3.6 Trial and Error

Clayton describes that as early as 1898, *Thorndike* published a theory of learning, based primarily upon animal experiments, such as the cat in a box. Later he expanded and developed this approach with applications to school situations. The unit of demonstrated or displayed behaviour was a relationship, an association or connection between sense impressions and impulses to action. Faced with a situation, the learner will engage in a number of responses eventuating in the one that 'solves' the problem. In repetitions of the situation, the incorrect responses will diminish and the correct response will become fixed. Learning, therefore, is a trial and error process. In the initial trials, there are a large number of errors, but as trials are repeated, there is no error and the result is success.

3.7 Insightful Learning

Kohler put a chimpanzee in a cage and suspended a banana from the roof outside the cage. Two sticks were placed inside the cage. Neither of the two was long enough to reach the banana. After some unsuccessful attempts, the monkey incidentally found that one stick fitted into the hole of the other, but not properly. This gave the animal a bright idea. It joined the two sticks firmly together and got the banana. This was not an exploratory type of learning involving conditioning or trial and error, but a sudden flash, leading to insight. 'Insightful learning' is common among human beings.

3.8 Learning by Imitation

Learning by imitation, happens by observing others doing things which one finds difficult to do himself and imitating them. Imitation helps to curtail errors, supplying cues for the learner. Speaking, writing, playing and numerous other skills are learned by observing others and repeating what they do. The pupil imitates the person he admires, one whom he would like to resemble. He identifies himself with the role model in the sense that he wants to be like him. According no *Nunn*, "Imitation is but the first stage in the creation of individuality, and the richer the scope for imitation, the richer the developed individuality will be." Imitation is never a complete reproduction. There is always variation indicating choice, preference for details and creativity.

3.9 Remembering and Forgetting

There are several factors and practices which influence remembering and forgetting. Remembering is an active process. Remembering is important for the pupil because by remembering what he has learnt, he can recall and learn more. Studying a material at a stretch is known as *massed learning*. When the material is learnt with intervals of rest, the method is called *distributed learning or spaced learning*. It has not been established that distributed learning is better than massed learning since unspread learning often leads to confusion.

Learning should proceed from the *simple to the complex*, from *part to whole* from general to specific, from concrete to abstract. Learning a lesson as one whole unit is known as '*whole learning*'. Dividing the lesson and learning the smaller units is termed *part learning*. Whole learning is more advantageous to the pupil, since he can comprehend the whole. However, if a passage is too long, dividing it into meaningful subgroups (paragraphs) will facilitate learning.

The more often a learned material is repeated, the better is the retention. The pupil must be encouraged either to recite or review often, the lessons learnt.

The meaningfulness of a lesson to be learned is the most important feature affecting the rate of learning and the amount of retention. *Guilford* demonstrated that *the more meaningful the material is to the pupils the greater is its retention*. Retention over various intervals of time, is greater for substance learning than for rote learning. Factual information is forgotten faster than the ability to explain, interpret and apply general principles. Therefore, *Guilford* has stressed the use of concrete rather than abstract materials and direct experience rather than second or third hand experience, particularly with young children.

All lessons should be made as meaningful as possible. It is purposeless to ask children to spell words, which have no purposeful meaning for them. Scientific facts are rapidly forgotten, unless reinforced by relevant experience. Dates and names are valueless as isolated facts. They must be incorporated into units which have significance for pupils. Meaningful organisation of material can be developed by attention to similarities and differences and by emphasis on the who, what, when, where and why of relationships.

Curves of forgetting generally show greater forgetting of verbal lessons as compared to those of motor skills. *Ebbinghaus's* pioneer work on learning and forgetting with the nonsense syllables which he invented in order to have learning tasks free of previous experience, showed a rapid initial drop followed by a gradual slide to nearly complete forgetting. The curve of forgetting varies considerably depending upon the extent to which school work has meaning, relatedness and organisation. There are also situations when overlearning or occasional recall occur.

3.10 Transfer of Training

Mastery of one skill may facilitate the learning of another skill. This is known as *transfer of training* (*learning*). *Thorndike's* experiments and experiences have proved that transfer of learning is not a universal occurrence.

The distinction between retention and transfer, rests upon the similarity or difference between the test situation and the learning situation. *When the situation in which learning is being tested replicates the situation in which it was learned, retention can be measured, but when the situation differs, transfer of training is being measured.*

The following factors appear to influence learning and its transfer:

1. The perceptual clarity of the task, in points of relevant cues and appropriate responses.
2. The meaningfulness of the material and the understanding obtained.
3. The context in which the skill or knowledge is acquired.
4. Conditions contributing to, or reducing the interference between tasks such as similarity of stimuli or responses, and degree of overlearning.

Ultimately, each aspect of the school curriculum must be seen as part of the total curriculum—the situations which provide learning experiences including those outside the school and its prescribed courses used for teaching and testing situations. They also include those that cater to individual differences, motivations, interests, attitudes, achievements and development.

3.11 Optimising Learning

Lacey's guidelines based on the principles of learning, emphasise that pupils learn most effectively when:

1. teaching is within the context of their previous experience.
2. an emotionally and intellectually stimulating environment is present.
3. they feel secure with the learning situation and have respect for the teacher.
4. multiple, concrete and first hand experiences are available as bases for concept formation.
5. they see the whole situation as well as the various parts in relation to the whole.
6. they are engaged in activities calling for critical thinking and problem-solving.
7. they participate and share actively in selecting problems and goals which have meaning for them.
8. learning experiences are planned in a meaningful, sequential pattern, in which every learning activity has a definite objective.

9. there is provision for differences in meeting the individual abilities, interests and needs.
10. meaningful practice reinforces sensory experiences.
11. the teacher plans learning experiences as carefully for attitudes and appreciations as for knowledge and skills.
12. learning gained in the classroom leads to purposeful action related to it and transfers readily to out-of-school situations, and
13. they participate in the evaluation of their learning experiences and receive emotional and intellectual satisfaction and a sense of achievement.

Since learning cannot be separated from teaching, good guidance and effective procedures are required of the teacher. She needs to apply knowledge of the principles of both teaching and learning, in planning the educational activities and more particularly for relating them to life experiences with a view to making the pursuits concrete and meaningful to the children.

4

Curriculum:
The Foundation of Teaching and Learning

4.1 Introduction

Methods of Teaching acquire a meaning only in the contextual framework of the curriculum, which the teachers attempt to transact. It is, therefore, desirable that the concept of curriculum, its diverse facets, the process of its development, its transaction, its review and renewal are deliberated upon.

Though, it will be incorrect to say, that the modern concepts and principles of curriculum are not well understood in India, we should have no hesitation in admitting that they have not found appropriate applications in the country. In actual application situations they have often been brushed aside as impracticable, expensive, time consuming and even sometimes dubbed as being not practicable.

There have no doubt been attempts at the scientific construction of curriculum in certain places but they are just a counted few. Despite these curriculum development based on technically sound principles and procedures does continue to be a neglected area in Indian education.

What are sometimes referred to as 'curricula' for certain courses, designed by the various agencies—the universities, State Departments of Education or the State Boards of Secondary Education, are just the enumeration of the topics of study. They are commonly known as *syllabi* and are nothing more than that. Even the topics of study in most cases do not stand defined in terms of desired parameters. It is then left to the prescribed textbook or the teacher to provide an operational explanation of a particular syllabus. In some cases now the educational agencies have started giving subject-wise instructional objectives in the beginning of the syllabi for the various courses. But, this is more ornamental than functional, because the objectives in most of such situations are superimposed on the already existing syllabi really reversing the sequence of the process. Above all even this innovation does not make them curricula.

It is no exaggeration to mention that even in teacher education courses where 'Curriculum' is the core concept, the courses of study stand enunciated in terms of topics to be covered through 'Papers' and no curriculum as such, based on fundamental principles of curriculum construction is developed and prescribed.

The main purpose of this chapter is to present a functional strategy for curriculum development which the educational agencies prescribing courses could consider adopting or adapting.

In this process, it will be attempted to spell out the concept of curriculum development as could be feasibly applicable in actual settings.

4.2 Basic Considerations

There are mainly three basic paradigms in curriculum construction. These are:

4.2.1 *The Individual* : Children, their probable age group, level of mental growth, background (family & social) as well as level of knowledge possessed aspirations etc.

4.2.2 *The Society* : This will include the social order, national economic policies, political system, cultural heritage philosophy of life of the nation etc.

4.2.3 *The Human Knowledge* : The existing store of human knowledge in various areas, which is fast growing and exerting an influence on our life-styles.

The above three considerations will provide the foundations of the curriculum and also be the most important of the sources of educational objectives.

4.3 Derivation and Statement of Objectives

The above basic considerations when spelt out are a pointer to the educational objectives. These overall objectives become the basis of deriving the objectives for different stages of education (primary, secondary, university). And finally the stage-wise objectives of education become the basis for developing instructional objectives of various subject areas and courses.

These instructional objectives will determine the real operational framework of the curricula for various courses. They will need to be conceived in all the three areas of pupil growth viz. the cognitive, affective and psychomotor. What is called the 'CAP' classification of instructional objectives is given as under for purposes of clarification.

4.4 CAP Classification of Educational Objectives

A composite Model of Taxonomies of Cognitive, Affective and Psychomotor Domains.

4.5 Pupil Growth

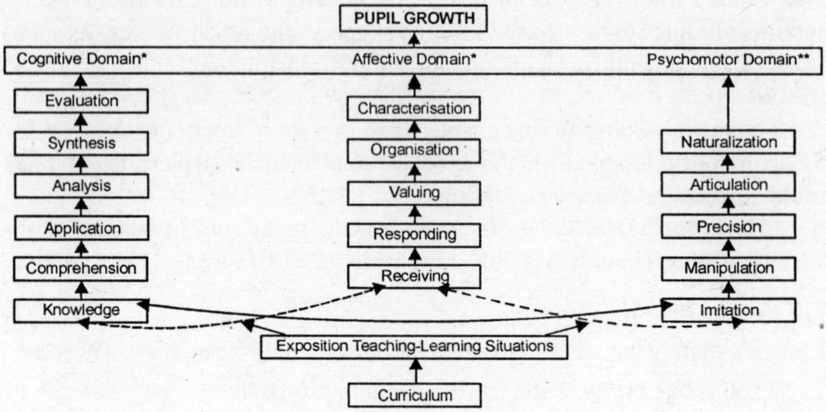

Diagram 4.1

* Proposed by B.S. Bloom, et al in *Taxonomy of Educational Objectives—Cognitive and Affective Domains*, David Mc Kay Company, Inc., New York.

** Proposed by R.H. Dave in *Developments in Educational Testing, Vol. 1*, University of London Press, London, 1969, p. 203-214. Also combined the three Domains into a Composite Model.

The Diagram 4.1 shows that when a child is exposed to a certain teaching-learning situation, the exposure is likely to generate growth in one or more aspects which could also be in varying degrees. This means that the growth will be cumulative and concomitant. Its measure will be identified in terms of the objectives.

In the situation stated above it will be necessary for the instructional objectives when stated and defined, to satisfy some criteria to motivate purposeful instruction and evaluation. This implies that they should be:

- stated specifically and in unambiguous terms.
- stated in terms of pupil behaviour (i.e., the way in which the pupils will be able to exhibit to us the achievement of the said objectives).
- stated with both the content and the modification parts (i.e., the behavioural changes expected on the realisation of the objective and the subject matter desired to be employed in the process).
- achievable with the available or procurable or manipulable resources.
- testable (i.e., for which evidences of growth could be obtained).

4.6 Identification of the Courses of Study

From the objectives, it will be logical to get to the designing of the subject courses considered necessary for their realisation. Though this is seldom done it is something that must be done. It is this traditional mistake which has rendered the existing educational system non-functional. *Courses are provided because they have existed in the past and not because they are needed today and for the future.* The malady of educated unemployment could at least be partially traced to the non-existence of this relationship between courses and future needs. Yet another extension of this is that we academicians do normally have only the 'college-capable' in mind, while we are planning for the school stage. The same phenomenon is repeated even in higher education where little or no attention is given to the vocational needs whose importance is in no way less that of the academic ones. Certain proficiencies would also be required to be developed among the students for the achievement of the objectives and these would suggest the courses for inclusion in the curriculum for subjects of different streams.

4.7 Developing Curriculum for the Different Courses

After the identification of the various courses of study and their respective objectives the next step is to develop a curriculum for each of these. While developing curriculum it has to be kept in mind that *curriculum is not a one man's job and certainly not the monopoly of the subject specialists as has been the case in the past*, in several places. Curriculum Development is a process requiring inputs from several areas of specialisation. These are mainly six specialised inputs required as is shown through the Diagram 4.2.

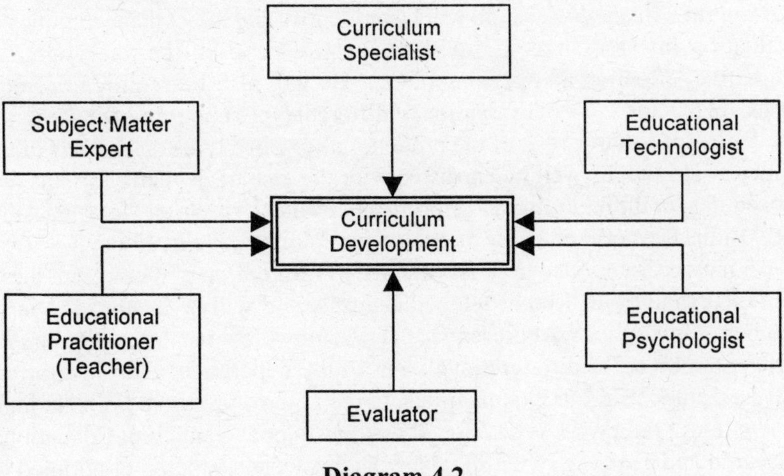

Diagram 4.2

Each one of these six has to play a distinct role. To state briefly the *curriculum specialist* will look after the general framework of the entire endeavour. He will help establish and ensure a feasible coordination between the different experts. The *subject matter expert,* who could be an individual drawn from higher education or University, will ensure that the content matter included is accurate and updated and that its organisation does not distort the facts. The *educational technologist* will see to it that the methodologies of instruction and modern aids to teaching (including technological ones) proposed are the most appropriate for the situations for which they are suggested. He will also be instrumental in establishing a relationship between the objectives, content and in instructional techniques. He could be a pedagogue drawn from a training college. The *educational psychologist* will scrutinise the potential of the proposed content and methodology for achieving the targets in respect of the expected outcomes. He will look to their appropriateness from the point of view of the mental level of the pupil-group and the likely adequacy of their preparation for the proposed intakes. The *educational practitioner* will indeed be the teacher, whose job will be to see that the objectives, content and methodology are all suitable for the students, that the objectives are neither pitched too high nor too low, that the content is graded and in line with the likely background of previous knowledge and competencies of the group and that the methodologies proposed can be employed either through the existing resources or those that can be easily manipulated or procured. He will also have to judge the implementability of the curriculum in respect, of the time-budget. Above all he will also be required to do a little introspection for finding out whether the average existing teacher can manage to impart, instruction as contemplated through the proposed curriculum. *The evaluators* job will be to identify and select the techniques of evaluation for assessing the quantum of growth in all the three domains (cognitive, affective and psycho-motor). He will also be required, in most cases, to develop tools of evaluation of different types and forms for assessing the degree of achievement of the predetermined objectives on the part of the students. He will as well be entrusted with the task of devising formats and procedures for the recording and reporting of evaluation data and for suggesting the various uses of the results of evaluation in different situations.

It may be mentioned here that the main presumption of the present thesis is that curriculum will be developed centrally and will be meant for a large number of institutions. At present each university prepares the curriculum for different subjects at different levels for all the departments and institutions that send students for its examinations. At the school stage in India, a National Curriculum Framework is developed by the National Council of Educational Research and Training (NCERT), New Delhi. This is adopted or adopted by different state level education agencies—the State Boards of School Education;

and of the State Departments of Education (Middle and Elementary stage). Since no structural changes are proposed through the proposals of this chapter, it may not be difficult to implement the suggestions contained in it by any agency involved in the process of preparing curriculum. It will, however, be necessary for these agencies to create conditions and provide the necessary infrastructure and facilities for the development of curricula which may satisfy the felt needs and help remove the imbalances that are commonly known to exist in them. They have also to realise that *returns in the field of education, are not as quick as they could be in industry.* The benefits of what we invest now, will be reaped only by the next generation and *our interest in the future generations will be estimated with the investments in terms of time energy we make for them.*

It is thus envisaged that a curriculum outline for a course will, in the main, incorporate the following aspects:

1. Objectives of Instruction.
2. Courses of Study.
3. Curriculum of each course.
   - 3.1 Specific objectives of each course
   - 3.2 Course content of the various units of a course
     - 3.2.1 Theoretical
     - 3.2.2 Practical
   - 3.3 Instructional materials
     - 3.3.1 For teachers use
     - 3.3.2 For students use
     - 3.3.3 For use by both students and teachers
   - 3.4 Instructional Methodology and Aids
   - 3.5 Scheme of Evaluation
     - 3.5.1 Continuous and Comprehensive School-based Evaluation for *improvement*
     - 3.5.2 External evaluation for *measurement*

4.8 Developing Curriculum Materials

Textbooks were probably the only item in this category used in a traditional set-up. Till recently they were developed solely by private individuals and the educational agencies simply selected a few out of the many submitted to them for a particular course. These were called 'approved' or 'recommended' textbooks and were used by students preparing for the courses concerned. However, at the school level many of them are now being developed by official agencies.

At the school stage, Teachers' Guides and Students' Workbooks entered the educational scheme in India only in the sixties. No deliberate effort was made to develop them earlier. Those that were available had been developed in foreign countries and were unrelated to the curriculum in use in India. Furthermore being imported they were expensive. This somehow created the wrong impression that even if they are developed in India, they would essentially be costly and out of the reach of the purchasing power of a majority of students and teachers. This fear was a constant discouragement for initiating any project for their development. Ultimately in the sixtees the National Council of Educational Research and Training, New Delhi, developed comprehensive curriculum projects. This was thus the first official agency in the country that planned and developed a wide variety of instructional materials. Besides textbooks, teachers guides, students workbooks, handwriting books and a reading readiness kit were developed. In Social Studies, teachers guides and instructional charts were developed to go with the textbooks. In Science, teachers' guides, kits of improvised and inexpensive apparatus (for demonstration and experimentation purposes) and laboratory manuals were developed in addition to textbooks.

The above description gives some of the main kinds of instructional materials, the development of which now needs to be explored further by the various educational agencies responsible for the different stages of education. The plea again is that the development of instructional materials of different kinds may be taken up as an integral part of the programme of curriculum development. It is not necessary for these educational agencies to create an elaborate top heavy machinery for doing this task but a core team will no doubt be necessary.

This will mean a deviation from the existing practice where the members of Boards of Studies in different subjects decide on the syllabus for courses in their respective subjects. Each Board of Studies or Committee of Courses, as it is sometimes called, works independently of the other. The situation yields lack of coordination and often the binding thread between the various courses is found missing. What is attempted to be made out here, is that curriculum construction as a highly specialised job which can best be done by an educational agency, through a centrally operated ongoing programme. This could be entrusted to what may be called the Academic/Curriculum Unit set-up within the organisation. It may consist of specialists in Curriculum, Evaluation, Instructional Materials, Educational Technology etc. This core body may coopt. specialists from other areas, as and when necessary, for accomplishing specialised jobs. At the present time it has become more necessary than ever before, to collaborate with *business and industry. This may not just be limited to consultation but their active involvement in the development of courses and their transaction for incorporating elements relevant to the needs of the job market.* But the sole responsibility for constructing the curriculum and having curriculum and evaluation materials prepared should rest with it. It will be only then that a coordinated curriculum development will be possible.

In such a set-up the Committees of Courses or the Boards of Studies, will take the form of the curriculum development committees for various courses at the school stage for example (adapting or adopting from the National Curriculum Framework in the Indian context). With the broadening of the concept of the curriculum, the services of persons represented on these committees will need to be utilised not only for the development of instructional and evaluation materials of various types but also for a variety of other academic endeavours. The proposal envisages that there may be two distinct divisions within the infrastructure of the educational agencies and the other for matters related to evaluation and certification. One of these may be incharge of curriculum and the other of administrative matters. Both the wings will of course, need supporting staff which will have to be provided. Academic work will thus acquire a status that it deserves. As could be seen the academic work has very wide dimensions and hence it does deserve better attention and position then what has so far been given to it, particularly by the examining agencies which by and large remain more than pre-occupied with the fire-fighting operations related to the conduct of examinations.

4.9 Developing Evaluation Procedures and Materials

Work on the development of evaluation procedures and materials has to go on simultaneously with that of the development of instructional methodology and materials. While the purpose and function of the latter, is to help the children realise the instructional objectives, that of the former is to assess the level of achievement of the same on the part of the students in the context of the inputs offered.

An evaluation programme to be so developed, will need to embody the following characteristics.

4.9.1 *Objective-based*—It should provide for the evaluation of all the related instructional objectives of the cognitive, affective and the psychomotor domains in a valid and a reliable manner. It should thus help gauge the strengths and shortfalls in pupil growth in a precise manner, not just for assessing and certifying the attained level of competencies but for further improving them through remedial measures.

4.9.2 *Continuous*—It should provide for a continued process of assessment instead of the usual periodical examinations which tend to test achievement only in one or two strokes. This will also help provide regular feedback to both students and teachers for improving their work and its quality.

4.9.3 *Comprehensive*—It should cover both the academic and the non/co-academic aspects of pupil growth and thereby provide a compelling motivation to the institutions in offering adequate and appropriate opportunities of the desired type, for developing the various competencies among pupils, some of which could otherwise have been overlooked.

4.9.4 *Use of a variety of techniques and tools*—As the evaluation programme will be designed for covering both the scholastic and co-scholastic aspects of pupil growth, it will need to exploit various types of testing situations. They may for example also need to focus on observation as an important technique of evaluation and necessitate the use of variety of unconventional tools of evaluation like check-lists, inventories, rating scales, observation schedules etc.

4.10 Curriculum Implementation

This is a crucial step. It is here that the use of the vast inputs in curriculum construction is made. This is mainly the teachers, jurisdiction where he is the master of the situation in manipulating or providing learning experiences to the students as envisaged by the curriculum. This is the stage of interaction between the curriculum on the one hand and the teacher and the students on the other. The phenomenon could be diagrammatically represented through the Diagram 4.3 below :

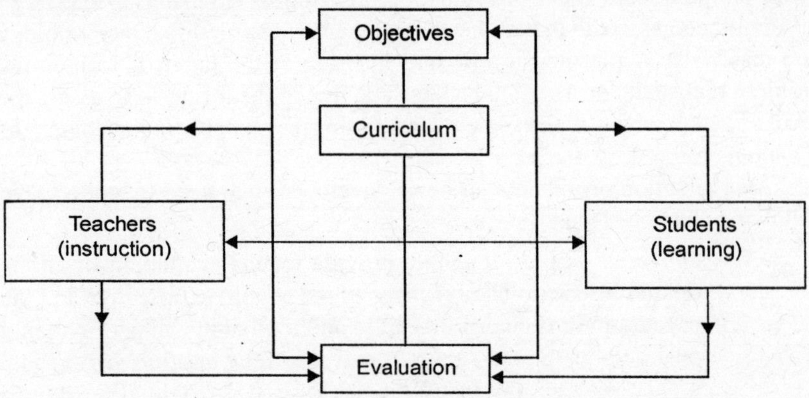

Diagram 4.3

Objectives are the anchor of the curriculum which in turn are the basis of the work of teachers and students. Teachers and students both work for the achievement of the objectives through the curriculum transaction which are ultimately evaluated through a well defined procedure of evaluation. The operation of this strategy could be called curriculum implementation and its process objective-based instruction and learning.

It may be mentioned here that several forces both internal and external influence the aforesaid process of instruction. *From the teachers point of view* they are his personal academic background and training, availability of resources and aids to instruction, his interest in and commitment for the job and the satisfaction he derives from its execution, etc. etc. *From the students' point of view* they are his interest in and attitude towards study, his level of achievement and growth, his previous preparation for assimilating the course, his future plans and his motivation etc. *From the point of view of both the teacher and the student*, it may be the ethos and the atmosphere of the school and the encouragement and motivation it provides besides the availability of instructional materials and their use etc.

Approach to instruction is yet another factor deserving attention in this regard. Normally while we educationalists view a teaching-learning situation, we are often guided in our thinking by the concept of the symmetrical normal curve and the stanine scale (this is being discussed in greater detail in the chapter on grading). We think that in a population only about 4% will get the top grade and another 4% will get the last one. This notion has overtaken our thinking so much that we often refuse to view the situation from another angle.

In fact a normal distribution of scores presumes chances and accidents. Indeed the distribution should not be normal if some carefully manipulated inputs are introduced in the process of instruction. It should then take a negatively skewed form. Thus we have reason to argue that *the closer a distribution is to the normal one, the more ineffective has our instruction been.* This logic advocated by Dr. B.S. Bloom of the University of Chicago is bound to be of great interest to the teacher and has the potential of adding to their confidence in picking up their instructional challenges. We should, therefore, have faith in enabling even the weakest student to attain the level of achievement of a bright student through well designed and implemented educational programmes and their concerted pursuit.

4.11 Curriculum Evaluation

This is the weakest link of the Indian curriculum development scene. It involves the tryout of the curriculum and curriculum materials to find out their adequacy and appropriateness for achieving the objectives. This is seldom done and even where it is attempted, it is not done as it should be. The try out could be *unitwise* as and when one is developed or that of the *full curriculum*. As a matter of fact both the above types of tryouts are necessary when a completely new curriculum is being developed. But sometimes only a partial revision of the curriculum is desired and in that case only that part of the newly introduced facet of the curriculum may be tried out.

In all these cases, however, it is sought to find out, as to how far the various elements of the curriculum and the procedures and practices implied through it, are effective in achieving the objectives set. More than one set of material and methods could also be tried out in this process for identifying the most appropriate one. Questions like the following could be sought to be answered through the tryout.

- Whether the objectives of instruction set are within the competence of the students to achieve?
- Whether one set of content matter or another is more adequate and or appropriate for enabling the students to achieve the objectives?
- Which one of the various methodologies tried is more suitable to be adopted as compared to the others?
- What instructional materials or sets of them help the students achieve the objectives better than others?
- Whether the scheme of evaluation is capable of providing valid and reliable result and whether the diagnosis made throught them can constructively help in the improvement of teaching and learning through the needed reinforcement etc., etc.?

The step is mainly contemplated to put the effectiveness of the curriculum to test before putting it into practice. The step of curriculum evaluation may no doubt mean substantial investment in terms of time, effort and money but it could save educational disasters which may mean losses multiplied several times over.

It may be mentioned that in an ideal scheme there should be a built in system of continuous review and revision (renewal) of the curriculum.

4.12 Conclusion

In conclusion it could be said that curriculum in the past has been a victimised outcome of social economic, political cultural and other influences. Serious efforts at the development of purposeful curricula to satisfy some of the felt needs are comparatively recent. Even when curriculum changes were contemplated and planned they were designed to fit into the existing organisational structure rather than to challenge it. *They were, furthermore, experience-based and any experimentation was foreign to the thinking on curriculum development.*

The proposals contained here are certainly not a cure for all the ills of curriculum development and implementation. They only give an approach for attacking the problems in the field. Several such approaches could be possible.

Curriculum development somehow which has normally been an ad hoc outcome of unanticipated changes in the past, *could well be compared to unplanned urban development where, in course of time, we are forced to live with short-sighted and short-term decision-making*. Let us then rise in unison to rescue curriculum from the above malady and make it worthy of meeting the challenge of preparing our children adequately and effectively for the twenty-first century.

5

Theoretical Paradigms of Educational Objectives

5.1 The Purpose of Objectives

Objectives are the starting points of any educational process and their understanding is a basic requirement for all teachers to be successful in their mission of teaching and testing students. With the goal of alround development of personality teachers ought also have an intimate acquaintance with the three domains into which the objectives stand classified viz., *Cognitive Affective and Psycho-motor*, which have been touched upon in passing earlier. They are the facts and concepts related to the objectives of the different domains which are attempted to be presented here.

Derivation as the first step towards proper development of educational objectives stands to gain in several ways by subjecting them to a proper framework of classification. It helps to view them as parts of a system rather than in isolation. It also increases their usability by providing clarity about their interconnections. A proper classification helps avoid overlapping among similar objectives in a list. They have to be properly delimited and defined. This further, helps in ascertaining as to how far the various aspects of a major objective have been covered by their specifications. A well laid out system of objectives is a must for an effective educational programme comprising curriculum development, instruction and evaluation. A system of classification is also essential for the pursuit of research, particularly in the fields of instruction and evaluation. Finally, a classification is very necessary for better communication among teachers on the subject of educational objectives without which all attempts at educational improvement may go waste.

5.2 A Snag in the Classification of Objectives

Each statement of an educational objective, as we know has two distinct components—*the modification part* and *the content part*. It is not easily possible to evolve a logical scheme of grouping objectives in a way that they cover the requirements of both these components. The subject oriented classification will tend to lean heavily on academic matters, whereas the behaviour-based classification will be mainly concerned with processes. Besides, it is also no easy task to synthesise demands of the different, categories of sources and evolve a balanced list. Such attempts have often ended in a very complicated list without much potential for practical application. Since the main business of education is to bring about a change in terms of behavioural outcomes, the choice naturally devolves upon the behavioural classification of objectives. While many attempts have been made in this direction much more has yet to be accomplished.

5.3 The Eight-year Study Model

One of the earliest systematic works on behaviour-based classification of objectives is witnessed in the evaluation programme of an Eight-year Study under the leadership of *Tayler*. Just for historical interest, the scheme of objectives as arrived at under this experiment is given below*:

1. The development of effective ways of thinking.
2. The acquisition of important information, ideas and principles.
3. The development of effective work habits and skills.
4. The development of increased sensitivity to social problems and aesthetic experience.
5. The inculcation of social rather than selfish attitude.
6. The development of appreciation of literature, art and music.
7. The development of increasing range of worthwhile interests.
8. Increased personal and social development.
9. Improved physical health.
10. The formulation and classification of a philosophy of life.

The procedure adopted for developing this ten category model of objectives was curriculum analysis and the conference method. The curricular objectives of the *thirty schools* under the study were sifted and regrouped keeing in view their behaviour homogeneity. However, the experimenters kept an open mind and were conscious of the shortcomings of their model. They felt that "the classification of objectives would be improved as evidence accumulates regarding the social significance of different behaviour patterns and regarding the correlation and consistency among various specific reactions classified under the particular type of a behaviour". A conference of specialists, teachers and administration was finally used for vetting the list tentatively drawn up.

5.4 Taxonomy of Educational Objectives

A number of models of classification of objectives have since been developed.

---

* Adventure in American Education: Volume III, Appraising and Recording Student Progress, p. 18.

The most convincing of these in the recent years has been the taxonomical model of educational objectives developed by *Bloom* and his associates. It has conceived and adopted a tripartite division corresponding to the three primary aspects of pupil growth-cognitive, affective, psycho-motor (knowing; feeling; doing).

A taxonomy is a classification scheme followed originally in biological sciences where plants or animals are arranged in increasing degrees of specificity (diminishing degrees of generality) on the basis of certain criteria, in a way that *each succeeding class appears to be telescoping out of or into the preceding one*, depending upon the direction of views, e.g., order, family genus and species. Likewise, when applied to educational objectives, the model should yield hierarchically arranged objectives in ascending or descending order of complexity or difficulty.

The taxonomy of educational objectives as developed by *Bloom* and his associates, is basically a judicious combination of educational, logical and psychological classification systems. The distinction between different categories is educationally significant. The terms have been defined precisely in a manner that earlier meanings are logically consistent among themselves. Lastly, the classification is kept constant with the correct psychological findings about the mental processes. This classification employs a decimal enumeration system. This classification still awaits empirical evidence in its support although it has already been subjected to a fair degree of logical validation.

5.5 Objectives of the Cognitive Domain (Bloom's Model)

The cognitive domain represents the intellectual component of mental life and is certainly the most basic one, from the point of view of education. A variety of attempts have been made to classify mental processes and one may come across a variety of terms indicative of it, e.g., logical reasoning, reflective thinking, productive thinking and such others. *Guilford's three-dimensional model* (operations; contents; products) of the structure of intellect (SI model) may be of interest in this regard. It attempts to classify intellectual operations into a hierarchical order—cognitive, memory, divergent thinking and evaluation.

In Bloom's taxonomy these operations or processes have been divided and arranged into the following six classes/categories:

1. Knowledge
   - Knowledge of Specifics
   - Knowledge of Methodology
   - Knowledge of Abstractions.
2. Comprehension
   - Translation

- Interpretation
- Extrapolation

3. Application
4. Analysis
   - Analysis of Elements
   - Analysis of Relationships
   - Analysis of Organisational Principles.
5. Synthesis
   - Production of a Unique Communication
   - Production of a Plan
   - Derivation of a Set of Abstract Relationships.
6. Evaluation
   - Judging in terms of Internal Criteria
   - Judging in terms of External Criteria.

The six categories of behaviours in the above scheme are obviously arranged from simple to complex. They have been further defined in terms of more specific behaviours.

Knowledge is taken to involve the recall of specifics, universals, methods, processes, patterns, structures, settings, generalisations, etc. The basic psychological process in use is remembering. This is distinguished from the remaining five which are together called intellectual abilities for the simple reason that the latter requires "organised models of operations and generalised techniques for dealing with materials and problems."

Comprehension which is next higher in the category of objectives is considered as the lowest level of 'understanding' equivalent of knowing what is being communicated and using the material or idea communicated "without necessarily relating it to other material or seeing its fullest implications."

Application is the third category which pertains to "the use of an abstract idea in a particular and concrete situation" and thereby arriving at a solution of a problem. There may be some difference of opinion about the limited scope of this objective and as such the use of the term, application for it. This may be defended on the ground that the word may be given an ad-hoc meaning by defining it adequately to connote the use of acquired knowledge in unfamiliar situations.

Analysis forms the fourth category and connotes the breaking down of a communication into its constituent elements, in a way that relationships or sequence or both of the components, of a set of ideas are made clear. Some people treat it as an equivalent of the objective of critical thinking which is only partly true. Analysis is an important component of critical thinking but the latter is something more. Analysis may lead to the identification of elements, relationships or principles.

Synthesis is the fifth category of objectives and involves the ability to put together the elements or parts in a way that a new pattern emerges therefrom. It has elements of creativeness.

Evaluation crowns all the categories and calls for the most complex mental processes necessary for judging a material, method or communication against a standard, internal or external to it.

5.6 Objectives of the Affective Domain—Krathwohl's Model

There is often a greater lack of clarity and unanimity among educationists with regard to the statement of objectives in the affective domain than in the cognitive one. The terms like interests, appreciations, values, attitudes are often assigned varying shades of meaning. The term appreciation for instance, may extend from awareness to profound aesthetic impact with a large spread in between. Apart from other factors accounting for the "erosion in respect of affective objectives in education" it is no doubt the lack of clarity about their scope and meaning which really turns out to be a very grave handicap in their proper pursuit. The taxonomy developed by Krathwohl seems to systematise these objectives into five broad categories given as under—

1. Receiving (attending)
   - Awareness
   - Willingness to receive
   - Controlled or selected response.
2. Responding
   - Acquiescence in responding
   - Willingness to respond
   - Satisfaction in response
3. Valuing
   - Acceptance of a value
   - Preference of a value
   - Commitment.
4. Organisation
   - Conceptualisation of a value
   - Organisation of a value system.
5. Characterisation by a value or value complex.
   - Generalised set
   - Characterisation.

Receiving is the lowest or rather the most rudimentary category of affective behaviour. At this level the learner shows sensitivity to certain stimuli. It is like the teacher catching the student's attention. Awareness, willingness to receive and the selected nature of attention are its important sub-levels.

Responding which is the next category, expects greater motivation and regularity in attention. It may also for practical considerations be described as 'interest' by which we mean a tendency to respond to a particular object or stimuli. Interest in turn, is evinced at three levels (1) compliance when expected, (2) voluntary response, and (3) response with a clear emotional tone.

Valuing is the third category which involves increasing internalisation of the sense of worth and identification with it. It indicates the motivation of behaviour not by deliberate desire but by the individual's commitment to the underlying value guiding the behaviour." This objectives may conveniently be called "attitudes". These objectives are "prime stuff from which the conscience of the individual is developed into control of behaviour."

Organisation forms the fourth category and connotes a system of values or attitudes. An individual's behaviour is not ordinarily motivated by a single attitude in isolation, but by an 'attitude complex'. Development of one's own code of conduct or standard of public life, may be an instance of the organisation of a value system.

Characterisation, the last of the categories, is reached when an individual is consistently found behaving in accordance with the values or attitudes he has imbibed, ultimately reaching a stage, when he has a consistent philosophy of life, of his own and an internal compulsion to pursue it.

The taxonomy of the affective domain may not appear quite hierarchical especially inasmuch as one order does not completely telescope into the other as a taxonomical characteristic, but surely presents an useful educational principle.

5.7 Objectives of the Psycho-motor Domain (Dave's Model)

The Psycho-motor Domain concerns itself with levels of attainment in neuro-muscular coordination. As the level of coordination moves up, the action becomes more refined, speedy and automatic. In this case five broad categories have been identified by R.H. Dave as given below:

1. Imitation
   - Impulsion
   - Overt repetition
2. Manipulation
   - Following direction
   - Selection
   - Fixation
3. Precision
   - Reproduction
   - Control
4. Articulation
   - Sequence
   - Harmony

5. Naturalisation
   - Automatism
   - Internalisation

Imitation accounts for the lowest level of psycho-motor behaviour. It starts as an inner urge or push or impulse. It is represented by "Covert inner rehearsal of the muscular system" which may be taken to be more of an action at the material level. Soon it may grow into an overt act with capacity to repeat the performance with very rudimentary coordination.

Manipulation is the next higher level of psycho-motor behaviour. It involves following direction, selecting certain actions in preference to others and acting accordingly. It marks the beginning of the fixation of operation and the end of initial fumbling in the manipulative actions.

Precision is the third category and is reached when reproduction of operations is carried out with speed and refinement, giving the learner the ability to control and adjust (increase, decrease or modify) his action in response to requirements.

Articulation which is the fourth category, can be said to have been attained when the learner is able to handle a number of actions in unison, keeping in view their sequence and rhythm. It involves coordination in action, i.e., right sequence in right proportion of time or at the right moment.

Naturalisation is the final stage which is the equivalent of perfect habituation ranging from automatisation to routilisation. At this level the performer does not expend any psychic energy in carrying out an operation. His actions are more or less automatic and mechanical and without any conscious thinking or planning, i.e., a mere reflex action.

The classification of objectives of the psycho-motor domain may not interest, in its entirety, the teachers of all subjects but in such curricular areas as writing, speech, driving, crafts, etc., it will find a very wide application. Unlike Cognitive and Affective domains the transfer value of an objective in the psycho-motor domain from one context to another may not be quite so pervasive.

5.8 Interrelationship of Different Domains of Objectives

The tripartite division of instructional objectives into domains is not water tight or an exclusive one. Firstly, the achievement in one domain is to a quite appreciable degree dependent on the learner's status in others. For instance, understanding (comprehension) may be a prerequisite for attaching proper value to an object or proper cognition, necessary for arousing proper interest. Similarly, interests and attitudes affect the quality of performance in both cognitive and psycho-motor domains. Comprehension again is a natural component of the precision level in the psycho-motor domain and similarly interests can be traced as affective components of almost all the cognitive proficiencies. Thus, there is some degree of parallelism in terms of readiness relationship between various categories. Lower levels of each domain come relatively closer to each other, e.g., knowing, receiving and imitating are very much interdependent among themselves. In the higher categories too, there is discernible parallelism. A particular category of one domain, as already illustrated earlier, may correspond to one or more of categories of the other.

The implications of the nature of inter-connectedness are many. For example, while planning the instruction for realising an objective, it may be considered as to how best the corresponding objectives of other domains can be exploited, fed or even protected. The affective domain it could be safely mentioned has grievously suffered on account of the over emphasis on teaching for the so-called glorious cognitive objectives as 'critical thinking' and 'problem solving' without caring for the emotive reactions simultaneously arising out of such mental exercises. Of the dichotomy of 'mastery' and 'transfer' objectives, the effective realisation of the latter, which in fact is of real importance, will immensely be affected by the manner in which the interconnectedness among the objectives of different domains, is handled.

Pupils' growth in respect of the three domains, as a result of the learning experiences provided, is *simultaneous*. But every learning experience does not result in the same quantum of growth in all the three domains. Thus, when a learning experience is planned and provided, it emits currents of growth in different domains, which finally settle down at different levels in the different domains. This variation in the potential of learning experiences for promoting growth leaves it to the initiative of the teachers to devise and offer an appropriate mix of learning activities for bringing about the desired behavioural changes and growth in the pupils in different domains.

It may also be mentioned that due to individual differences the same learning experiences may result in different levels of growth in the three domains among different individuals. This highlights the need for individualised instruction.

The three taxonomies could be called the CAP (Cognitive, Affective and Psychomotor) classification of objectives.

The usefulness of the taxonomical classification of instructional objectives is also sometimes disputed. It, therefore, appears necessary at this place to summarise below some of the uses to which it can be put particularly in achievement testing:

1. Since categories in the Taxonomy are arranged on the principle of graded complexity, the scheme is very helpful in identifying the meaningful level at which the learner is functioning, especially in view of "the upper and lower limits of the same category as well as in the context of the nature of the next higher and lower categories."
2. The techniques and tools of assessment can be relevantly decided upon, developed and deployed. Their categorisation thus becomes

easy and clear. The form typology, which has so much grip on the minds of the teachers now, can be very profitably replaced by the objective-based one, as a much desired change.

3. It will be helpful in translating into practice the principle of comprehensiveness of evaluation by ensuring proper realisation of various aspects of pupils' growth: cognitive, affective and psychomotor.
4. The evaluation of the evaluation devices in terms of their validity will be facilitated.
5. The evaluation may prove very helpful in arriving at the meaningful synthesis of various dimensions of pupils growth. Identification of areas of inter-relationship among the three domains may be of particular significance in this regard.
6. The logical nature of categorisation helps in identifying and grading teaching-learning situations, which can be an important source of selecting proper testing situations and deciding their sequence too.
7. Curriculum development and preparation of instructional material should profit from such a scheme of classification in many ways. Preparation and analysis of textbooks based on well defined objectives may prove to be a big improvement.
8. The classification through its well defined criteria "will provide a bridge for further communication among teachers, between teachers and evaluators, curriculum and research workers, psychologists and other behavioural scientists."
9. The taxonomy has also opened new avenues for research in education. To name a few, the re-evaluation of objectives should be the immediate reaction, such as finding out the relationship between different domains, categories and sub-categories. Empirical validation of the Taxonomies besides being a worthy research in its own way, will open new vistas of work. The problems of retentivity and recession in learning on different objectives may be an equally fruitful project. Teachers may also be motivated to undertake experimentation on objective-based teaching and testing. The scope is likely to become more wide and varied in course of time.

For purpose of the discussion that follows in this document, Bloom's taxonomy in the Cognitive Domain, Krathwohl's taxonomy in the Affective Domain and Dave's taxonomy in the Psycho-motor Domain have been taken as the basis. The above mentioned taxonomies of the three domains are, however, not followed in the '*letter*' but only in '*spirit*'. The adaptations it may be mentioned, are an outcome of the suggestions received in the course of discussions with a very large number of students, teachers, teacher-educators, educational psychologists and sociologists, educational administrators, educational planners in India, spread over a span of more than five decades.

The main criteria for these adaptations was their suitability to the national environment in its various facets. Attempts were therefore made to check that the objectives identified for classification in each of the three domains were realisable through the curriculum, textbooks, educational resources, commonly available as also the competencies of the teachers and the students to attain them.

In regard to the objectives of the Cognitive Domain they have been limited to the first three of the steps of Bloom's taxonomy, viz., knowledge, understanding and application with analysis, synthesis and evaluation compressed and dovetailed into application. This has been done because the average teacher is likely to find it difficult to discriminate between them and consequently to appropriately tackle them either for purposes of teaching for realising them or for evaluating them with the precision with which they have been originally enunciated by Bloom particularly so in social sciences.

The objectives of the affective domain again have also been condensed in the present document. They have firstly not been presented in the nomenclature proposed by Krathwoh but just limited to 'interests' and 'attitudes' and personal attributes which are commonly understood terminologies.

The objectives of the psycho-motor domain have been reduced to the muscular skills related to the subject of study. Basically, these are such as require the abilities of '*precision*', '*precaution*' and '*proportion*' needed in undertaking activities like experiments, drawing sketches and diagrams, pursuing performing arts.

5.9 The Author's Contribution to the Taxonomies

As we have seen, the taxonomies of the Cognitive, Affective and the Psycho-motor domains present the phenomenon of vertical growth of the individuals in the three domains individually and collectively.

In the above context the author has expounded the theory of *sequential horizontal relationship among the three domains.* When anybody acquires some acquaintance (cognitive impression) about something, it often triggers an appreciation (affective impact) of the thing, learnt. The overflow of these feelings then moves beyond emotions propelling some fulfilling (psycho-motor) action.

This sequential horizontal relationship, among the three domains can be easily and effectively explained through a commonly observed phenomenon. We observe (cognition) some likeable characteristics of a child., we get impressed by them (affection) and then we instinctively hug and kiss it (Psycho-motor action).

6

The Practical Dimensions of Educational Objectives

In the context of the aforesaid theoretical framework, it is desirable to turn to their operational implications and applications in life situations.

6.1 The Sources of Educational Objectives

The philosophy of life is, in fact, the main source of all facets of all our activities including education. Educational targets to get derived from this very fundamental foundation. The main of these are the:

- The social order and its diverse linkages with life e.g. we in India and orient do not discard and reject the past, we assimilate it. This has important implications for life and also for education.
- The economic structure too, is an important determinant of educational targets which naturally differ in countries following capitalistic, and socialistic societies.
- The political system too exerts a powerful influence on educational targets and practices, bringing about wide variation in the democracies and dictatorships.
- The cultural heritage is again an undeniable factor that determines educational targets, which involves pride in ones past.
- The existing store of human knowledge is another factor as we know many things now which we were looking for in the past. This masks a shift of ground and focus of educational targets.
- Educational targets cannot also ignore the individuals for whom they are enunciated—their age, maturity level, previous knowledge etc.

6.2 The Levels of Educational Objectives

There is a distinct hierarchy among the educational target consisting of :

From top to bottom it implies a journey from whole to parts for example there could be many aims in a goal, many objectives in an aim and many specifications in an objective.

It also at the some time presents a phenomenon of a movement from general to specific. For example a *goal* could be 'making a good man'. Now this could have different interpretations in different situations and in different ideologies. An *Aim* in this very context could be 'making a good citizen.' Even this could mean differently in different societies. The allegiance of a good citizen in a dictatorship could be to the dictator, in a communistic state to the party, and so on. An *Objective* in the same backdrops could be making a judicious voter who will take an objective decision about whom to vote for. The next in the chair are *specifications*. They indicate the applied side of objectives giving what a student will be able to do to demonstrate that he has achieved a particular objective.

This hierarchy can be diagrammatically presented as under:

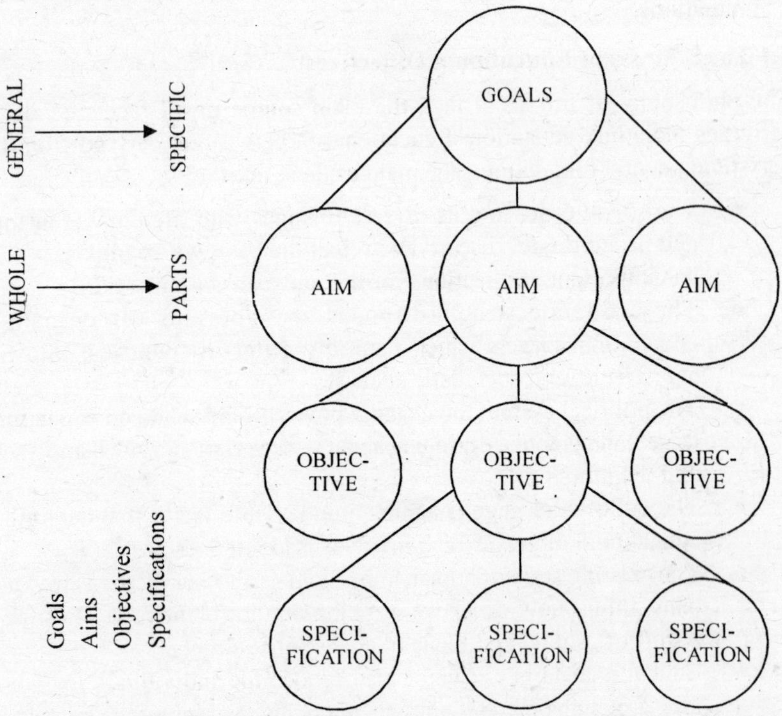

It is at the level of objectives that targets become tangible and realisable through educational inputs and testable through evaluation for judging the quantum of gain.

Specifications of different objectives in many ways, are competencies which become the basic ability elements for being focused upon for being achieved as also the basis for formulating evaluation situations and testing tools.

6.3 The Statement of Educational Objectives

Objectives in fact indicate that level of targets which are tangible for being handled in educational processes. Educational objectives are therefore to be stated.

The statements of objectives are, therefore, governed by some characteristic conditions. These are briefly enunciated below:

- Objectives have to be stated in concrete terms without vagueness or ambiguity.
- The statement of objectives have to have both the *modification* and the content components i.e. the changes desired to be realised in pupil behaviour (competencies) and the *content* through which they are proposed to be realised.
- Objectives must be aligned to the subject for which they are meant.
- Objectives must correspond to the level of abilities of the students.
- Objectives ought to be stated in terms of pupil behaviour and in terms of teacher behaviour ('to acquire' the ability of ... and not 'to help children to acquire').
- Objectives must be achievable.
- Objectives must be evaluable.

6.4 The Definition of Objectives

For purposes of being constructively utilised objectives do need to be broken down into parts. The parts ought to wear a behavioural garb in respect of the students. These parts are called *specifications* and are derived in answer to the question as to what would students be able to do to demonstrate to us that a student has achieved a particular objective. Let us take the example of the objective of 'understanding' in social studies.

Statements of the Objectives

To develop an understanding of facts, terms, concepts, principles, hypothesis, trends etc. in social studies.

Specifications of the Objectives

To demonstrate that a student has achieved the above objective, a student will be able to:

- discriminate
- compare and contrast
- give examples
- classify
- identity relationship
- defect and correct errors.

These specifications as already mentioned are competencies which need to be developed and which deserve to be tested for enabling us to know about the quantum of growth as a result of the educational inputs selected and provided.

7

Managing Student Groups

To succeed as a teacher, one has to possess a number of attributes of different types. Among these one of the most important is to deal with groups because in most of the situations, he has to teach groups in classes. Thus he does not just impart knowledge or enable students to acquire competencies, but also to *manage the groups* in all these processes of teaching and learning.

The groups of students in different classes could have some affinity by virtue of having been together in earlier classes with forged affiliations but otherwise the group is quite often quite heterogeneous coming from different family backgrounds social and cultural classes, income groups, family professions each espousing different values. The intellectual attributes of the individual students too are different.

The teacher, however, is required to tackle the whole group in a large class with more dissimilarities than similarities. He is therefore left with no choice but to choose a middle of the road path with little opportunity for individual attention.

7.1 Characteristics of Student Groups

The students in a class possess the *inherent traits* of children of their respective age-groups. Each one of them particularly in the lower classes is desirous of putting his best foot forward, each interested in *attracting the attention* of the teacher and others through his achievements and behaviour. They are also normally imbued with the dominant spirit of competition. All of them with only exceptional exceptions *live in the present* with future beyond their imaginations. All of them appreciate praise and detest admonitions and these become powerful influences for whetting motivation to learn and progress or for depressing it. They are also inherently impatient.

Differences among them exist in respect of the degree of diligence, emotional satability, possessiveness, spirit of initiative, spirit of social service, language patterns, attitude towards taking things seriously or casually and so on. These, however, usually carry the stamp of the home background.

7.2 Desired Characteristics of Teachers

The management of such heterogeneous groups as classes are, is by no means an easy task and the teachers too should possess and demonstrate some qualities of head and heart for winning over children through love, affection and consideration than through fear or punishment. S/he should possess these qualities which may make the teacher, a role model for the students. The main of these attributes could be safely mentioned as:

- Interest in the welfare of the students
- Helpfulness
- Treating all students equal
- Guidance in educational and personal matters
- Tolerance
- Forgiveness
- Mastery over the subject etc.

They are attributes of personality like these that bring students close to the teachers and help in promoting and accelerating the growth of students.

7.3 The Responsibility of the Institution

The institution therefore has also to become a coherent unit for helping children grow in desirable directions. To one and all in the institution, the development of total personality of students has to become their core concern.

It will not just be the scholastic growth of students but more so their non-scholastic development, which will need to be focussed upon. Enabling children to earn high examination scores and grades will therefore have to be just one of the many goals to achieve, with the development of a whole and a good individual as the central target.

In this context the student behaviour will have to be observed and guided not just in the classrooms but also in the library, the laboratories, the play ground, during school functions and cultural programmes, in the course of excursions and picnics, study visits, inter-school meets and competitions and so on. The traits of personality observed in these informal situations are more relevant for success in life than only in examinations. It is, therefore, that guiding students in conducting themselves in these situations assumes great importance. Observations in these situations being not for awarding marks or grades but for further improving growth in diverse personality factes assume, a position of strength in the scheme of education.

Observation of behaviour in the above situations will also not just be the responsibility of the teachers but also of the peers. *Self-evaluation* could also be encouraged by introducing an activity of letting students write a daily diary stating the desirable things done by him/her on a particular day and something which s/he should not have done. The latter instances will be *conscience awakening measures* and instruments for developing values in children.

7.4 Maintaining Discipline

The Teachers will also need to help students adhere to disciplinary norms and inculcate desirable *group manners*. In this regard, students will have to be trained for things like—

- Inculcating dignity of labour
- Taking ones turn in queue
- Speaking one at a time
- Permitting others to speak
- Raising hand with elbow on the desk
- Not interrupting others when they are speaking
- Accepting ones mistake and not repeating it
- Taking victory and defeat with equanimity
- Appreciating the point of view of others
- Helping others in difficulty or pain
- Following the rules of the game
- Honouring the decision of the referee or the teacher
- Being clean, punctual and regular.
- Learning to live together in cooperation and peace
- Taking pride in ones home, school and country

and so on.

It is of utmost importance to train the group through drills related to the demonstration of the above competencies for making them a part of the regular life style of students.

7.5 Rewards and Punishments

With a complete ban on corporal punishment appreciation and rewards of different degrees remain as the only means of motivating students. These could take the form of adjectives like 'Good' 'Very Good' etc. or of prizes for excellence at school functions. *Reprimands though still permissible should be rare and never in public*. Praises should be given in public.

Counselling through discussions with the erring students is a safe and a sure remedy which can make students realise their mistakes and for resolving not to repeat them.

Close contact with the parents and soliciting their cooperation in solving problem related to their children could be very helpful. These contacts yield best results, when they are informal and frequent.

7.6 Mock Parliaments and Courts

The organisation of Mock Parliaments for discussing and formulating rules for maintaining discipline in schools are good inputs for enabling the appreciation and implementation of disciplinary norms.

Similarly the holding of Mock Courts *for deciding hypothetical cases related to discipline* in schools are helpful in injecting ideas of discipline and for creating desirable attitudes, among children.

7.7 Conclusion

In all problems of group dynamics it has to be understood by the teachers that they are dealing with immature beings who are unable to discriminate as to what is good and what is bad for them. The present is all that concerns them. They are impatient to wait for a prospect or promise of a future gain. They are also sensitive creatures for whom small gains or small losses make a magnified impact in terms of happiness and despair. Furthermore while their pleasure at a gain may be short-lived their unhappiness at a loss could be lasting.

These are things that ought to be kept in mind, while maintaining a balance, in the group dynamics and for further improving upon the quantums, the facets and the pace of growth.

8

Enriched Teaching for Improved Learning

Learning, is the core determinant of growth and the sole path of progress. Our main effort, therefore, ought to be to make it enabling empowering and enriching.

8.1 The Fundamental Foundations

As already mentioned in passing earlier objectives are the anchor points of both learning experiences and evaluation. As the teacher must be thoroughly acquainted about 'both these' they are being briefly discussed below:

The most important understanding, which the theoretician and practitioner of education ought to develop, is the intrinsic relationship between the instructional objectives, learning experiences and evaluation techniques. Teaching is planned so as to achieve the objectives set in advance and evaluation techniques help us know the extent to which the inputs provided have been effective in helping pupils attain the desired goals.

Objective-based instruction and objective-based evaluation thus form the crux of all educational programmes and practices of educational institutions. The relationship is generally presented through the following well-known Diagram :

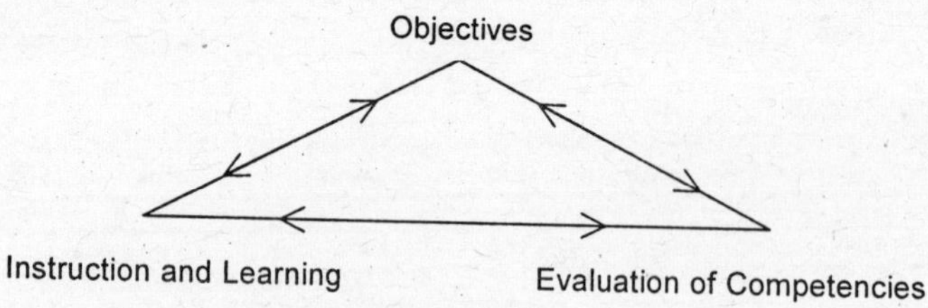

Diagram 8.1

First of all let us examine the mental processes involved in the achievement of instructional objectives. The whole process of instruction indeed ought to be geared to this end. Tracing the steps of the process, we can say that *teaching* becomes successful only when learning takes place. *Learning* takes place through experiences. *Experiences* consist of the absorption of ideas through different senses. *Senses* react to external situations (*stimuli*) for absorbing ideas. These situations are made up if pupils' activities. *Pupils' activities* are thus the starting points for the attainment of objectives.

Based on the gains of participation, in the teaching-learning activities, the evaluation instruments are designed for assessing the degree of the realisation of the expected goals. The analysis of pupil performance reveals the shortfalls in performance or hard spots in learning if any. The process is then reversed and the learning experiences are examined, revised and re-provided for the effective realisation of the goals. If it is considered necessary even objectives are modified, to make them realistic—both achievable and evaluable.

Objectives, as we know, have two specifications the 'competence' specification and the 'content' specification. Both these specifications converge on to a central point which we call a *teaching-learning situations*. These situations as the synthesis of the two aforesaid specifications of objectives, become the basis for designing instructional programmes and evaluation strategies in respect of both the content and competency specifications of the objectives.

The extension of the model also shows the relationship between evaluation and learning. This process can be expressed as under :

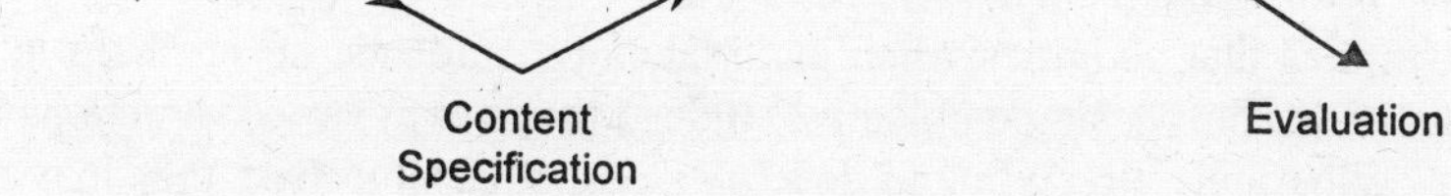

Diagram 8.2

Coming back to the learning process, it could be stated that it is not possible to provide all the possible activities in a particular instructional programme for all student groups. A selection is imperative. The selection is primarily made on the basis of some considerations, like, the objectives desired to be achieved, the time and the resources available and the maturity level of the pupils.

In order to clearly visualise, the relationship between objectives and pupils' activities, let us for a while study the following table, giving the activities and the corresponding objectives that each can help achieve and try to draw some conclusions from it:

PUPIL ACTIVITIES	*OBJECTIVES*
Execution of Practical Work	Understanding, Skill
Organising an Exhibition	Interest, Appreciation, Application, Skill
Excursions /Field Trips	Knowledge, Understanding
Discussions	Understanding, critical thinking
Lectures	Knowledge, Understanding
Dramatisation	Comprehension, interest

The generalisation which can be easily drawn from the above table are as under :

- Different activities lead to the realisation of different objectives or conversely it is not possible to realise all the objectives through a single activity.
- For the achievement of one objective, it may be necessary to employ one or more activities or conversely one activity may, at the same time, lead to the achievement of more than one objective.

8.2 Principles of Objective-Based Instruction

These generalisations lead us to some of the very important principles of objective-based instruction. These are:

8.2.1 *The Principle of Relevance*

This implies that the teaching-learning activities chosen for being pressed into service, should be relevant to the objective and possess the potentiality of achieving it. As it is not possible for all the activities to help in the realisation of all the objectives, they will have to be carefully selected to conform to the need of the situations.

8.2.2 *The Principles of Concomitant or Collateral Learning*

This implies that activities when undertaken by students, do not help in the realisation of only a single objective. Indeed they act in varied directions and while deliberately attempting to develop a particular objective, they may also help achieve some other objectives simultaneously, in an incidental manner.

8.2.3 *The Principle of Adequacy*

This implies that the activities selected should be adequate for achieving the objectives of instruction, comprehensively. This adequacy in respect of activities is achieved through the selection of relevant activities in adequately sufficient number, the frequency of their repetition and the spacing of these learning experiences.

8.2.4 *The Principle of Variety*

As a corollary of the above three principles, it could be said that for accomplishing the desired objectives, it is necessary to choose and use a variety of activities.

8.3 Methods of Teaching

The above principles lead us, almost naturally to a discussion on teaching methods which could be defined as *the systematic organisation of activities that result in learning and thus in the achievement of the desired objectives of instruction.*

Teaching methods can be sub-divided into two categories :

(a) The Standard Methods of Teaching, and
(b) The Specific Methods of Instruction designed for achieving certain emergent purposes.

The standard methods of instruction are quite well known. The activities to be pressed into service in the process of instruction, through them are almost fixed. These designated activities are followed sequentially almost in a ritualistic manner. The objectives that are possible to be achieved through such methods are also commonly known.

The specific methods of instruction on the other hand, are a product of teachers' ingenuity for achieving the specific purposes they may emerge in the course of teaching or those that the teacher may deem necessary. These are original in their nature and involve a unique organisation of activities with a view to achieving specific goals desired to be realised by the teacher in the process of teaching. They do not admit any rigidity either in the sequence of the steps or in the number or kind of the activities to be used.

Objective-based instruction would mainly follow the latter of the two methods, though efforts can be made to incorporate some of the features of the formal methods of instruction as well.

8.4 Planning Enriched Objective-Based Instruction

Objective-based instruction can be divided into the following main operational steps:

- The preparation and use of objective-based instructional material.
- Planning instruction in keeping with the objectives.

  This planning may consist of the preparation of:

  (a) a year's plan
  (b) a term's plan
  (c) a unit plan
  (d) a class period plan

In planning for objective-based instruction, the preparation of an yearly plan is very important. It is the first step for *preparing a time-budget* for covering the course. A teacher is allotted a number of periods for covering the given specific quantum of the subject matter. As an initial step of planning, the whole content area is divided into different sub-units and allotted periods in terms of a time-budget in the instructional programme. Here the measure of emphasis will be determined by the proportion of resources, energy, time etc. proposed to be pressed into service for achieving the objectives. This plan can be hypothetically presented through a table like the one given below based on the supposition that there are six major units of content to be covered and that eighty class periods are available for accomplishing the task.

Domains of Development →	*Cognitive Areas*			*Affective Areas*		*Psycho-motor Areas*	*Number of Class Periods*
Objectives →	*Knowledge*	*Under-standing*	*Application*	*Interests*	*Attitudes*	*Skills*	
Units of Content ↓							
U_1	✓				✓		15
U_2		✓		✓			10
U_3	✓		✓			✓	25
U_4		✓			✓		15
U_5	✓		✓				10
U_6	✓	✓		✓		✓	5
					Total		80

Diagram 8.3

The next step in the planning of instruction is the preparation of teaching units. These units are generally prepared by experts with the help of teachers, and are supplied to teachers. Teachers however should always remain the master of the teaching operations and must never become slaves of the teaching units handed down to them. Teachers are supposed to make use of these units according to their needs and requirements. Resourceful teachers can also prepare their own teaching units, if they have time and facilities. The preparation of lesson-plans is the subsequent step. From a teaching unit a teacher can prepare lesson-plans for each class period according to need and convenience.

It will not be out of place to re-emphasise here that *educational objectives as mentioned earlier are derived from several primary sources, chief of which, are the level of psychological development of the child, the social order, the economic environment the political system, the cultural heritage and the existing store of human knowledge in the society in question*. From the overall educational objectives, are derived the *stage-wise objectives* which become the basis for curriculum development of the different stages of education. From the stage-wise objectives, in turn are derived the *subject-wise objectives* of teaching which become the basis of the development of the curriculum plans of particular subjects at a particular stage. These subsequently help and guide the preparation of unit-plans and lesson-plans. Taking the processes in the opposite direction it could be said that the achievement of the different lesson-wise objectives leads to the achievement of unit-wise objectives, the achievement of different unit-wise objectives leads to the achievement of different subject-wise objectives, the achievement of the subject-wise objectives leads to the realisation of stage-wise objectives and these finally lead to the achievement of overall objectives of education.

The above discussion leads us to conclude that there is a parallelism between testing and teaching-learning which can be diagramatically represented as under :

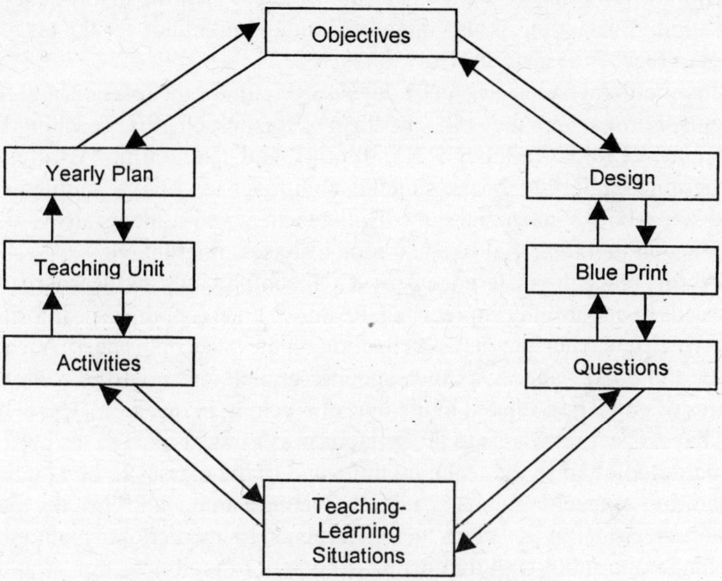

Diagram 8.4

8.5 Nature and Purpose of Instructional Material

Suitable instructional material is an essential prerequisite for ensuring enriched instruction. There has, of late, been a phenomenal explosion of knowledge. In a good many cases different subjects and topics have assumed new dimensions and meanings. In many places, however, there is a paucity of aids and materials having relevance to related classroom instruction. Syllabi in different subjects are also often very sketchy and generalised in nature. They do not indicate the exact scope of subject-matter desired to be taught and tested. Textbooks also continue to be very deficient in many respects.

New types of instructional materials and ways of structuring different subjects and topics of study, leave nothing which is not teachable. Methods of instruction, however, well-conceived will also remain ineffective without a solid grounding in the subject-matter, which is basically provided by instructional materials.

Furthermore, evaluation also will fail to appropriately test the objectives, unless the objectives like understanding of major ideas, skills and attitudes are drawn from the solid base of the subject-matter. Activities too in order to be purposeful must fit into the context of what is to be taught. These activities will lose their significance unless teachers have a complete perspective of all the dimensions of the subject-matter.

The main available source of subject-matter to both teachers and students is instructional material. Instructional material to be effective has but to incorporate enriched content material, which is helpful to the teacher in curriculum transaction. It also ought to contain guidelines for the teacher on 'What to teach?' as also on 'How to teach?'

Instructional materials can be developed both for the teachers and for the students. For teachers they take the form of Resource Units, Teaching Units, Reference Books, Teacher's Handbooks and Curriculum Guides, etc. Instructional materials for the students comprises textbooks, supplementary books, workbooks, magazines, etc. Both teachers and students also make use of some common material like textbooks, atlases, internet etc.

At this place the difference between Teaching Units and Resource Units also needs to be carefully appreciated. Resource units contain basic information from which a teacher can make a selection on the basis of his need. A teaching unit on the other hand lays down specific guidelines about the content and process of education related to the unit of teaching in question. The teaching units have direct relevance to the syllabus prescribed as also to the periods of instruction allotted to the teaching units and to the classes to be taught. The preparation of teaching units is a crucial venture and needs both the mastery of the subject-matter as well as the skills related to instructional methodology. Teaching units should not duplicate the content of textbooks nor should they be a mere compilation of materials culled from advanced books. They have to be specially tailored to specific needs.

The syllabus of the entire year is first to be split into a number of viable units. Each one ought to be autonomous in some ways—in respect of subject-matter, a sequence and relationship with what has gone before and what is to follow in the scheme of instruction should not be overlooked. One teaching unit may be further split into more than one teaching lessons.

The contents of teaching units are merely suggestive. The teachers may use them flexibly according to the needs and exigencies of actual classroom situations. Length of descriptive statements is not a guiding criterion of a good teaching unit. Its usability and the support it offers to the teachers are the real yardsticks for judging its utility.

8.6 A Suggestive Format of a Teaching Unit

The format of the teaching unit is not rigid. It also need not be uniform in all the subjects and at all levels. However, a broad outline is suggested below.

8.6.1 *Introduction*

The introduction of the teaching unit should bring out the significance of the topic, its conspicuous character or novelty, its implications and relevance in life. It is to be based on what the students have studied before and also becomes the basis of what the content of the present unit is.

8.6.2 *Specific Objectives*

A teaching unit must indicate specific objectives of the topic to be taught. These will comprise the understanding of major ideas, application of knowledge, development of skills, the desired interest and attitudes as expected outcomes of the learning of the unit in question. The formulation of specific objectives is based on the general objectives envisaged in the study of the particular subject.

The formulation of objectives has to be precise, clear and their wording has to be spelled out so as to be comprehensible and indicative of what is significant for learning in respect of the content unit in question. Formulation of objectives is also very crucial, because they give a sense of direction and a perspective to our entire approach of presentation of content, incorporation of activities and evaluation. They should indeed be stated in terms of 'specifications' of the objectives, as to what a student will be able to do, to demonstrate that s/he has realised the objective in question.

8.6.3 *Content Analysis*

The content analysis given in a teaching unit as mentioned earlier should not merely reproduce the content given in the textbooks. It should unfold details more vividly and in the correct perspective, which will make teaching graphic and powerful. It may contain extracts from original sources or enriched materials which may not be within easy reach of the teacher. The content may even contain materials not necessarily falling within the precise preview of specific major ideas, but which may provide appropriate links in the continuity of its sequence or in supporting it.

Major ideas, which are, in a way, basic concepts come to be the basic learning points, which are supposed to be internalised by the students while some peripheral things could be permissible to be forgotton. Some 'Major Ideas' in social sciences could be:

- Ashoka's administration symbolised a centralised monarchy.
- Raja Rammohan Roy brought modernity to Indian education.
- A citizen has both rights and duties.
- Industrialisation has brought problems in its wake.
- Early civilisations grew in river beds.
- Scientific developments have not always been for the good of mankind.

The content should be authentic and up-to-date. If it deals with controversial issues, it should present the different conflicting view points objectively. If it has a generalisation, it should be fully substantiated by given data. The content ought to err on the side of comprehensiveness rather than on too much simplification or generalised form of global presentation.

8.6.4 *Teaching Hints and Activities*

Instruction in order to be effective must be objective-based and center round *pupil's activities.* These activities should be purposeful. They should flow out of the content aimed at the realisation of objectives. Suggestion in this regard must be specific and in the context of the subject-matter. They should outline the process of instruction, the teacher's role as also the student's activities and the approaches to their execution. If discussion is suggested, the stages of its actual conduct and various possible questions to be deliberated upon, ought to be broadly indicated. The hints to teachers should be specific. Assignments whenever suggested need also be detailed out. They should be creative and not routinised and repetitive.

8.6.5 *Evaluation of Competencies*

Evaluation is an integral part of instruction. It has to be continuous and built into the total teaching-learning process. It ought to be objective-based and comprehensive covering both scholastic and non co-scholastic aspects of pupil growth. It should also be valid (accurate) reliable (dependable), objective (just), and practicable (feasible). The questions should not merely test memory. Teacher's mastery of the subject-matter however is essential for framing questions properly. In evaluation various procedures and tools of evaluation should be utilised in a bid to fully realise the instructional objectives, in the Cognitive Affective and Psycho-motor domains.

8.6.6 *Reference Material*

This section of a teaching unit should indicate the books which the teachers/ students may consult on the topic. The list should not be unduly ambitious. It should be complete—containing full specifications of authorship and publishers, year of publication, edition, relevant chapters, pages etc.

8.7 Conclusion

To conclude, it may be said that enrichment of instruction for improved learning will remain a vague slogan till we impart to our teachers greater competence and mastery in the use of instructional materials through pre-service and in-service teacher-education programmes. Development and supply of skillfully prepared teaching units is an important step in this direction.

Objective-based evaluation and objective-based instruction are the two sides of the same coin. Preparation of good teaching units needs the cooperation of the teacher, the pedagogue, the subject expert and the evaluator and this ought to be solicited in letter and spirit.

A diagramatic representation of objective based instruction is given in Diagram 8.5.

8.8 Objective-based Instruction: A Diagramatic Representation

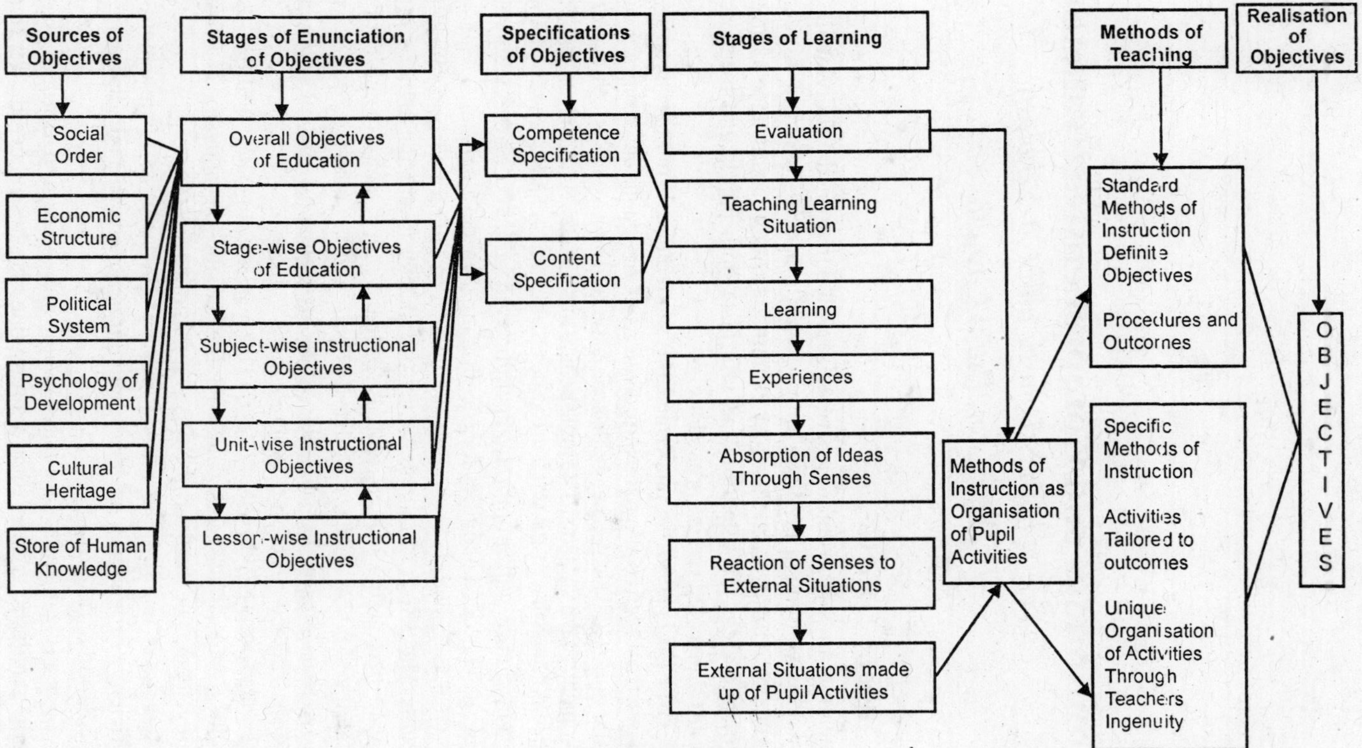

Diagram 8.5

9

Continuous and Comprehensive Evaluation

Covering both Scholastic and Co-Scholastic Aspects of Pupil Growth

9.1 Historical Overview

Education aims at promoting alround development of the individual. This alround development involves both scholastic and co-scholastic aspects of personality. However, because our examinations, take cognisance of only the scholastic areas, all attention and efforts of both pupils and teachers are primarily invested on this area alone.

The NPE 1986/92 has pinpointed, this shortcoming of our education system and given a directive about the introduction of Continuous and Comprehensive Evaluation (CCE) covering both scholastic and non-scholastic areas of the personality of the students. The logic behind this directive is that if some abilities, skills and qualities of the students are to be evaluated and reported for public consumption, it will prompt the institutions to initiate concrete action about offering the needed activities for encouraging their development.

CCE is aimed at correcting the current imbalance in our educational pursuits. The term '*Continuous*' emphasises that the evaluation of the identified areas of personality is a continuous '*process*' rather than a combination of isolated unconnected '*events*'; that it is built into the total teaching-learning process as its integral part and is thus spread over the entire span of an academic session. The second term '*Comprehensive*' implies that it attempts to cover different aspects of personality beyond the academic ones i.e., abilities, skills, qualities, interests, attitudes, values outdoor activities etc. and not just academic achievement. The third term '*Evaluation*' implies that the purpose of the total endeavour is not just the measurement of the level of achievement and proficiency of students but also their improvement through diagnosis and remediation/enrichment.

Such a scheme of school-based evaluation, in addition to stimulating the pupils' scholastic growth, aims at promoting his physical health, developing in him desirable personal and social qualities, building in him desirable attitudes and values, helping him cultivate and nurture his interests by providing opportunities of acquiring skills and proficiencies through participation in various co-curricular activities.

9.2 Dimensions of the Scheme

9.2.1 *Scholastic Aspects*

Curricular Areas

Techniques of Evaluation
- Written Examinations
- Oral Examinations
- Practical Examinations

Tools of Evaluation
- Question papers
- Unit tests
- Projects
- Surveys

Periodicity of Evaluation
- Twice in an academic session

Coverage
- For all students

9.2.2 *Non-scholastic Areas*

Health Status
- Height in relation to age
- Weight in relation to height
- Chest Expansion
- Eyesight
- Hearing

Techniques of Evaluation
- Medical Check-up
- Observation by the teacher

Tools of Assessment
- Height and weight charts weighing machine, measuring tapes

Periodicity of Assessment
- Twice in an Academic Session

Coverage
- For all Students

Personal and Social Qualities
- Regularity
- Punctuality
- Discipline
- Habits of cleanliness
- Initiative
- Co-operation
- Sense of Responsibility
- Deligence

Techniques of Evaluation
- Observation

Tools of Evaluation
- Anecdotal records
- Rating Scales

Periodicity of Evaluation

- Civil Consciousness
- Spirit of Social Service

Interests

Literary Interests
- Recitation
- Debates
- Creative writing
- Extra Reading

Scientific Interests
- Exploration
- Experimentation
- Science Club activities

Cultural Interests
- Music
- Dance
- Dramatics

Artistic Interests
- Drawing
- Painting
- Sculpture
- Artistic Embroidery

Attitudes
- Towards teachers
- Towards school-mates
- Towards school programmes
- Towards school property

Values
- Dignity of labour
- Honesty

- Twice in an Academic Session.

Coverage
- The first four personal and Social Qualities to be assessed in respect of all students and the rest only when evidences are available.
- A student may choose only one activity from any one of the areas of *interest* for being evaluated, though he may participate in as many as he likes.
- A student is to be rated on all *identified attitudes.*
- In regard to *values* a student will be evaluated only when evidences are available.
- In regard to co-curricular activities *Games and Sports* are to be compulsory for all students and they will be rated on any one of them selected by the student. In addition a student can choose any one other activity for evaluation, available in school for being rated.
- A student could participate in additional activities other than those selected for evaluation. While these will not be rated, his participation in them will be indicated in the certificate.

- Courage
- Courtesy
- Tolerance
- Forgiveness
- Team Spirit

Co-Curricular Activities

- Games and Sports
- Gymnastics
- Swimming
- Scouting
- Gardening
- Craft
- Adventure Activities

Note: *Evaluation in respect of Academic Achievement and Health status will be in numerical terms. In the rest of the areas proficiency will be evaluated in terms of grades on a five point scale (ABCDE). The grade "E" will, however, not be awarded to any student as it indicates failure.*

9.3 Operational Strategy

The schemes envisages the issue of an independent certificate by the school. The scheme will cover :

- Level of academic achievement attained in school
- Health Status
- Personal and Social Qualities
- Interests
- Attitudes and values
- Proficiency in outdoor co-curricular activities

The Certificate of School-based Evaluation will be issued as a supplement to that of Board Examinations, on a format prescribed by the Board.

The Board's certificate of external examination will contain a footnote stating that "*There is another certificate of School-based Evaluation being issued by the school on a format prescribed by the Board, which should also be taken cognisance of in judging the total personality of the student.*"

9.4 Salient Features of the Scheme

The scheme elevates the status of the schools by making them equal partners with the Board, in evaluating (and certifying students for public consumption), the abilities and potentials of the students through an independent certificate.

The official recognition given to the school certificate through the footnote on the certificate of external examinations, will naturally lead to an extensive use of this certificate by the institutes of higher education as also the prospective employers.

The delegation of the aforesaid authority to the schools for issuing a certificate for public consumption, as a supplement to that of Board Examinations, will also go a long way in improving the tone of the institutions.

The scheme successfully counters the common criticism of public examinations that they focus only on scholastic areas by bringing different non-scholastic facets of personality within the gamut of evaluation.

The *scheme also does away with the innumerable malpractices associated with internal assessment (where the marks awarded by the schools are arithmetically added to those of external examination for determining the students' final level of achievement)* by providing for a separate presentation of external and school marks through two independent certificates.

The simplicity and built-in flexibility of the scheme makes it applicable to all types of schools and does not increase the work-load of the teachers as it only means systematisation of the tasks he is already doing.

The scheme also pursues and toes the age-old dictum that those who teach must also test.

9.5 Evaluating Growth in Co-Scholastic Areas

The Tools of Assessment

Two assessments are proposed in an academic session, for purposes of being recorded in the certificate, with Anecdotal Record Form and Rating Scales as the main tools.

Use of Anecdotal Records

Anecdotal Record Forms are basically used for collection of evidences. They ought to be freely available in the Principal's office and the staff room. They can be filled in by any member of the staff of the school on the observation of a particular noteworthy behaviour. They could assume the following form :

ANECDOTAL RECORD FORM

Name of the Student:........................ Class:.......... Section:.................

Date of Observation:.........................

Occasion & Place	Anecdote as Observed (A Factual Account)	Teacher's Comments (If any)
Teacher's Signature.. Date........................		

The Anecdotal Record Forms have then to be passed on to the class teacher, who will keep on collecting them and maintain a record about each such receipt with signature of the person forwarding each filled in anecdotal record form. The Anecdotal Record Forms are basically aids to memory and spread the observation-net wider. They assume special importance because many of the facets of personality have only to be rated when evidences about them are available.

Use of Rating Scales

Rating scales are the main tools of evaluation for assessing co-scholastic aspects of pupil growth. Five point rating scales are recommended to be used. In such a rating scale (A, B, C, D, & E). A rating of "E" which is supposed to correspond to failure is not proposed to be used at all and the students may be classified into only four categories (ranges of competencies).

In some cases, e.g., in Personal and Social Qualities only one Rating scale will be required to be used as illustrated below in respect of 'Discipline'.

RATING SCALE FOR DISCIPLINE

E — Rarely or never obeys rules and regulations

D — Occasionally obeys rules and regulations but is not courteous

C — Usually obeys rules and regulations and knows his responsibilities

B — Obeys rules and regulations, most of the time, knows his responsibility but is not always courteous

A — Always obeys rules and regulations, accepts the role assigned to him and encourages others to do the same and is courteous

In some other cases as in activities related to interests and other co-curricular activities, there may be more than one evaluative criteria on which it may need to be evaluated for example in 'Dramatics' they may be:

- Make up
- Acting
- Dialogues
- Emotional Appeal

In such cases rating scales would need to be developed for each evaluative criteria and for arriving at the composite overall grade in respect of the activity to be recorded in the certificate the following procedure could be used :

Numerical Value of Different Symbolic Grades	*Symbolic Grades Obtained by a Student on the four Evaluative Criteria*		*Numerical Grades Corresponding to the Symbolic Grades obtained by a Student*	*Derivation of a Symbolic overall Grade*
A = 5	Make-up	B	4	4 + 4 + 5 + 4 = 17
B = 4	Acting	B	4	17 + 4
C = 3	Dialogues	A	5	= 4.25
D = 2	Emotional Appeal	B	4	= B
E = 1				

GRADE RANGES

E	D	C	B	A
0.6←→1.5	1.6←→2.5	2.6←→	3.6←→4.5	4.6←→5.5

As 4.25 falls within the grade range of grade B, the final symbolic grade for recording in the certificate is B.

With a view to ensuring uniformity in the standards of assessment, the rating scales may be developed centrally by the examining agencies and supplied to the teachers.

9.6 Assessment in Scholastic Areas

Recording of assessment in scholastic areas (for purposes of certification) too is required to be done twice in an academic session; These will, in fact, be two half yearly entries. Two such entries will be possible in class IX and only one in class X. In lower classes two entries of assessments may be done in the course of each academic session.

In operational terms, the assessments will be continuous and spread over the total span of the academic year. *The evaluation situations could consist of tests, assignments, project work, field work, surveys etc. and not just tests.* The weightages to these evaluations, in terms of percentages of marks could be as given hereunder during different spans. While the exercises may by themselves carry a higher weightage individually, the obtained scores will need to be reduced to the given percentages in respect of the particular span of time. The hypothetical example supposes that the academic session would start in July and end in April with May and June as the period of summer vacations. The horizontal lines show the points of time for recording of evaluation results and the vertical lines the spans of attainments to be covered and their respective weightages. In institution level evaluation 50% marks could be taken as the level of eligibility for promotion to the next class.

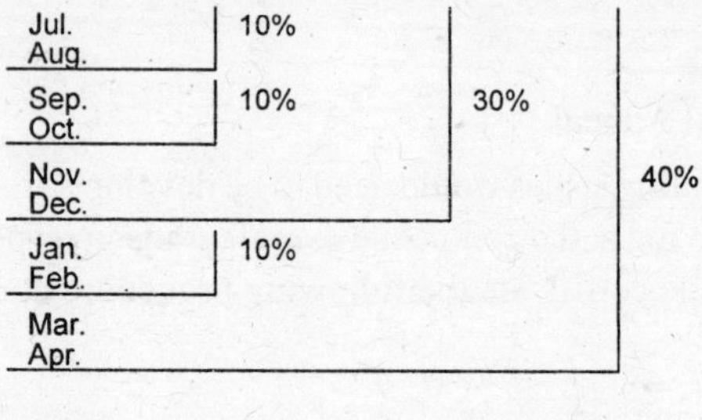

9.7 Assessment of Health Status

This will be done twice a year and will basically consist of those aspects which a teacher can manage on his own. A measuring tape and a weighing machine are the only instruments to be used. Height and chest measurements will be done in terms of meters and centimeters and weight in terms of kilograms and grams.

Charts giving age and height in respect of males and females and those giving norms height and corresponding weight will be required to be used and these could be supplied to the schools by the Department of Education.

In the remarks column any special thing like a physical deformity could be mentioned.

If a Medical Examination by a Doctor is done, the aspects needing the attention of the parents could be communicated to the parents by the class teacher/Head of the school on the basis of medical advice.

Ratings of Interests, Attitudes, Values and Co-Curricular Activities

These will be evaluated through rating scales and the ratings entered in the certificate.

Administrative Procedure for Determining Ratings for Entry in the Certificate

While objective evaluations will be available in some cases like height, weight, academic achievement and in some physically measurable co-curricular activities, it is desirable to minimize subjectively in evaluation to as great an extent as possible. While in some cases Anecdotal Record Forms will be available and in other cases the general observations may be the basis of assessment of participation and proficiency in different activities. It is, therefore, proposed that for deriving/determining the final ratings for certificate entry, the head of the school may nominate another teacher for working with the class-teacher.

9.8 Format of a CCE Certificate

(Example: Secondary Stage)

School Profile

- School Logo
- Name of the School
- Full Addresses and Telephone/Fax Number
- Board to which affiliated with Affiliation Number
- A brief description of the School
  - Year of Establishment
  - Type of School
  - Physical & Social surroundings and the school campus
  - The type of population being catered to

Pupil Profile

- Name of the student
- Admission/Enrolment No.

- External Examination (if any) cleared with year and Roll No.
- Sex (Boy/Girl)
- Date of Birth
- Guardian's Name (Father/Mother)
- Permanent Address

Level of Academic Achievement (In Percentage)

Subject \ Assessment \ Class	Class	
	First Assessment	*Second Assessment*
I Language		
II Language		
Social Sciences		
Sciences		
Mathematics		
Additional Subject (If any)		

Health Status

Aspect \ Assess-ment \ Class	Class							
	First Assessment				*Second Assessment*			
	Height (in cms)	*Weight (in kg)*	*Chest Normal (in cms)*	*Chest Expanded (in cms)*	*Height (in cms)*	*Weight (in kg)*	*Chest Normal (in cms)*	*Chest Expanded (in cms)*
Additional Remarks (If any)								

Personal and Social Qualities

Sl. No.	Quality \ Assessment \ Class	Class	
		First Assessment	*Second Assessment*
1.	Regularity		
2.	Punctuality		
3.	Discipline		
4.	Habits of Cleanliness		
5.			
6.			
7.			

Interests

Types of Interest Literary/Scientific/ Cultural/Artistic etc.	*Selected Activity*	*Class… … …*	
		First Assessment	*Second Assessment*

Additional Interest Related Activity/Activities in which Participated (Without Rating)

Type of Interest	*Activity / Activities*

Attitudes and Values

ATTITUDES

Sl. No.	*Class / Assessment / Attitudes*	*Class… … …*	
		First Assessment	*Second Assessment*
1.	Towards Teachers		
2.	Towards School Programmes		
3.	Towards Schoolmates		
4.	Towards School Property		

VALUES

Sl. No.	*Class / Assessment / Value*	*Class… … …*	
		First Assessment	*Second Assessment*
1.			
2.			
3.			
4.			
5.			

Outdoor Curricular Activities

Sl. No.	*Class / Assessment / Activities*	*Class... ... ...*	
		First Assessment	*Second Assessment*
1.			
2.			
3.			
4.			

ADDITIONAL CO-CURRICULAR ACTIVITY/ACTIVITIES IN WHICH PARTICIPATED

Sl. No.	*Activities*
1.	
2.	
3.	
4.	
5.	
6.	

Dated:.....................

Overall Remarks

____

____

____

____

Signature of Class Teacher

Principal's Observations

____

____

____

____

Principal's Signature

10

Preparing Questions of Different Forms

In any comprehensive programme of educational reform, improvement of examinations and the improvement in the quality of the question papers is a foregone conclusion. Individual questions would, therefore, have to be framed in such way that when put together in the form of a question paper, they fulfill the requisites of a good measuring instrument. We may make use of essay type, short-answer type, very short answer type and objective type questions or some of them together but they should all conform to and satisfy the characteristics of a good question of the given form. This is discussed below :

10.1 Characteristics of Good Questions

Objective-Based

A good question should be framed on a predetermined objective and it should test the concerned ability effectively. Questions may sometimes test more than one objective. It may also test one or more specifications of a particular objective on which that question is based. In case a question attempts to test more than one objective, it is designated as one testing the highest objective in the hierarchy which it aims to test.

Content-Specific

The content on which a question is based is closely related to the objective being tested. The framer of the question, has, therefore, to take into account the topic or the sub-topic he is going to prepare a question on. He should see that a question samples exactly the same area of content, which is desired to be tested through it.

Form of Questions

Essay type, short-answer type, very short answer type and objective-type questions are the main forms of questions in use. In a question, the form depends considerably on the kind of ability as well as the nature of the content desired to be tested. Some forms are more suitable than others for testing certain abilities. Essay-type questions for example, are more suitable for testing abilities like organisation of thoughts, analysis, interpretation etc. Therefore, a judicious mix of the appropriate question forms will have to be attempted, while setting questions which may finally be woven into a question paper. A decision about this has to be made while preparing the design for the question paper itself.

Wording of Questions

To bring objectively in evaluation, there is need for using clear, precise and unambiguous language while framing questions. Use of unfamiliar and difficult terminology may be avoided so that the comprehension of the question itself may not become a problem for the students by even influencing their difficulty level. A question should be so worded that by-and-large, all students as also examiners may make the same meaning out of it, about the scope and length of the expected answer. Here special care is to be taken to avoid the use of stock, phrases like describe, elucidate, discuss or write short notes on, write an account of, write a report on, what do you know, etc. What is expected to be written by the students has to be explained to them in unabiguous terms, while wording the questions themselves.

Structuring the Situation

In writing different questions, selection of an appropriate situation is an important step in the framing of questions. Textbook situations could be alright for testing knowledge. Other situations discussed in the class may be suitable for testing knowledge or understanding. But to test application of knowledge, some unfamiliar situations will need to be identified or even concoted. Although in such cases situations are likely to go beyond the textbook yet they should be in keeping with the ability levels of students and related to the content studied by them. It will be advisable if the teacher collects such situations and keeps a record of these so that they may be available to him as and when needed.

Estimated Difficulty Level

While writing a question the framer of the questions should be conscious of the estimated difficulty level of the question in relation to the ability of pupils for whom the question is meant. The difficulty level of a question usually depends upon the complexity of the mental processes involved (objectives) in responding to it, the area of the content desired to be tested and the time available which can be spent for answering it. The difficulty level of a particular question can be estimated fairly well in advance by an experienced teacher. Actual difficulty index, however, is possible to be calculated only after the question has been really tried out and its responses analysed. Multiple choice questions are amenable for such calculations. However, an experienced teacher can easily estimate the difficulty level in approximate term. Such decision determine the proportionate questions of varying estimated difficulty while preparing question papers.

Discrimination Value

It is not possible to estimate the discriminating value of a question unless it is tried out. Nevertheless when some novel situations are involved and common place questions are avoided, the questions definitely go a long way in discriminating the bright students from the weak ones. Questions at either extremes of the difficulty continuum are poor discriminators, while those in the middle are found to be more effective in this respect.

Delimiting the Scope of the Answer

The question framer or paper setter should ensure that while constructing a question s/he gives due thought to the expected answer. S/he is also required to develop an outline of the expected answer alongwith the marks to be devoted to each part of the expected answer as part of the marking scheme. This is desirable to be done at the same time as the preparation of the question. This would reveal the weaknesses (if any) in the wording of the question itself. It should be specific and precise in language so that the scope and length of the expected answer stands clearly delimited and defined.

Key/Marking Scheme

In case of objective-type questions, the key must be prepared alongwith the questions. In case of long answer, short answer and very short answer questions, outlines of expected answers and the marking scheme has to be prepared. Weightage in terms of marks to each value-point or aspect of the expected answer has also be indicated.

A question framer or paper setter, while constructing each question, should be conscious of the various dimensions of questions discussed above as also the other considerations and rules for framing different forms of questions.

10.2 Forms of Objective-Based Questions

Objective-based questions are questions designed to test different objectives of teaching and testing. They could assume different forms of which objective type questions are one. The other three varieties being Essay Type (Long Answer Type), Short Answer Type and Very Short Answer Type. All the forms (types) of questions, test some objective/ability/competency/proficiency. Thus *all objective type questions are objective-based, though all objective-based questions are not objective type questions.*

Questions could broadly be classified into different forms/types as under:

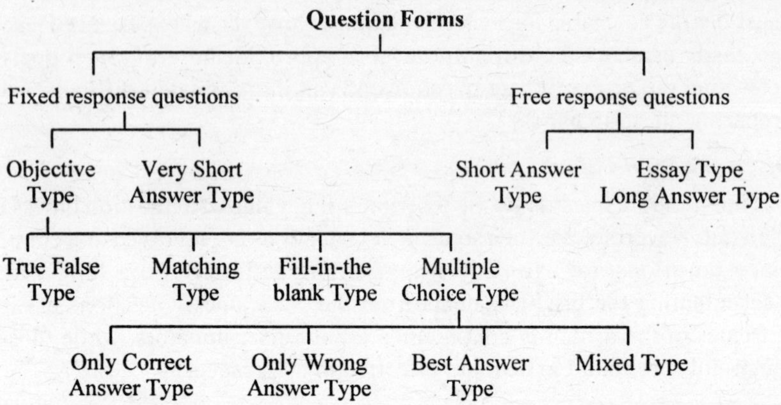

It is intended here to discuss different forms of questions in terms of their characteristics, their strong and week points and the rules governing their preparation.

It has already been mentioned that depending upon the objective (ability) and the content area (subject matter) we can select the form of the question (essay type, short answer, very short answer or objective type).

The most commonly used tools of evaluation in the written tests are the questions which are generally of two types – the free response type and the fixed responses type. The long answer/essay type questions which are basically free response questions have been in use for quite some time. They used to be the sole variety of questions in traditional question paper. Now with the realisation of the shortcomings of these questions (as proved through research studies both in India and abroad) and their adverse effects on the accuracy, dependability and objectivity of examination results, short answer questions which also fall under this category are also being increasingly used. Fixed response questions (Very Short Answer types and Objective type) are those where the answer is fixed and any deviation from the expected answer is taken as incorrect. In free response questions as compared to this situation the examinee exercises freedom to manipulate his answer in his own language.

The long answer or free response type questions are still being used but in limited numbers, only for testing those abilities which other forms of tests cannot effectively test.

Operational descriptions of questions of different forms are attempted below:

(i) Objective Type (*Multiple Choice* with four alternatives).
(ii) *Very Short Answer (VSA)* questions usually carrying one or two marks and requiring an answer in one word, one phrase or one

sentence or one or two steps of mathematical calculation. They need about a minute to answer.

(iii) *Short Answer Questions (SA)* carrying two to four marks which require answers in about 25 to 50 words or involve four to six steps of mathematical calculation. Each of these questions usually require 3 to 5 minutes to answer.

(iv) *Long Answer or Essay Type Questions (LA/ET)* which require answers between 100 to 400 words or upto a maximum of ten or more steps of mathematical calculation. These may carry 5 to 15 marks.

(v) In languages the composition questions require the students to discuss certain themes using their own vocabulary, usage, syntax with originality and in their own style. These questions would also need to be given a rough time limit based on the expected length of the answer. Therefore, the length of the answer will also be required to be approximately indicated as part of the wording of the question itself in the question paper. A rough and the ready formula is to determine the length and the mark allocation in a proportionate manner. Roughly speaking 5 marks could be allocated for an answer expected to be written in 100 words.

10.3 Preparing Long Answer or Essay Type Questions

These questions are considered to be easy to prepare and administer in the traditional scene. They also offer quite a lot of freedom to the examinees who can use their own language and style of writing. These questions require examinees to choose the language, select the facts, organise the ideas for presenting a response to the question asked in the way they choose.

These questions provide examinees an opportunity to analyse, synthesize, re-organise, integrate, synthesize and evaluate situations, as also to investigate, interpret them for drawing conclusions for justifying or negating a particular stand.

They have the potential of testing the originality and creativity of the particular examinee. Thus they can most effectively test those abilities and mental processes which are not possible to be tested through any other form of questions.

Shortcomings

Despite the positive points the long answer or essay type questions are also imbued with some very serious shortcomings. While they provide freedom to the examinee, they also provide freedom to the examinee. Thus they breed subjectivity in scoring. Quite often they are criticised and quite rightly so, for introducing a substantial element of unreliability in scoring.

Besides, there is also another serious shortcoming and that is that because they require long answers, they also need longer time to answer and because they need a long answering time, only a few of such type of questions can be asked in a given time. Again because they can only be few, they are able to test only a small part of the prescribed syllabus. The use of such questions, in question papers, more often than not, leads to selective study and selective teaching, which in turn endangers the validity (or accuracy) and reliability (or dependability) of the result, because of restricted and poor sampling of the content.

In this background, therefore, while long answer questions are incorporated in the question papers, their number and the quantum of marks devoted to them are deliberately restricted to the barest minimum.

In spite of these shortcomings the long answer type questions continue to be used in examinations, because as already mentioned *they can test those abilities which no other form of question can effectively evaluate* e.g., the capacity to weigh ideas, to argue in favour or against a proposition, to establish relationships, to critically analyse situations, to judge the implications of a given phenomenon and so on. These questions also promote self-study with insight.

Some Guiding Principles for Preparing Long Answer Questions

Preparation of good essay type or long answer questions is not an easy task. Some tips for preparing this type of questions are spelt out below:

- Long Answer or Essay Type questions because of their limitations, should be set to test only those instructional objectives, which are not possible to be tested by other forms of questions.
- Essay questions should be prepared for specifically testing the mental processes or learning outcomes implied by the objectives in view.
- These questions ought to be so worded that the scope and approximate length of the expected answer is clear to the students.
- Maturation level of the examinees must be taken into consideration while constructing an essay/long answer question. Length and nature of answer will differ from class to class. For example, questions requiring discussion, interpretation, summarisation or evaluation may be asked in higher classes, whereas those testing abilities like listing, describing, selecting etc. may be considered suitable for lower classes.
- Outline answer of each question with value points to different parts of the expected answer also needs to be specified as part of the marking scheme. This should be done at the same time as drafting the questions themselves. After framing the question, revert back to the language of the question and check that it would evoke the expected answer from the examinees. In case it does not do so, changes may be introduced in the wording of the question in question, so that it may be ensured to yield the expected answer.

- The use of directional words or phrases like the following be systematically avoided:

	Or
Elucidate	Relate
Exemplify	Evaluate
Criticise	Weigh
Discuss	Examine
Justify	Write an essay on ....
	Write short notes on ....
	Write a report on ....
	What do you think of ....
	What do you know about ....

  The purpose of these words or directions is not clearly understood by students and also sometimes by examiners. What the student is expected to write in the answer, should therefore be clearly and unambiguously stated instead of these unintelligible directional words and phrases.
- This will also contain the tendency of the students to write all that they know about that topic, instead of responding to the requirements of the questions.
- The question ought to be worded in such a manner that each question presents a definite problem. Though the student should be provided freedom to choose the language and style this should be exercised within the dimensions and parameters which may be indicated by the wording of the questions.
- The marks that each question carries should not be indicated against them as a whole (e.g. 10). They should be clearly distributed among the various aspects of the expected answer or various expected abilities attempted to be tested and indicated as say (2 + 4 + 4).
- The questions should not be repeated vertatim from among those asked in previous examinations or lifted from those given/listed at the end of the chapters of the books/work-books.
- The questions set may not just be direct questions, answers to which may be found directly in the books and could be lifted as such from a particular portion of a book. The questions should also invariably present situations or problems which call for thinking rather than just recall and reproduction of memorised information.

Scoring of Long Answer Questions

Essay/Long answer type questions in the traditional set-up are prepared quickly but they take a much longer time to answer. Furthermore though easy to prepare, they are difficult to answer, mark and evaluate.

A detailed marking scheme, giving outline answers and value points in terms of marks for different aspects or facts of the expected answer (desired to be taken into consideration for purposes of evaluation) have to be prepared alongwith the framing of questions and adhered to in letter and spirit while evaluating answers.

These aspects of an answer required to be evaluated should be made known to the students in the question paper itself e.g. there may be situations where spelling mistakes, may be taken into account for deducting marks and others where the opposite may be true.

Correction of a sample of scripts by all the examiners at the time of Co-ordination Meetings and the modification of the marking scheme prepared by the paper setter, wherever considered necessary, needs to be meticulously done for finalising it. This would iron out ambiguities regarding the interpretation of the wording of a question and thus ensure objectivity.

As far as possible scoring of essay/long answer type questions should be done on an *analytical* basis. *Impressionistic* scoring may be done only in cases where it is absolutely unavoidable.

However, the directions in the question paper may clearly indicate to the students, the major points of emphasis in the scoring pattern. They could even be built into the language of the questions themselves or form part of the general directions. Furthermore, if a diagram or an illustration is required to be given by the students as part of the answer, it should be clearly mentioned in the question and not left by the paper setter to the initiative of the student or the imagination of the evaluator.

In the marking scheme, which may be finalised for the evaluation of scripts, the aspects and the sub-aspects or the steps of the process of the expected answer be clearly spelt out. Each of these may be given a definite weightage e.g. in a given situation, and wherever applicable its analysis, interpretation and drawing of inferences may be allocated separate weightages. Similarly, if spellings, language style, coherence, and unity of presentation deserve to be given independent weightages these also should be known to the students. In short the students should know what is expected of them, what will enable them gain marks and what will make them to lose them.

In mathematics the steps of calculation and weightages to them be clearly indicated in the marking schemes.

10.4 Preparing Short Answer Type of Questions

Short answer questions present a compromise between the long answer and objective type questions. They enjoy the advantages of both the types of questions.

While the long answer questions suffer from lack of objectively and reliability, the short answer questions are technically better off in regard to these criteria.

On the other hand while the objective type questions are largely unable to test abilities like expression, organisation and synthesisation of ideas, the short answer questions possess at least in a limited measure the capability of testing these abilities.

As these questions enjoy the advantages of both essay and objective type questions, without their disadvantages, to some extent the short answer questions have come to be increasingly used in examinations.

A rule of thumb used in many examinations is the provisions of a weightage of 50% marks in a question paper to short answer questions and an equal distribution of the rest of 50% between the long answer and the very short answer/objective type of questions.

Short answer questions too have always to be carefully structured, so as to require specific and to the point answers. They should neither be vague in their wording nor should they encourage or admit vague and global answers. This is what differentiates them from the traditional, open-ended short note questions indicating themes without enunciating the dimensions of the given themes expected to be tackled by the examinees, like "Write short notes on democracy", where a student does not know as to how long or how short the short note has got to be on such a topic like democracy, on which books can be written. A short answer question therefore should not be confused with the traditional short note question.

The construction of short answer questions also requires lesser level of competence in preparation as compared to the objective type questions.

While the limits in regard to length/dimensions of short answer type questions could vary quite a bit, they cannot be precisely defined. Still some rough and a ready explanation of their physical dimensions is attempted here.

Short Answer Questions normally require:

- A 30 to 50 words answer
- an answer with upto 6 steps of mathematical calculations

They usually have 2 to 4 credit points and they approximately need 3 to 5 minutes for answering them.

Thus there can be many short answer questions in a question paper covering a larger proportion of the syllabus, than what long answer questions can possibly accomplish. With this increase in the length of the test they tend to provide a more reliable/dependable estimate of an individual students proficiency and potential.

For example a short answer question could be worded as under :

History : Give two evidences to substantiate that Clive was the real founder of the British Empire in India.

English : Write a paragraph in about 50-60 words on trees. You could use some of the following words:

Beauty Utility

Pleasure	Forest
Branches	Shade
Twigs	Fruits
Birds	Logs

A long answer question could also sometimes be converted into short answer questions with great advantage as illustrated through the following example.

Usual Form of Long Answer Question

Give a brief account of various theories of organic evolution. (Essay-type question)

Modified Form (Short-Answer Questions)

(i) Name the various theories of organic evolution.

(ii) Which theory in your opinion better explains the mechanism of organic evolution? Give two reasons.

(iii) Write two fundamental principles on which the theory of Lamarck is based.

(iv) How does d'Vries' theory differ from that of Weismann's.

Such questions can be profitably used in both external and internal examinations. They also ensure better reliability, because such questions are more definite and specific and can be scored more objectively. They also cover a larger segment of the syllabus as we can have a number of such questions in place of a single essay type question. Therefore, they draw upon a wider range of students achievements than the usual essay question do. They also ensure adequate sampling of content and thereby help improve the validity of the question paper.

It is, therefore, desirable that we should encourage the use of such questions in our examinations to improve their validity and reliability and objectivity.

10.5 Preparing Very Short Answer Type Questions

Very short answer type of questions have been discovered as a possible substitute to objective type questions. While they can be assessed as objectively as objective type questions, they do not present as many conditions or rules to be satisfied in construction as the objective type questions do.

Very short answer questions require an answer in one word, one phrase or at the most one sentence. They have *just one or two testing points and* thus ensure the same level of *objectively* in scoring, as it exists in the objective type of questions. Normally they are assigned just one or two marks and need about a minute to answer.

In view of the small answering time and low mark weightage, many such questions can be set in a question paper by using a very small quantum of marks. They can also be spread over a larger chunk of the prescribed syllabus thus improving upon the *reliability* of a question paper.

Somet mes when the forms of questions are classified as *Selection type* and *Supply type questions*, the very short answer type of questions are classified among the 'supply type questions' because unlike most of the objective type questions, the answer has to be supplied by the student and not just selected from the given ones.

Very Short Answer type questions could assume a number of forms. Some examples of these related to English are given below :

Fill-in-the-blank type:

I am not satisfied .... your answer

Completion Type:

I was to worried. ....

Analogy type:

Soyabean: Protein :: Rice:

Location type:

Show the location of Sydney on the outline map of the world

Transformation type:

Questions on

Reported speech
Voices
Synthesis
Transformation of Sentences

Usage type:

Use the following words/phrases in your own sentences :

Break/Break up
Look/Look after

Question type:

What is a mole?

10.6 Preparing Objective Type (Multiple Choice) Questions

Objective-based and objective type tests are often confused with each other. It, therefore, needs to be stated again that when a question is framed with deliberate attention to the objective (ability) which we want to specifically assess it is an objective-based question.

But when a question is designed to provide a measure of student's achievement in objective rather than a subjective manner, we call it an objective type question.

There are various forms of objective type tests. Two alternative questions, which are commonly known as *true/false* or yes/no type is the oldest of the objective type of questions in use. *Fill-in-the-blank type* questions are the other commonly used variety of questions. *Matching type* items have two or more columns. In a two-column matching question for example, we can give principles on one side and the illustrations-based on those principles on the other. The student is required to write the matching number of the principle involved against the related illustration or example given. Among these the *master-list type* of questions consists of two parts. One is the list of closely related terms, concepts etc. which form the alternative and are called the master-list. Then it is followed by another often a longer list consisting of a number of statements pertaining to the master-list and the student is required to relate each statement with the corresponding one, of the master-list for identifying the right response. *Multiple Choice Items* are those in which a statement or question is followed by normally four alternatives out of which the student is to select the correct one.

The form of objective type tests commonly used for examination purposes is the *multiple choice type* of question. It consists of a stem which may be in *the question form or in the form of an incomplete statement* followed by a number of words, pharases or statements which answer the question or complete the statement. The students' task is to select from the given alternatives the one which correctly gives the answer. The effectiveness of the item should depend on how well the item has been framed, to test the desired objective. The following points may be kept in view while structuring a good multiple choice test item.

Suggestions for Writing Multiple Choice Test Items (questions)

A multiple choice type item, as already mentioned comprises a '*Stem*' in the form of a statement or a question followed by four (or five) *alternative* choices or distractors. The whole item when constructed must make complete sense and be accurate in respect of language and information.

The following are some suggestions for framing such items:

1. It should be ensured that there is only one choice/alternative which is correct or the best. Alternatives which are overlapping with one another should be avoided. The response should be agreed upon as the best or the most suitable one from among the plausible ones given, by competent critics.
2. The stem of the item should be comprehensive enough to contain the central problem by including in it as much of the item as possible. The alternatives should not contain anything which could have been put in the stem.
3. The pupil should not be required to copy the correct response but only mark or write the serial number of the alternative to answer the question.
4. The use of the text-book language should be avoided. The rote learner should be mislead by using familiar or stereotyped phrases as distracters.

5. The stem and all the alternatives should be made as succinct and consistent as possible.
6. It should be explored if a better item can be obtained by turning round a partly formulated question into an answer and the answer into the question.
7. All the choices provided ought to be sufficiently plausible to be selected by a fair proportion of the examinees. Both correct and incorrect choices, should be homogeneous in their mode of expression, physical length and other external characteristics. The distracters should represent errors commonly made by the students, who are to be tested.
8. Each choice (alternative) should be studied for any possible irrelevant clues. For doing this the following steps are suggested.
   (a) The correct response should not be consistently longer or consistently shorter in length than the incorrect ones.
   (b) All choices should be grammatically correct and consistent with the stem whether in a question form or in that of an incomplete statement. The use of singular and plural number, tenses etc. should not be allowed to serve as clues.
   (c) The choices may be arranged in a logical order, if one exists; otherwise they should be arranged in the alphabetical order.
   (d) The position of the correct answer in the series ought to be chosen entirely at random. The first and last places should be used as often as any of the intermediate places.
   (e) No part of the stem should follow the distracters.

To conclude it may be said that while the multiple choice type of questions are used in examinations, other form of *objective type questions could be effectively used as teaching devices* for initiating discussions in class. Such discussions could greatly help in consolidating ideas. These objective type questions other than the multiple choice questions can surely be used upto class two even in examination situations as well.

The multiple choice type of questions are also used in examinations because, there are a variety of statistical measures available for calculating their characteristics/qualities like the Difficulty and Discrimination indices. Various types of sophisticated statistical analysis have also been evolved.

11

Setting Balanced Question Papers and Unit Tests

11.1 The Backdrop

There are various *techniques* of testing like Written Examinations, Oral Examinations, Practical Examinations, Observation. Each of these techniques uses different tools of 'testing'. For example we use observation schedules, check-lists, inventories, rating scales and question papers as *tools* of evaluation in different techniques as per need. Among these the question papers and tests are the most commonly used of the tools.

While tests and question papers are the basic tools of evaluation in written examinations, they are also used for other techniques.

As public/external examinations are the most common types of examinations used and since they are predominantly written examinations, question papers have become the most important of the tools of testing.

The traditional form of question papers used to suffer from a variety of flaws which have been attempted to be overcome as a part of the Movement of Examination Reform Programme of the NCERT where in the author played a crucial note. These reforms, however, have been by and large limited to the school stage and the universities do still by-and-large use the traditional form of examinations in a substantial measure. In some places these school level reforms have also influenced university education.

Examination Reform at the school stage has been influenced by the latest developments in the science of evaluation which have revolutionised education in respect of its concept, content and process. Earlier it was thought that anybody who knows a subject can teach it, anybody who can teach can also test. These notions no more hold ground with the evolution of the Science of Pedagogy and the Science of Evaluation. In fact both pedagogy and evaluation have germs of science and art.

Without getting way-laid into the wider realms of pedagogy and evaluation let us revert to the central theme of Setting Balanced Question Papers.

11.2 Shortcomings of Traditional Question Papers and their Remediation

Some of the main shortcomings that had come to infest traditional written examinations particularly because of the pattern of question papers were:

- Over-emphasis on memorisation
- Subjectivity
- Poor Content Coverage and
- Some administrative shortfalls

Let us now take up these one by one and analyse the nature of the shortfall its implications on teaching and testing and the measures for overcoming them.

11.2.1 *Over-Emphasis on Memorisation*

The questions contained in the traditional question papers were mainly focussed on content where the examinees were supposed to *memorise and reproduce.*

Since we tended to *teach what was tested rather than testing what we taught*, the development of higher abilities like understanding, application analysis, synthesis, critical thinking, evaluation were almost completely overlooked. Education so imparted, turned children into parrots and mechanical beings rather than creative not just in examinations but also often in their future lives. While this served the needs of the foreign rulers for developing lower and middle level workforce, for running a colonial administration, they have turned out to be utterly inadequate for the emerging demands of independent India.

It has been because of this that the *ability* dimension has been forcefully added to the *content* facet in testing. In addition to the sub-division of the content (topics and sub-topics), objectives (abilities/competencies) too have been identified in respect of each subject and these further sub-divided into specifications. For example the objective of comprehension/understanding has been divided into its constituent components like discrimination, classification, comparison and contrast, identification of relationships, giving examples, detecting and correcting errors etc. These ability sub-divisions have thus now become integral and focal components of testing devices (questions) besides content. The phenomenon has encouraged schools to try to develop the higher mental abilities also, besides memorisation—recognition, recall and reproduction, which in the good old days used to be almost the sole ability tested because of the main focus on the memorisation of content.

Furthermore in the traditional scheme of things the focus was predominantly on the mental abilities. The reformed system also attempts to cover the *total personality consisting of the abilities of the head (cognitive abilities), of the heart (affective abilities) and those of the hands (psycho-motor abilities)*. Taxonomies of these objectives too now stand developed as discussed earlier in the chapter on objectives. Evaluation of different cognitive, affective and psycho-motor abilities is being taken up as a part of Comprehensive and Continuous School-based Evaluation.

Testing in written examinations through question papers, however, mainly covers the cognitive area and only partly the psycho-motor and the affective areas of personality. In developing balanced question papers, objectives desired to be tested in the concerned subject are listed and weightages allocated to each of them (in terms of marks) on the basis of the relevance of a particular objective in the subject in question. For example in subjects like Geography and Biology a substantial chunk of marks would be devoted to 'skills', in subjects like Physics and Chemistry to Application of Knowledge, in History to Knowledge and so on.

The next step is to construct questions equivalent to the allocated weightages to content and objectives. In this process the choice of the form of question will be an important criteria for example, for testing the ability of expression, a long answer/essay type question and not an objective type question has to be chosen to be constructed. Furthermore each form of question has to follow some rules which have already been discussed separately in the chapter on preparing questions of different forms.

All these measures help overcome the over-emphasis on memorisation by systematically including questions testing higher abilities in the question papers in due proportion.

The steps will also help improve the validity of the question papers.

11.2.2 *Subjectivity*

Traditionally subjectively too has been a great shortcoming of the written examinations. It operates mainly at three levels. *Subjectivity of the question paper setter* used to operate in a wild manner particularly because the question paper setters enjoyed complete unrestricted freedom to pick up or drop any item from the syllabus for setting question papers and nobody could question their authority. The questions were basically factual and the directive words like 'elucidate', 'illustrate', 'elaborate' were indiscriminately used. Invariably there was a short note question giving themes like 'Democracy' on which books could be written.

This unlimited freedom stands checked now because the paper setter is now given a 'Design' (Format appended) of the question paper to be set and clear instructions given about the language of the questions, their unambiguous/specific wording indicating the precise scope and length of the expected answer. The paper setter is also now required to develop a marking scheme indicating the parts of the expected answer and the marks to be allocated to each part. This curbs the paper setter's vagaries and helps him correct many mistakes in the questions on their own.

While the format of the design is appended to the chapter, it is pertinent to mention its main parts which are:

- Weightage to objectives
- Weightage to major areas of content

- Weightage to different forms of questions
- Scheme of sections
- Pattern of options

In addition to this the paper setter is also required to prepare a '*Blueprint*' (Format enclosed) for setting the question papers. This indicates the precise placement of each question in respect of objective and topic attempted to be tested by it, the form in which it is to be framed, and the marks it carries. This makes him check the comparability/compatibility of the design with the blueprint, and of the blueprint with the questions, and of the questions with the marking scheme. The question paper setter besides preparing the blueprint, the questions, the marking scheme is also required to prepare a question-wise analysis (format appended) which is yet another check for him to conform to the paradigms of each question he has prepared. This table incorporates the following details about each question or part thereof.

1. Objective and specification tested
2. Content Area (topic & sub-topic) covered/tested
3. Form of the question
4. Marks carried by the question
5. Estimated difficulty level (easy/average/difficult)
6. Estimated time for answering

Subjectivity of the Examinee

This too is a common phenomenon and occurs mainly because of the vague wording of the questions where the student himself has to interpret about what he has to write. In response to the questions in the traditional question papers anything and everything could be written. Students therefore chose to write all that they knew about that topic rather than answering the question as such.

With restrictions on the language of the questions which has now to be precise and pinpointed, exactly spelling out the scope and length of the expected answer, the examinee now precisely knows what is expected of him to write and what the parts of the answer have to be, how long the answer has to be and what marks each part of the answer would carry. In the new question papers the marks carried by different questions are not given as say 10 in all, but the marks to parts of the expected answer as well like (2 + 4 + 4).

Subjectivity of the Examiner

This too has been a common phenomenon and one which stands scientifically proved. The technical term 'Standard Error of Measurement' owes its origin to it.

Edwin Harper's study 'Hundred Marking Ten' in 1967 done at Allahabad proved that marking variations operate within a range of 5% and 8% and in more than 50% of the cases, they are likely to be more than 5%.

The NCERT study of 1998 where 20 examiners evaluated the same

10 History answer scripts of Class XII of a particular Board, did not have any different story to tell. The scripts and the examiners were both randomly selected. The examiners evaluated these zeroxed scripts when they were actually evaluating the actual answer scripts of the same subject, of the same examination, using the same marking scheme, which they were expected to follow in evalualting these zeroxed scripts.

The marks awarded out of 100 by the most lenient and the most strict of the *twenty examiners* to the same ten scripts were as under:

Script No. / *Examiner*	*1*	*2*	*3*	*4*	*5*	*6*	*7*	*8*	*9*	*10*	*Mean*
Marks Awarded by the Most Lenient Examiner	50	66	23	.35	37	74	54	53	39	37	46.8
Marks Awarded by the Most Strict Examiner	21	28	02	10	14	43	23	19	05	07	17.2
Difference Between the Two	29	38	31	25	23	31	31	34	34	30	29.6

The position could only be worse twenty years back. Though things have no doubt improved with double checking a lot still needs to be done.

A concrete measure taken by the Council for the Indian School Certificate Examination (CISCE) is that though a marking scheme already stands developed by the paper setter, each Deputy Head Examiner is required to evaluate 20 or so scripts. This is followed by a discussion in the course of the *Coordination Meetings*, only after which the marking scheme to be used is finalised. Another suggestion could be for the Boards to make it compulsory for all affiliated school to depute teachers for purposes of evaluation for continuation of their affiliation to the Board. This is because the good schools do not send their teachers for evaluation. The non-availability of examiners in adequate numbers also forces the Boards to give more scripts for evaluation to each examiner than what should ordinarily be given for doing justice.

There should also be a provision for appointing some additional hands at the evaluation centres, who may only check that the totals are correct, that all parts of answers have been evaluated, that marks to all parts of answers have been individually awarded and that the marks have been correctly posted on the cover page of the script and also on the mark sheet. They should also check that the member of supplementary sheets indicated are all there. The Deputy Head Examiners in-charge of evaluation centres should also actually check the sample of scripts they are supposed to check and not just initial them as a formality. He and the checker should ensure that the marking scheme is being followed for evaluation in letter and spirit so that the errors of measurement can be minimised.

With the above measures the objectivity will become possible to be ensured to a large extent.

11.2.3 *Inadequate Content Coverage*

When no 'Designs' and 'Blueprints' were used the situation was alarming. Comparatively it is better but a lot still needs to be done. It is *poor content coverage that leads to selective study and selective teaching.* The provision of options further aggravates the problem. Suppose there are 20 topics in the syllabus, 16 are covered by the question paper and a student can attempt full 100 mark questions if he attempts questions on 12 topics and he can pass if he gives correct answers to questions on 5 topics. In this case

20 Topics	imply	100%	Full coverage of content
16 Topics in the question paper	imply	80%	Apparent coverage of content
12 Topics which can yield full marks	imply	60%	Actual coverage of content
5 Topics for passing the examination	imply	20%	Real coverage for passing

In this commonly witnessed situation a student can easily omit 40% of the syllabus and yet aspire to get the highest possible marks. One needs to study just 20% of the course content to pass. Is the situation not shocking?

This is not all about options which do lead to selective study and selective teaching. They also make examinations a farce.

The traditional question papers normally used to have about 8 questions and the instructions used to be "All questions carry equal marks attempt any five". These *overall options* meant that any question could be substituted for any other. The presumptions that the situation made were that:

- if an examinee knew one topic it was taken that he knew any other.
- all questions tested the same ability and same content.
- all questions needed the same answering time.
- all questions were pitched at the same estimated level of difficulty.

all of which could not stand any of the above tests.

In addition, in such a situation, different students attempted different sets of questions – in effect, different question papers. If A got 40 marks, B got 50 and the C got 60 it *could not be said* that C is first, B is second, and A is third because all the three of them have not been subjected to the same tests. The situation is similar to the one when a student X does 1.83 m. long jump, Y does 1.22 m. high jump and Z 2.44 m. high pole vault, where one cannot say who is first, who is second and who is third.

Options could, therefore, be provided if the questions given as options.

- cover/test the same content/topic
- test the same objective/ability
- are of the same form
- are pitched at the same estimated level of difficulty
- take the same approximate time for answering
- carry the same marks

Satisfying all these conditions at the same time is not just difficult but near impossible for ensuring equivalence among options.

There are *overall options* like all questions carry equal marks, attempt any five, *internal option* within questions like write short notes on any three of the given five and *alternate options* of the this or this type.

A rule of thumb in this regard if options have to be offered is

Objective Type Very Short Answer Type Short Answer Type	No options
Long Answer Type	Alternate internal equivalent options

It, therefore, appears necessary that major areas of content may be identified and each given an appropriate weightage (marks) out of the total marks for the question paper for preparing questions on these weightages which could be determined on the basis of :

- the importance of the particular area in the subject
- the difficulty level of the area
- the time needed for covering the theme in teaching and learning

These weightages would stand indicated in the 'Design' prepared by the examining agency and should be appropriately reflected in the grid of the 'Blueprint' prepared by the question paper setters. Questions could then be framed on that basis. This is a technical exercise and cannot be done by anyone and everyone without training in the concept and techniques of evaluation with particular reference to setting of question papers, which should be arranged to be organised and become essential eligibility criteria for being appointed as question paper setters.

11.2.4 *Administrative Inadequacies*

Question paper setters, have but to be trained in the Concept and Techniques of Evaluation with particular reference to the Technology of Setting Question Papers to execute the technical job assigned to them.

Detailed instructions should also be prepared and issued to the question paper setters, besides of course the design.

Three question papers based on the same design should be prepared at the same time. This should be a team task with the team of three consisting of *a content expert,* a *pedagogue and a practising teacher*. All the three should be given the same design for preparing their own blueprints and question papers on them. The three of them should then come together to discuss and finalise the three question papers, their respective marking schemes and question-wise analysis of their papers. The content expert would be able to check the accuracy of content of the questions, the pedagogue the technique of framing questions and the practising teacher the appropriateness of standard of the questions. The three sets of such question papers and related material be then packed and sealed separately. One of these may be picked up for the annual examination, the other for the supplementary examination and the third may be kept for a possible emergency. The three papers based on the same design will be parallel at the level of the design and hence substitutable.

Another administrative measure relates to the situation where a significant portion of the question paper/test may be consisting of objective type and very short answer type questions with some questions of the other forms as well. In this situation if the section with objective type and very short answer type questions remains with the examinees' for longer than necessary there could be a likelihood that they may try to check their answers with their neighbours. It is, therefore, desirable that the question paper be divided into two sections one with objective type and very short answer type questions and the other section may have short answer and long answer questions. Both the sections may be administered together but the one with objective type and very short answer type questions be collected earlier at the end of the prescribed tight time limit.

Adequate publicity for carrying the public opinion along about this strategy will also be necessary for a general acquaintance about the merits of the proposal.

11.3 Steps of the Action Plan

In respect of each question paper the following action points related to different sequential steps will need to be taken:

1. Preparation of a Design of the question paper to be prepared by the examining agency/institutions.
2. Preparation of a blueprint based on the design to be prepared by the question paper setter. Format to be supplied by the examining agency alongwith instructions.
3. Transfer of blueprint details on to the item sheets with one question on each answer sheet with the details about objectives, specifications, topic, sub-topic, form, marks expected, answering time and estimated difficulty level in respect of each question filled in. The marking scheme with expected outline answers and marks to different parts of the expected answer written on the back side of the item sheet. Adequate number of item sheets to be provided by the examining agency alongwith instructions.
4. Papers for writing the consolidated question paper and consolidated marking scheme to be also provided to the paper setter.
5. Format/Proforma for the preparation of question-wise analysis be also supplied to the paper setter alongwith the instructions.

FORMAT OF A DESIGN QUESTION PAPER/TEST

Subject : ....
Unit/paper : ....
Class : ....
Time : ....
Marks : ....

Weightage to Objectives:

Objective	K/KE	U/CO	A/EX	S/AP	Total
Percentage of marks	....	....	....	....	....
Marks	....	....	....	....	....

Weightage to Forms of Questions:

Forms of Questions	E/LA	SA	VSA	O	Total
No. of Questions	....	....	....	....	....
Marks Allotted	....	....	....	....	....
Estimated Time	....	....	....	....	....

Weightage to Major Content Areas:

	Units/Sub-Units	Marks
1.	....	....
2.	....	....
3.	....	....
4.	....	....
5.	....	....
6.	....	....
7.	....	....
8.	....	....

Scheme of Sections : ....
....

Pattern of options : ....
....

Estimated difficulty level:
Difficult : .... % marks.
Average : .... % marks.
Easy : .... % marks.

Abbreviations : K (Knowledge), U (Understanding), A (Application), S (Skill)
KE (Knowledge of Elements of Language), CO (Comprehension), EX (Expression), APP (Appreciation)
E (Essay or Long Answer Type), SA (Short Answer Type), VSA (Very Short Answer Type), O (Objective Type – Multiple Choice)

FORMAT OF A BLUEPRINT

SUBJECT: ______________ CLASS: __________

UNIT/PAPER: ______________ MAXIMUM MARKS: __________ TIME: __________

OBJECTIVE / FORM OF QUESTIONS / CONTENT UNITS/SUB-UNITS	ELEMENTS OF LANGUAGE				COMPREHENSION				EXPRESSION				APPRECIATION		TOTAL
	KNOWLEDGE				UNDERSTANDING				APPLICATION				SKILL		
	E	SA	VSA	O	E	SA	VSA	O	E	SA	VSA	O	E	SA	
SUB TOTAL															
TOTAL															

Notes: Figures within brackets to indicate the number of questions and figures outside the brackets to indicate marks

* Denotes that marks have been combined to form one question.

Summary:

Essay (E)	No.	Marks	Pattern of Options ....
Short Answer (SA)	No.	Marks	
Very Short Answer (VSA)	No.	Marks	Scheme of Sections ....
Objective (O)	No.	Marks	

ITEM SHEET FORMAT

Front Side of the Item Sheet

S.No. ....

Objective	....	Topic	....
Specification	....	Sub-Topic	....
Form	....	Expected	
Estimated	....	Answering Time	....
Difficulty Level	....	Marks	....

Question : ....

....

....

....

....

....

....

Reverse Side of the Item Sheet

S.No. ....

SCORING KEY

QUESTION NO.	1	2	3	4					n
KEY									

MARKING SCHEME

EXPECTED OUTLINE ANSWER	MARKS TO EACH ASPECT	REMARKS

QUESTION-WISE ANALYSIS

S. No.	OBJECTIVE	SPECIFICATION	TOPIC	SUB-TOPIC	FORM	ESTIMATED DIFFICULTY LEVEL	MARKS	ESTIMATED ANSWERING TIME

12

Methods of Grading Pupil Performance

12.1 Emergence of the Idea of Grading in India

A discussion about grades has but to start from the concept of marks, as a move from which they are taken to be more desirable departure.

Marks and grades are both approaches for identifying/determining presenting/declaring the judged level of attainment or competency or potential of an individual in a particular activity/area.

Apart from this similarity both the concepts have marked differences.

'Marks' are points on the spread of a distribution while 'Grades' indicate the slots or ranges within which the proficiency level of an individual is judged to lie in respect of a given quality or ability.

When we use 'Marks' as indices of the level of performance, we normally use a 101 point scale (0-100). In using 'Grades' we use a much smaller scale say a nine or a five or a three-point one. In the situation, where marks are used the likelihood of mis-classification of the levels of competencies of individuals, or of their potential is also therefore much greater than when we use a much smaller number of grades.

In awarding 'grades' as compared to marks we are also much more confident about the accuracy of our decisions. The swinging in decisions which often generate chance elements also naturally get crossed over. It is because of this that approximations in terms of 'grades' are considered as more valid and reliable than 'marks' which proclaim precision. One cannot just vouchsafe that an individuals' mathematical or linguistic ability is exactly say 57% and nothing more or less or that the honesty of an individual is say precisely 68%. One can only be general and not specific in such assessments.

There are, of course, human attributes that lie beyond the range of any technique or tool of evaluation to assess. *Grading therefore is an honest confession of our inability to assess human qualities with precision.*

12.2 Why Grading?

To just say that the National Policy on Education NPE 1986/92 has recommended the replacement of marks with grades is not enough for convincing others to advocate it. One has to go into the reasons have led to this recommendation. In fact there are variations in the clientele taking the examination in different years. Teachers always say that a particular year's batch of students is better or not so good as that of the previous year. Clear evidences of this were found when students pursuing a 10+2 pattern went to colleges as compared to the previous batches who had been educated in the 8+3 pattern.

Apart from the variations in the clientele taking the examination, there are also marked variations in the *ranges of marks* obtained by the students in different subjects due to the *mark yielding nature of the subject* (e.g. English 30-80 and Mathematics 0-100). Further-more the standard of question papers in the same subject also varying from year to year. This goes against the sacrosanct use of the same cut off scores (33%, 45%, 60%), year after year in all subjects.

12.3 Grading and Concept of Pass and Fail and Award of Divisions

In view of the above logic the use of a 33% level of attainment for clearing the examination in each subject, also does not stand the logic.

The concept of pass and fail and of the award of 'Divisions' is alien to the concept of grading as grades are awarded subject-wise without aggregation.

Grade Point Average

When the practice of awarding grades in place of marks is adopted grade point averages could be calculated if it is necessary for granting *admissions* or for awarding *scholarships*. Even raw scores could be used, if necessary in such cases. In such a situation the numerical values of the obtained symbolic grades in all subjects is added up and divided by the number of subjects graded.

Suppose the symbolic grades and their corresponding numerical value on a nine-point scale is as under. It needs to be observed that letter/symbolic grades could assume different forms.

Symbolic Grade	I	H	G	F	E	D	C	B	A
	E	DE	D	CD	C	BC	B	AB	A
	E	D_2	D_1	C_2	C_1	B_2	B_1	A_2	A_1
Numerical Value of Grades	1	2	3	4	5	6	7	8	9

Also suppose there are six subjects and the symbolic/letter grades on a nine-point scale obtained by a student in the six subjects are as under:

Subject	*No. 1*	*No. 2*	*No. 3*	*No. 4*	*No. 5*	*No. 6*
Obtained Symbolic Grade	B	C	A	D	C	B
Numerical Value of Grade	8	7	9	6	7	8

$$\text{GPA} = \frac{\text{Sum of the numerical value of the letter grades in all subjects}}{\text{Number of subjects graded}}$$

$$= \frac{8+7+9+6+7+8}{6} = \frac{45}{6} = 7.5$$

A GPA will be able to give a value up to two decimal points which should satisfy the need.

In special cases as per need some additional weightages could be provided to one or more subjects. The procedure of calculating GPA with cognisance to the weightages will, however, remain the same.

12.4 Methods of Awarding Grades

There are various approaches of awarding grades which deserve to be explained for the choice of the one to be adopted in a particular situation.

Diagrammatically these approaches can be presented as under:

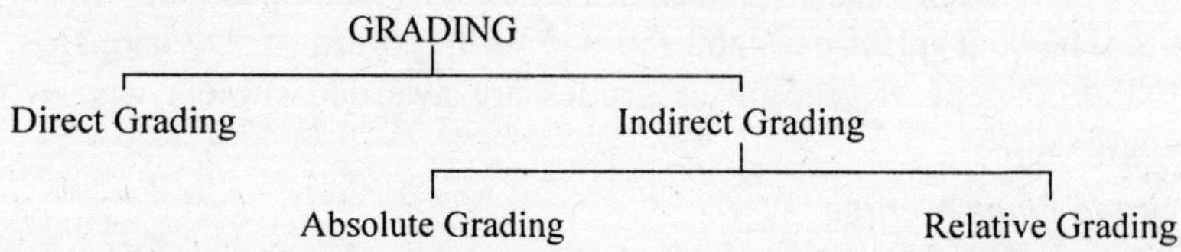

Deciding about the Scale to Follow

In each of the above situations, it is desirable to first decide upon the scale to follow.

The scales normally used have middle points as in a three-point or a five-point or a nine-point scale.

A Three-Point Scale

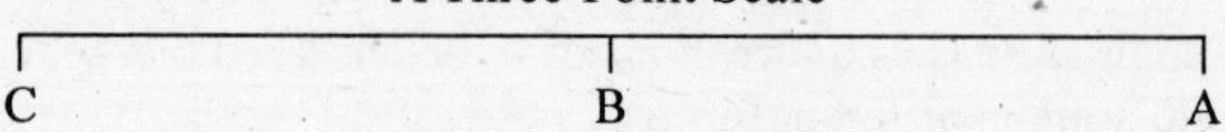

A Five-Point Scale

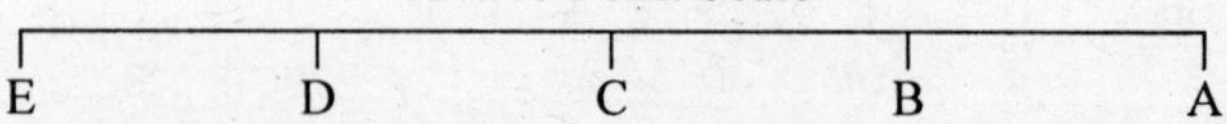

A Nine-Point Scale

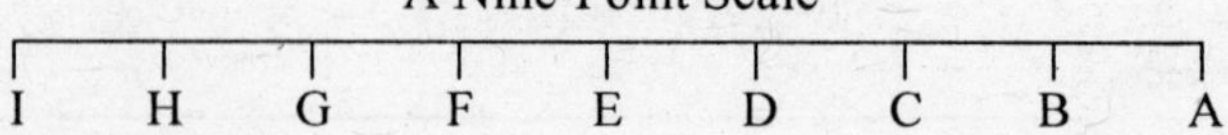

With the increase in the number of points in a scale the discrimination becomes finer. While choosing the scale one has to take a decision on the basis of the fineness of discrimination desired.

12.4.1 *Direct Grading*

In direct grading *each piece of performance or a part thereof, is required to be individually graded.* Grading is done on the basis of the criteria evolved by the evaluators or those forwarded to them by the examining agency (University or Board). Usually letter or symbolic grades (A B C D ...) are used in Direct Grading.

After the award of Direct Letter Grades the numerical value of each grade (as per the scale selected) has to be tabulated and added up. This sum of the numerical values of obtained grades is then divided with the number of questions or parts evaluated in an answer script, for the calculation of GPAs. This total is again converted into a letter grade for obtaining an overall index of performance of the student in that particular question paper in terms of a symbolic grade.

This by itself is a tedious process and it is difficult to check and make needed corrections. The current practice of awarding marks is itself infested with mistakes of totalling. In the event of the introduction of Direct Grading such mistakes are bound to multiply and checking the accuracy of the calculations, will be a near impossible exercise. The problem will be unwieldy and unmanageable particularly in large-scale examinations as in Boards and Universities.

It is because of this that Direct Grading cannot be recommended or adopted in large-scale public examinations and particularly so when the number of questions in the question papers are many.

Direct Grading is also devoid of transparency and is infested with chance elements and subjectivity which could severely undermine the credibility of examinations.

In institutional situations of in-house evaluation, however direct grading could be used subject to the condition that:

- the number of items to be evaluated are few.
- the number of students whose performance is to be evaluated too are few and manageable.
- the grades awarded have to stay as such without the need for making necessary calculations for obtaining a GPA and again converting the same into grades.

Situations like project work which have an independent identity could admit direct grading. However, if it is a part of a subject with a particular weightage for it out of the total marks of a subject the problem would become difficult.

A similar problem would also arise in respect of question papers where questions may carry different marks.

12.4.2 *Indirect Grading*

Indirect grading is *grading through marks*. In this practice the usual procedure of awarding marks to the units of performance continues. This being something to which the evaluators and teachers are already used, this is not likely to create any problem.

Indirect Grading can assume two forms:

- Absolute Grading and
- Relative Grading

Absolute Grading

Absolute grading is the one where the boundary scores for different grades stand decided in advance of the examination.

In fact the practice of declaring students as pass or fail and of awarding divisions and distinctions is a known example of Absolute Grading as illustrated below:

75% and above marks	Distinction
60% to less than 75% marks	First Division
45% to less than 60% marks	Second Division
33% to less than 45% marks	Third Division
Below 33% marks	Failure

As mentioned earlier the indicators of overall levels of performance will not be comparable because of reasons for which the replacement of marks by grades has been recommended.

Such decisions about boundary scores for different grades will invariably be ad hoc and arbitrary because they would be decided in advance of the examinations and normally for all subjects alike, particularly because the same score in different subjects is not equivalent and comparable. In fact the recommendation of the NPE for the replacement of marks with grades is a reaction against the practice of absolute grading using sacrosanct cut of scores for all subjects and all examinations uniformly.

The procedure takes marks on their face value irrespective of the errors of measurement due to chance element and subjectivity.

Even though the procedure has a diagnostic value and the students can make efforts for achieving the highest grades, the system of absolute grading cannot be technically recommended or accepted for adoption as it has evident shortfalls whose remediation was indeed called for, while suggesting the replacement of marks by grades. Any cut-off boundary scores for grades, decided in advance of the examination, does not take into account the actual performance of the students in a particular examination.

An example of Absolute Grading on a nine-point scale is given below:

Letter Grade	*Numerical Value of the Grade*	*Range of Marks*	*Description*
A	9	90% and above	Outstanding
B	8	80% to less than 90%	Excellent
C	7	70% to less than 80%	Very Good
D	6	60% to less than 70%	Good
E	5	50% to less than 60%	Above Average
F	4	40% to less than 50%	Average
G	3	30% to less than 40%	Below Average
H	2	20% to less than 30%	Marginal
I	1	Below 20%	Unsatisfactory

Evidently, in such a scheme of things, there may be no top grades in some subjects and more of them in some others implying thereby that only some subjects can breed talented students and not others.

Relative Grading

Relative Grading is another approach of Indirect Grading but is quite a contrast to its other sibling of Absolute Grading.

Unlike Absolute Grading where grade ranges are decided in advance of the examinations and applied to all subjects for all years, the boundary scores in Relative Grading are determined,

- after the examination has already been held.
- on the basis of the range and distribution of the obtained scores.
- for every subject at each examination separately

In relative grading, therefore, grade ranges keep on changing for each subject, in each examination, of each year, as they are based on the range and pattern of distribution of obtained scores.

Decided in this manner, *Relative Grades, successfully overcome problems of the variations in the mark yielding nature of different subjects, variations in the standards of question papers of different years and differences in the groups of examinees taking the examination in different years.*

Relative Grading is based on the premise that whenever any population of students is subjected to a particular test for testing any attribute/s ability or abilities through any mode—written oral or practical—and their scores plotted on a graph, the true level of achievement in this graph would take the form of a symmetrical bell—shaped Normal Probability Curve.

In actual practice, however, there are *errors of measurement* which lead to differences in the 'true' and the 'perceived' levels of attainments and the obtained curve is not usually 'normal' but a 'skewed' one. This also happens because we usually work on samples (rather than population) which are much smaller than the population, which would have yielded a normal curve of distribution. The obtained curves, therefore, are found to be skewed positively or negatively. These obtained curves are negatively skewed if a larger number examinees obtain higher marks and are positively skewed when a larger number of candidates obtain lower scores.

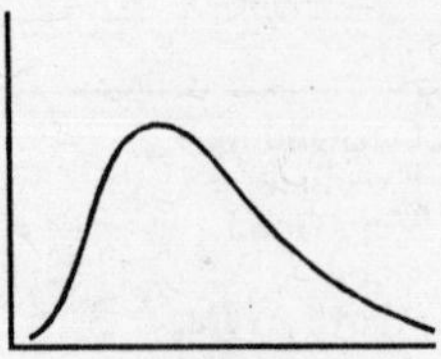

Positively
Skewed Curve

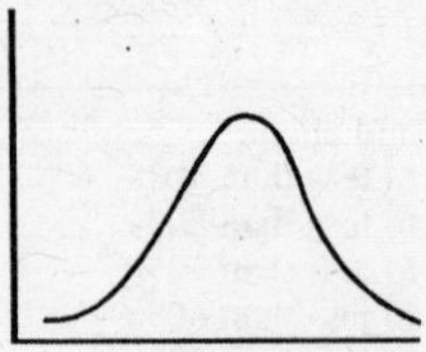

Normal
Probability Curve

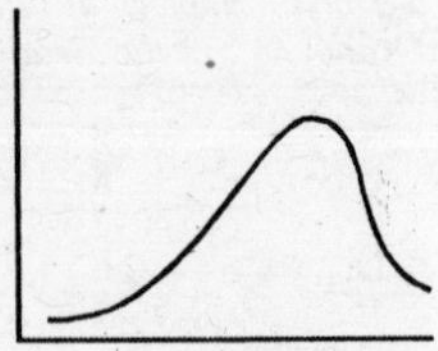

Negatively
Skewed Curve

If then the obtained curve were to be converted into a normal curve it would allow us to scientifically categorise the obtained curve into grades. It is because the obtained curve is infected with a number of shortfalls explained earlier which account for differences between the perceived and the true attainments, the element of skewness is ignored for practical purposes of awarding grades and taken as if it is a normal one.

In regard to the choice of a scale for categorising students attainments or potentials, our choice in large-scale public examinations falls on the *Stanine Scale*. This term is a contraction of 'standard nine'. It is a scale evolved by the Air Force in World War II for categorising professional levels of proficiency of its workforce on different abilities into nine grades. The scale has come to be universally used in educational and some other situations.

In using this scale the entire distribution of obtained scores is divided into nine equal parts 1 to 9 with a mean of 5 and a Standard Deviation of approximately 2 units. The Stanine scale, clusters together the two tail categories at either end of the distribution for bringing the categories to the convenient number of nine instead of eleven. The measure does not make any significant difference because the number of students whose performance falls in the two tail-end categories is insignificantly small.

The percentage-wise distribution of students falling in each of the nine grades in a Stanine Scale follows a symmetrical pattern representative of a normal curve and from either the top of the bottom it is

4% 7% 12% 17% 20% 17% 12% 7% 4%

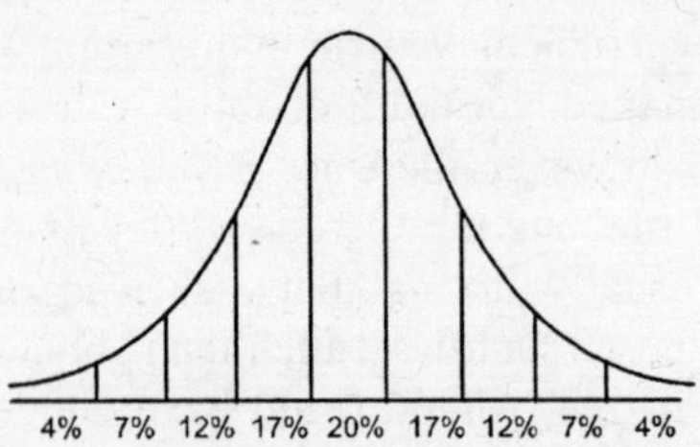

Symmetrical Curve

These percentages represent the approximate rounded off area of the curve covered by a particular grade if the curve is sub-divided by vertical lines drawn from the demarcating points for grades, on the base line representing the total distribution. These points on the base line are situated at a distance of ½ a Standard Deviation from one another in a stanine scale.

These are proportions (rounded off to the nearest whole value) which would be formed in the corresponding ½σ intervals in a normal distribution. The area relationship under the normal curve would show that 9.9 per cent of the area lies between the Median and a point, one quarter of a standard deviation away. Hence 2 × 9.9 = 19.8 per cent or 20 per cent lies in the Median interval.

The percentage to be assigned to grade D is similarly determined from the tables. The area from the mean to three quarters of a standard deviation above the mean contains 27.3 per cent of the area under the normal curve. Subtracting 9.9 per cent from this it is found that 17 per cent of the scores above the Median lie in this slot. The other percentages, are determined similarity.

In the case of a Stanine scale the grade-wise distribution will be as under:

Grade-wise Distribution in a Stanine Scale

Symbolic or Letter Grade	*Interval*	*No. of Cases*	*Numerical Grade Value*
A	1.75 σ to ∝	4%	9
B	1.25 σ to 1.75 σ	7%	8
C	0.75 σ to 1.25 σ	12%	7
D	0.25 σ to 0.75 σ	17%	6
E	-0.25 σ to 0.25 σ	20%	5
F	-0.75 σ to -0.25 σ	17%	4
G	-1.25 σ to -0.75 σ	12%	3
H	-1.75 σ to -1.25 σ	7%	2
I	- ∝ to -1.75 σ	4%	1

In case however we decide to use a five-point scale, again, in a large population the measurement scale will have to be divided into five equal parts where the numerical grade values for the symbolic grades will range from 1 to 5 with a mean of 3 and a standard deviation of approximately one unit. Grade-wise percentage of cases in this situation will be as under:

Grade-wise Distribution in a Five-Point Scale

Symbolic or Letter Grade	*Interval*	*No. of Cases*	*Numerical Grade Value*
A	1.5 σ to ∝	7%	5
B	0.5 σ to 1.5 σ	24%	4
C	-0.5 σ to 1.5 σ	38%	3
D	-1.5 σ to -0.5 σ	24%	2
E	-∝ to -1.5 σ	7%	1

It could be mentioned that even though the Stanine Scale is widely accepted to be used, examining agencies could devise their own scales on the basis of their curves of distribution e.g. one examining agency has decided on the following scale for relative grading.

A+ A A–	Top Next Next	2% 6% 12%	20%
B+ B B–	Next Next Next	15% 20% 15%	50%
C+ C C–	Next Next Next	12% 10% 8%	30%

12.5 Grading in School Situations

While grading pupil performance in school situations, the prime pre-requisite of 'population' (large numbers) is conspicuous by its absence. Hence some compromises in the aforesaid idealistic and scientific procedures will need to be struck.

First of all it needs to be appreciated that when the performance of students has to be classified into different categories a nine point scale may become impracticable. This is because the number of students will be small and a number of grade slots may remain unfilled. Use of a five-point scale will therefore be advisable in school situations.

The type of schools, based particularly on their management (govt. schools/govt. aided schools/local body or municipal schools/private unaided schools) will also demonstrate different patterns of skewness. The schools or school categories will, therefore, need to devise their own situation-specific systems of grading.

While Absolute Grading is inadvisable in large-scale public examinations schools could, even devise and designs their own procedures of subject-wise absolute grading. These, however, will need to be worked out class-wise and subject-wise on the basis of past statistics about obtained scores of students. The devised formula, however, will need to be periodically reviewed for a possible revision if and when and where necessary.

In the Report Cards, however, the mark ranges for different grades in different subjects will need to be presented on the reverse side of the certificates for a better public appreciation.

Schools could also use direct grades wherever feasible.

The school grades should desirably be awarded on a five-point scale or even on a three-point one, in view of the special limitation of small numbers.

It is certainly not desirable for schools to blindly copy the situation of external examinations by using a nine-point scale because it is not practicable.

A *compromise formula*, which is neither completely scientific nor totally unscientific, could be proposed as a practicable proposition. In each subject at a particular examination the highest and the lowest obtained scores be identified. The lowest score be substracted from the highest score. This figure may be divided by four. The number so obtained may be substracted from the highest score five times, one by one. These numbers will give the boundary scores for the different grades and marks falling within these, be awarded the corresponding grade.

13

Evaluating Teaching Effectiveness

Teacher effectiveness, is the most important facet of educational effectiveness, yet it is rarely attempted. This aspect is proposed to be discussed in this chapter.

13.1 The Need

Educational evaluation is a process of estimating and appraising the degree and dimension of achievement and abilities.

Evaluation of educational practices is a process of estimating and appraising the proficiency of the teachers in conducting educational practices. In other words, it is a process of appraising the application of educational theory into practice.

In some situations the outcomes of education are available only in qualitative terms and the outcomes of evaluation are expected in quantitative terms particularly for purposes of grading and classification. To get over this problem an approach is being proposed and suggested here.

13.2 Scope of Evaluation of Educational Practices

Educational practices and the activities related to them can be classified as under:

- Curricular activities related to the subjects of instruction, which are organised with a view to achieving the objectives of the scholastic domain.
- Activities related to the non-scholastic areas or those related to the other school programmes and practices. The purpose of organising these activities is to ensure those aspects of pupils' growth, which though important goals of the instructional programme, cannot be achieved through the teaching and learning of subjects alone.
- Activities related to diagnosis, prognosis, review, motivation, guidance, evaluation etc. The very title of each of these activities itself explains the purpose and importance of their position in the curriculum.

13.3 Purpose of Evaluating Educational Practices

There may be several purposes or functions for which the evaluation of educational practices may be taken up. The area of Teacher proficiency is being selected here to illustrate the proposed approach. Three *purposes of Teacher Education programmes* are being stated here by way of an example:

- To discover the degree of competence developed by the teacher in initiating, organising and improving the educational practices and to diagnose the strengths and weakness of his students for further guidance.
- To make a prediction about the likely educational practices which a particular teacher can best organise as a regular teacher in a school.
- To certify the teacher competencies about the level of his proficiency in initiating and organising a particular educational practice.

13.4 Procedure of Evaluating Educational Practices

Objectives

A good Teacher appraisal programme attempts to find out the degree of proficiency attained by the teachers in the various programmes and practices incorporated in a the various programmes of the institutions. It is, therefore, essential at the outset to identify the most prominent of teacher competencies to be subjected to evaluation, these are lasted below:

- To develop an understanding of the subject to be taught, the objectives of teaching it and the methods and techniques best suited for teaching it.
- Familiarity with the different philosophies of education and to acquire the ability of evolving a sound philosophy of his own.
- An understanding of the different aspects of pupils' development and behaviour and the factors related to them.
- An experimental attitude towards teaching and faith in the teaching profession.
- A motivation for one's professional growth.
- Acquisition of skills in planning and executing teaching-learning activities through observation, participation and actual teaching under observation/supervision.
- Familiarisation with the salient features and problems of Indian education with reference to the different stages of general education, i.e., primary, secondary, university or professional education.
- Ability to organise activities related to both scholastic and co-scholastic areas as also other programmes and practices.
- Acquisition of the knowledge of evaluation procedures and skill in

developing and administering tools for evaluating pupil behaviour continuously, comprehensively and for applying measures for improvement.

The above illustrative list can be further elaborated and some additions can surely be made to it.

Evidences

In order to evaluate teacher competencies it is necessary to collect evidences about the professional growth of the individual teacher in relation to the objectives. For this purpose a teacher will have to consider issues such as the following:

- What techniques and tools should be employed for evaluating different abilities in a given situation.
- What method should be used for obtaining evidences so that a variety of expected educational outcomes can be incorporated in the scheme of evaluation. This would also involve the sampling of situations.
- How much time should be spent on this task.

Taking the illustration further *to the specific area of classroom teaching*, it could be said that this area of evaluation comprises the following aspects of evaluation.

- Class management:
- Pupils' co-operation
- Teacher's expression
- Teacher's subject-matter competence
- Activities incorporated in the instructional programme.
- Use of aids
- Evaluation.

These aspects of evaluation should be very clearly specified. Their enumeration should cover the entire gamut of the subject. They ought also help him in locating the most adequate tool for the assessment of each of the aspects. This would also imply the use of a variety of tools as the same tools may not prove to be effective for evaluating all the aspects of each area.

Developing Evaluative Criteria

For each aspect of evaluation detailed out, it will be necessary to develop evaluative criteria to make the assessment specific and accurate.

Taking the point still further, it could be said that if *subject matter competence* of the teacher is taken as an aspect of evaluation, its evaluative criteria could be:

- Correctness
- Relevance and
- Richness

It will then be in respect of these evaluative criteria that the degree of proficiency of a teacher will be judged.

Collection of Evidence

After having developed the evaluative criteria for each area of evaluation, the next natural step will be the collection of evidences for evaluation on the basis of the identified criteria.

One of the most common techniques for the collection of evidences in the present situation will be *planned observation.* Other possible techniques could be interview, assessment of records of the process of execution and the outcome. In order to be able to collect usable evidences, it will be necessary to select or develop appropriate tools.

Taking the illustration still further it could be said that if subject matter competence is the aspect to be evaluated and if its correctness, relevance and richness are the criteria for evaluating it, the evidences could normally be collected from the following sources:

- Lesson plans for evaluating the degree and kind of preparation made by the teacher for teaching the particular lesson.
- Performance in actual teaching situations.

Evidences so obtained could be summarised in qualitative or quantitative terms. Qualitative evaluation based on the summarisation and interpretation of the evidence collected, is quite common. It can be obtained from the study of the lesson notes, the observation of lessons and the prepared teaching aids.

Evaluation in qualitative terms is not only possible but is also likely to prove of greater practical utility though it is not usually attempted probably because of the natural resistance to change. But in view of its scientific foundation, *a quantitative assessment of proficiency in educational practice based on qualitative evidences is likely to yield a more commonly acceptable measure.* It will also make comparisons possible and easier to make. Such a conversion of qualitative evidences into quantitative indices has, however, to be based on a scientific basis.

Summarisation of Data

Summarisation of data—So that the data collected could be used for educational ends, it is necessary that it may be appropriately summarised and interpreted.

Summarisation of data as already mentioned could either be in qualitative or quantitative terms. In qualitative terms it could focus on a particular individual aspect in respect of a specific ability. In quantitative terms, it could be summarised through a tool like a rating scale on which ratings could be awarded to different individuals for the degree of their accomplishment in a particular aspect of evaluation.

13.5 PREP INDEX and its Derivation

How a quantitative measure of a qualitative outcome could be obtained is illustrated below. The proposed tool is a Rating Scale. The following description further stretches the example of subject matter competence of a teacher already mentioned earlier.

A nine-point rating scale with five points defined is devised for evaluating each of the aspects on the basis of the abilities assessed on identified evaluative criteria. The following is an illustration of such a scale developed for assessing subject matter competence.

8. Fully correct, completely relevant and very rich
7.
6. Rare evidences of incorrectness or irrelevance and richness
5.
4. Usually correct and relevant and moderately rich
3.
2. Several evidences of incorrectness and irrelevance and poor content
1.
0. Mostly incorrect, irrelevant and very poor content

Such scales will need to be devised for all specified aspects of evaluation. The ratings on these scales could then be translated into a profile. Thus while evaluating a complete lesson suppose it is found that particular student teacher has been rated as follows on nine-point rating sale for in respect of different aspects;

Class Management	5
Pupil's Co-operation	3
Expression	4
Subject matter competence	7
Activities incorporated	5
Use of aids	3
Evaluation	4

These ratings could then be translated into a profile like the one given below :

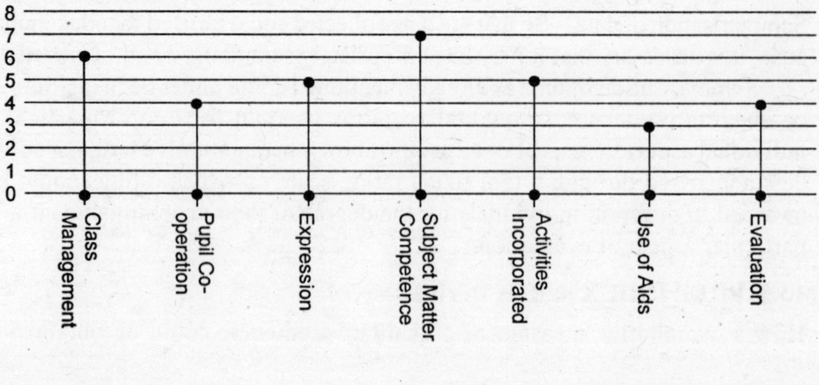

Such profiles will prove to be of very great help not only to the evaluator but also to the teacher himself for making his own self-evaluation. Giving profiles from time to time, will enable the teacher to judge for himself, his own strengths and weaknesses in specific aspects of evaluation and the progress that he may have made between one point of time and another in respect of each one of them individually.

The representation on these profiles could be quantified by the following method to arrive at the *Index of Proficiency in Educational Practice* (PREP INDEX)

Suppose there are 75 marks in all out of which teacher has to be evaluated and the different weightages to each of the aspects of evaluation are as given in the table as follows. Suppose also that on each of these aspects of evaluation the respective scores obtained out of eight (the points 0-8 on the scale), are also as indicated in the table, the PREP INDEX will be calculated as follows:

S. No.	*Aspects of Evaluation*	*Weightage to Aspects*	*Scores on the Rating Scales*	*Weighted Scores*
1.	Class Management	10	5	50
2.	Pupil Co-operation	5	3	15
3.	Expression	20	4	80
4.	Subject-matter Competence	10	7	70
5.	Activities incorporated	10	5	50
6.	Use of aids	10	3	30
7.	Evaluation	10	4	40
	Total	75	31	335

Total of weighted scores = 50+15+80+70+50+30+40 = 335

Maximum scores out of which the total weighted scores have been obtained = 8 × 75

(8 being the maximum point of scales and 75 the total weightage to all the aspects of the particular area of evaluation)

= 600

Score = 335/600

PREP INDEX = 335/600 × 100

= 55.83

Thus 55.83 is the Prep Index of the particular teacher in regard to teaching competency.

In the same manner as explained above, 'Prep Index' or the Index of Proficiency (PR) in Educational (E) Practice (P) could be calculated for each aspect of evaluation and will help the evaluator in the different ways in which this data can be used.

13.6 Use of Evaluation Data

Evaluation data, as we know, could be either qualitative or quantitative. Both these forms of data can be used for a variety of purposes. These are:

Diagnosis

Educational practices are incorporated in school programme with a view to achieving some well defined educational objectives. The achievement of these objectives leads to pupil growth in desirable directions, in organising the various school programmes and in conducting educational practices, to ensure pupil growth as enunciated through the objectives. The extent to which he is successful also needs to be evaluated. The primary purpose is to identify the strengths and weaknesses of a particular teacher so as to guide him in making better progress and in achieving higher successes.

Self-Evaluation and Guidance

Evaluation of educational practices, particularly in regard to the development of profiles and derivation of the Prep Index, in respect of each aspect of evaluation for a particular teacher, serves another very important purpose of self-evaluation and self-guidance. This also provides him motivation for achieving better success on subsequent occasions.

The evaluator also finds himself on a better footing to assess the teacher on the basis of the evaluation data referred to above. As the evaluator would specifically know a particular teacher's hard sports, he can be more precise and more effective in giving him guidance.

Certification

Certification in regard to the degree of competence achieved by him in different areas of evaluation is also one of the most important functions of evaluation data. The derivation of the PREP INDEX will again prove to be of a more valid measure of proficiency than the arbitrary assessments based on vague perceptions which are very often attempted. Certification on the basis of this data will not only be more valid and reliable but also more meaningful to the employer for being used for different purposes.

Prediction

The evaluation data could also be used for the purpose of prediction as to what a particular teacher is capable of accomplishing.

13.7 Conclusion

Evaluation of educational practices was mostly undertaken in the past in an arbitrary manner, endangering both the reliability and validity of the measurements. The development of a Methodology for Evaluating Educational

Practices has therefore been a long felt need. The fore-going discussion is an attempt at developing such a methodology which could be applied to all educational practices. Evaluation done on the basis of such a methodology will, it is hoped, yield data which will be more accurate; specific and meaningful than the one arrived at through the usual arbitrary conclusions of a few individuals who may find it difficult to overcome their biases while making assessments.

This could as well be a valuable approach for assessing practice-teaching lessons in teacher's colleges. The format of the profile could be printed in a corner of each page of the criticism book and the faculty members observing the lesson could just put in the dots and the student teacher may then calculate the Prep Index. This may be in addition to the written observations.

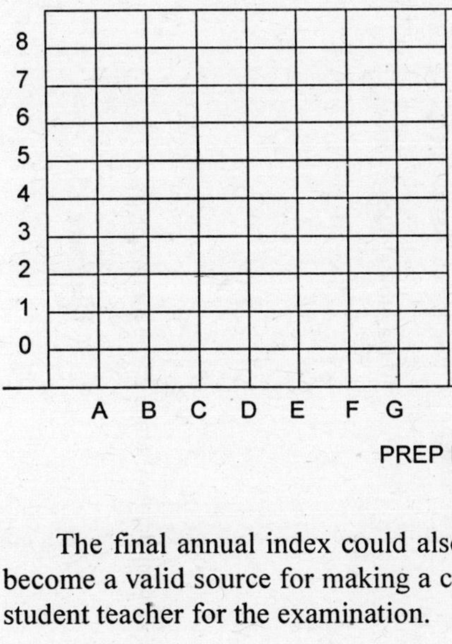

INDEX

A. Class Management
B. Pupil Co-operation
C. Teacher's Expression
D. Subject Matter Competence
E. Activities Incorporated
F. Use of Aids Evaluation

PREP INDEXs

The final annual index could also then be calculated on this basis and become a valid source for making a conclusion, about the final grade of the student teacher for the examination.

Adapted from the chapter contributed by Dr. R.H. Dave & Dr. H.S. Srivastava for "Evaluating Teacher Effectiveness" brought out by the ETS, Princeton (New Jersey), U.S.A.

13.8 Methodology of Evaluating Educational Practices (A Graphical Presentation of steps)

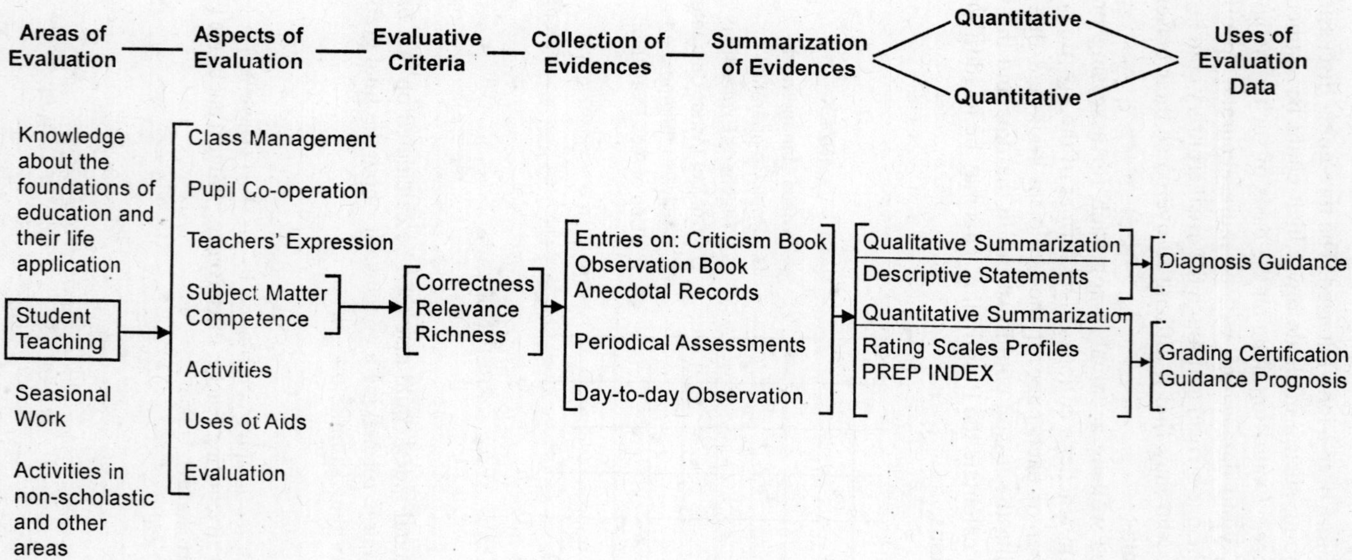

* Selected as illustration for explaining different steps of the methodology

Diagram 13.1

PART II

SOME CONVENTIONAL TECHNIQUES OF TEACHING

Introduction

A teaching technique, method or approach connotes the manner of curriculum transaction. There are many of these and such a one should be selected for a particular teaching situation which:

- is aligned to the age-group of the concerned students,
- is found to be of interest by the students,
- is based on their previous knowledge and experience of the students,
- is within the ability of the children to pursue,
- can motivate children for further learning on their own,
- enhances pupils' competencies by imparting enablement, empowerment and enrichment to the students,
- encourage learning initiatives of self-directed learning among children, and
- help in the realisation of objectives.

Not all methods are suitable for all situations. The choice of a method will have to depend among other things on the children being taught, the teachers own abilities, the facilities available.

Some of the main of the commonly used of these are described below alongwith their diverse manifestations and the approaches of their effective use.

14

The Lecture Method

This '*Tongue and the Ear Method*' is, by and large the most widely used method of teaching and learning and consists of dispensing of information by the teacher to the students. The teacher is active and the student is passive. The method conceives that the completion of the prescribed course content by the teacher in this fashion, is the main purpose of education. The teachers proficiency is judged by the quantum of information transmitted and not by its assimilation by the students. *Teaching thus becomes both the means* and *the end and learning not the core concern.*

The lecture method is the most economical method. More information can be transferred to the students in a given period of time than by any other method. To be fruitful the lectures must be supplemented by some other methods or aids or activities. Active participation of the students, in the process of learning helps in augmentation, acceleration and internalisation of learning.

Socrates distrusted the lecture method on the ground that the lecturer puts ready-made ideas into the minds of pupils, without giving them a chance to explore and experiment for drawing their own conclusions and thereby discover their own potentials. To Socrates questions are a powerful means triggering thinking besides being powerful instruments of evaluation. The Socratic method aims at leading pupils (through self-evaluation) from 'unconscious ignorance to conscious ignorance' through an ironic or destructive stage of questioning and then reading them on to 'truth' through a constructive stage of further questioning.

There are two essential steps involved in the lecture method:

- Lecture Preparation
- Lecture Presentation

14.1 Lecture Preparation

Preparations for using the lecture method of teaching are not easy by any chance. It means the collection and compilation of information from different sources. Systematic organisation and sequencing is an important subsequent part of this exercise.

The prescribed course content and the maturity level of the students is the basic foundation of this endeavour. *What has gone before and what is to follow determine the direction and dimensions of preparation.*

Time Budgeting is another basic necessity because the course has to be completed within the time available. The number of lectures that can be delivered is thus determined on the basis of the time available. This in turn becomes the basis of the decision about how much of the content can be put into a lecture.

The teacher has also in the process to identify *the hard spots in learning*, in the subject matter, covered through a lecture and be amply prepared for clarifying the related ideas for overcoming them.

The teacher has also to collect the latest references, statistics, information about latest developments beyond the text books for enriching the process of his teaching to enable students to overcome the related hurdles.

14.2 Lecture Presentation/Delivery

To make an impact, the presentation has but to be effective. And to be effective it has to have some *distinct characteristics*. Some main of these are described below:

A lecture though called a lecture, should not just be a one way traffic but *an amplified dialogue with pupil participation*. Studding and punctuating the ideas with examples and augmenting them with new ideas can save them from being reduced to monotonous monologues which they often become.

An *attention capturing introduction* can also prove helpful in retaining pupils' attention and this has to be very carefully prepared.

Couching the lecture in appropriate words and catching phrases are useful fodders for whetting the cutting edge for the students.

Speech and delivery are other criteria for success and this implies clarity of thought, simplicity of words, as also good pronunciation, intonation, articulation and above all fluency.

Graded sequence of presentation which may carry students from known to the unknown, from concrete to abstract, from general to specific, are well tried prescriptions for effective teaching.

Emphasis on anchor points and definitions even at the cost of repetition become important measures for the assimilation of knowledge on the part of the students. This is also of great help to the students in jotting down points to remember.

Proceeding to the *next point* after making sure that the *previous one* has been well understood is a confirmatory test of successful teaching. This could be ensured by recapitulating what is taught through pointed questions and cross questions. In fact the students too ought to be encouraged to ask questions to clarify any misgivings they may have. The clarifications given are, in fact, a better teaching device than just lecturing and the teacher should welcome interruptions by students in this regard.

Alertness of students has but to be ensured in the course of lectures and one of the easiest methods is to ask questions in the course of the lectures and these questions should be so distributed over the class as to retain student attention althrough, with a constant apprehension that the next question may be asked of any of them.

A *congenial climate* is conducive to learning. It should always be a friendly atmosphere that should permeate the classroom. It is desirable in this context to address students by name.

There are also some ***don'ts*** in this regard. The teacher should never try to show off by mentioning facts and terminology which the students cannot understand. He should address students in their face, watching their eyes and their forehead wrinkles which are great indicators of their having understood or having not understood the ideas communicated. The teacher should neither chew nor swallow words. He should also not speak to himself but to the class. The lectures from a pulpit or a public dais are to be differentiated form those in the classroom. A clergy-man or a political leader can call it quits after a lecture which a teacher cannot as the lecture is a means to the end of learning and not an end it itself. A teacher has but to ensure that he has communicated what was necessary and that it has also gone down the throats of the students. Even enabling students to learn and understand is not enough, they should also be enabled to use that knowledge in unfamiliar situations. The teacher therefore has to work with that ultimate goal in mind..

15

The Discussion Method

There are issues where there is a likelihood of differences of opinion or problems admitting different solutions or some conceptual confusions needing clarifications where some consensus is required to be obtained. These are to be put up for discussions.

15.1 Discussions

- permit students to freely express their view points
- stimulate group thinking
- enable students to agree to differ from other co-students.
- promote public speaking.

15.2 Teacher's/Leader's Role

Discussions must always have a leader, a role which the teacher could assume himself or he may delegate that position to some student.

In case it is necessary or is considered desirable, a class may be divided into groups for discussion on the theme as a whole or on sub-themes and each may have its own leader.

The leader in such situations would need to execute the following responsibilities:

- ensure that everybody gets an opportunity to speak and to be brief
- honour the time limit
- pacify heat in contradictions.

15.3 The Process of Discussions

A discussion starts with an introduction by the leader, who must make a thorough advance preparation not just for presenting the theme, but more so to intervene and make the concluding remarks. The theme should then be presented comprehensively, highlighting the differing view points.

In the course of discussions it is always the leader who is addressed and not another member of the group as a part of the *discussion decorum and etiquette*. Speakers should be given a clear idea of the time constraint and be tactfully reminded/interrupted whenever necessary.

The leader should also not allow the discussion to get derailed. Deviations from the focus of the discussion needs to be promptly checked.

The leader should not necessarily intervene after each observation unless absolutely unavoidable. The students should take their turns one by one. The leader should resist the temptation for intervention and go on jotting points. He may make his balancing concluding observations at the end to save himself from imposing his views on the group. A black-board summary, in telegraphic language, is always helpful for highlighting the conclusions or focal points. This is helpful in consolidating and internalising learning.

No student should ever be snubbed but listened to with respect. Freedom of speech and an informal ethos, are guarantees for success of discussions. Humour always eases tense moments and deserves to be inducted like 'commas'. In the event of confusions the black-board should come to help.

15.4 Pre-requisites for Effective Discussions

With the goals clearly defined and the road map drawn, the discussion should at its close, impart to every participant a feeling:

- of having contributed to the joint effort.
- of taking the conclusions convincingly as his own.
- of having gained a clearer picture of the situation than before.
- of realising that there are also points of view other than his own.

Discussions imply both listening and speaking. Listening has to be patient and speaking relevant. Being attentive to whatever any member of the group speaks and to understand what is meant to be conveyed by the speaker, enables a pin pointed and meaningful response, which is always appreciated by everybody.

Logical presentations and responses always needs the marshalling of ones own arguments. Ones own classify about the term of discussion is very necessary and for this some self study is always called for. In fact a habit of general reading, always comes to the aid of everybody and this ought to be constantly persued.

16

Demonstration

16.1 Introduction

Demonstration as a method of teaching is used in practical subjects like Physics, Chemistry, Biology, Mathematics, Geography, Home Science. It is used by itself or as part of a lecture.

Demonstration by the teacher or a professional or a student demonstrates to the learners the steps of the *process* in executing a task for ensuring the quality of the outcome or *product*. Experimentation on ones own is the follow up of demonstrations.

Demonstration is able to explain the do's and the don'ts of the process of performance or a practical task, more convincingly than any oral description, because *demonstration is an action picture*. An old *Chinese proverb says that one picture is worth a thousand words* and demonstration, therefore, is much more than that.

16.2 Demonstration as a Teaching Device

Demonstration as such is a valuable teaching device and as an action-cum-demonstration lecture, it brings to the fore the precise relationships between apparatus, materials, articles, machinery and appliances and the methods of handling them. *Necessary precautions in avoiding damage and accidents, of avoiding wastage, of the meticulous maintenance of equipment, of their orderly arrangement for ensuring ease in locating them when required also get automatically highlighted.*

Demonstrations serve as models of laboratory work by the students independently. They bridge the gap between theory and practice, stimulate thinking and motivate further learning through exploration and experimentation on the part of the students.

Demonstrations require special seating arrangements for the students so that everybody can see as they are performed. Specially designed class-rooms with rows in stair-steps, or semi-circular in shape are considered appropriate as in an amphitheater.

16.3 Preparation for Demonstration

In preparing for demonstration, the demonstrator must brush-up his knowledge about the theme and its relationship with others going before and coming after it, to be able to answer questions students may ask. This will also give him the confidence in performing the experiments for the demonstration. He should also be relaxed and friendly in the course of the demonstrations and should display an infectious vitality and enthusiasm.

An *inventory* of the equipment required must be made and a checklist for checking not just their availability but also their workability should be ensured. While it is often proposed that the best of equipment should be used for demonstrations it is desirable to use, the like of the same which the students would be using in real situations. This will impart greater confidence to the students when they perform the experiments and exercises on their own.

16.4 Prerequisites for Demonstration

The most appropriate height of a demonstration table is supposed to be 75 cms or 30 inches. The length and width of the demonstration table would depend on the kind of demonstration. Usually the traditional demonstration halls mentioned earlier have large-sized fixed demonstration tables with taps and sinks and drawers. Appropriate lighting and seating arrangement will need to be ensured for adequate visibility of the demonstration. A rehearsal of the total operation about how to begin, how to proceed and how to conclude is a valuable preparatory exercise. This practice about what to say and what to do, will lead the teacher to better success.

The main steps of preparation in this regard will, therefore, be:

- preparation for the presentation (oral).
- arrangement of the apparatus/equipment to ensure easy accessibility.
- checking seating lighting and other arrangements.
- rehearsal of the total operation.
- the wordings of the questions.
- the black-board summary or bullet points.
- the special points of significance and relationships to be highlighted.

In case it is possible for the students also to do some experiments/or parts of experiments simultaneously, it can be a useful teaching method.

The demonstrator should also simultaneously clarify all misgivings of students, for a clearer understanding and for avoiding any subsequent confusions.

16.5 Limitations of the Demonstration Method

Demonstration as a method of instruction, also has some *limitations*. It proves to be an expensive proposition financially. It also takes quite a lot of time. Furthermore, it presumes that all students learn at the same speed. It is, therefore, that it is proposed that demonstrations and practical work by studens should go on simultaneously.

17

Observation

Observation is basic to learning, enquiry and discovery. It is the process through which pupils can be stimulated to learn.

Observation helps pupils:

- to develop the ability to see phenomenon and processes as they exist and operate and to note important details, which otherwise might be overlooked.
- to develop an objective approach and to participate efficiently in individual or group work.
- not just to 'see' but also to critically perceive and realise what they see. This augments what they learn from the book.

Directed observation can be carried out by an individual pupil or by small or larger groups. Individual observation offers broader experience as a learning technique, than group observation, since greater amount of competency, independence and responsibility, are developed in the individual pupil. Participation in activities such as field trips, video films, exhibitions, promote group observation.

17.1 Preparation for Making Observations

The pupils ought to be given an orientation about the situation in which observation has to be made and what exactly they have to observe. In fact giving them a list of things to be observed is very helpful.

Some situations in which observation has to be made may be natural and others contrived or simulated. Specific activities facilitate learning through observation. Sometimes for consolidation of learning, drill by way of repetition of activities may be necessary. Repetition may also be needed for arriving at generalisations.

17.2 Process of Observation

All observations must be recorded without lapse of time immediately and accurately. Observation sheets/schedules prove helpful in this regard as the fact/phenomenon observed can be entered easily and quickly in the relevant column, which may even save future labour of classifying information.

Attention is the key to accurate observation, which leads to learning. Children should not talk among themselves during the process of observation. Students should also be asked not to maintain a casual detached attitude while observing. No questions may be asked by the observers or the teacher or the other students in the course of observation as the phenomenon observed are mostly fleeting. All questions, doubts, apprehensions may be jotted down to be presented during the discussion time allocated for discussing the observations.

Observations made should be discussed after the process is over. In this session all the things observed by all the students may be listed and the similarity of their views on a particular issue, may then be summarised and conclusions drawn to reinforce the understanding of pupils about the observations made by them. When their observations are confirmed, by others too, that will give them confidence about the accuracy of their observations as also in their ability to draw conclusions on their own in subsequent situations.

17.3 Observation of Individuals

They are not just the facts and phenomenon that are to be observed but also the behaviour of the students themselves. In fact many aspects of personality, need only observation so as to be evaluated. The areas of personality attributes, attitudes and values etc. can only be observed, in different situations. There situation have therefore but to be provided by the institutions in a systematic manner. These situation should not look like external unrelated interventions but built into the entire teaching learning process as an integral part.

The areas of physical competencies in outdoor co-curricular activities to require only observation for being judged. In fact the ways in a student behaves in them unmistakably reveals many traits and attributes of the individual besides the level of proficiencies attained in them.

The insight that observation provide are authentic evidences for being used for different purposes.

As a subject of evaluation, they also require different types of assessment tools like rating scales and the collection of evidences would require anecdotal record for prompt, on the spot recording of the kind and degree of attainment.

18

Problem-Solving Method

Any method of solving a problem scientifically, involving thinking, reasoning planning and execution by following logical steps is a scientific method. The process of problem solving results in the development of *cognitive abilities, affective qualities, attitudes and psycho-motor skills*. It is in this context that the 'Problem-Solving Method' is called a scientific method.

RISK explains problem solving as "a planned attack on a difficulty, perplexity or problem to find a satisfactory solution". ROSS interprets problem solving as an educational device whereby the teacher and the pupils attempt in a conscious, planned and purposeful manner, to arrive at an explanation or solution to some educationally significant difficulty.

A problem occurs in a situation in which a felt difficulty to act is realised. It may be a mental difficulty or a physical one, slowing or blocking the path of progress for reaching the goal. It may therefore impress upon the pupils (who may meet it) as needing a solution and is recognised and realised by them as a challenge to be picked up and squarely met.

18.1 Characteristics of a 'Problem'

A problem in an educational setting ought to possess and actually possesses some distinct characteristic spelled out below:

Emergence from a live educational setting: The problem is normally related to life or education and is, therefore, normally within the ambit of common experience of the pupils.

Focussed in nature: The problem identified as the subject of instruction/ learning ought to be clear, definite, understandable, interesting, aligned to the age group of the pupils, within the capability of the learners, and based on the knowledge they already possess. Above all, it ought to be thought provoking.

Of practical utility: The problem should have a practical value and the outcomes/solutions ought to be taken as of practical utility by the pupils. This would motivate the pupils to demonstrate diligence and perseverance in investing efforts for solving them.

Related to the curriculum: To be pursued purposefully the problem must be a part of the curriculum to realise the goals of which, is the prime concern of the students.

Within the range of the time budget and resources available: The process of problem solving as a method of teaching/learning should not put unnecessary strain on the finances of the institutions. At the same time it should also be possible to accomplish the total task, within the available time.

18.2 Approaches to Problem Solving

Basically, there are two main approaches to problem solving with different and contrasting procedures:

- the inductive method, and
- the deductive method.

The *Inductive Method* carries the thinking process from particular to general situations. Conclusions by way of generalisations are arrived at from particular principles and concrete examples. An example of inductive problem solving could be that "As Vitamin C dissolves in water and is easily destroyed by heat, a generalisation could be drawn that all foods rich in Vitamin C should be cooked in minimum amount of water, for the least possible amount of time and heat."

The *Deductive Method* carries reflective thinking from general to particular/specific. For example when students find that in dry summer the desert coolers substantially bring down temperatures inside the rooms, they draw the inference, through deduction that the heat outside leads to the evaporation of the water of the cooler pads and thus causes loss of heat which makes the air passing through the wet pads cooler, which in turn cools the rooms.

In classroom situations, simulated/hypothetical problematic situations could also lead to integrative learning and in this manner reinforce the knowledge and the skills among the students.

Two other important methods also help reinforce the problem solving method and could be safely mentioned here in passing.

Heuristic Method: Heurism is derived from the Greek concept of 'Heurisken' which means finding out. This can be an important approach for problem solving or for the discovery approach. It aims at making students more observant, accurate, truthful, thoughtful and dexterous. The method lays the foundation of self-education and helps promote the spirit of enquiry and research among pupils.

Discovery Method: Problem solving involves scientific enquiry which is a search for truth and knowledge. The emphasis in problem solving too is on search rather than mere acquisition of knowledge. This scientific method is also referred to as the discovery approach to teaching and learning. The method was spearheaded by PIAGET in Switzerland and BRUNNER in Cambridge Massachusetts.

Learning by discovery implies experiencing a sense of achievement and personal aggrandisement. Discovery is the identification and recognition of a relationship between:

- ➢ an idea and an observation

- two ideas
- two relationships

BRUNNER mentions four following advantages of learning by discovery:

- increase in intellectual potency
- shift from extrinsic to instrinsic rewards
- learning the heuristics of discovery
- memory processing

18.3 Steps of the Problem Solving Method

The main steps involved in using the Problem Solving Method could be listed as under :

Sensing or selecting the problem: The teacher should help the students to identify the problem to be solved by analysing the hurdles and handicaps posed by it. Necessary motivation for solving it should also thus be generated among the students. Students should also be enabled to be alert in spotting and recognising the problems as and when they crop up in different situations.

Defining (Interpreting and delimiting) the problem: The problem selected should be fully understood by the learners. The nature of the problem should help in charting the path for overcoming it. The feasibility of the action plan is governed by the ability of the students and the availability of the needed resources.

Hullfish and Smith suggest the following questions to be raised in defining a problem:

- What exactly is the problem? Can it be broken into sub-problems?
- Does the problem bear any similarity to any of those encountered in the past?
- In what fundamental ways is the problem similar to others
- In which ways does the particular problem differ from the others
- What do differences imply—new approaches?
- Is it necessary to redefine the problem in view of the above?

Collecting and evaluating relevant information/data: After the problem has been defined and interpreted in collaboration with the pupils, they should be prompted to list the information needed for solving it and to commence the process of its collection. With a view to initiating this, the teacher may identify:

- the sources from which the information can be collected—books, documents, reports etc.
- the personnel—experts and functionaries to be consulted.

The collected information should then be checked for its:

- appropriateness and relevance,
- adequacy and
- applicability in the given situations of the problem.

Formulating alternative solutions and selecting one: Different possible approaches for solving the problem could then be listed and their pros and cons discussed. This process of churning would enable the identification of the one most suitable. Tentative solutions could also thus be arrived at.

Arriving at the final solution: The next natural step is to pool together the possible solutions. These may then be discussed thread bare from different angles, for reaching an appropriate solution. At this point of time, teacher's indepth knowledge and ingenuity will be called for, for guiding students to reach apt and appropriate judgemental inferences.

Testing the validity of the solution arrived at: The validity of the solution finally arrived at, could be arrived at through:

- the application of the hypothesis to new situations
- further exploration, experimentation and investigations
- additional investigations for gathering new information.

Teachers constructive help and guidance would but be necessary throughout the process of problem solving.

18.4 Problem Solving and Project Method

Inspite of a host of similarities the problem solving and project methods do stand out prominently in respect of marked differences.

Problem solving requires a solution in thought or action or both. Project Method on the other hand aims at the successful completion of a task or unit of work.

Problem solving could be taken up as project work but a project need not always be a problem solving exercise.

18.5 Merits and Limitations of Problem Solving Method

The pursuit of the Problem Solving Method imparts valuable personality attributes to the students. The limitations of this method however, mainly relate to logistics and the perpetual paucity of resources.

The Problem Solving Method prompts pupils to learn by doing, a process through which they learn to think, to reason and to develop initiative. They also acquire valuably desirable work habits and self-reliance. As problem solving requires a higher order of mental abilities, it also helps students develop mental self-discipline.

The main limitations of the problem solving method are that it is time consuming both for the teachers and the students and hence cannot be used extensively and frequently. Paucity of resources too often become hurdles in using it. Quite often when problem solving is used as a method of teaching the elaborate and intensive focus it requires, turn out to be the only mental activity with others relegated into the background and in fact they get grossly neglected. The teacher has, therefore, to use his discretion in establishing the needed balance among different methodologies of instruction. He has particularly to guard against the situation when he may assign problems without the problems coming from the students as that kills their interest.

19

The Herbartian Steps

19.1 Historical Overview

John Friedrich Herbart (1776-1841), the German educational philosopher was both by birth and education an educationist. His grandfather was the Rector of a Gymnazium (a German School) at Oldenburg, Herbart's native town. His father was a lawyer and Privy Counsellor there. Herbart's mother is known to be a rare and a wonderful woman, who was able to assist her son with Greek and Mathematics and provide direction to his educational pursuits.

Just before graduation he became a tutor to the three sons of a Swiss Governor. During this span of two years (1797-1799) he was required by his patron to prepare a bi-monthly written report about the methods he used and about the progress and conduct of his students. This was Herbart's only experience in Pedagogy.

While in Switzerland Herbart met Pestalozzi and was greatly impressed by the educational principles propounded by him.

Then on resuming his interrupted university course he developed his own ideas from Pestalozzianism and put them into writing as well.

Following this, he lectured on pedagogy at the University of Gottingen from 1802 to 1809 and brought out his book 'General Pedagogy'. In 1809 Herbart was called upon to the chair of philosophy at Konigsberg as practically the successor of the illustrious Immanuel Kant. Kant died in 1804 and was succeeded by Traugott who resigned in 1809 to accept the chair at Leipzig.

It was at Konigsberg that Herbart took to documenting his ideas to become the first example of being an educational psychologist and philosopher, developing the educational process from the point of view of a teacher with the evolution of his concept of the '*apperceptive mass*' as the core doctrine of his educational philosophy. According to him it is in accordance with apperception that a teacher can secure the interest and attention of the pupil to any new idea and have him retain it. The teacher can make or modify his apperception masses or system of ideas in such a way that it can be apperceived or incorporated with the old in educative instruction.

19.2 The Originally Proposed Steps

The Herbartian steps to instruction propounded by the philosopher are widely used in different parts of the world until this day. They are:

- clearness (absorption)
- association (reflection)
- system (coherence)
- method (application/active reflection)

19.3 The Subsequent Adaptations

Subsequently Herbart's noted disciple ZILLER divided the step of 'clearness' into 'preparation' and 'presentation' and a more recent Herbartian REIN added 'Aim' as a sub-step to preparation. The names of the other three processes have also now been changed by subsequent Herbartians for giving greater lucidity and significance to them. The five formal steps of instruction are now given as:

- Preparation
- Presentation
- Comparison and association
- Generalisation
- Application

These steps are based on his concept of three primary functions of the mind as knowing, feeling and willing and incorporate his concepts of 'apperceptive mass', 'concentration' 'correlation' and multisided interests and project his philosophy that to 'instruct' the mind is to 'construct' it.

The above five steps could be described as under:

Preparation: Before starting to introduce new ideas it is necessary to mentally prepare children for the new intake. What the children already know is to be related to what is planned to be taught to them. The most common and also the most appropriate method is to ask them some questions about their previous knowledge which may logically or sequentially lead them to the new one. This step has essentially to be a brief one. The statement of *Aim* has to be an important part of it.

Presentation consists of relating and connecting new information with the old one, by dividing it into sections if necessary. Links between what is already known and what is purported to become known, as also the subsequent areas of content, have thus to be established. The degree and quantum of learning, desired to be imparted by the teacher and acquired by the students is an important decision to be made at this stage.

The subject matter becomes the focus of attention of both the teacher and the taughts. The presentation made by the teacher has but to be logical, sequential, clear, and focussed, involving lecturing, narration, description, demonstration and discussions participated by pupils. Repetition is also resorted to for internalisation of learning and the themes are also attempted to be integrated with those of other subjects and with life for creating, promoting and retaining the interest of the pupils in the subject. Developmental questions play an important part in this process.

Comparison or Association is the stage for consolidating learning by attempting to relate old knowledge with the new through comparisons and contrasts for establishing closer relationships between the two. The process is also aimed at arousing pupils curiosity for learning more, about the theme as also for leading them to think creatively.

Generalisation is the stage for putting together through recapitulation (revision) the facts and principles dealt with, during the earlier stages and for drawing of inferences and generalisations by the pupils with the teacher remaining in the background. Such pupil-based initiatives make learning abiding.

The Application stage attempts to demonstrate to the pupils that knowledge acquired has a vital relationship with life. The pupils mind at this stage shuttles between specific facts and phenomenon to generalisations and back to the specifics. At this stage the pupils ascend from the individual to the universal stage of knowledge and are enabled to acquire the ability for applying the generalised knowledge to specific individual situations.

19.4 Conclusion

Through these steps which go by his name Herbart attempted to demonstrate that philosophy is not just a macro-level concept but can also be applied at the micro-level as well.

Herbartian steps, in fact, present a blended amalgam of the principles of teaching and learning. That is why, they have been holding the ground for nearly two centuries now. Being easy to understand and practise they are a valuable guide for the teacher in preparing a teaching plan. Based on psychological principles they present the outline of a sequential action plan.

As they have been tested by time, suitably modified with experience they propose a predicable approach to teaching.

Just as with the passage of time modifications have been introduced in the steps, they can be further altered to suit emergent needs. Their value however will still remain.

PART III

SOME UNCONVENTIONAL TECHNIQUES OF TEACHING

Introduction

Emancipation from Formal Education

Formal education, has somehow come to imply only the use of the traditional methods, the main of which have been discussed in the preceding section on techniques of teaching. Besides, there are also some other *unconventional methods*, the use of which is more an exception than the rule. These approaches nevertheless possess a powerful potential for imparting learning, which is easily digestible by the learners, to become an internalised part of themselves. This is because most of them involve the active involvement of learners in the process of the acquisition of knowledge and other competencies. These methods also enrich the learners because they become *participatory crusades of learning*, where individuals are enabled to learn through the joint outcomes of their individual efforts or the labour of their teams and the contributions that each one makes to the learning programme.

As the approaches are basically learner-based, the teachers stand to gain, by way of saving on their time and effort in dishing out information to the students. This must, therefore, be an additional motivation for the teachers to use them for economising on their work load, and at the same time, successfully reaching their sole goal of ensuring abiding learning on the part of the students.

Furthermore, the freedom and flexibility that these allow both to the teachers and the taughts, does not shackle the learning process by any rigid rules or standardised procedures. This is something that often turns the frequently caused pain of learning into a joyful pursuit.

Some of the main of these approaches are attempted to be explained below in general terms. The teacher should feel free to make the needed adaptations in them to suit the special needs of their specific situations.

20

The Project Method

The Project Method is based on JOHN DEWEY'S pragmatic philosophy of experience and experimentation, which brought a new dynamism in education. It transformed the dull monotonous and often purposeless class-room teaching into one that made it vibrant and imparted vitality to it. Dewey said that '*Education should not only be for life but through life*'. He was keenly aware of the gap between a pupil's life in school and his life in the society. He insisted that in an efficient educational system this gap should be bridged. The project method is an attempt to bring society into the school.

William Kilpatrik defines the project as a "unit of whole hearted purposeful activity, proceeding in a social environment." *Stevenson* defines a project as "A problematic act carried to completion in its natural setting." *Ballard* states that "a project is a bit of real life that has been imported into the school." A project is thus related to real life, its problems and their solutions in the social environment.

20.1 Types of Projects

According to *Kilpatrick* projects can basically assume four forms:

The Producers' Type: In a producers type of project the emphasis is on actual production or development of material, or object or article.

The Consumers' Type: This type of project consists of various experiences like reading listening and evaluating things.

The Problem Type: This type of projects involve problem solving requiring the exercise of mental processes.

The Drill Type: This type of projects involve learning mainly by repetition of the processes like learning vocabulary, spellings etc.

20.2 Principles Involved in the Project Method

The principles governing the project method are:

Purposefulness: A project must be meaningful and purposeful to the pupils. This offers incentive and motivation to the pupils to learn and yields them the satisfaction and gratification at having been successful in accomplishing the tasks.

Activity centredness: A project is woven round some activity and offers opportunities to children to learn by doing by getting involved in the activities. They are also required to plan, think, evolve strategies of functioning and in accomplishing tasks independently, with a sense of achievement and flulfilment.

Life centredness: A project is planned around an actual life situation which is specially created/simulated in the school environment. The situations so created enable children to demonstrate their special abilities competencies, capacities and talents.

Based on experience: Experiences lead to abiding learning, as the learning that so accrues is self-acquired. The child also learns the value of team work and participatory learning and the resulting social and democratic values.

Freedom: The process of learning through the project method, offers full freedom to children to exercise their initiative and ingenuity in planning and executing the steps of the process on their own. Such freedom enables children to express themselves fully and freely. Incidentally this also helps them develop a sense of accountability for their activities.

Utility: Utility of the knowledge and experiences gained, through personally initiated and executed tasks, yields children the satisfaction of having realised something, which is of utility in life. This imparts meaningfulness to the educational ventures undertaken.

20.3 Steps in the Project Method

Quite like some other approaches, in Project Method too children learn by doing. The teacher's job is to provide a situation which may give pupils a spontaneous urge, to carry out the project according to their interests, attitudes, aptitudes, competencies etc.

Project situations can be provided both inside the classroom and outside. The *project situations* can be provided through:

- conversations on different topics
- discussions on different themes
- pictures
- video films
- story-telling
- excursions
- educational tours

With the seeds of situations sowed, the steps of proceeding on the projects have to be pursued, which are as under:

20.4 Proposing and Purposing a Project

The teacher proposes a project and enunciates the purpose. The latter serves as a motivating device as the children discover its usefulness and its compatibility with their respective interests and capacities to work for.

20.5 Planning the Project

Planning could be ideally done by the students themselves but in regard to the younger folk, some hints could be offered by the teacher, who may keep on watching them do things on their own. In fact the students may be encouraged to think of alternative approaches for realising the same goal and then to select the one that they consider most appropriate. This paves the way for the internalisation of the idea, which serves well in later life situations where an individual has but to learn to be flexible in weighing situations for taking ones own decisions.

The students also come to learn that whatever they may have planned, need not always be rigidly followed even if the plans do not work. The concept of 'mid-way corrections' for realising success is a valuable mental attitude of accepting the need for making changes in plans and finally making them.

20.6 Executing the Project

The freedom of project execution too is the prerogative of the pupils. It gives them the joy of doing things on their own, as per their self-developed plans. Distribution of responsibilities among themselves is another valuable step which enables pupils to put in their best to their respective (often self-chosen) tasks. While the project execution goes on, the teacher mainly remains an observant on-looker, ensuring that the pupils get all the materials they need and that all precautions are in place, so that the children do not get hurt in any way. He has also to establish a balance between the over-enthusiastic and the comparatively inert pupils. Encouraging and guiding the latter can yield them confidence and enthusiasm to work and effectively contribute to team effort.

20.7 Evaluating the Project

While evaluation is considered to be a teacher's activity the pupils can also be motivated to assess their own efforts and the resulting outcomes themselves.

The teacher should try to evaluate the project from the academic angle, diagnosing and identifying the outcomes of the project in real terms by way of the development of competencies by the pupils, cooperation in team work, voluntary willingness to make a contribution to the project while in process, identification of gainful outcomes in terms of the developments and whetting of *interests* and *abilities.*

The pupils too can undertake a self-evaluation of the gains, the new things learnt, the capacities improved, the insights into various operations gained, the confidence in oneself and motivation for further improving ones competencies. The teacher should in fact lead them to such realisations.

20.8 Shortcomings of the Project Method

Project method though a great educational innovation does suffer from some shortfalls the main of which are stated below:

It is a *time consuming* method of learning and teaching. It is also *not applicable to all the subjects and all the themes therein.* The teacher cannot always think of completely original themes for projects and therefore quite often they become repetitive.

20.9 Conclusion

Inspite of the shortcomings, the project method remains a very useful method of imparting abiding learning through personal experiences. Its great value in concept formation and development of valuable life relevant attitudes cannot be underestimated.

21

The Laboratory Method

21.1 Introduction—Learning by Doing

Pupils learn by doing. The laboratory method helps pupils to learn by doing. In experimental subjects experience in the laboratory becomes an important segment of pupils' total experience. It is the best method of providing pupils a clear understanding of any process. Laboratory experience under teachers' supervision is the first step for the development of manipulative and managerial skills among the students. Personal involvement in experimentation promotes the development of a spirit of inquiry, capacity for reasoning, exploration for purposes of acquiring the needed information and objectivity in observation as also faithful recording of observations, and rational deduction of inferences.

21.2 Support Material for Laboratory Work

The laboratory method even in science subjects, suffers from the handicap of the availability of sufficient items of apparatus, but now thanks to the NCERT, some Science Kits have been developed. Each kit has apparatus for twenty students to perform experiments individually. The basic idea behind prompting this venture is to provide inexpensive aids to experimental science education. In these kits, every item of glass apparatus which could be converted into plastic has been so converted, eliminating the fear for their replacement in case of breakage, if it was glass and thus of repeated financial investments. The fundamental premise for developing these aids/items of experimentation is to educate students in *concepts* rather than insisting on *accuracy* of results.

The Science kits are also a way of reaching the rural schools where adequate infrastructure is not available. The kit has taken the form of a box with a handle at the top. This can be stowed in any corner of the classroom thus eliminating the need for a special cup-board for storing the equipment. The apparatus is all stored in the drawers and chemicals on the shelves of the kit box. The kit has two doors, both in the front. One has hinges that brings the inner door from top to bottom and this can serve as a demonstration table. The outer cover is hinged in a manner that it opens up on one side. This side that opens up is painted black and can be used as a black-board, where even that is not available. Now however things have improved. The innovation of the development of science kits however, still remains an ingenious thing for overcoming constraints and handicaps.

As experimentation is usually time consuming, it is desirable to allot two consecutive class periods for it.

21.3 Forms of Laboratory Method

The laboratory method could assume three forms:

- Experimentational
- Observational
- Productive

The *experimental mode* helps explain, illustrate or to prove principles by enabling students to explore, experiment and draw conclusions. These conclusions become abiding acquisitions of the students. This mode also helps in creating in students an instinct for verifying facts and phenomenon.

The *observational mode* is again based on personal deductions not just based on experimentation but on personal observations. Exploration becomes the chief means for making observations. Observations of this type could be illustrated by the inferences on characteristics of growing children of different age groups.

The *productive mode* consists of creating a tangible outcome like the production of a simple item like a pin tray in wood work, a candle in wax-work or a frock in tailoring (home science).

The laboratory method starts and ends with activities. It starts with an introduction by the teacher establishing a relationship between theory and practice. The pupils are enthused to make and promptly put down their observations as they make them. The laboratory method could be used both for individual and group teaching. The latter, however, is the common practice.

A *first aid kit* is, however, a perpetual part of all laboratories for meeting emergencies.

21.4 Process of Laboratory Work

In performing experiments students are always advised to go strictly by the oral instructions given by the teachers and the directions contained in the manuals and instruction cards.

In the process of experimentation, the teacher goes round and supervises the work of individuals or groups and helps those that need it. If there is a common mistake being committed by them, he draws everybody's attention and makes necessary suggestions.

21.5 Post Experiment Discussion

After the process of experimentation is over, discussions are the concluding step. The common experiences and differences are discussed and the teacher finally helps them to get to accurate conclusions.

22

Programmed Instruction

22.1 The Purpose of Programmed Instruction

Programmed Instruction promises to increase the effectiveness of mass instruction. Through this approach individual instruction is possible to be provided to pupils in an effective manner than what is possible for any single teacher to do.

The uniqueness of programmed instruction lies in the fact of its not just being a device of teaching but more so as a scientific approach applicable to different levels and sectors of education.

Skinner and his colleagues at the Harvard University conducted research experiments to study the behaviours of pigeons. They managed to teach these docile little creatures to do certain tricks and also to play a form of Table Tennis.

The basic principles guiding the experiment of teaching pigeons were:

- If rewarded whenever a pigeon made a right move, it learns a new one more quickly.
- A complicated feat must be taught through small steps and just one at a time with each subsequent step being graded to become an easy one.

22.2 The Structure of Programmed Instruction

Skinner once visited his daughter's fifth grade Mathematics class and noticed that pupils' attention wandered away from the inefficient classroom instruction. He grew indignant at what he saw in the classroom and developed a fifth grade Mathematics course based on the principles used in teaching pigeons and other small animals.

In programmed instruction, the subject-matter is broken down into a sequence of small steps. The sequence and steps must be determined much more carefully and skillfully than what is possible for an ordinary learner to do. The steps must be small enough for the learner to move from an easier one to the next more difficult one easily, with a minimum of error. Mistakes are costly, as they have to be unlearned. Trial and error learning must be reduced to a minimum. The ideal programmes would result in no mistakes. Constant success reinforces past learning and motivates further effort.

Programmed instruction may take many forms depending upon the subject, and the objectives desired to be achieved. The most common form in academic subjects is to present certain carefully-worded data in a '*Frame*' or viewing space. Each Frame calls for a response.

In programmed teaching/learning, a school subject is broken into simple, easy graded progressive steps and presented as questions, which the pupil must answer. The pupil would be kept active with the process of continuously answering of questions. The reward would be that of knowing at once if he was right or wrong, and if the subject was programmed in its logical order, he would rarely be wrong. The pupil would need to work alone, concentrating on the questions as they emerge, writing his own answers. A mechanical device or a '*teaching machine*' is a device used for the purpose. It presents an exercise or a problem to a pupil, induces him to respond and reveals to him whether or not his response is correct. Many machines require that incorrect responses be corrected before the pupil can be allowed to continue. Most teaching machines use the tutorial or the *Socratic method*. They ask questions, wait for answers and then let the pupil know whether or not he is right. They induce the pupil to think and work for himself. This is how the 'Teaching machine movement' came into existence. Instruction by '*Teaching machines*' *is called programmed learning or self-instruction*. The material may be presented through any device—a machine or a book.

22.3 The Operations of Programmed Instruction

In general, programmed material consists of a series of small units called '*Frames*'. Each Frame is based on knowledge already possessed by the pupil and each Frame also adds a small increment to this knowledge. Each Frame contains one or more blanks to be filled in by the pupil in a sentence—completion fashion. The blank in a Frame calls for a response that the pupil is able to make either because he learned how to make it, in the settings of the previous Frames or because it is made possible by the Frame currently confronting him. The pupil reads each Frame and then fills in the blanks. The type of reading required by a Frame ensures active and continuous manipulation of the ideas, described in it. This type of concentrated and focussed reading reinforces learning in contrast to passive reading, without a need for active manipulation of the ideas that make up the subject-matter.

The genesis of programmed learning can be summarised thus:

- Small steps
- Thoughtful reading
- Active responding
- Immediate confirmation

- Reinforcement
- Self-paced learning

There are different styles or systems of programming. The *'linear'* programming, associated with the work of Skinner, is a single track programme because the pupil goes directly in a straight line through the material from beginning to end. The *'intrinsic'* programming associated with the work of *Crowder* is a branching programme. It is a method of programming material that directs the erring pupil along certain corrective pathways, before he is permitted to proceed to the next step in the programme. Introducing remedial or explanatory loops of review passage into a programme helps the learners who need them, while the swifter learners can skip the entire practice.

Research findings show that programmed instruction helps to accomplish consolidation of learning at every level, from pre-school to graduate or professional level. It is useful for slow learners as well as mature superior pupils. It can teach a variety of subject-matter, such as mathematics, statistics and language and variety of skilled, behaviours like, rote-learning, paired associated learning, application of formulae, formation of concepts and 'thoughtful' reading.

22.4 Conclusion

Developing a 'programme' is not easy. It requires not only mastery of and insight into the subject but also planning preparation and sound training. The nature of the programmed instructional material is such that *it cannot be easily transplanted from one country to another*.

One of the important factors in the use of programmed material is, that programmed material need not substitute the textbooks or the teacher as only certain parts of a text is programmed. The textbook could thus remain largely intact.

Teaching machines can never replace human teachers, however indispensable they may become. Factual learning which comprises the content of most programmes is only one means to some important cognitive processes, associated with intuitive, judgemental and problem-solving behaviour.

23

Think-Tank Sessions

23.1 Connotation

Think-tank sessions imply joint/collective loud thinking on a common issue or problem. The theme selected could be real or hypothetical.

23.2 Requirements

Normally placards, with questions, phrases and statements on the selected topic are prepared with the help of students. These are such as to force people to think.

23.3 Physical Arrangements

Students sit in groups (circles or semi-circles) to deliberate in-depth on the given theme. Each group has its own placards on the same theme.

23.4 Purpose

To reflect in-depth on a topic, analysing it, delving into the causes (if any), discussing implications, suggesting alternative solutions, pondering on the pros and cons of each solution in terms of immediate outcomes as also long range impact and identifying the most suitable one, pre-occupy the students as they engage themselves in dialogues to exchange views without any heated debate or argumentation.

23.5 The Process

Students are divided into groups of 10 or 15. The purpose is explained to them along with the working dynamics. The students are required to do reflective thinking. Each student may explain the meaning and connotation of the contents of his/her placard. Placards are also circulated among different groups for encouraging different view points on the same issue. New ideas are also thus initiated.

23.6 The Gains

It is possible to get different view points on the different facets of the same theme. With every student desirous of saying something new, it becomes a race in creativity of thought and speech. Students are also enabled to learn about how the same problem, can be viewed from different angles. It also helps impart to the students the most valuable conviction that theirs is not the only view, and also not essentially the only correct one. With no inhibitions, students are also able to come out with their thoughts which they may not normally express. This prompts them to experience the exercise their right for having their own respective opinions about different facts and phenomenon.

Think Tank Sessions basically are exercises in collective thinking on the issue in question. Though different members of the team may hold different members of the team may hold different view points, because of the different exposures and experiences they may have had; they entertain the common target of charting the most appropriate road map for reaching the same target. In fact, different view points enrich the thinking process. the suggestions are invariably constructive and forward looking.

The realization of likely pitfalls and a discussion about the gravity of each, in regard to their potential for dislocating the proposed plans, gives valuable pointers for avoiding them through care in advance planning.

The development of placards on the identified theme also becomes a good training ground for being **creative with catching brevity.** To concentrate the content of many sentences into small slogan like statements is by itself a valuable ability to inculcate which can stand people, in good stead, in life.

Further more, when one coins a catchy statement for a placard, he follows a particular line of thinking the interactions, that follow enable the individual to learn about other possible meanings and interpretations of what he has written as well. This process and the discussions enlighten everybody in the group and by so learning from others, one acquires a clarity about his own motions.

Further more, "Think Tank Sessions" also successfully offer to each member of the group, a sense of cohesion and unity as a team working towards the same goal. The outcome, in terms of conclusions thus does not remain any single individuals work but that of the entire group and the group as a whole, takes it to be its work with a sense of achievement and satisfaction.

This also creates a sense of interdependence among members who then have **no egoistic hesitation in consulting others.** Such attitudes are conducive for welfare of the institution, agency or organisation the individuals work for the, so emanating personal harmony naturally also results in professional harmony.

24

Seminars

24.1 The Meaning

A seminar is an in-depth discussion on a topic under the guidance of a teacher or a leader.

24.2 The Prerequisites

Being an indepth discussion, a seminar is normally preceded by a study of the theme in advance.

24.3 The Setting

A circular or a semi-circular seating arrangement for an in-house seminar is considered appropriate. For formal seminars, there may be a dais for experts to sit and seats for the audience in the front.

24.4 Operational Steps

The date for the seminar and the topic are announced in advance. Normally, the students jot down their misgivings (if any) about the different aspects of the theme earlier. Some of them may have already prepared a brief presentation about their explorations.

24.5 The Process

The teacher or the leader briefly introduces the topic and supervises the discussions, allowing time to everybody to have a chance to speak. The thematic organisation is also the leader's responsibility. S/he also makes inputs/corrections wherever needed, and ensures that the major aspects of the theme are covered.

Different ideas and points of view are then presented and discussed thread-bare, covering the minutest of details. For everybody, it is an opportunity for clarifying ones conceptual confusions.

24.6 The Gains

Even though the whole class may participate, the situation in seminars is informal, and students have no reservations about expressing their opinions. The cross-fertilisation of ideas is very educative as everybody is eager to share whatever new s/he may be knowing about the topic, or whatever opinions s/he may be holding about it.

The theme being a part of the curriculum, the learning so accruing is unique and more enriching than classroom teaching or individualised learning.

Seminars normally display an academic inclination. With the prior timely announcement of the theme everybody may have had an opportunity to study the theme. In the process, he may also have jotted down his own misgivings about which he needs classifications.

The study of different books and materials by the students may also have exposed them to different view points of the authors. The presentation of these view points naturally enriches the deliberations of the seminar.

While a consensus may or may not be possible, to be arrived it, a seminar does become a platform for participatory learning. The discussion at the seminar becomes such an enriching experience that no student normally wants to miss a seminar while he may not mind missing a lecture.

The thread bare analysis of the theme in question, through contribution pouring in form all sides, enables the participants to gain from the labour and explorations of their other peers, which they on them own may never be able to do.

It is always useful to ask students to write briefly about the points they may have made in the course of the seminar. A small group could them be constituted to arrange the ideas sequentially in a logical order in the form of a summary paper. The sources from which different ideas may have been called out will be valuable reference points for those who may like to know about the particular aspects of the theme.

Seminars offer a valuable opportunity for **library research** and help inculcate the ability of **learning how to learn and self directed learning**. The ample scope for showing off ones own exploits, is by itself a powerful motivation for the students to acquire indepth knowledge and to present it publically before the whole group/class/seminarians. These presentations of individuals, often leave good impressions on others about the deligent and intelligent homework done by the individual and enhances his prestige in the group. This becomes an incidental gain.

25

Panel Discussions

25.1 Connotation

A group of persons are selected to discuss an issue among themselves. The panelists could be both outside experts and/or faculty members.

25.2 The Setting

There is normally a dias where the coordinator and the panelists sit, and there is the audience. Panelists normally do not exceed five.

25.3 The Requirements

The chairman/coordinator directs the presentations. He also sets time limits for the panelists to speak, and provides the links between the presentations of different panelists. He initiates the discussions and also concludes it.

25.4 The Process

A topic is decided in advance. Panelists who are experts in the field are selected and invited to present their view points on the identified theme. After the chairman has introduced the panelists and the theme he asks each one of them to make brief presentations. Threads from the ideas expressed are then picked up, and discussions start among them. Sometimes even after the introduction of the theme, if it admits different view points or controversies, the discussion starts straight away with inputs coming from different panelists. Towards the close, sometimes, the audience is also permitted to ask questions which are responded to by the panelists.

25.5 The Gains

It is an opportunity to hear experts speak on a theme. The differences of opinion on the subject come to the fore, and as points are normally made with reasons they are very enriching.

'Panel' discussions are normally organised on themes where view-points may be varied. Panel discussion provides an opportunity to the members of the audience who could be students, to analyse the facts for themselves and draw their own conclusions.

Panel discussions are held on specialized themes and the panelists are experts in that field. Quite naturally, the experts would be having different experiences and backgrounds which will come to bear on the presentations they make.

Sometimes as a matter of planning the different panelists may be requested to focus on different facets of the theme of discussion. This helps avoid avoidable duplication. However, the main theme being the same some overlap is bound to be there. But, the panelists, on their own, by to avoid it on the basis of the presentations of earlier panelists.

The discussions among the panelists after the presentations are basically technical and the students as the audience have to pick up things relevant to their needs. Sometimes when the panelists enter into technicalities quite a few things go over the heads of the audience, the students. It is therefore desirable to brief the panelists in advance for remining within the range of understanding of the students for whom really the panel discussion has been arranged.

It is however always desirable to record the presentations and the deliberations. These presentations being by specialists are surely likely to be of interest and use to other working in the field. With the permission of the panelists, these could be widely circulated, after editing by the panelists themselves.

While selecting the panelists it is always desirable in the setting of an educational institutions not to include rivals who may contradict everything that the rival may see. This vitiates the ethos and destroys the purpose of the discussion by becoming a wordy battle ground.

After the presentations, discussion and the question answer session, time must be saved for brief concluding statements by the chairman.

26

Symposium

26.1 The Connotation

A symposium is a discussion on essays prepared and presented by some selected individuals (students or experts) on a particular theme/topic.

26.2 The Physical Arrangement

It could be a semi-circular or classroom arrangement.

26.3 The Requirements

Students or experts are selected, and after being assigned topic, are asked to prepare brief papers for presentation. As normally the total time available for a symposium is limited, they are asked to prepare brief presentations.

26.4 The Process

The students or experts who have prepared the essays on the theme make presentations one by one, as called upon. As the presentations are made, the others jot down the questions to ask. The rest of the period is devoted to questions and answers.

26.5 The Gains

The topic being the same, each speaker is anxious to prepare the best essay by consulting the largest possible number of sources. The exercise thus motivates students (in an institutional symposium) to undertake library research. As the time is limited, they also learn to be brief in their writings, so as to include everything that is relevant, in the smallest possible space. The essay has to be drafted as a speech and so has to have new facts, convincing arguments and reasoning. Stage shyness is also got over in this exercise of public speaking/reading. Those who write and read papers also incidentally get the needed training in responding to questions orally. So, besides written expression, oral expression too finds an opportunity for being demonstrated, of which promptness to marshall arguments is an important part.

It is desirable to ask students to write essays by turns. The teacher could initially come to the help of those who may not be proficient in writing and speaking, and enable them to subsequently do things on their own.

A symposium is basically an all student affair. The selection of a theme well in advance is necessary for the students to prepare their own essays for presentation. In symposia the themes selected are mostly those of common interest reflecting common concerns/problems.

Quite naturally each student selected to write an essay and to present his own point of view and the approach for solving the common problem. **Practicability of the suggested solutions** will, of course, be the central focus. No theoretical impracticable approaches will therefore be appreciated. As each one would have a slake in the solutions suggested he will analyse it in the context of his own interests. This will make it necessary for the suggestions to satisfy the majority of not all.

As this will involve presentations on the basis of written essays those writing them will need to ensure all the requirements of written expression. To add to this, the ability to present a reasoned point of view will also be called for. The pros and cons of different possible approaches will also need to be examined and the final solution suggested, will also have to be supported by arguments. This will be no easy job.

It will be desirable not to select the same students for writing essays and presenting them every time. Students should take turns in executing this valuable learning exercise which has many things to teach students.

After the presentations have been made there should also be an open house for the audience to raise questions. Those who may have made presentations could of down the points related to his presentation and then each of the four or five should respond. The concluding note however should be given by one of the teachers. This teacher should try to balance different view points and focus on points of agreement rather than points of disagreement.

27

Library Research

27.1 The Concept

Library Research implies systematic exploration and investigation for discovering/establishing facts on identified themes.

27.2 The Requirements

Access to a library with books on the selected topic. Time-table for

- Consultation
- Presentation
- Discussion
- Summarisation

27.3 The Process

The theme is identified and given to the class. The class has then to be divided into groups not by choice but by selection. Each group is allotted a sub-theme to work on. Time-table for collection of material, group presentation, class discussion and summarisation is intimated. The groups then go about their business. Each student takes his notes about significant points from the books/documents studied.

The students then come back to their respective groups, where the collected material is analysed, synthesised and evaluated for the preparation of the group reports. The points of the group report are jotted down and the member of the group with a facile pen prepares the draft of the group. The report is then read to the group and approved by it. This is then presented by the writer/group leader.

The Group Reports on different sub-topics are then presented and discussed. The suggestions made, and the ideas that emerge in the course of the discussions are incorporated in the group reports and a final report on the whole topic weaving in the different group reports is prepared and formally written.

This report and any other material which may have been prepared by the groups is then put up in an exhibition.

27.4 The Gains

Library research is a valuable experience in participatory learning which saves time, and at the same time is enriching. It is good training for the concept of *Frontline Curriculum* where say 90% syllabus remains relevant for four or five years and 10% changes every year or two. As no books are available for this 10%, teachers too become co-learners with students in the process of exploration. Students, while browsing through books, are able to realise the richness of the topic. They also learn to analyse ideas, synthesise them and evaluate them. This also often motivates them to learn more about the theme.

Library Research is always an enriching exercise. In fact the old time practice of allocating library periods in the timetable served a great motivating force for children to explore the world of books. He may not necessarily read every book in the library but "browse" through it. This will imply looking through the table of contents and turning the pages just like that for identifying an interesting chapter an attractive picture or an educative diagram. It is quite likely that the students, would be able to find some chapters of books or books themselves to study further.

This in fact will be the beginning of self learning which is an important attribute for success in life.

Library Research is surely not an aimless exercise of browsing through the books but a focussed one before the theme is taken up in class and necessarily after the theme has been completed. Collection of additional knowledge about the same theme will surely be an enriching exercise as it would help the student gain further insight into the topic which will make the content more meaningful to him.

Consultation of other textbooks for the same class and the same subject not prescribed by the school could be a very valuable exercise. Students for example could select the exercise in mathematics textbooks for purposes of drill for the mastery of the theme.

Consultation of children's encyclopaedias would surely be a useful exercise in widening the knowledge horizons of students.

The magazines subscribed by the school library could lead the student, to some interesting reading material which may motivate the students for further wheeling his interest in self reading.

28

Photo-Language Session

28.1 The Meaning

Photo-language sessions involve giving expression to thoughts, ideas, feelings, emotions evoked by photographs or pictures.

28.2 The Prerequisites

The collection of photographs, pictures related to the selected topic in the first step. As everybody looks at the pictures attentively, and tries to mentally analyse what they depict and reflect on them in terms of the ethos of their contents. The atmosphere naturally is reflective, because what is attempted to be caught are thoughts and feelings that the pictures or photographs exhale.

The time for viewing these pictures or photographs is also rationed, say two or three minutes.

So that all the students are able to view them closely. The class is then divided into groups of say ten students each who are normally seated in a semi-circle for watching the set of pictures presented to each group.

28.3 The Process

As mentioned, sets of pictures/photographs related to the central theme are given to each group. The leader of the group shows the pictures/photographs given to the group one by one to the whole group. Students are given time to observe them in silence and jot down in telegraphic language the things they observe. The leader then asks the students to give their reactions to the details observed in the pictures without any inhibitions or reservations. The students then individually write their observations. These observations are then compiled picture wise. The pictures and photographs are then circulated to the other groups where the same operation is repeated. All the groups then come together. Each picture or photograph is then presented one by one and each group presents its report on that one by one. The variation in the perception of different groups about the same picture or photograph are by themselves enriching experiences. If time permits a discussion on each could also follow.

28.4 The Gains

The exercise promotes the habit of close observation and the ability to mentally translate the depictions/details into feelings, and these into words. The exercise empowers students to reach out their thoughts to the affective domain and thereby to sensitise the students to certain needs and situations. This also helps students to channelise emotions and to communicate them.

Photo-language Sessions sound like something new but even in the good old days there used to be a question on **Picture composition.**

The broad purpose in the two exercises is the same i.e. the translation of one form of presentation into another. Even in mathematics this type of translation exercises among tables, diagrams and graphs is quite common.

The Photo-language Session focus on language for interpreting the contents of pictures. The projective techniques in Psychological Testing like the Thematic Apperception Test use the interpretation of pictures for judging attributes of personality.

Coming back to Photo-language Sessions, it could be said that this involves the varied interpretations of the contents of the pictures by different individuals. The exercises what the power of intricate observation of pictures for giving them a meaning. The different observations on the same picture enable students to learn about the points they missed to observe and interpret. This thus becomes a learning exercise by itself.

With all the pictures, allied to the common themes the scope for differences in interpretation does no doubt get narrowed down but still some elements of if do remain.

The ability to write what one sees is the main ability attempted to be developed.

The exercises become difficult because of the depiction of emotions and likely related activities. This requires not just close observation of dialects but also of the expressions and gestures depicted by the pictures.

To be able to do that, one must have a good backup acquaintance with vocabulary and usage for which extra reading becomes a stand by asset.

29

Surveys

29.1 The Connotation

Surveys connote detailed study by collecting information and analysing it to discover some new facts, or to reinforce the existing knowledge, or to confirm and verify some stated idea or principle.

29.2 The Requirements

Selecting a topic and allotting its facets to different groups.

29.3 The Physical Arrangement

Informal and flexible.

29.4 The Process

Dividing the class into groups and the teacher holding separate meetings with different groups to explain to them the objectives, areas of exploration, places to be visited, information to be collected and people to be interviewed, the diagrams to be drawn etc.

The groups may be given specific time budgets for doing the job.

The students may maintain notes of the things they observe, the things they learn and the conclusions they draw. Groups then make their presentations to the whole class (all the groups) and prepare a written report for exhibition along with tables, charts etc. prepared in the course of their work.

29.5 The Gains

The students do not receive information collected by someone else but collect it on their own, which by itself is very aggrandising. They learn how to collect, tabulate, and interpret the information they may collect for drawing their own conclusions. This makes the inferences more meaningful to them. They experience the thrill of discovery and also come to realise that team work can do many things which individuals by themselves cannot singly do. They also gain faith in their conclusions and take the established principles to be really true and valid, having been experimentally verified by them.

Surveys as such are a valuable teaching device. They enable children to acquire first hand knowledge form primary sources, to compile and organise it and to draw their own conclusions form it. The so derived inferences become the self-earned part of an individual's knowledge and being so, turns out to be his abiding permanent treasure. The Engel's law of consumption in economics for example if it is memorised it can slip out of the memory after some time, but if it is derived though a survey of different levels of people (say an executive, an office assistant, a labourer) about the proportion of their income they spend on food, clothes, shelter, and entertainment, it will be never forgotten by the individual student.

Further more surveys bring students closer to realities of life enabling them to gather personal experiences about the life in their environment. This too is a permanent gain making the individual realistic in this statements or decisions.

The tool through which data for surveys is collected and the hurdles that come in the way yield insights which other situations cannot impart.

Further more the student also learns about the importance of little bits of information when he reaches a solution where for want of a small piece of information he feels disabled in reaching conclusions.

Surveys in fact become enjoyable when the student has an eye on the end result and hopes to collect information for substantiating an existing tenet or for disproving it. In this process, exceptions always attract his attention and these prove the rule.

Surveys should not be undertaken as a formality but should be purposeful and the purpose when firstly understand by the students what their motivation by igniting their interest in them.

30

Participatory/Group/Team Learning

30.1 Introduction

Participatory learning is an innovation mothered by necessity. Eventhough an outcome of compulsions to practice, it has started paying valuable dividends by way of:

- speeding up the process of collection of educational information as compared to individualised endeavours.
- consolidation and internalisation of self-acquired learning as compared to teacher dispensed information.
- reduction of teacher's workload and more particularly, his speaking load.

These gains are not just encouraging but enticing and tempting to be pursued.

30.2 The Genesis of Participatory Learning

In 'Participatory Learning' it is not just each student who pursues his course of action for acquiring the gains of learning. It is the group or team that pursues learning as a joint venture by sharing responsibility, replicating the concept of 'division of labour'.

30.3 Prerequisites of the Approach of Participatory Learning

A well equipped School Library/Laboratory

30.4 The Process of Participatory Learning

The process of participatory learning consists of the following flexible and adaptable steps:

- Announcement of the theme/topic to the class by the teacher.
- Taking the class to the library to browse through the books on the subject and identify those that deal with the given topic.
- Dividing the class into viable groups.
- Distributing the books to the groups.
- Loud reading of the concerned theme from the books by students in

their respective groups by taking turns. This could be done in the course of any decided span of time and at any place they decide, with each member of the group taking his/her own notes.

- Return of the groups to the class in the next scheduled period when the teacher may, in consultation with the students, draw-up on the black-board, an outline of the sub-themes of the main theme and throws them up for a discussion.
- Taking up each such theme for discussion one by one, with students contributing whatever the books they consulted, contained. Different points of view or approaches could thus emerge.
- Simultaneous development of black-board summary by the teacher.
- Concluding observation by the team/group leaders and the teacher.

Participatory Learning has infact become the need of the hour particularly because knowledge is growing every fast and becoming redundant faster. An individual cannot all by himself explore the many sources that contain knowledge. Therefore a division of labour is a valuable innovative approach. If a number of students set out to collect information about a particular theme in a planned manner, almost everybody will be discovering something not know earlier. The compilation of this knowledge and its presentation to the group will be enriching to one and all of them. Every member of the group will also thus derive a unique satisfaction for contributing to the common pool of knowledge. This will become a meaningful exercise to everybody because of the eagerness that will automatically get generated in each one. There will thus be a beggaring of both **competition for advancement and cooperation for strength.**

Particularly or team learning will not thus be restricted to only library research but could take the form of **surveys, projects, exploration, experimentation etc.** It will offer examples of situations where students will learn without being taught even though the teacher will remain as a planner and a guide in these activities. Even the teachers would stand to learn from these initiatives of the students and he would always be looking forward to what new the students may discover through their strides.

It needs to be specifically pointed out here that when there is a teacher student interaction in the course of a teaching learning session, the concentration of the students is minimal. When this becomes a student-student interaction the level of this concentration improves and when it is the interaction of the student with himself (as in self learning and self-directed learning episodes) the concentration is at its highest level.

30.5 Conclusion

Thus the claims stand more than realised with children learning much more than what they could ever have dreamt of, while pursuing learning individually. All the students can take pride in contributing to the theme in his own way. The process leads to abiding learning, and the students do not usually forget what they learn. The teacher too saves time and labour.

The approach is simple, easy, effective and economical. It is also an encouraging proposition aligned to the standard of the class. Institutions would however need to have a good library. The method could be usefully used from class VII/VIII onwards.

31

Action Research

31.1 The Concept

Action research is in fact a problem solving strategy in the teaching process. Whenever and wherever a hard spot is identified, that situation becomes the starting point of Action Research. The problem that arises has first to be analysed for getting to its source. Steps for overcoming it are then designed. The action is instant and so it disallows any snow balling of the confusion or lack of clarity that may have emerged. Action research is not any theoretical construct but a practical approach specifically designed for the specific situation. The approach therefore is a hand maid of the teacher who exercises full freedom and flexibility in designing and implementing a situation specific strategy for making teaching amenable to learning.

31.2 Designing of Steps

The teacher being the master of the situation designs the exercise as per his own thinking in the hope of solving the problem through it. In the process he often breaks down a complex situation into smaller sub-situations and helps pupils move on step by step, wherein the success they realise at each step gives them the confidence for realising success in the subsequent steps. This also leads to a better consolidation of learning in the pupils. This approach for realising the goal is termed as Action Research Hypotheses.

Both the strategy and the targeted goals can change midway at the discretion of the teacher on the basis of the need for change experienced by him. Action Research thus admits immense flexibility and adaptability.

Success in a particular situation in action research does not go to enunciate a principle or a theory or a generalisation, particularly because it is based on situation specific ingenuity of the teacher. This characteristic differentiates it from basic or fundamental research as in Action Research the teacher and in some measure the students become the sole judges of the effectiveness of the approach in realising the anticipated success.

31.3 Operation of Action Research

Action research, is an informal methodology and satisfaction of the teacher and the students is the measure of success which does not offer any quantitative enunciation.

The outcomes of Action Research are also not normally presented formally as the findings result in self-assuring experiences, which may encourage other teachers to devise their own approaches for solving the problems they may face from time to time.

Unlike fundamental research where the findings are normally used subsequently by others in action research there is no time gap and the teacher is both the designer of the approach and its follower. Thus he is both the producer and the consumer of the research. He also thus translates his knowledge of theories into practice.

Action Research admits a very wide operational scope. It can be used in any teaching, learning or testing situation and at any step or juncture. It can also serve as a useful tool of management of different operations for making them effective.

Action Research bears a striking similarity with micro teaching. In fact the diagnoses of shortfalls is the starting point of both. In the former the purpose is transmission of ideas to others (pupils) in the latter it is for self-improvement. Improvement however is the common goal.

Though an invariably successful strategy it often turns out to be time consuming but the time spent becomes an investment because internalisation of learning, leads to faster learning of subsequent steps. The time saved thus compensates for the extra time spent.

Though the conceptual terminology of Action Research introduced by *Stephen Corey* sounds new there is nothing new about it as teachers have all along been using it for transmitting knowledge to the pupils. It is in fact common sense which is not uncommon in its utilisation. Corey, however, gave a formal shape to this informal approach.

PART IV

SOME ANCILLARY TEACHING-LEARNING FACETS/SITUATIONS

32

Assignments and Work at Home

32.1 Assignments as Consolidation of Learning Exercises

Assignments constitute that part of the instructional activity which are aimed at consolidating previous learning and for laying the foundation for future learning in an effective manner. Assignment helps in the planning and organisation of ideas when both the teacher and the pupils prepare for the next step. It is a co-operative experience in which the teacher is a sympathetic director or guide and pupils willing participants.

The assignment method is also based upon the principles of learning by doing. It provides opportunities to pupils to work independently in the class or laboratory and in the course of study by themselves. Pupils are thereby helped to develop the habit of extra study. They learn how to consult references and collect data and information.

The assignment method is an economical one because pupils in a class could be given different assignments, depending upon their interests and abilities. Each pupil can work at his own speed. The weak pupils do not stand in the way of bright pupils. Students can refer their difficult *experiences* to the teacher who is in a position to give individual attention.

32.2 Characteristics of Assignments

The success of the assignment method depends upon how well the assignment is drawn, and how well-equipped the library and laboratory are for assignments to be allotted to individual pupils. Some problems encountered in using the assignment method in the schools, are a heavy curriculum which cannot be finished within the limited time available. Dearth of books and references, non-availability of literature on all topics and the tendency for some pupils to copy from others are some of the main problems faced.

Assignments should be challenging to enthuse pupils and enable them to explore and experiment. The problem of copying by the weak pupils can be eliminated and solved by asking oral questions and at times requiring them to write short answers in the class to know whether or not a particular concept or principle has been understood.

Assignments as a technique of teaching, are yet to be recognised in education. The significance of the assignment method is based on the premise that the desire for self-learning is more important than that of learning through teaching. It is pupils' attitude towards learning that matters, and not the courses of instruction, however well organised they may be. In the words of DOUGLASS and HUBERT, "The assignment represents one of the most important phases of teaching". If good assignments are prescribed, pupils can and will study independently with success; but with poor or routine assignments they will fail to profit.

Assignments rouse children's interest, stimulate their thinking, elicit their co-operation, encourage initiative, clear-up misunderstandings, develop insight and boost morale. They help pupils to outline the work to be undertaken in the future with new and wider avenues and to discover facts and phenomenon. Assignments thus supplement class-room teaching. They provide the teacher an opportunity to augment learning through extra study. Assignments are of two types:

1. Home assignments
2. School assignments

Home assignments include writing of answers to questions or undertaking of tasks assigned by the teacher. School assignments could take the form of performing experiments in the laboratory and answering questions put forth by the teacher in the class. According to Yoakam, assignments may be of the old type or the new type. Those assignments which have been long in use, such as prescribing the number of pages, paragraphs, topics, themes, exercises, questions and experiments are of the old type. In contrast the new type of assignments include the project activity and problem solving. The new type ones are the outcome of the shift of focus from teacher-directed study to self-directed learning.

A good assignment must be related to the topics learned at school. It should be brief, clear in purpose and flexible. It should aim at realising the goals, prescribed in such a way that it stimulates reflective thinking and gives freedom to pupils to discover facts for themselves, appealing to the curiosity of the pupils, as also thought-provoking and challenging and aligned to the age, intelligence and abilities of pupils.

32.3 Steps in Giving Assignments

The *first step* is to analyse the prescribed course and allot suitable assignments within the time at disposal. With the calendar and course requirements, the teacher should find out the total number of assignments which could be undertaken by the students within the working days in a year by a particular class. The *next* step is to list the assignments and lay down the objectives for each assignment, with the co-operation of the pupils and guide them through the following stages :

1. *Reference to previous experience*—If for example, the previous lesson was 'planning the house', references should be given from the previous lesson, to motivate and prepare the pupils for doing worthwhile assignments. The assignment could relate to a study of different designs observed by them at home or in the school. While giving such references for the assignments, the teacher should see that the books suggested are within the comprehension ability of the pupils.
2. *Discussion*—The teacher can organise a discussion on any suitable topic. Various proposals for the execution of the assignments could be then suggested by pupils. The teacher should guide the discussion indicating the time allotted for completing various parts of an assignment.
3. *Explanations and clearing difficulties*—Any doubts and difficulties regarding the assignment will be cleared by the teacher.
4. *Distribution of tasks*—Suggested activities like collection of pictures, making models, writing essays will be distributed to the pupils either individually or in groups. When assignments are part of class work, the teacher will offer on-the-spot guidance.
5. *Starting the activity*—Pupils take up the assignment as a new project.
6. *Evaluation*—Assignments should then be evaluated jointly by the teacher and pupils for positive results and for offering further motivation through diagnosis and remediation.

32.4 Work at Home

Home work is independent work which the pupils do at home, to supplement the instruction received at school, away from the atmosphere of the class room, in the midst of home surroundings. As a practical teaching device, home work is a step towards self-education. It enables the pupil to use his own resources and work without external help and supervision.

Home work facilitates formation of habits, of independent effort, self-study and work habits. It accelerates the advance of pupils in their studies and gives opportunity to teachers for securing more effective co-operation from parents in the education of their children.

In order that home work may be effective, it should be graded. The nature and amount of home work must be determined by the pupils' capacity and allowing time for play. Home work should never be considered as a punishment. All the subjects in the curriculum must get due share of home work.

33

Organisation of Exhibitions

33.1 Introduction

Exhibitions too are important aids to teaching. Exhibitions involve the display of a variety of two or three-dimensional objects for communicating different ideas and pieces of information to the observer. An exhibition therefore has immense educational value.

As they are the pupils who participate in preparing the exhibits, setting them up and explaining them, they not only learn new concepts but also consolidate their learning. Interesting exhibits also motivate pupils to explore further and obtain new information.

33.2 Basic Principles of Organising Exhibitions

- Have an overall theme. The exhibits should have an educational value, should always have a message to convey which may be possible to be immediately perceived without the need to read it. The message should be brief, crisp, clear and have an appeal. It should effectively convey the central idea and project the unity of the display.
- Locate the exhibit centrally at an easily accessible place.
- The settings of the display should not be crowded using bright colours and strong broad lines.
- Use movement if possible.
- Follow artistic principles—proportion, balance, colour, shape, rhythm.
- Some exhibits have to be just seen, others understood. What has to be read should be placed at the appropriate eye distance.
- Label the exhibits properly. Labels should be possible to be read from a distance. Labels should be of uniform pattern and style.
- Display only latest up-to-date material, old, soiled and dust settled items should not be displayed.
- Give optimum dramatic effect—setting lighting etc.
- Have the exhibits of all children displayed. Parents will be interested

in seeing the exhibits prepared by their children. Judicious use of colour and illumination help capture the attention of the viewers.

- Use the principles of advertising even in an educational exhibition as the objective of all advertisements is to sell ideas.
- Survey the place allocated and the material and accessories available. A map of the place be prepared and location of objects decided.
- Train students to explain exhibits. They should be level-headed, respectful and intelligent for giving pinpointed appealing answers to questions asked.
- Use a variety of display techniques for reaching ideas to many people to save time of the viewers, for appropriately targeting the viewers and to make them think.

33.3 Characteristics of Exhibits

- Exhibits should involve as many senses for appreciation as possible—visual, audio, tactile
- Colour imparts attraction to the exhibits and should be judicioι sly used particularly because colours also convey different attributes.

  Yellow – prosperity
  Red – danger
  Brown – monotony
  Green – production
  Grey – submission
  Orange – cheer
  Black – sorrow

- Motion in exhibits is great attraction but all cannot have that. Soft background instrumental music adds interest to an exhibition.
- Provide for at least some opportunity to the viewers to touch, turn, press operate, open as that can sustain their interest in the exhibition.
- None can compel a person to look at an exhibit except the exhibit itself.

As mentioned earlier, harmony, balance, artistically designed setting are crucial for making an appeal.

Exhibitions need not always be an elaborate affair. There could even be exhibitions put up by different classes to share with the students of other classes. For example, the conclusion of a project the class concerned may present the process and outcomes of the same.

Such events could also bigger a healthy competition among classes for sharing with others what they may have accomplished and which they may consider is worth sharing.

The classes or groups of students of representations of different houses could even produce a magazine periodically spurring creativity and innovation among students.

34

Educational Field Trips and Excursions

34.1 Introduction

Field Trips and Excursions enable on-the-spot study of different things/facets of the environment by putting the school on the wheels. Children are enabled to come face to face with realities. Field Trips and Excursions, offer such experiences which though necessary for learning cannot be brought into the classroom. They give meaning to classroom learning through personal observations and experience.

34.2 Purposes of Organising Field Trips

Field-trips and Excursions serve a variety of educationally fruitful purposes. They enable the pupils:

- a changeover from routine activities.
- to gain first hand experience about facts and phenomenon they study and investigate.
- to critically observe and scrutinise things for arriving at personally made conclusions which are never forgotten by them.
- to obtain clarifications about different concepts and processes.
- to launch on self-directed educational activities.
- to broaden and change attitudes in desirable directions.
- to discover areas of interest other than the existing ones.

Educational trips assume three main forms:

- *Field trips* are taken to places of the neighbourhood like a post office, a fire station, a construction site.
- *Excursions* to places where people live or work. They are outside the school but not very far from it. They may take a day or half a day. They may include visits to a bakery, a poultry farm, water purification plant, a nearby factory or a manufacturing unit like a sugar factory, a power generation plant, a museum, a zoo, a monument and so on.
- *Study Tours* are normally of longer durations and cover wider or distant areas. They may also involve long journeys.

34.3 Organisational Steps

There are some common essential steps for organising educational trips excursions/tours:

- *Identification of a trip*. This is done for different classes as per their curricular needs. The purpose of the trip is also simultaneously defined and impressed upon the pupils before commencement.
- *Planning* : Advance planning is a pre-requisite for a successful trip. This involves:
  - ➢ detailing of objectives of the trip in the context of its relationship with the curriculum.
  - ➢ listing of places to be visited and of details to be observed.
  - ➢ drawing-up an itinerary with dates and timings.
  - ➢ contacting the authorities for obtaining permission to visit the proposed sites.
  - ➢ obtaining the permission of the head of the school and the parents.
  - ➢ collecting necessary finances.
  - ➢ making arrangements for travel transport and accommodation.
  - ➢ delegation of responsibilities to the students during the trip.
  - ➢ collecting information about places to be visited.
  - ➢ collecting necessary material/equipment etc.
  - ➢ preparing a 'medical help kit'.
  - ➢ offering do's and don's to the students.
  - ➢ holding a stock-taking meeting every evening.
  - ➢ including sight seeing to make the trip interesting.
  - ➢ advising students to carry essential items.
  - ➢ asking students to carry note books for on the spot observations and cameras available.

34.4 Post-Trips Exercises

After the trip, on return to school some other often overlooked items of action are:

- writing thank you letters to all those who were helpful.
- reporting to other classes about the trip.
- writing poems, stories for the bulletin boards about the trip.
- convening PTA meeting, for acquainting them about the highlights of the trip.

Field Trips and excursions could be used for several other useful purposes. Surveys of different kinds for collecting first hand information is one such potential use. In fact, when an individual himself collects informations and draws his own conclusions, this learning becomes abiding. The survey or also acquires valuable insights about different things in the process of collecting, compiling analysing and interpreting information. No text book or any other enrichment material can offer, this kind of enlightenment. The student thus constructs his own set of tenets which yield him a sense of achievement.

35

Educational Aids—Support Material

35.1 The Genesis of Teaching Material and Aids

The singular target of the teacher is to communicate ideas to the pupils in a manner that they assimilate them. Towards this end, he makes a mental picture of the ideas and transforms this mental picture into words. This communication often suffers from shortfalls, at both the ends. Sometimes this linguistic transmission of their mental picture is not as effective as it should be. While the teacher may feel that he has been successful, he may really not have been so. The result is that the pupils are not able to comprehend the communicated ideas properly and may miss the points made.

The situation can be resolved if the teacher does not solely depend on oral communication and supplements it with other media of communication. These other media are commonly referred to as Audio-Visual Aids.

35.2 Utilisation of all Senses for` Learning

Senses constitute the main link between man and the environment—the surroundings physical, mental (intellectual) and moral. Vibrations of assimilation get stimulated through experiences and perceptions arising from the senses.

Senses transmit information about the environment to the individuals. These channels could be through touch, taste, smell, hearing and sight and all of them influence the mind.

The aids that impress upon the mind through the sense of hearing are referred to as 'audio-aids', while those which impress through sense of sight as 'Visual Aids'. The aids which impress upon the mind through both sight and hearing are known as Audio-Visual Aids. These aids transmit their respective images either directly or indirectly, pictorially/graphically or symbolically. All these support materials called teaching aids, help students not just in learning but more so in assimilating what they learn easily and abidingly as well.

35.3 Purposes of Instructional Aids

Audio visual aids serve a variety of purposes. They:

- reinforce and consolidate teaching and learning.
- accelerate the teaching-learning process.
- help pupils assimilate learning easily and effectively.
- evoke and maintain pupil interest.
- reduce the teachers' work load particularly their speaking load.
- help transforming abstract concepts into concrete realities.
- promote the interplay of different senses in the acquisition of learning
- impart joy to learning.

Educational aids and support materials assume a variety of forms.

Audio Aids like:

- Radio
- Television
- Recordings

Visual Aids:

- Graphic Aids
- Pictorial material
- Diagrams
- Maps
- Charts
- Sketches
- Display Boards
- Flannelograph
- Bulletin Boards
- Three-dimensional models
- Working models
- Internet
- CD ROMs/Discs
- Projective Aids—Films, Film-strips, Video films
- Video
- Internet

The main purpose of the Teaching Aids is to supplement information for facilitating comprehension of ideas, concepts' facts, etc. They save space and the labour of long explanations.

35.4 Situations for the Use of Teaching Aids

Use of these aids at appropriate junctures is as important as their quality. Their relevance to the content is equally important and they should always be accompanied by appropriate explanations, so that they are able to communicate effectively.

Normally, when we talk of teaching aids, we think about the material which may already be available for reinforcing the process of teaching. There is the other type of material also which is instantly produced by the teacher, by way of an example or a diagram for satisfying an instant emergent need in the course of teaching. Such aids to introduction are produced by the teachers when their students encounter some hard spots in learning. The teacher, in such instances thinks of an example which may resolve the difficulty of the students. He may even draw a diagram on the blackboard to explain the concept for bringing it home to the students.

These illustrations through instantly produced often prove to be more powerfull than the ones developed in advance in response to anticipated needs of the teacher in the course of a particular lesson.

While teachers continuously develop such material, no record is normally kept of them. It will be very useful of the teachers make it a point to document them. They can constitute an important part of remedial programmes.

36

Edgar Dale's Cone of Experience

Dr. Edgar Dale has classified and arranged audio-visual aids in a pictorial form, called the 'Cone of Experience'.

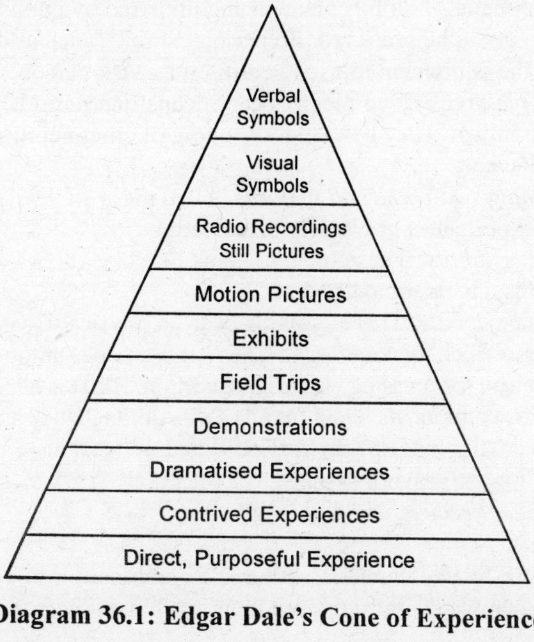

Diagram 36.1: Edgar Dale's Cone of Experience

The cone is a visual aid which helps to explain the inter-relationships of various types of audio-visual materials and illustrates their 'positions' in the learning continuum. *At the bottom of the cone, Dr. Dale has placed the most concrete and direct experiences and at the top the most abstract ones. Heading from the bottom these experiences are*:

1. *Direct, purposeful experiences:* These are realities as we experience them first hand—going to the bazaar, preparing a meal, repairing a piece of furniture, giving a party at school for mothers etc.

2. *Contrived experiences:* A contrived experience differs from the original in size, or in complexity, or in both. We use a working model in order to make pupils understand easily the real/original of the model, e.g. a model of a loom to show how cloth is made, models of childrens' toys, models of the human body, etc.

3. *Dramatised experiences:* Dramatic experiences help to get closer to realities that are not easily accessable or available at first hand. For example, acting the role of a Head Master/Principal.

4. *Demonstrations:* A demonstration is a visualised explanation of an important fact, or idea, or process.

5. *Field trips:* Excursions or field trips are taken to see life situations and how other people do things. Pupils might be taken to a house that is being built to see the construction.

6. *Exhibits:* There are two general types of exhibits, the 'ready-made' and the 'home-made'. Exhibits planned and prepared by pupils with the help of the teacher, are to be preferred. Preparing exhibits, such as different types of models or the equipment to use in caring for a sick person.

7. *Video pictures*: Video pictures can reconstruct periods with dramatic intensity and realism. They help understanding of other peoples' lands, ideas materials and events.

8. *Recording-radio and still pictures:* All of these are less, direct than the audio visual experiences previously discussed.

9. *Visual symbols:* These include items like blackboard and chalk, flat maps, diagrams, charts, models etc.

10. *Verbal symbols:* These symbols bear no physical resemblance to the objects or ideas which they represent. The term iron does not look like an iron or feel like an iron for pressing clothes like an iron. But it is a term we use that has more or less common meaning for all of us. Although they are abstractions, we use these verbal symbols with every other audio-visual material on the cone.

An old Chinese proverb says:

If I see, I remember
If I do, I know.

The most effective communication is a combination of seeing, hearing and doing. When visual aids are used along with demonstration they make a deep impact.

37

Using Questions for Teaching

37.1 Introduction

Teaching and testing are two basic components of every instructional programme. They are dovetailed to the instructional objectives which provide directions for both. *Teaching is the criterion behaviour against which testing is validated.* Testing on the other hand also validates the whole teaching-learning process by providing relevant evidences about the degree of its effectiveness in realising the objectives. Thus teaching and testing not only motivate students' learning, but can also be used as a means to effective instruction, through a regular feed-back mechanism.

Questions are mainly used for testing the achievement of pupils. At the same time it is not unusual to find students solving the question papers of previous years before the examination. As the questions in traditional public examinations used to generally test rote learning, students memorised answers to expected questions in order to pass the examinations. In this chapter an attempt is made to highlight the *role of questions in classroom instruction.* Examples from some selected subjects of the curriculum have been taken to indicate the objective, specification, topic, problem, previous knowledge assumed, teachers' activities, pupils' activities and additional tasks. The teachers should ensure that he prepares his students adequately for this type of questions by suitably adapting his teaching. The test items presented in regard to different subjects will give them an indication of how he may shift emphasis in teaching-learning procedures from rote memorisation to real internalisation as displayed through comprehension and expression.

Every teacher should keep in view specific instructional objectives while teaching and testing, which should go hand in hand. Test items are normally used for determining the attainment levels of students. While using any such item in the classroom, the teacher himself should be very clear about the objective on which it is based, and also about the kind of expected learning outcomes. This will make him look back to the knowledge already imparted and also to fill in the gaps in learning. In the light of these gaps he can reinforce his teaching for improved learning on the part of students.

Use of question is one of the means the teacher can profitably use in classroom situations. However, it must be borne in mind that testing is no substitute for teaching.

37.2 Some Examples

Some examples in different subjects on this unfamiliar theme were developed by the then Examination Reform Unit of the NCERT in 1977. A few of these have been summarised and are being presented here.

37.2.1 *English*

Topic

The Happy Prince: (Author: Oscar Wilde)

Question

If God had asked His Angel to bring only one most precious thing from the city instead of two, what would he have brought? Give reasons. Your answer should be limited to about 100 words.

Objective

- The student reads the story entitled 'The Happy Prince' with comprehension.
- The student writes answers to questions based on the text correctly and effectively.

Specific Learning Outcomes

In respect of the above story:

- ◆ *Comprehension*

  The Pupil:

  - locates important events, facts and ideas.
  - reads between the lines.
  - identifies relationship between objects and events.
  - critically examines and evaluates events, actions, ideas, and feelings in the light of their outcomes.

- ◆ *Expression*

  The Pupil:

  - uses appropriate vocabulary and structures.
  - culls and presents only relevant ideas and facts in logical order.
  - avoids unnecessary repetition.
  - organises ideas, facts, etc. appropriately into paragraphs and other forms of presentation.
  - displays imagination in writing.

Previous Knowledge

For being able to answer the above question, it is assumed that the students are:

- thoroughly acquainted with the story 'The Happy Prince'.
- acquainted with various events that occur in the story.
- able to appreciate the values of love, sacrifice, and service.
- able to organise their ideas and thoughts in a logical order.

Teaching-Learning Activities

- The students will be asked to read the story 'The Happy Prince' silently in the class.
- They will then be asked the above questions.
- They will be guided to identify significant events in the story.
- The likely reasons for bringing the two possible objects by the angel will be discussed in the class.
- The students will debate on the significance of the two possible alternative decisions on the part of the Angels.
- The students will critically examine and evaluate both the possibilities and reach their own conclusions.
- The teacher will guide them in substantiating their respective points with examples from the story.
- The teacher will help the students in expressing their ideas effectively.
- The teacher will help them to organise and arrange details in a logical sequence and coherent presentation so that the answer becomes effective.
- The students will then write the answers to the above question.

Follow-up Activities

The teacher may plan to undertake one or more of the following activities:

- The teacher, while correcting the answers, should note their mistakes and discuss them in the class.
- He may ask the students to write an imaginary incident in which the little swallow again helps the 'Happy Prince' in his service to humanity, in the event of the lives of both of them restored to them.

37.2.2 *Physics*

Topic

Relative Density-Law of Floating Bodies

Question

A cork weighing 10 grams can just sink into water when a load of 40 grams is placed over it. What will be the relative density of the cork?

Objective

The students apply their knowledge of law of floating bodies, in the new situation.

Specific Learning Outcomes

The pupil:

- analyses the situation to identify the principle underlying in the given problems.
- makes some hypothesis regarding laws of floating bodies etc.
- establishes relationship between mass of displaced water and the cork with the load placed on it.
- predicts the effect of increase or decrease in load placed on the cork.

Previous Knowledge

- Definition of density and relative density.
- Archimedes' principle.
- Density of water is 1 gram/c.c.
- Mass = Volume × Density.

Teaching-Learning Activities

- The teacher presents the problem listed above after teaching Archimedes' principle, laws of floating bodies etc.
- The students try to understand the problem, analyse it and try to know what is given and what is required.
- The teacher helps the students to analyse the problem further and formulates the following hypotheses:
  (i) The weight of the floating body is equal to the upward thrust of the liquid.
  (ii) The volume of the displaced water is equal to that of the body inside water.
  (iii) The upward thrust is equal to the weight of water displaced.
- On the basis of the above hypotheses, the students find that the mass of water displaced is equal to the total mass of the cork and the load placed on it i.e. (10 + 40) gms. = 50 gms. Hence, the volume of the displaced water = 50 c.c. which is, therefore, the volume of the cork. The students finally find that the relative density of the cork = 10/50 gm/cc. = 0.2 gm/c.c.
- The teacher asks the students as to what will happen if more load is placed on the cork.
- The students find that since the mass of the body is greater than that of the displaced water, the body cannot float, but will sink completely.
- The teacher asks a further question of the students as to what will happen if a weight less than 40 gms. is placed on the cork.

- The students argue that in above case the weight of the body (cork) being less than that of the displaced water, the body will float and some portion of the body will be above water.
- The teacher advises the students to remember that Archimedes' principle cannot be applied if the liquid is not in equilibrium.

Follow-up Activities

The pupils:

- arrange the experiment to get the results checked and comment on arrangements made by other friends.
- prepare similar question taking other factors as unknown: volume, mass etc.
- comment on questions prepared by friends. For example, if the problem is to find the relative density of the load put over the cork, then it cannot be solved.
- prepare similar questions taking a liquid other than water and then realise that the one additional data viz. the density of the liquid is needed to solve the problem.
- try to solve similar type of more complicated problems like a situation when the cork is immersed in a mixture of two liquids whose densities are known.

37.2.3 *Biology*

Content Unit

Levels of Organisation: (Concept of cell tissue organ and system)

The illustration given here deals with the concept of cell, tissue, organ and system. The question that follows is only one example of only one type which can be made use of in teaching as described below. The purpose is to emphasise and explore the possibility of using a question as a device of teaching. It is only through the discussion of relationships in each alternative that students arrive at the correct answer and learn about the concepts involved.

Questions

The relationship between cell and tissue is almost similar to the relationship between:

A. ptyaline and starch.
B. liver and the gall bladder.
C. carbohydrate and fat.
D. ectoderm and endoderm.
E. organ and the system

Objective

The student comprehends the concept of cell, tissue, organ and system with respect to human physiology.

Specific Learning Outcomes

The pupil:

- recalls different levels of organisation of life and recognises the structure of cell and of different tissues and organs of digestive system.
- identifies relationship among cell, tissue, organ and the system.
- compares different units of life.
- cites examples of tissue, organs and the system.
- observes and interprets correctly the given diagram or a slide showing transverse section of some organs.
- draws inferences about the given or observed situations involving different types of relationship.

Previous Knowledge

Students are already familiar with the following:

- The cell as the basic unit of all living organisms.
- Elementary idea of tissue.
- Elementary idea of digestive system.
- Proximal constituents of food.
- Structure of multicellular animals like coelenterates.

Teaching-Learning Activities

- The teacher poses the above problem in the class.
- He explains the relationship involved in the cell and tissue for further clarification. He helps the students to recall that cell is the basic unit of life and the tissue is composed of a group of such cells. Therefore, cell is a component of the tissue which is a larger unit of life.
- Pupils study the problem, recall the structure and function of cells and tissues. They also try to identify relationship between the two concepts and may give different answers to the problem stated.
- The teacher analyses the responses; takes note of the various categories of answers and discusses each choice with the students to enable them to establish relationship in each case. He educes with the help of students that in alternative 'A' the relationship is that of an enzyme and the substance digested; in 'B' it is that of a production and a storage unit; in 'C' it is that of two constituent units or components of a common substance (food) while in 'D' the relationship is spatial, i.e., external and internal positions of an organ.
- Pupils make comparisons of the relationship between cell and tissue with each of the relationship observed in each of the cases A, B, C and D and recognise that none of these relationships is similar to the one between cell and tissue.

- Pupils are especially asked to study the choice 'E' which may be the plausible answer in this case. They examine the functional relationship between organ and system.
- Pupils find out the different organs that go to make up a system just as cells go to make up a tissue. Thus they establish that the relationship between a cell and tissue is the same as between organs and the system thereby arriving at the correct choice.
- Teacher then asks pupils to interpret the relationship between tissues and the organ on the basis of relationship established by them between organ and system.
- Pupils interpret the overall relationship among cell, tissue, organ and system.
- Teacher then shows to the class different charts of animal and plant organs showing different tissues and cells comprising the tissues, for students to observe and identify the various levels of organisation.

Activities in the practical class

Teacher guides the students to open the viscera of the frog and helps them to:

- observe the various organs found inside the body of the frog.
- recognise some organs which form one system e.g. digestive system and see which organs combine together to form that system (digestive system in this case).
- examine the microprepared slide of the T.S. of one organ made up of various tissue (e.g. stomach).
- interpret the internal structure of the stomach and infer relationship between tissues and organs.
- In the prepared slide of T.S. of stomach, the students examine one layer under the high power of the microscope and find out similar type of cells in the layer and draw inference that a group of similar cells form a tissue and tissues form the organ.

Follow-up Activities

- Pupils are asked to examine simple or isolated cells of an animal like Amoeba or a plant like Chlamydomonas.
- Pupils would examine a group of cells forming simple tissue, say in Hydra.
- Pupils may be asked to examine different tissues in an organ in any microprepared slide, say T.S. of intestine and report their observations regarding relationship between the two.
- Teacher suggests to his pupils to prepare a chart depicting a particular system of an animal as also the organs, tissues and cells separately indicating relationship among them.

- Students are asked to discover and record other similar relationship that they might observe or locate from different sources.

37.2.4 *Mathematics*

Topic

Polygon

Question

The quadrilateral obtained by joining the middle points of the adjacent sides of any quadrilateral is a

A. square
B. rhombus.
C. rectangle.
D. parallelogram.

Objective

The student applies his knowledge of the relationship between the straight line joining the middle points of any two sides of a triangle to the third side to find the solution of the problem.

Specific Learning Outcomes

The pupil:

- identifies relationship between the line joining the middle points of any two sides of a triangle to the third side of it.
- compares among different types of polygons.
- draws the inference that the required figure is a parallelogram.

Previous Knowledge

- Terms and concepts: Triangle, quadrilateral, square, rectangle, rhombus, parallelogram.
- Relationship; (a) The line joining the middle points of any two sides of a triangle is parallel to the third side and is equal to half of it. (b) A parallelogram is a quadrilateral having opposite sides parallel.

Teaching-Learning Activities

- The teacher presents the problem after teaching the theorem regarding the relationship between the straight line joining the middle points of any two sides of a triangle to its third side.
- The students try to comprehend the problem, analyse it and understand what are given and what is required.
- Pupils recall appropriate relationship and processes given above.
- The teacher ascertains through questions whether the students have a clear concept about a parallelogram and know the relationship between the opposite sides. The teacher explains the concept of

parallelogram, in case he finds that it is not clear to the students. He helps them to understand that a rhombus is a special parallelogram whose all four sides are equal, a square is a special type of rhombus whose one angle is a right angle and a rectangle is a special parallelogram whose one angle is a right angle.

- The students are asked to draw the figure according to the problem and measure the length of the opposite sides of the quadrilateral obtained by joining the mid-points of the adjacent sides of the quadrilateral.
- The students find that the opposite sides are equal and parallel and conclude that the figure is a parallelogram, and that the choice 'D' may be the correct answer. The possibility of the alternatives A, B and C being stated by the students as the correct answer is, however, not ruled out.
- By actual measurement of all the sides of the quadrilateral so formed, the students find that all are not equal and thus it cannot always be a rhombus or a square because all the four sides may not always be equal.
- By the measurement of one of the angles of the same quadrilateral, the students also find that it is not always a right angle. Hence, they conclude that the aforesaid figure is not always likely to be a rectangle.
- Students arrive at the conclusion that only 'D' is the correct answer.
- After the students have verified through a practical exercise that 'D' is the only correct answer, the teacher then asks the students to give an analytic proof of the proposition. He ascertains through questions what is given in the problem and what is to be proved. He also asks them about the method for proving it.
- Students give different answers to the problem stated.
- The teacher then tries to help him in arriving at the conclusion that this can be achieved only by joining the diagonals of the given quadrilateral.
- The students find that each pair of opposite sides of the inner quadrilateral is parallel to each diagonal of the given quadrilateral and is equal to half its length. They come to the conclusion that opposite sides of the given quadrilateral are equal and parallel.
- They find out that the two diagonals of any quadrilateral need not always be equal. Hence, all the sides of the quadrilateral obtained by joining the mid-points of the given quadrilateral need not be equal. This eliminates the possibility of answers A and C.
- The students find that the diagonals of any quadrilateral need not always intersect at right angles. Hence, the sides of the quadrilateral

under discussion also need not always be at right angles. This eliminates the possibility of answers A and B.

- They finally arrive at the conclusion that the obtained figure is a parallelogram and thus D is the only correct answer.

Follow-up Work

- Students are asked to prove analytically similar problems based on the above concept.
- They are asked to draw similar figures taking square, rectangle, rhombus, trapezium instead of any quadrilateral.
- They are asked to find out the nature of the quadrilateral so that the figure obtained by joining the mid-points of the adjacent sides turn out to be a square, or a rectangle, or a rhombus.
- They are required to find whether the obtained figure can be none of the four alternatives suggested in the problem.

37.2.5 *Geography*

Content Unit

Geography of India: Climate (Monsoons).

Question

Compare and contrast the summer and winter monsoons in India with respect to their causes, direction of winds, duration and areas of occurrence.

Objective

The pupil exhibits an understanding of the role of the monsoons.

Specific Learning Outcomes

The pupil:

- discriminates between such terms as summer and winter monsoons. South-west and North-east monsoons. Advancing and retreating monsoons, bursting of monsoons etc.
- interprets climatic data presented in different forms.
- analyses the effect of the northward shifting of the thermal zone in the summer season and its retreat in the winter season.
- compares the effect of the shifting thermal equator on the surface weather and conditions in the upper atmosphere.
- establishes relationship between temperature and pressure conditions in the atmosphere in summer and winter.
- establishes relationship between distribution of rainfall and various factors which affect their regional distribution.
- draws inferences about the sources of air-masses and direction of winds.
- selects relevant facts to explain the similarities and dissimilarities in weather and climate conditions in different parts of India.

- predicts weather conditions in different parts of the country during winter, summer and monsoon seasons.

Previous Knowledge

It is presumed that the pupils already know the following:

- The latitudinal and longitudinal position of India.
- Major relief regions of India.
- Seasons.
- Distribution of summer and winter temperatures and its relationship with pressure systems prevailing in these regions.
- Relationship between pressure systems and wind systems.
- Ferrels law.
- Cyclones tropical and temperate.
- Seasonal and annual distribution of rainfall.

Teaching-Learning Activities

- Teacher illustrates with a relief map, rainfall map and temperature map of India the temperature and pressure conditions of India in the different months, and the shifting of the centres of low pressure pockets.
- Pupils observe the facts and explain the changes in wind direction in relation to the occurrence of the monsoons.
- Teacher poses the problems of the vagaries of rainfall distribution in the country in all seasons and explains the relationship between intensity of low pressure and 'bursting of monsoons' and the march of the monsoon winds in the country.
- Pupils identify on maps regions of heaviest rainfall in the different months and explain the real difference in occurrence of rains from June to September on the west coast and October to March on the east coast.
- The teacher highlights the phenomena of 'reversal' or 'retreat' of monsoon conditions and its relationship to distribution of temperature and pressure conditions. Thus the classification of monsoon winds as summer and winter, wet and dry or North-east and South-west is explained.
- Pupils identify from a world climatic regions map the other areas which experience monsoons and the causes of such an occurrence. They differentiate the Indian monsoon from the Malayan monsoon and the Japanese and North Australian monsoons.
- Pupils identify from temperature and rainfall data of a few places in India, the regions of which they are representative.
- Teacher organises a discussion on the effect of monsoons on growing seasons in different parts of India and the problems created by

monsoons, of flooding and erosion and steps to counteract such destruction. Similar discussions on the role of monsoon in respect of (i) irrigation facilities (ii) forestry (iii) crop production, (iv) distribution of population etc. could also be arranged.

Follow-up Activities

Practical work

- Preparation of maps of India showing seasonal distribution of rainfall, temperature, pressure wind direction, particularly during the spans June to September and March to October.
- Preparation of maps of the Indian Ocean showing distribution of pressure and direction of winds in different periods especially January, March, May, June, September and November.

Discussions and Group Work

- Effect of seasonal variation in rainfall on crop production.
- Problem of famine following failure of rainfall in different parts of India and steps taken to counteract this.
- Relationship of forests and rainfall.

The above illustration is just one of the many approaches in which a question could be tackled and used as a basis for teaching. The other activities which have potentials for using a good question as instructional material are (i) self-study or assignment (ii) group study project (iii) classroom discussions on topical news etc.

PART V

TEACHING OF SPECIFIC SUBJECTS

Methods of Teaching Different Subjects

While the preceding discussions on the conventional and the unconventional techniques are broadly applicable while teaching different subjects, each subject is unique in its own way having its own characteristics. It is this that calls for specially designed adaptations of these approaches to suit the specific nature of the content of different subjects. In some subjects some approaches may yield better results and in some others other approaches.

Furthermore as applications of different subjects in life and their position in the scheme of studies (curriculum) also vary and their objectives of teaching too are different. This in turn accounts for significant differences in the methods of teaching and learning of different subjects as also the utilization of different curriculum materials and aids. The entire process of curriculum transaction thus gets influenced by these internal and external factors.

It is this that is attempted to be spelled out in this section in respect of different main subjects of curriculum.

In respect of each subject among other things, the conceptual framework, the objectives of instruction and the methods of teaching have been enunciated.

38

Teaching of the First Language

38.1 The Genesis of the First Language

Work has been going on for years on the development of teaching and testing material in Mother Tongue. The concept of the subject, therefore, first needs to be deliberated upon Multiplicity of languages with their own literature and scripts in India pose a real problem in this regard. This has been laudably attempted in the monograph on the Principles of Preparation and Evaluation of Textbooks in Mother Tongue brought out by the NCERT. The statement (which deems mother tongue to be the first language) reads as under:

"The broad areas for the use of mother tongue are day-to-day life. It is used in the home, market, office, educational institutions and social and cultural gatherings. Naturally, one of the main differences between mother tongue and other subjects being taught in the schools is that mother tongue is concerned with as many aspects and needs of human life as are possible, while any other subject is concerned with that aspect only on which it stands. *Secondly*, the sources for materials for mother tongue are manifold, while those of any other subject are relatively limited. Mother tongue collects its materials from all those areas where it is used. *Thirdly*, mother tongue helps in the learning of all other subjects being taught in the schools, while other subjects have consideration of their respective areas only. Thus, the content in mother tongue is very comprehensive in nature compared to those of other subjects. Besides this, mother tongue communicates with all other subjects. While other subjects display relationships with only a few subjects, particularly those allied to their respective areas mother tongue pervades all of them."

Two main aspects of content which mother tongue receives from daily routine life, formal education and the social and cultural aspects of life are the *linguistic content and the ideational content*. Mother tongue has some ideational content of its own, e.g., cultural and mythological themes, scenic beauty etc., but it borrows a lot of ideational content from other subject areas, both in social and natural sciences. Then, the ideational content which is expressed with the help of linguistic content also adopts some forms and formats. These forms and formats of the content are borrowed from actual life but in literature they adopt more sophisticated forms.

38.2 Instructional Objectives of First Language and their Specifications

Instructional objectives lay down the parameters of both teaching and testing and cannot be missed from any discussion the methods of teaching a subject. In regard to First Language: these have been listed stage-wise.

1. To acquire the knowledge of (a) elements of language, (b) ideational content, (c) different forms and formats of literature and (d) different forms of composition. (S)*
2. To acquire the ability of comprehending whatever he/she listens to. (PMS)*
3. To acquire the ability of comprehending whatever he/she reads. (PMS)
4. To acquire the ability of expressing oneself orally. (PMS)
5. To acquire the ability of expressing oneself in writing. (PMS)
6. To acquire the ability of translating from the second language to the First Language and vice versa. (S)
7. To develop the ability of appreciating the literature of the First Language. (PMS)
8. To bring-in originality in written expression. (PMS)
9. To develop an interest in mother tongue and its literature. (PMS)
10. To develop healthy and desirable attitudes. (PMS)

Objectives and their Specifications

38.2.1 *Objective: To acquire the knowledge of (a) elements of language, (b) ideational content, (c) different forms and formats of literature and (d) different forms of compositions.*

Specifications of the Objective	*Expected Behavioural Changes*
(i) *Elements of Language*	The student will be able to:
Phonology, including pronunciation	1. recognise (PMS) 2. recall (PMS)
Graphics, including spellings	3. detect the errors (PMS)
Vocabulary, including lexis and semantic structures	4. discriminate (PMS) 5. relate (PMS)
Structure, including phrases and semantics	6. classify (MS) 7. compare (PMS)

---

* *Note*: P = Primary stage classes I–V
M = Middle or Upper Primary classes VI–VIII
S = Secondary classes IX–X and Senior Secondary classes XI–XII.

Grammar, including parts of speech, word-formation and agreement	8. analyse (PMS) 9. synthesise (MS) 10. illustrate (MS)
(ii) *Ideational Content (PMS)*	*Expected Behavioural Changes*
a. Cultural values b. Life experiences c. Mythology d. Elements of character e. General knowledge f. Facts and fiction	All those described in (i) above
(iii) *Forms of Composition*	*Expected Behavioural Changes*
• Written Expression a. Precis (S) b. Story (PMS) c. Biography (PMS) d. Letter Writing (PMS) e. Dialogue (PMS)	All those described in (i) above
• Oral Expression a. Dialogue (PMS) b. Oral reading (PM) c. Interview (S) d. Lecture (MS) e. Debates and discussions (MS) f. Puzzles (PM) g. Rhymes (PM)	
(iv) *Forms of Formats of Literatures*	*Expected Behavioural Changes*
a. History of the literature of mother tongue (S) b. Synchronic study of different forms and formats of literature (S)	All those described in (i) above.

38.2.2 *Objective: To acquire the ability of comprehending whatever he/she listens to.*

Specifications of the Objective	*Expected Behavioural Changes*
Forms of Listening Comprehension Material	
a. Oral reading (PM) b. Dialogue (PM) c. Debate (PM) d. Elocution (PMS) e. Speech (PMS)	This student will be able to: 1. listen patiently. (PMS) 2. follow the etiquette of listening to others. (PMS) 3. listen with concentration. (PMS)

f. Directions and instructions (PMS)
g. Recitation (PMS)
h. TV programmes (PMS)

4. remain open-minded to receive the ideas of others. (MS)
5. understand the meaning of words, idioms and phrases in a given context. (PMS)
6. comprehend the sense according to the stress, accent and intonation. (S)
7. know the theme of whatever he is listening to. (PMS)
8. grasp the important facts, ideas and feelings. (PMS)
9. understand the relationships among the facts and ideas. (PMS)
10. get at the gist of whatever he listens to. (PMS)
11. get at the central idea. (PMS)
12. follow the mood of the speaker. (PMS)
13. appreciate the style of expression. (PMS)
14. appreciate the ideas and feelings. (S)
15. evaluate the facts, ideas and feelings. (S)

38.2.3 *Objective: To acquire the ability of comprehending whatever he/she reads.*

Specifications of the Objective

Forms of Reading Comprehension Material

a. Stories (PMS)
b. Novel (S)
c. Dialogue (PM)
d. Drama and one-act plays (MS)
e. Essays (PMS)
f. Biographies (MS)
g. Poetry (PMS)
h. Newspapers (PMS)
i. Magazines (PMS)

Expected Behavioural Changes

The student will be able to:

1. read patiently (PMS)
2. read with concentration. (MS)
3. remain open minded so as to receive the ideas of others.
4. read with correct pronunciation, proper accent, stress and intonation. (PM)
5. read keeping in view the punctuation marks. (PMS)
6. read with speed according to the nature of the topic. (MS)
7. read with proper speed and at appropriate pitch according to the context. (PMS)
8. read aloud according to the feelings expressed in the material. (MS)
9. understand the meaning of the words, idioms and proverbs in a given context. (PMS)
10. understand the value of the words, idioms, proverbs and phrases in a given context. (MS)

11. give a proper heading to whatever he reads. (MS)
12. grasp the important facts and ideas. (PMS)
13. understand the relationships between facts, ideas and feelings. (PMS)
14. get at the central idea. (PMS)
15. get at the gist of whatever he reads. (PM)
16. follow the mood of the writer. (MS)
17. appreciate the style of expression. (S)
18. evaluate the facts, ideas and feelings. (MS)
19. realise the relative importance of facts, ideas and feelings. (MS)
20. compare the material read with what he had read earlier. (PMS)

38.2.4 *Objective: To acquire the ability of expressing oneself orally.*

Specifications of the Objective

Forms of Oral Expression

a. Dialogues (PMS)
b. Speeches (PMS)
c. Debate and discussion (PMS)
d. Recitations (PMS)
e. Directions and instructions (PMS)

Expected Behavioural Changes

The student will be able to:

1. speak in an audible voice. (PM)
2. speak with proper speed according to the context. (MS)
3. speak with correct pronunciation and proper accent, stress and intonation. (PMS)
4. speak with proper pauses. (MS)
5. speak with fluency. (MS)
6. use the words, idioms and proverbs according to the context. (MS)
7. use the words, idioms and proverbs correctly. (PMS)
8. use simple and idiomatic language. (PMS)
9. use grammatically correct language. (PMS)
10. give proper sequence to words, phrases and clauses in a sentence, according to the meaning and sense desired to be conveyed. (PMS)
11. frame various types of sentences correctly. (PMS)
12. present the relevant materials. (MS)
13. maintain the sequence. (MS)
14. maintain the coherence. (MS)
15. maintain the unity of the topic. (S)

16. speak with proper gestures. (MS)
17. repeat only when necessary. (S)
18. bring brevity in his oral expression. (S)
19. follow the etiquette of oral expre-ssion in different contexts. (PMS)
20. use various styles according to the subject matter and the context. (MS)

38.2.5 *Objective: To acquire the ability of expressing oneself in writing.*

Specifications of the Objective

Forms of Written Expression

a. Letter, application (PMS)
b. Essays (PMS)
c. Biographies (PMS)
d. Stories (PMS)
e. Dialogues (PMS)
f. Directions and instructions (PMS)

Expected Behavioural Changes

The student will be able to:

1. write legibly. (PM)
2. write in a given context with the desirable speed. (MS)
3. write correct spellings of words. (PMS)
4. use the punctuation marks properly. (MS)
5. frame paragraphs. (PMS)
6. use grammatically correct language. (PMS)
7. use the words, idioms and proverbs in accordance with the context. (PMS)
8. use the words, idioms and proverbs correctly. (PMS)
9. use simple and idiomatic language. (PMS)
10. give proper sequence to words, phrases and clauses in a sentence according to the meaning he wants to convey. (PMS)
11. frame various types of sentences correctly. (PMS)
12. present the relevant material in his expression. (PMS)
13. maintain the correct sequence. (PMS)
14. maintain the coherence of language. (MS)
15. maintain the proper unity of the topic. (PMS)
16. repeat only when necessary. (S)
17. bring brevity in the written expression. (S)
18. Follow properly the technique of different forms and formats of written expression. (PMS)
19. express himself through a variety of forms of written expression.

20. use the style according to the topic and forms and formats of written expression. (S)

38.2.6 *Objective: To bring-in originality in the written expression.*

Specification of the Objective

Forms of Written Work

a. Essays (PMS
b. Stories (PMS)
c. Dialogues (PMS)
d. Letters (PMS)

Expected Behavioural Changes

The student will be able to:

1. select the forms of composition appropriate for the topic and the ideas and feelings to be expressed. (MS)
2. express the ideas and feelings experienced by him. (PMS)
3. express effectively the ideas and feelings experienced by him. (MS)
4. give new shape to language with the help of imagination to the ideas acquired and feelings experienced by him. (MS)
5. express in one's own way the ideas acquired and feelings experienced by him. (MS)
6. Use the language and style according to the topic and context. (S)

38.2.7 *Objective: To develop the ability of appreciating the literature of the first language (MS).*

Specifications of the Objective

Forms of Textual Material

a. Stories
b. One-act plays
c. Essays
d. Poetry
e. Biographies

Expected Behavioural Changes

The student will be able to:

1. find out the validity and invalidity of the facts. (MS)
2. find out the appropriateness of the ideas and feelings. (MS)
3. find out the portions of literary beauty. (MS)
4. appreciate the beauty of literature. (MS)
5. appreciate the form and style of expression. (MS)
6. appreciate the beauty of the words and other forms of expression. (MS)
7. recognise the metre and figure of speech involved. (MS)
8. identify and appreciate the beauty of symbolic expression. (MS)
9. recognise various shades of meaning. (MS)

10. analyse the language and the style. (MS)
11. evaluate the language and the style. (MS)
12. compare various forms of literature from the point of view of language and style. (MS)

38.2.8 *Objective: To acquire the ability of translating from the second language to the first language and vice versa.*

Specifications of the Objective	*Expected Behavioural Changes*
Forms of Material for Translation	The student will be able to:
a. Basic language b. Target language c. Content expressed in the base language	1. give appropriate synonyms in the target language for the words and phrases in the base language. (MS) 2. give appropriate equivalents for the idioms and proverbs of the base language into the target language. (MS) 3. give appropriate sentence structures in the target language for those of the base language. (MS) 4. avoid the use of structural words of the base language unnecessarily in the target language. (MS) 5. use the structural words necessary for the target language though they may not be present in the base language. (MS) 6. maintain the sequence of ideas in the base language. (MS) 7. maintain and transfer the mood and sense of the base language into the target language. (MS)

38.2.9 *Objective: To develop an interest in the first language/mother tongue and its literature.*

Specifications of the Objectives	*Expected Behavioural Changes*
Forms of Material	The student will be able to:
Language and literature	1. read books other than the text books. (PMS) 2. memorise good poems. (PMS) 3. contribute to the school magazine. (MS) 4. participate in literary programmes in the school. (PMS) 5. collect photographs of literary figures. (MS)

6. collect photographs of literary importance. (S)
7. participate in literary programmes outside the school. (S)
8. collect literary magazines and articles.
9. make a library of his own. (S)
10. become a member of literary societies. (S)
11. promote the taste for literature in his friends. (S)

38.2.10 *Objective: To develop healthy and desirable attitudes (PMS)*

Specifications of the Objective	*Expected Behavioural Changes*
Forms of Attitudes	The student will be able to:
a. Faith	1. develop love for literature.
b. Respect	2. develop love and respect for one's culture and that of others.
c. Love (for literature, country and human beings)	3. have respect for the ideals of different societies.
d. Sensitivity	4. develop love for the people of the country and those of world at large.
e. Consideration for others	5. have sensitivity to the immediate and global environment.
	6. entertain and profess the ideas and feelings in line with the desirable attitudes.
	7. act in conformity with the desirable attitudes.

38.3 Approaches to the Teaching of First Language

The aforesaid genesis and the corresponding content carry our thinking to the following implications for designing instructional strategies for the first language.

One of the implications of the above mentioned objectives for teaching the first language is that the teaching programme should be organised in such a way as may enable a student to achieve that level of proficiency in the first language which may help him in conducting his daily life, getting formal education and participating in the social and cultural life of the community. For that matter, only the knowledge of the discrete units of the contents of the first language will not do. These components are to be integrated. The integration of linguistic content, ideational content and different forms and formats of literature will help the child to comprehend whatever he reads. This will also pave the way for integration of linguistic content, ideational content and different forms and formats of expression–oral and written–used in daily life and will help the child in expressing himself, both verbally and in writing, and in comprehending whatever he listens to. This integration of different component marks a very important point of difference between languages and other school subjects from the point of view of teaching. In other school subjects, the content becomes all the more important. But in language teaching, in addition to the knowledge of all these elements of content, proficiency in the skills, viz., listening and reading, comprehension and oral and written expression should be developed in the students. Then, certain interests and attitudes are also to be developed through the teaching of the first language, which are its special concern and are necessary for the social and cultural life of the child. We may call all these as instructional objectives of the mother tongue, which may be the first language too and will include knowledge, skills, interest and attitudes.

As already indicated above, the child uses the first tonguage which is quite often the mother tongue in almost all the contexts—formal as well as informal. While he uses it, he learns it, but it is certainly not true that the more he uses it the more he learns it. Quality of learning does not wholly correspond to the frequency of use. If it were so, only the routine use of mother tongue would have been sufficient for learning it, and there was no need of teaching it in the schools. But the need of formal teaching of the first language or the mother tongue has been felt for long, for literature and language as well. The purpose of the language programme is to provide formal training to the students in the linguistic skills which informal and routine use of language does not fulfill. In the context of all this, in the programme for teaching mother tongue, the instructional materials occupy a very important place. These instructional materials may be textbooks, supplementary readers, workbooks and other materials prepared by the classroom teacher. Of course, the textbooks though only one of these materials, are the base upon which the programme of teaching of mother tongue is built up on.

The First Language, though normally the Mother Tongue and *the first among equals in the family of curricular offerings*, has somehow got relegated to the background to become the tail end of priorities. This by no chance is an accident, but a conscious diversion being taken by the students because the pragmatic concepts of utilitarianism have completely overtaken, overpowered and enslaved them. They have unfortunately come to believe that the study of their native tongue is not going to be of any help to them in the avocations that await them for ascent in life, and that it will only mean learning for learning sake, a concept which has got buried deep in the debris of present day materialism. Somebody in a lighter vein observed that the youngsters these days use mother tongue only to hurl abuses on each other.

All this, however, does not change the traditional status of the mother tongue, and one can still find enthusiasts pursuing studies passionately. These are the people who are not just preserving but also contributing to promoting the growth of valuable literature in our languages.

It could be safely mentioned that the literature of our ancient languages is a rich repository of our culture, which, in spite of all onslaughts of the so-called modernisation. we are unable to wean away from the milieu of our very existence.

In mother tongue there is everything that one can think of in regard to language—Prose, Poetry, Drama, Novels, Short Stories etc. that have to be studied, but with a difference. Everything is for detailed study. One has not only to learn peripherally, but in depth. Knowing the names of the authors and poets is not enough. *One has to know about their life and family, even significant turning points of their life, their other contribution to literature before and after the events in question, the choice of their themes, the underlying thread of their works (if any), their style, the audience or clientele to whom their work is addressed, the contemporary society of their times and the impact it made on their work.*

Even this is not enough. In the contents of their works one has to identify not just what has been said, but has been *conveyed without being said, not the apparent but the veiled ideas, not events but their implications, not the actions but their motives, and above all, not just their thoughts but also their underlying feelings.*

All this is not easy and can be an outcome of the joint efforts of the teachers and the taughts. Quite often, participatory learning could be resorted to where students with teachers guidance, could distribute themes, areas, books, poems etc. among themselves for detailed exploration, and then pool together their respective exploits and share them with others in joint sessions. In this situation, quite like those of quests related to the *Frontline Curriculum,* the teacher too becomes a co-learner with the students. Such group exercises, besides being time saving, are also very enriching for one and all of those that participate in the venture, because they are able to get hold of such a treasure of knowledge which they can never acquire through individual striving. Such group/team exercises generate and whet the interest of the students for further study of literature, some of whom may also finally turn out to be scholars, authors and poets and add to the existing literature to further enrich it.

The rigour of grammar too is a part of the study of all languages. In fact it provides the foundation of language and enables a better appreciation of the wording, the style and the diction. The students must, therefore, be enabled to enjoy the alliteration, the rhyming and should also be able to identify and appreciate the 'feet' and the 'meter' in the poems.

The student should also be able to brand a particular poet or author or dramatist or novelist as one of 'beauty', of 'fancy', of 'philosophy', of 'nature'.

He should also then be able to classify them into such different categories on the basis of sound reasons and valid evidences.

A comparative study of the different works of a writer and of similar works of different authors, is an instinct worthy of being ignited within a student.

The appreciation of puns, metaphors, similes and other figures of speech is a must, for an indepth study of the works of any author, and background knowledge of these is a must for the purpose.

Teaching of the first language easily admits both 'standard' and 'specific' methods. While the standard methods have been described in the sections on Techniques of Teaching, the specific ones are those that the teacher designs himself for meeting different emergent situations. In teaching Kabir, he could arrange a video taped session or if possible, show them on video the film on the life of Kabir. The anecdotes of life of such 'ideals' get immediately settled in the minds of children and become quotable quotes.

The teacher could present a poem which may have multiple meanings. This may be given to the students to study carefully and to identify the different meanings conveyed, and their implication in life.

In **dramas** again, the students must be enabled to gain an insight into the plot, to be able to quote phrases and sentences and pieces of dialogue to substantiate the points they may endeavour to make while answering the questions.

Essays too will demand creative writing with a rich thought content. By and large, the given themes for the essays will call for reflective thinking. It will not be proper to expect only descriptive or narrative essays from students particularly so in secondary or senior secondary classes. The teacher will need to train students in planning the essay by developing an outline in advance. Time spent on this preparation will impart better sequence, greater coherence, and a more natural transition from one idea to another. Such an investment of time always pays off.

Short Stories too should not be taken to be like the grandmothers' tales. They normally convey much more than what is clear to the eyes or the ears. Knowing the facts and events is certainly not enough. The thought content of the stories, the messages they convey, the morals they exhale are their core kernel. These are not found on the surface but one has to dig deep to reach them. This is exactly what is necessary, and students must be enthused to accomplish that.

Prose, Poetry, Drama have already been covered earlier, and it will only suffice to say that students should get so inextricably interwoven with the contents of these works that they may feel the injustice done to any body in them as that done to them, they may exhilarate at the dramatic justices occurring, they may weep at the sorrow of others and feel happy at the happy turns in the plots. They should also be trained to 'reflect' on what they have read and learnt and on the applications and implications of the learning on their own lives. This is one of the surest ways of realising the worthwhileness of the educational ventures in languages.

Discussions, Recitations and Contests in such areas create and promote the proficiency in public speaking and help students get over stage shyness.

To sum up, it could be said that the teaching of the first language should not just be limited to teaching of prescribed books, but should get extended to a variety of exercises and activities that make learning meaningful and enriching.

Note: It is desirable that the language teachers go through both the chapters on the first and the second language for getting a comprehensive idea.

39

Teaching of the Second Language

In life situations, students do not just study the first language but also other languages described as second and third language. The difference in the teaching and learning of first, second and third languages in more that of degree rather than kind. In the present context however we will not move on to the teaching of the third language, but conclude the issue of language teaching only with the second language.

39.1 The Significant Significance of Second Language

The commonly chosen second language where the mother tongue is the first language in English. Indian languages other than mother tongue and other foreign languages like French, German and Japanese usually find a place among the third languages taught.

S.N. Saha a former colleague of the author, while writing about textbooks in English as a second language deliberated on the significant significance of English and developed a brief note, which is worth being reproduced here:

"English has retained a place in the educational and official structure of India. It has thus, to its credit, the recognisable national importance. It is important for other reasons also. No nation today, however great, can rely solely on its own indigenous share of social, cultural and technological inventions and development. Nations, as much as individuals, share their mental and material acquisitions and thereby profit immensely. Understandably, learning another language is a significant enterprise directed towards ensuring a more intensive experience and wider view of the world. And it is more so when the language concerned is a living tongue like English, which is rich in literature—humanistic, scientific and technological." What is more, as the *Radhakrishnan Commission* emphasised: "English is the means of preventing our isolation from the world, and we will act unwisely if we allow ourselves to be enveloped in the folds of a dark curtain of ignorance. A sense of the oneness of the world is in the making, and control over a medium of expression which is more widespread and has a larger reach than any of our languages today will be of immense benefit to us."

So at present and in the foreseeable future, the demand for foreign languages will be increasingly felt, and they will continue to occupy an important place as an important part of the curriculum. People, for example, will need to communicate in English and to read books in English and decode from them. They will need English, which will give them access to the romance of modern industry and commerce, transport and communication, engineering and technology. Therefore, as a curricular subject, a second or the third language should be treated like any other curricular subject in so far as it should be taught well and learnt well. Similarly French as a foreign language is today studied in India by the largest number of people next only to English, German and Japanese too are being increasingly learnt. But learning a *second language* is basically different from learning other curricular subjects in so far as it is not so much an intellectual experience for the learner as a living emotional experience. It is to be learned with the heart and with love. And it is possible when the learner has the feeling that he is doing something with the language which is worth doing for its own sake. This leads to some basic considerations in the learning of a second language which could be a foreign language or another Indian language vis-à-vis the learning of the native tongue.

Nature and Scope of Learning a Foreign Language, whether first or *second, implies a system of patterned social behaviour*. It is, therefore, not realised in the abstract: it is realised as the activity of people in situations, either in its spoken or in written form. *Mackey* calls language a system of systems with the complex of *relationships between the system of sounds, the system of words, the grammatical system and the system of context or meaning*. So learning a language is a very complex process, with its complex interlocking of patterns, and the demand for their optimum coordination, control and internalisation by the learner. Yet it remains true that *an ordinary, normal child learns his native language more effortlessly*. The answer to a child's facility in his native language is attributed to his constant exposure to situations evoking his behaviours, hours of practice, his motivation, instant rewards of success, etc. In fact, the world of the child is a linguistic world. There are a myriad items in it, thousands of configurations, untold situations, unlimited experiences and emotions, which insistently clamour for expression. This is an indispensable stimulant in the learning of his language. So the child's learning of his native language is an inevitable process. But how differently a child learns a second foreign language! *While success of the child in mastering his native language is more or less taken for granted, the circumstances and success of the second language cannot be predicted so easily*. A child is forced to learn the first language because he has no other effective way to express his wants, to name things, to express his sentiments and sensations. In learning another second language, this compulsion is largely missing. Again, with the first language the child's mind is thought of as a 'tabula rasa' where the patterns become impressed, whereas the second language is perceived through the habitual channels of his native language. Coupled with this, the child's motivation for learning a second language may not be as high. He may have only an hour or two a day to wrestle with his second language, and that also in the classroom, whereas he has all day, every day to acquire the first one. There is also a certain amount of interference and negative transfer. Even learning the first language and gaining mastery over it is a stupendous task. A child simply could not, in a life time of learning, exhaust the lexical wealth of any language, nor could he put into actual practice, the infinite possibilities available to him from the abundant productivity of the language. Indeed, no method can teach the whole of a language. No native speaker knows all of it. If this is true in respect of the first language, how much more so it is for a second language. Hence in the second language, there is the inescapable need for abstraction from the total manifestation of language, its phonology, syntax, lexis and contexts, which will adequately serve the purpose of learning another language.

39.2 Purpose of Learning the Second Language

In this context the purpose of learning the second language needs to be clearly defined. As discussed above, the second language learner is at a disadvantage as compared to the infant learning his native language. However, comprehensive the course, the fact remains that the average second language learner, is not normally able to acquire the same competence in the language as he has in his native tongue. Speech being the foundation of the language, adequate opportunities should no doubt be provided to the children to cultivate it, so that *they are able to carry on comprehensibly a conversation in the second language on a topic fully within the range both of his own experiences and interests, and well within the range of active command of vocabulary and structures postulated by the syllabus*. However, this objective of second language learning, though very important, should not be stretched too far, since most children have very limited opportunities of hearing the language spoken and of speaking it. To be realistic, proficiency in reading easily and with understanding books in a second language within a prescribed range of vocabulary and sentence structures and growing readiness to proceed to a more advanced reading stage, that of reading unsimplified texts, particularly those bound up with the learner's personal studies and interests, and also the ability to write clearly and with ease on any familiar topic, seem to be the *most reasonable objectives of the second language learning*.

At the school stage in India except in the schools affiliated to the Council for the Indian School Certificate Examination (CISCE) and in a few other states English is taught as a second language. In CISCE, English is both the first language and the medium of instruction right from class I. In most of the State Boards of School Education, the study of English, though not compulsory, is an invariable first choice for a second language of almost all the students. There are also many instances, where the standard of both the first and the second language is almost the same.

39.3 Objectives of Teaching the Second Language

The Boards of School Education which take English as the first language, and those who accord a similar status to it, could look up the objectives of the first language for being guided in the development of curriculum and its transaction. Most of the others could take the objectives of teaching the second language for purposes of teaching and testing. These are enunciated below:

Instructional Objectives of Second Language

1. The student understands the language when spoken at normal conversational speed.
2. The student speaks the language correctly.
3. The student reads aloud passages and poems in the language correctly.
4. The student reads the language silently with comprehension.
5. The student writes in the language correctly.
6. The student develops an interest in the language.

(*Note*: All these objectives will operate within the range of structures and vocabulary prescribed for various stages.)

Objectives and their Specifications

39.3.1 *Objective: The student understands the languages when spoken at normal conversational speed.*

Specifications of the Objective:

To demonstrate the achievement of the above objective, the pupil will be able to:

1. recognise the characteristics of speech sounds of the language.
2. recognise stress and intonation of the language when spoken, and follows their significance.
3. recognise the meaning of words, phrases and sentences in the concerned context.
4. grasp the idea or ideas in a piece of connected speech.
5. follow the sequence of ideas expressed or events narrated—live or over the T.V.

6. recognise relationships between objects, person's ideas, events etc. occurring in speech or in passages read out to him/her.
7. grasps the substance and the central idea of a connected speech.

39.3.2 *Objective: The student speaks the language correctly and effectively.*

Specifications of the Objective:

To demonstrate the achievement of the above objective, the pupil will be able to:

1. use proper pronunciation, stress and intonation.
2. use appropriate words, phrases and sentences.
3. use appropriate pauses in speech.
4. use varied types of sentences.
5. present his ideas in proper sequence.
6. acquire reasonable speed and flow in speech, suited to the situation.
7. use conventional greetings and modes of address.

39.3.3 *Objective: The student reads aloud passages and poems in the language correctly.*

Specifications of the Objective:

To demonstrate the achievement of the above objective, the pupil will be able to:

1. pronounce words correctly.
2. pause wherever necessary.
3. use proper accent and rhythm.
4. use proper intonation.
5. maintain reasonable speed and flow.
6. read according to the sense expressed in the material.

39.3.4 *Objectives: The student reads the language silently with comprehension.*

Specifications of the Objective:

To demonstrate the achievement of the above objective, the pupil will be able to:

1. display reasonable speed in silent reading.
2. grasp the meanings of words, phrases, and sentences from the context.
3. locate keywords, phrases, and sentences,
4. locate important facts and ideas.
5. identify relationship between objects, ideas, events, facts, characters, etc.
6. infer the meaning, ideas and the message of a passage.
7. infer the mood of the author or character.
8. interpret ideas, events, traits of character, etc.

9. gets at the central idea of a piece.
10. evaluates events, actions, and expressed ideas, feelings and views/opinions.

39.3.5 *Objective: The student writes in the language correctly.*

Specifications of the Objective:

To demonstrate the achievement of the above objective, the pupil will be able to:

1. use appropriate words, idioms and structures.
2. use varied sentences.
3. spell words correctly.
4. use capital letters and marks of punctuation correctly.
5. make appropriate use of connectives such as 'and', 'but', 'so', 'therefore', 'otherwise', etc.
6. present only relevant ideas and facts.
7. present his ideas logically.
8. avoid unnecessary repetitions.
9. organise ideas, facts etc. into paragraphs.
10. introduce a subject, develop it and end it well.
11. give a suitable title.
12. display imagination in writing.
13. follow techniques of different forms and formats of written expression.
14. write a neat and a legible hand with reasonable speed.

39.3.6 *Objective: The student acquires knowledge of the elements of language and the textual content of the language.*

Specifications of the Objective:

To demonstrate the achievement of the above objective, the pupil will be able to:

1. recognise, recall and locate sounds, stress, intonation and rhythm in sentences.
2. recognise, recall and use structural words, content words, sentence patterns, spellings, capital letters and marks of punctuation.
3. recognise and recall events, facts, ideas from the text.

39.3.7 *Objective: The student develops an interest in language and literature of the language.*

Specifications of the Objective:

To demonstrate the achievement of the above objective, the pupil will be able to:

1. read books, newspapers and magazines of the language on his own.
2. listen to radio and television broadcasts and see films in the second language.

3. listen to speeches, debates, discussions, plays, songs etc. in the language.
4. take part in debates, discussions, plays etc. in the language.
5. collect or remember lines from poems and quotations from prose in the language.
6. converse in the second language outside the class when there are opportunities.
7. write reports, stories, letters, etc. in the second language on his own.
8. make use of dictionaries, thesaurus and other reference books in the language.

39.4 Teaching of Second Language

It may be specially mentioned that in the teaching of any second language, the emphasis would only be marginal in literature, appreciation of poetry, study of various authors and poets and their style. Hence the focus will be on:

- Elements of language
- Reading and listening comprehension and
- Oral and written expression.
- Appreciation, in a limited manner, with the core goal being communication.

The content of the curriculum will consist of:

Prose
Simple Poetry
Short Stories
Biographical sketches
Letters
Dialogues.
Dramas
Novels and
Exercises in Elements of language—grammar usage etc.

All these will, however, be simple with the main purpose of developing competencies related to day-to-day transactions in communication.

39.4.1 *The Direct Method and the Translation Method*

There are basically two traditional methods of teaching a second language.

The *Direct Method*, consists of acquainting the pupils with vocabulary and usage by introducing objects and situations. This is more suitable when they are being introduced to a new language, particularly in lower classes. As children grow-up and catch the language, communication becomes an effortless affair, just as walking is to us today, which was difficult at first.

The *Translation Method*, on the other hand, uses Mother Tongue as the medium of instruction where the meanings of words and usages are communicated to the students in the Mother Tongue. This used to be the most common method of teaching until the new techniques started being used.

The *Direct Method* is naturally a slow method and is time consuming, both for the teachers and the taughts, but it does lead to abiding enablement in using the language. The *Translation Method* takes lesser time, but the linguistic facility acquired by the students gets infected by the mother tongue, often in an adverse manner.

The pronunciation, intonation and accent of the teacher, too, play an important part in helping students to develop similar linguistic prototypes. It is, therefore, of utmost importance that the teacher particularly of a second language too must communicate not just in grammatically correct language, but also with correct pronunciation, intonation, accent, stress etc., because the children too would learn accordingly. It is because of this that the students are advised to listen to news bulletins on the TV in the concerned second language.

39.5 The Facets of Second Language Teaching

The central focus of attention in regard to different aspects of the prescribed course content also deserves a specific mention.

Prose lessons are normally woven around themes and these ought to be comprehended by the pupils, with particular reference to the meanings of words, phrases and idioms in the context. The apparent and the hidden meaning too should be understood by the pupils. The paragraphing and the sequencing of the text ought also be understood well by the students and so well that they may be able to answer questions based on them simply and correctly.

Poetry in second languages is simple, where the element of appreciation is not pitched at a high level as compared to the first language courses. However, the thought content, the display of the finery of feelings, the flights of imagination are all there to be grasped. Poetry, it is said, is not taught but caught and so it leaves one thinking and full of perceptions, which are often unexplainable in regard to the impact they make on the mind. This feeling embalmed outcome of the study of Poetry, is an all pervasive, unimpregnable, and indivisible entity, and it is therefore advisable that it is not be dissected to be taught like prose. A poem is a coherent entity and it is this wholeness that creates an overwhelming influence on the mind. Dissection of the parts of poems, tears the poems into parts and robs them of their poetic spirit and soul. This should never be attempted because what is desired to be communicated is not just thought and meaning, but more so the feelings they are imbued with, and the ethos that enrobes them.

Drama too, is sometimes a part of Second Language courses. These, however, are not classical ones, but usually consist of extracts of scenes or summaries like Tales from Shakespeare, or sometimes one act plays or scenes from them or small dramatic skits. Irrespective of the physical form in which they stand prescribed in courses, they are by no means meant to be for detailed study, in second languages. The expectations from the students in this area will therefore be that they should know:

- the name of the dramatist.
- the story woven into the drama, its turns and twists.
- the characters and their characteristics, their relationships, as also their cordiality or strains.

The questions asked of the students in examinations too are by-and-large factual and straight.

Novels in a second language course can only be for supplementary reading where again the students would not be expected to acquire any indepth knowledge of the social, economic, political or cultural setting that the story may have been built upon nor even about the contemporary literature or society. What they are supposed to know about dramas viz. the author, the story and the characters will be just adequate in respect of novels as well.

Short Stories either incorporated in the prescribed textbooks or in supplementary readers too will need very general acquaintances with their different facets. Anybody who may have just gone through them once, and possesses fairly adequate communication abilities, should be able to answer the general questions that may be asked on them.

Biographical sketches are often part of the texts. The students are expected to know the place of birth, the family background and composition, education, his professional life, his significant contributions, his successes and failures and his personal social and humane qualities. The short biographical sketches often capture the interest of the students and motivate them to collect more information about the individual. The biographical sketches, more often than not, communicate valuable values that the character/individual cherished and pursued, and the causes he stood for. The biographed individual's character do sometimes, become role-models for the students, which serves well the justification for their inclusion in the courses.

Dialogues too, often find a place in the prescribed courses. These, besides the gist, also communicate colloquial language to the students, which enables them to appreciate the difference between formal and informal conversations. The status of those conversing, displays the etiquette and manners, as also the modes of address demonstrated during the dialogues. Of importance for understanding, are the figures of speech used, the sarcasm imbued, the directions/orders given, the submissions or requests made, in the course of the dialogues as also the underlying spirit. These in fact are the things that students should focus on and not just understand, but also subsequently, use effectively in their own dialogues as per the demands of different situations.

Picture compositions are also sometimes part of the prescribed courses. The picture represents a person, place or thing in a given setting. The student is expected to pick up the ethos of the setting and the sense from the picture and to describe it in his own words within the required length. Such a reproduction of visual perceptions, in equally picturesque words, is the competency expected to be demonstrated. They are not just the facts, but the embalmed thoughts and the germinating imagination, imbued in the pictures which has to be captured, and the student is rewarded through higher examination scores for these abilities.

Letter Writing is the most common of the kinds of written communication. Letters could be *formal* and *informal*. In formal letters and communications all the formalities have to be formally adhered to, not just in spirit, but also in letter. The format for these letters is fixed and prescribed. The mode of address and the conclusion depends upon the person being addressed, his relationship (official) with the writer and his comparative status. The content has to be related to the given situation, and the words and the language therefore become the main focus of attention. Its body should contain all the required facts and figures, or answer to all the conceivable questions that the addressee may want to know in that regard. Inspite of everything else, the language should be cordial and courteous. The letter should indicate the completeness of the background information one may be possessing and desirous of sharing, with a view to evoking a positive impression of professionalism.

Elements of language constitute the foundation of any course on any language. They are the soul of communication. Eventhough formal grammar is no more advocated to be taught, applied grammar has come to take its place. The attempt, therefore, is to teach the elements of language through usages, rather than rules and principles. This is taken to be a more progressive departure, from mechanically learning and applying rigidly formal rules of grammar to increasingly flexible stances of usages.

Steps in Teaching Prose and Poetry

Traditionally, the following steps have been successfully used in teaching prose and poetry:

- Model Reading by the teacher with correct pronunciation, intonation, emphasis, pauses and so on.
- Loud Reading by the students with mid-way corrections by the teacher.
- Developmental Questions by the teachers, responded to by the students on the pieces read.
- Guided summarisation by the students about the genesis of the content.
- Recapitulative Questions
- Application Questions on aspects related to the central theme.

All these are quite well known steps and they do help realise the objectives of teaching and learning.

Teaching Other Areas of Content

Apart from prescribed textbooks dramas, novels, short stories, biographical sketches and the like in second language students are supposed to cover these mainly through self-study. They could then seek clarification from the teacher in the class. The teacher should then ask questions, distributing them over the whole class to confirm that the students have grasped the things mentioned earlier.

Teaching of Elements of Language

Practical exercises in respect of different elements ought to be given, for purposes of teaching supported by drill and subsequently those of testing.

Correction of mistakes and their discussion serves as a great remedial measure, and examples given by the teacher further reinforce and consolidate learning.

Apart from these, the techniques of teaching mentioned earlier could also be pressed into service for further rejuvenating learning and making it lasting.

40

Teaching of Mathematics

Mathematics is an undeniable ingredient of school curriculum because it is the basis of living and of transactions in day-to-day life.

40.1 Place of Mathematics in School Curriculum

Mathematics has helped man to quantify ideas, to be precise and to utilise spatial concepts in his day-to-day living. Its place in the sciences and in the practical arts, from the informational and computational standpoints as well as its cultural significance, make it indispensable in our life. In a society which is rapidly transforming itself into an industrial and technological society, mathematical literacy is essential for every citizen. In General terms the purpose of mathematics education at the school stage should be:

(a) to cultivate a mathematical way of thinking, i.e., in terms of carrying out experiments with numbers and geometric forms, making hypotheses, verifying them with further observations and experiments, generalising them, trying to find proofs and making abstractions, etc.

(b) to quantify their experiences of the world around them and to understand the process of applying mathematics to real life situations.

(c) to learn the basic structures of mathematics through unifying concepts, and to motivate the learning of structures through applications and concrete situations, and

(d) to study mathematics on their own, and to develop a taste and feeling for mathematics.

One of the basic aims of teaching mathematics in schools is to inculcate the *abilities of quantification of experiences around the learners*. Towards this end, carrying out experiments with numbers and forms of geometrical figures, framing hypotheses and verifying these with further observations from inherent part of mathematics learning. It would also include generalising these findings with proof through repeated ventures and developing competencies for solving problems. Mathematics helps in the process of decision-making through its application in real life situations—(familiar as well as un-familiar). It contributes to the development of precision, rational and analytical thinking, reasoning, positive attitudes and aesthetic sense. Apart from being a distinct area of learning, it helps enormously in the pursuit of other disciplines which involve analysis, reasoning and quantification of ideas. Study of mathematics also provides ample opportunities for making conjectures, testing and building arguments about their validity and also in raising new questions about different related issues. Understanding of the basic structure of mathematics leads to a much better appreciation of the scope and power of mathematics. The mathematics curricula must develop an appreciation and understanding of the contribution of Indian mathematicians alongwith those of other countries. This would develop a sense of self-esteem and self-confidence amongst the learners.

While determining the curriculum in mathematics, it must be kept in mind that majority of learners would need to apply mathematical skills and competencies in their life and work situations. A smaller number of students, of course, would go in for higher education. The curriculum therefore, needs to strike a balance between the learning requirements of both the groups.

40.2 Objectives of Teaching Mathematics at the Elementary Stage

At the elementary stage the objectives to be focussed upon for being acquired are:

Counting and Measurement

The pupil:

- identifies sets and their members.
- compares areas and masses of different shapes and sizes.
- demonstrates measurement of length, area, time, temperature and volume using relevant instruments.
- orders numbers.
- determines number relationships.
  distinguishes differences between estimation and measurement of objects and phenomena.
- selects situations when measurement and estimation are to be used for determining length, weight, area, distance, size, etc.
- compares, measures and makes inferences about the variables.
- designs tables for recording data.
- prefers to be accurate in measurement.
- appreciates the need to measure for interpreting relationships between phenomena.

Symbolic Skills

The pupil:

- recognises the significance of conventional units of measurement, signs, symbols, etc. to express his ideas.
- translates unique signs and symbols into verbal form and vice versa.
- interprets the given figures, maps, graphs, flow-charts, etc.
- selects appropriate signs, symbols and units to express his ideas.
- expresses his ideas through the use of appropriate diagrams, graphs, maps, etc.

Fundamental Numerial Operations

The pupil:

- carries out oral calculations with ease and speed.
- carries out written calculations at a reasonable speed.
- draws geometrical figures and graphs with ease and accuracy.
- reads and interprets tables, charts and graphs correctly.
- solves problems involving fundamental numerical operations.
- transforms verbal expressions into symbolic form and vice versa.

40.3 Instructional Objectives of Mathematics at the Secondary and Senior Secondary Stages (Class IX and XII)

In concrete terms, the objectives of teaching Mathematics at the school level, with particular reference to the secondary stage as under :

1. To acquire the knowledge of terms, concepts, symbols, definitions, principles, processes and formulae of Mathematics.
2. To develop an understanding of terms, concepts, symbols, definitions, principles, processes and formulae of Mathematics.
3. To apply the knowledge and understanding of Mathematics to unfamiliar situations or new problems.
4. To acquire competencies related to (a) computation, (b) drawing geometrical figures and graphs and (c) reading tables, charts, graphs etc.
5. To appreciate the role of Mathematics in day-to-day life.
6. To develop an interest in Mathematics.
7. To develop scientific attitude through the study of Mathematics.

Objectives and their Specifications

40.3.1 ***Objective: To acquire the knowledge of terms, concepts, symbols, definitions, principles, processes and formulae of Mathematics.***

Specifications of the Objective:

To demonstrate the achievement of the above objective, the pupil:

1. recalls and reproduces.
2. recognises.

40.3.2 *Objective: To develop an understanding of terms, concepts, symbols, definitions, principles, processes and formulae of Mathematics.*

Specifications of the objective

To demonstrate the achievement of the above objective, the pupil:

1. gives illustrations.
2. detects errors and corrects them.
3. compares.
4. discriminates between closely related concepts.
5. classifies items as per criteria.
6. identifies relationships among the given pieces of information.
7. translates verbal statements into symbolic ones and vice versa.
8. estimates the results.
9. interprets.
10. verifies results.

40.3.3 *Objective: To apply the knowledge and understanding of Mathematics to unfamiliar situations or new problems.*

Specifications of the Objective:

To demonstrate the achievement of the above objective, the pupil:

1. analyses and finds out what is required.
2. finds out the adequacy, superfluity or relevance of data available.
3. establishes relationship among the data.
4. selects the appropriate method for the solution of problems.
5. suggests alternative methods.
6. generalises (i.e. reasons inductively).
7. infers (i.e. reasons deductively).

40.3.4 *Objective: To acquire competencies related to (a) computation, (b) drawing geometrical figures and graphs, and (c) reading and interpreting, tables, charts, graphs etc.*

Specifications of the Objective:

To demonstrate the achievement of the above objective, the pupil:

1. carries out oral calculations with ease and speed.
2. carries out written calculations with ease and speed.
3. handles geometrical instruments with ease and efficiency.
4. measures accurately.
5. draws freehand figures with ease.
6. draws figures to specifications or to scale.
7. draws figures accurately.
8. reads tables with speed and accuracy.
9. interprets graphs, tables, etc.

40.3.5 *Objective: To appreciate the role of Mathematics in day-to-day life.*

Specifications of the Objective:

To demonstrate the achievement of the above objective, the pupil:

1. appreciates the role of Mathematics in solving problems of life and of other branches of Science.
2. appreciates the symmetry of figures and designs.
3. appreciates qualities like brevity and precision exactness through the study of Mathematics.

40.3.6 *Objective: To develop an interest in Mathematics*

Specifications of the Objective:

To demonstrate the achievement of the above objective, the pupil:

1. reads literature on Mathematics.
2. writes popular articles on Mathematical topics for the school journal.
3. solves Mathematical puzzles.
4. participates in the activities of Mathematics Club.
5. gives short cuts for solving the problems.
6. invents mathematical problems.
7. brings to the teacher additional problems not related to the syllabus.

40.3.7 *Objective: To develop scientific attitude through the study of Mathematics.*

Specifications of the Objective:

To demonstrate the achievement of the above objective, the pupil:

1. accepts a proposition only when logically proved.
2. examines all the aspects of a problem.
3. points out errors boldly if convinced.
4. accepts mistakes without hesitation.
5. respects the opinions of others.
6. keeps an open mind and does not regard any argument as final.
7. develops the habit of logical thinking.

40.4 Methods of Teaching Mathematics at Different Stages

The first ten years of schooling are to provide general education to all the pupils. Therefore, mathematics as per the National Policy on Education 1986/92 is to be compulsory for all students up to Class X.

While redesigning the teaching of mathematics, it is also necessary to take into consideration the role of modern technological devices in the teaching-learning process, particularly in the context of the emergence of educational computing and learning through the understanding of the interplay of variables including cause effect relationships.

Pre-Primary Stage

At the pre-primary level, it is visualised that many play-way activities have relevance for the development of number concepts among children. When the teacher draws the attention of children to number of fingers, toes, play equipments, individuals at home, chairs, legs of chairs, etc., or when they are involved in use of money, counting of objects, comparing and matching of collections of varying sizes, measurement of length, mass and volume etc., they learn the concepts of numbers, shapes and sizes informally.

Primary Stage

At the primary stage, learning of mathematics should lay the foundation for mathematical thinking about the numerical and spatial aspects of the objects and activities which the children at this stage are required to deal with. The pupils should master basic mathematical vocabulary, symbolism and computational skills related to numbers, geometrical figures, money, time, measures of length, mass, volume, etc., and be able to apply them to day-to-day problems in their immediate environment. They should also develop simple drawing skills and measuring skills. Learning by doing (with concrete materials) should be the main method of learning at this stage.

At the primary stage, the child should also be introduced to numbers, the fundamental operations related to them and their elementary properties. Concepts of length, width, time, area and capacity should be developed, along with the units of measuring these. The child should gain familiarity with geometrical forms and figures, and also with an elementary notion of algebraic symbols. Simple applications of the fundamental operations and arithmetical processes to everyday problems should also find an important place in the instructional programme at this stage.

In the first two years of the primary stage, i.e. in Classes I and II, children need to form some basic pre-number concepts related to size, length, mass etc. They also need to sharpen their skills of classification, grouping and sequential thinking. These provide them with a sound foundation for learning numbers and developing competencies of addition and subtraction. The content of mathematics will therefore need to be built around the immediate environment of the child.

In classes III to V, the child should be introduced to numbers and fractions as a concept. The four fundamental operations—addition, subtraction, multiplication, division, and computational skills related to them too need to be mastered on numbers and fractions. The concepts of length, mass, capacity, money, time, area and volume as well, have to be developed along with the units of measuring these. The child should gain familiarity with geometrical forms and figures, and be able to appreciate patterns and symmetry in the environment. Simple applications of arithmetical processes too should find an important place at this juncture.

Upper Primary Stage

At the upper primary stage (Classes VI to VIII) the pupils should acquire further knowledge and understanding of facts, concepts, principles, etc., related to commercial mathematics, mensuration, descriptive statistics, practical geometry and fundamentals of algebra. They should develop proficiency in using tables and ready reckoners etc., in solving problems. The problems presented should however be realistic, informative and data-based, and should be selected from different sources like trade, commerce, industry, agriculture, population studies, etc. There should be practical work in the mathematics laboratory/work-room/open field consisting of geometrical drawings, for estimation, and measurement of lengths, areas and volumes, and verification/ demonstration of geometrical facts with simple teaching aids including paper folding/cutting etc. The pupils should thus be enabled to read and interpret data from statistical tables and graphs. Mathematics upto the upper primary stage, should be mainly functional. The study of arithmetic, including commercial mathematics, should be completed to a very large extent by the end of the upper primary stage. Introduction of simple mathematical signs, international terms and symbols may also at this stage be introduced as a curricular objective.

At this stage, the number system will also need to be extended to real numbers and their operations. The students should be made familiar with the language of algebra and linear equations, and inequalities in one or two variables introduced to his thinking. The concept of sets and their notations, as also the elementary concepts of statistics, too should be developed. The application of arithmetical processes to problems of daily life may be further extended, and properties of triangles, quadrilaterals and circles, and area of regular figures and solids may be developed on practical lines.

The upper primary stage should be confined mostly to the study of essentials of mathematics in day-to-day life. The students may be encouraged to gain proficiency in oral/mental mathematics useful in day-to-day life activities as well as in solving problems with accuracy and speed. Furthermore, the students should be able to read and interpret data from statistical graphs/ charts/diagrams, and develop skills of drawing, model making and measuring.

Secondary Stage

At the secondary stage (Classes IX and X), a beginning should be made for the transition from functional mathematics, studied till the upper primary stage, to the study of mathematics as a discipline in appropriate forms. The (logical) proofs of prepositions, theorems, etc. should be introduced at this stage. The pupils should acquire knowledge and understanding of concepts, symbols and processes related to algebra, geometry, elementary trigonometry and statistics. The treatment of algebra should be simple, but the basic algebraic skills such as addition, substraction, multiplication, division, factorisation, etc. of algebraic expressions, should be mastered by the pupils. The pupils should also develop the ability to solve problems through algebraic methods. Geometry, including the experimental geometry, studied upto the upper primary stage, should be taught in the form of formal geometry with theorems and proofs. Proving results in the geometrical problems (riders) should be emphasised. Arithmetic and mensuration should be reinforced in the form of application of logarithms and of algebraic equations. The treatment of trigonometry should be elementary and sufficient to solve simple problems like those of 'heights and distances'. Practical work including simple projects, computation with calculations, use of ready reckoners and tables, working with computers could be an integral part of mathematical learning at the secondary stage. The most important part of computing is the concept of logarithms. The pupils should be introduced to the concept of computing, logarithms algorithm and flow-charting. However, at this stage, the scope should be limited to reading and interpreting flow-charts and preparation of simple flow-charts.

With regard to the common core components in the school curriculum and the related values, the most valuable contribution that mathematics should make directly is towards the inculcation of the scientific temper through the development of analytical thinking and reasoning.

In Classes IX and X, real-life problems should be handled by the students. The knowledge of algebraic processes should be systematised and extended. The idea of proof should be developed, and elementary theorems on triangles, parallelograms and circles taken up. The introduction of trigonometric ratios and the use of descriptive statistics along with measures of central tendency and dispersion should be made at this stage. The history of mathematics with special reference to India, and the nature of mathematical thinking should permeate the entire course.

The level of the general course should be high enough to provide the base for advanced study in later years, and also to equip the individual with the necessary competence to be able to tackle day-to-day problems. But this does not rule out the possibility of offering some units at higher level for talented students.

Senior Secondary Stage

The subject downs a disciplinary hue at this stage. The teaching and learning could also enter the arena of abstractions with imagination playing a critical role. The different aspects of the subject would become subjects themselves and will need to be treated as such.

41

Teaching of Environmental Studies

41.1 Concept of Environmental Studies

Environmental studies in the past used to be a part of the course for primary classes (I-V). The study of the subject in view of its importance has now been extended upto the Senior Secondary Stage wherein the subjects of sciences and social sciences are projected in a coherent integrated and unified manner for making a better and a more focussed impact.

Technically, the concept of Environmental Studies reflects a conglomeration of the subjects of Sciences and Social Sciences presented in an inseparable integrated form, which could be called a '*compound*' and not a '*mixture*'.

The instructional objectives, the content and the methods of teaching cannot therefore be separated into those of sciences and social sciences. This is, therefore, the manner in which the subject is proposed to be treated here. An example will help to clarify the point. If a topic like 'transport' is proposed to be included in the course, it will be taught as History of Transport, Geography of Transport, Physics of Transport, Chemistry of Transport, Biology of Transport, Mathematics of Transport and so on. This type of treatment will be quite different from the one commonly meted out to such themes in the past by dividing them into Rail Transport, Road Transport, Air Transport, Sea Transport, Inland Water Transport and so on.

41.2 Content of Environmental Studies

General Science Facet

The topics of study are not different from what they are in their respective disciplines, *but their treatment is entirely different.*

An outline of a possible course in Environmental Studies could be spelt out as under:

1. *Earth Related Sciences*
   - Our Universe
   - Air, Water, Atmosphere and Weather (pollution, degradation ozone layer etc).

- Rocks, Soils and Minerals

2. *Physical Sciences*
   - Energy (conventional and unconventional sources)
   - Natural and Technological and Industrial wastes
   - Environmental disasters and their prevention (ozone layer, greenhouse effect, global warming)
3. *Biological Sciences*
   - Living things
   - Plant life/Agriculture
   - Animal life
4. *Science, Technology and Development*
   - Man and Environment
   - Development and environmental crisis

Though apparently reflecting a Science approach, these topics are treated not just as scientific disciplines but in terms of their cultural, social, economic, ecological, technological implications and concerns, and their relationship with other subjects of the entire environment and with life.

Social Sciences Facet

In Social Sciences facet, an outline of a possible course in Environmental studies could be:

- Indian Society and Environment
- Population and Environment
- Human Activity and Environment
- Liberalisation and Globalisation

Again, the environment as a whole used to be the subject of study, not just from the Historical, Geographical, Economic, Sociological points of view, but also from that of Physics, Chemistry, Biology and even Mathematics.

In both the Science and the Social Science facets, they are not just the subject related themes, but their applications and implications that constitute the areas of study. This relationship with different aspects of life in fact provides meaning to the themes, because they are taken to be not as abstract but concrete entities of relevance to the day-to-day life, a fact which evokes the interest of children in the things they learn as part of Environmental Studies.

At the Senior Secondary Stage also the subject has to be treated in an integrated manner as the following divisions would indicate:

- Man and Environment
- Environment and Development
- Environmental Pollution and Global issues
- Energy

- Biodiversity
- Environmental Management

It may be mentioned that the subject of Environmental Studies even goes beyond sciences and social sciences and even attempts to cover different aspects of life and living.

41.3 Objectives of Teaching Environmental Studies

The objectives of teaching Environmental Studies too, like its content, are not disciplinary but integrated. It is, therefore, that they are also stated differently and defined comprehensively in a fusionistic perspective.

The objectives of Environmental Studies, quite like other subjects, are activity based, but these activities are simple, with small graded progressive steps, which are strictly aligned to the age group. This is because in the quest for realising the objectives, students should be encouraged and enabled to move from success to success. *In the formative years, any unsuccess is more disheartening and even more threatening and dissuading.* They give up quickly, and such a point should not be allowed to occur because a single set-back or derailment may then need four times the labour for restoring the child's confidence for bringing him on the rails.

It is with this point of view that the following objectives have been worked out. The specifications indicate what a student will be able to do, to demonstrate that he has attained the particular objective.

41.3.1 ***Observation:*** To develop the ability to explore the world around them with specific purposes, to recognise and identify objects so as to find relationship between new and observed facts, using all their senses. (This process does inculcate a sense of personal satisfaction in knowing and exploring the environment through direct experience.)

Specifications of the Objective:

To demonstrate the achievement of the objective, the pupil will be able to:

1. recognise the properties of objects and phenomena using the senses of sight, sound, taste, smell and touch.
2. recall the properties of objects from previous experiences.
3. identify objects, events and changes occurring in the environment.
4. distinguish objects on the basis of their properties, and develop a habit of noting minute differences and changes in the characteristics of objects and phenomena.
5. voluntarily seek new information about the physical and social environment.
6. develop curiosity to see new objects of the environment.

41.3.2 ***Classification***: to develop the ability to discriminate, order, arrange, give sequence, observe events, using given or chosen criteria in order to compare phenomenon. (The process develops an awareness of the diversity of systems and the importance of ordering and interpreting phenomena).

Specifications of the Objective:

To demonstrate the achievement of the objective, the pupil will be able to:

1. describe differences between objects and phenomena on the basis of given or chosen criteria.
2. distinguish between objects and phenomena on the basis of similarities and differences.
3. order objects on the basis of one or more criteria.
4. identify and name properties which could serve as the basis for possible classifications.

41.4.3 ***Counting and Measurement*****:** To develop the ability to identify the purpose of measurement, to select which type of measurement would most appropriately serve the purpose and how the measurement is to be taken and recorded in order to make inferences about relations between variables in the environment.

Specifications of the Objective:

To demonstrate the achievement of the objective, the pupil will be able to:

1. identify sets and their members.
2. compare items of different shapes and sizes.
3. demonstrate the ability of measurement using relevant instruments.
4. order numbers.
5. determine number relationships.
6. distinguish differences between estimation and measurement of objects and phenomena.
7. select situations when measurement and estimation are to be used.
8. compare, measures and makes inferences about the variables.
9. design tables for recording data.
10. prefer to be accurate in measurement.
11. appreciate the need to measure for interpreting relationships between phenomena.

41.3.4 ***Use of Space-time Relationship*****:** To develop the ability to identify relationships in the social and physical environment between movement of time and the changes that occur in social and physical processes.

Specifications of the Objective:

To demonstrate the achievement of the objective, the pupil will be able to:

1. recognise specified objects in relation to other objects.
2. identify direction and movement of objects in space.
3. interpret trends and the changes in environmental phenomena.

4. compare changes in the spatial position and relationships between physical and social phenomena over time.
5. develop tentative generalisations to explain changes in social and physical phenomena over space and in time.
6. appreciate the dynamic nature of natural and social systems and develop awareness of the diversity and constant change of social and physical processes.

41.3.5 ***Experimentation and Investigation*****:** To develop the ability to pose questions which require investigation, to suggest and use procedures, to collect, organise and interpret data, to derive generalisations. (Considering the stage of development of the child, the experiments would range from simple to complex).

Specifications of the Objective:

To demonstrate the achievement of the objective, the pupil will be able to:

1. pose questions and identify problems which are likely to be answered by investigation, experimentation and exploration.
2. suggest possible or tentative conclusions.
3. establish possible relationships between variables.
4. construct and/or assemble relevant apparatus for experimentation.
5. prepare appropriate tools for investigation.
6. conduct experiments and investigations systematically.
7. show perseverance in undertaking experiments and investigations.
8. skilfully manipulate instruments.
9. obey safety regulations.
10. voluntarily undertake care and maintenance of tools, materials and living things.
11. Practise honesty in reporting results.

41.3.6 ***Analysis and Interpretation*****:** To develop the ability to identify the relationships between different variables, to infer cause and effect relationships and to deduce conclusions derived by investigation and experimentation.

Specifications of the Objective:

To demonstrate the achievement of the objective, the pupil will be able to:

1. organise data efficiently.
2. recognise central themes/issues and assumptions.
3. compare trends and patterns of observed phenomenon.
4. infer relationships between different phenomena.
5. establish relationships between variables.
6. suspend judgements till adequate data is available.
7. form a habit of systematic enquiry.

41.3.7 *Generalisation and Prediction*: To develop the ability to formulate generalisations, draw conclusions, verify facts and predict consequences on the basis of analysis and interpretation. (The appreciation of using enquiry to form hypotheses and critical judgement of evidences is an outcome of this process).

Specifications of the Objective:

To demonstrate the achievement of the objective, the pupil will be able to:

1. deduce relationships between variables.
2. verify conclusions with further evidences.
3. extrapolate trends, implications, assumptions based on obtained data and previous knowledge.
4. derive principles on the basis of relationships between variables.
5. appreciate the need to revise opinions and conclusions on the basis of newly available facts and evidences.
6. support ideas and arguments with sound and logical arguments.

41.3.8 *Communication*: To develop the ability to express through writing, speech and action, relevant observations, conclusions and arguments. (The requisite skills to understand and use information through the development of the skills to read, listen, see, locate and relate information effectively is an expected outcome of this process.)

Specifications of the Objective:

To demonstrate the achievement of the objective, the pupil will be able to:

1. use relevant new words, sounds, actions, tools and instruments correctly.
2. translate observations, conclusions into suitable means of expression.
3. precisely describe objects, phenomena, trends, experiments, procedures through words, sounds, drawings, writings and demonstrations.
4. locate relevant sources of information from the environment.
5. voluntarily participate in group activities.
6. willingly share ideas and accepts arguments and ideas of others.

41.4 Methods of Teaching Environmental Studies

The methods of teaching Environmental Studies are directly related to the objectives enunciated, and consist of observation, exploration and analysis of environmental phenomenon like the 'nature watch', which at the primary stage may consist of items like the daily observation and recording of:

- timings of sunrise and sunset.
- the minimum and maximum temperature of the day.
- the direction of the wind.

- the state of the sky (cloudy/clear).
- the amount of rainfall recorded.
- any special weather related phenomenon (like a dust storm).

The children may then be enabled with the help of the teacher to draw conclusions about weather from the collected evidences.

The main methods of teaching environmental studies could no doubt be listed, but it will be the teachers' initiative and ingenuity which will determine the approach that s/he may decide to use in a particular situation because they will mostly be practical exercises done by the students, which may be introduced to children by the teacher.

These activities could be related to:

- observation
- exploration
- experimentation
- analysis of outcomes of experiences (projects, surveys etc.)
- establishment of relationships (environmental degradation)
- Interpretation of facts and phenomenon
- Drawing conclusions, and
- Presentation of findings
- Translating one form of presentation into another.

These, basically, will be the methods of teaching in respect of the themes prescribed in the curriculum.

The approach is often concentric where the same theme is taught in the next class in greater detail.

41.5 Evaluation in Environmental Studies

Evaluation is Environmental Studies at the elementary stage, for example, will be activity-wise consisting of the outcomes of activities in both kind and degree.

Observation will be the main technique of evaluation with a variety of related tools that may be decided to be used for ensuring accurate, dependable and just assessments. Some of the main tools could be:

- Inventories
- Check-lists
- Observation Schedules
- Rating Scales

These evaluations will need to be a continuous process of which the recording, compilation, analysis and interpretation of evidences aimed at meaningful declaration of result, will be the main components.

Beside, the quantitative evidences, there would naturally be host of qualitative ones to be taken care of. While evaluation in the former case could be done in terms of marks it would be desirable to use grades in respect of the qualitative ones. In classes I–V, where Environmental Studies is to be taught, symbolic grading (A B C D & E) on a five-point scale could be safely suggested.

Evaluation in Environmental Studies will also heve to have a diagnostic stance and remediation in this regard will have to be prompt and consist of on-the-spot correction, so that the shortfalls do not snow ball. The impartation of ability to succeed will positively reinforce the learning process and yield confidence and self-assurance to the students, raising their morale for better and higher success.

At the Secondary and the Senior Secondary Stages the subject could be evaluated through written examinations and some practical exercises.

42

Teaching of Social Studies

In view of the wide variations, in the treatment of science and social science subjects, particularly because they are supposed to follow an integrated approach upto class X and a disciplinary approach at the senior secondary stage, both the types of treatments are being presented—social studies and general science as integrated subjects as also in the form of individualised disciplines subsequently.

42.1 Place of Social Sciences in the School Curriculum

The study of the social science component of general education is of critical importance in facilitating the learner's growth into a well informed and responsible citizen. It should aim at developing in him/her an understanding of his/her physical and social environment, both immediate and remote, in terms of time and space and appreciation of the cultural heritage of India and of various cultures of the world. The study of the immediate physical and social environment should help him/her in developing an understanding of the interaction of man with his physical and social environment, and with the related institutions—social, economic, political etc.—through which human beings inter-relate with one another and function in the society. The study of social sciences should also aim at enabling him to see the present in the perspective of past developments for evolving a perspective for the future.

Similar to the study of physical and natural environment in science education, the study of social environment in social sciences should have three aspects, namely, *learning about the social environment, learning through the social environment and learning for the social environment*. This would mean that a pupil will learn, for example, about the social customs, cultural heritage, history of the society etc. through observation, exploration and scientific study of social phenomena and events and imbibe an urge for preservation of what is good in our culture and improvement of existing socio-economic cultural set-up.

Social science is perhaps the singular curricular area which can prove to be the most effective tool for providing education in the context of all the core components indicated in the NPE-86/92. Special care should, therefore, be taken in designing the curriculum in social sciences so as not to overlook any of the core components.

The component of social sciences is integral to the total quantum of general education upto the secondary stage. It helps the learners in understanding the human environment in its totality and in developing a broader perspective and an empirical, reasonable, and humane outlook. It also helps and enables them grow into individuals with necessary attributes/skills, so that they could participate and contribute effectively in the process of development and nation-building.

The curriculum of social sciences in schools will draw its content mainly from geography, history, civics, sociology, anthropology and economics. Together they provide different facets of the human society, over space and time and in relation to each other. It helps the learners in understanding the contemporary society better. Social sciences education also aims at providing students with essential knowledge, skills and attitudes necessary for self-development.

In order to make education in social sciences meaningful, relevant and effective, the concerns and issues of the contemporary world would need to be kept in the forefront. As such, the needs and challenges of today must be responded to suitably. *Globalisation and liberalisation on the one hand, and localisation on the other*, are going to have tremendous impact on the future society. These have already brought about many economic and social challenges and opportunities which need to be addressed effectively for building a strong and a cohesive Indian and World Society. It also calls for developing intelligent learners, who are prepared to face new challenges and adjust to unfamiliar situations. In a democratic set-up with decentralisation of power, local governance such as 'Panchayati Raj' has gained importance. It aims at raising the levels of participation and involvement of people in governance. In order to make optimum utilisation of resources for development, the local governance has to be more responsive and efficient. A well-designed social sciences curriculum would help learners '*think globally and act locally*'.

In a world of ever-increasing knowledge, selection and organisation of the content areas assume great importance. The social sciences curriculum has thus to be comprehensive, and yet not heavily loaded with information. Interrelatedness of ideas must be kept in view. It would also be desirable to emphasise the process of learning and thinking, rather than mere acquisition of facts.

These themes may be drawn from Geography, History, Civics, Economics and Sociology in a balanced manner and suitably graded—simple to complex immediate to remote and general to specific.

The study of Indian civilisation and its rich cultural heritage along with other world civilisations and their interconnections may be the major area of study drawn from history. The constituents of social sciences have their own distinct characteristics and hence deserve independent treatment in their own right. This is being attempted hereunder starting with their respective objectives.

42.2 The Concept of Social Studies

The school as an important social institution has to discharge its responsibility in the context of the purposes that society desires to fulfil through it. One of our avowed national goals is the *establishment of a vital democracy* through the development of an enlightened and responsible citizenry imbued with an abiding faith in democratic principles and processes. The school undoubtedly has to play an important role in the achievement of this aim, and undoubtedly a large share of responsibility is to be shouldered by the subject which goes by the name of Social Studies. Educational theory holds that the school is responsible for the education of the child, and that this responsibility cannot be fragmented and the fragments allotted to special fields of knowledge. It nevertheless, is also true that particular subjects must assume primary responsibility for the realisation of one or more of the general aims of education. Social Studies thus becomes the specific subject which has primary responsibility in helping to develop a body of devoted, active, well-informed and discriminating citizens, who participate effectively, and of their free will, in the affairs of the locality, the State, the Nation and the World.

Social Studies is a field of study which deals with man, his relations with other men, and his environment. One of the primary concerns of Social Studies, therefore, is to promote an understanding of man's ways of living, his basic needs, the activities in which he engages to meet his needs—social, economic, cultural and political—and the institutions he has developed.

Over and above this, Social Studies keeps before itself, the all-pervading educational purpose of developing a national and scientific approach to social problems and issues. This can be fulfilled only by fostering in the learners, the ability to discern the point at issue, to sift the relevant from the irrelevant, to marshal ideas in a logical sequence and to express themselves with lucidity and effectiveness.

By and large, Social Studies seeks to further the objectives that a general education programme attempts to attain, and therefore, it is to be regarded as an indispensable part of general education.

The Social Studies syllabus can be organised in a variety of ways, so long as its content, organisation and teaching methods do not stand in the way of achieving the purpose to be attained. Thus, both the 'integrated' approach, which it seeks to use and the organisation of the components of social science subjects as independent subjects can be pursued. This is often attempted to be done by combining the knowledge and skills provided by the many social science subjects in a good social studies curriculum proposes.

Social and technological developments are constantly exerting diverse influences on social studies and as such:

- The concept of Social Studies as an area of study too has been changing ever since its inclusion in school curriculum.
- The study of man in his environment has become the central theme of Social Studies.
- It is more of an integrated approach than a disciplinary one. Hence it draws its content from various social sciences.
- Social Studies is concieved as a dynamic subject and helps to build, defend and strengthen democracy.
- The concept of Social Studies largely determines the scope of the subject, and to a great degree, the techniques of teaching it.

Social sciences are the most suited areas of study for integrating almost all the core components of the curriculum. Emphasis, however, has to be laid more on the economic, political and social aspects of human environment, especially of the contemporary world, for nurturing a national identity, equality of sexes, removal of social barriers, fundamental rights and fundamental duties and human rights including the rights of the child, may be suitably integrated with related themes. Its teaching must be objective and *free from all kinds of stereotyped images, biases prejudices and superstitions.*

Field work, project work and group activities should preferably form the basis of teaching and learning in social sciences. Projects having direct links with the local community may be encouraged. Economic and politico-legal literacy, grievance redressal systems and consumer education deserve to be promoted through it.

Although pre-primary and primary education naturally does not deal with the study of social sciences, and is part of Environmental Studies, social development of the child surely remains a major objective to be achieved at this stage of education. To attain this objective, a variety of activities and programmes are directed at providing ample opportunities for a child to interact with other children, and with his physical and natural environment. Education at this stage aims at, along with other things, developing in the child *desirable social attitudes and manners, which would prepare him for a healthy social participation and sensitise him to rights and privileges of others.*

There are and can be different approaches to the treatment of social studies in the school curriculum. The most common of these is enunciated below. In Grades I and II, the child could be introduced to the environment as a whole, without making any clear-cut distinction between natural and social elements that go into its making. It could be called Environmental Studies. In Grades III–V, while the environmental focus should continue, the physical and social aspects of the environment could be introduced into social studies as a broad and composite area of study, parallel to integrated general science. The social studies at this stage should widen the child's mental horizon from his/her home, school and neighbourhood to the state, country and the world. Stories and narratives about major aspects of our cultural heritage and great personalities, events and developments that have acted as major influences in shaping the life of man in India and elsewhere may also be a part of the curriculum.

At the Upper Primary Stage, the study of social sciences could comprise the study of history, geography, civics and related contemporary issues and problems of the society. The learner at this stage should be initiated into the study of India's past in all its major aspects such as social, cultural and scientific development. He/she should also be helped to appreciate diversities in the ways of living and interdependence of various regions of India and the world. He/she should know the civic and political institutions and be enabled to understand contemporary social and economic conditions and problems. Social skills, civic competencies and a national perspective would thus motivate him to inculcate desirable attitudes to participate in the task of social and economic reconstruction.

The components of the environment and their interaction may be studied in terms of processes and patterns. The learners may be encouraged to investigate and undertake studies pertaining to various physical and man-made features, phenomena and events. They may be enabled to recognise simple patterns such as rainfall distribution in the country and patterns of agricultural and urban land uses.

The learners need to be helped to understand and appreciate India's cultural heritage along with some of the other ancient civilisations of the world and their interconnections.

The contemporary society, including the social, political and economic institutions of India and of some other countries and their functioning, the administrative system, urbanisation and economic social and industrial development may be some other areas to be included. In addition to academic skills, social skills and civic competencies may be developed to help them grow and participate effectively in day-to-day life situations.

At the Secondary Stage, the study of social sciences could assume a more diversified approach comprising elements of History, Geography, Civics and Economics to promote an understanding of contemporary India. He/she could be introduced to the stages of development of human civilisation and to the historical forces that shape it the contemporary historical perspective of India's heritage, and the struggle for freedom should also be focussed upon. The other social science subjects should help him/her in understanding Indian society, polity and economy and the social, economic and political challenges facing the country. The study of social sciences at this stage should also develop his/her understanding of contemporary world problems, and of India's role in relation to problems like world peace and international cooperation, decolonisation and safeguarding of human rights.

42.3 Objectives of Teaching Social Studies

The formulation of the objectives of Social Studies is crucial for:

- the development of curriculum and curriculum material.
- the transaction of the curriculum with a view to realising the targets set.
- the identification of appropriate evaluation techniques, and for the construction of evaluation tools.

These objectives can be enunciated as under:

To acquire the knowledge and understanding of:

- ➢ the diverse cultural streams that have come together and influenced each other to form a composite Indian culture.
- ➢ the continuous part of global developments which Indian culture has been.
- ➢ the nature of the assimilation of modern developments in the Indian society as an integrated Indian culture.

To acquire an appreciation that:

- ➢ change has been the essence of social history.
- ➢ change for the better is an outcome of the cooperative effort of the people.
- ➢ change of lasting value has not been imposed from outside but has emerged from within the culture—sometimes even assisted by external causes.
- ➢ change has been a reciprocal phenomenon, where India has both contributed to, and received from, other cultures and peoples.

To strive for sharing the benefits of scientific and technological developments with all, without any discrimination.

To effectively utilise the scientific methods in solving our problems.

To appreciate the need for providing appropriate avenues for the fruitful and enjoyable use of leisure, which has come to be available because of technological developments.

To espouse a patriotic pride based on a fair and just appreciation of the past and hope for a bright future.

To learn to be tolerant and respectful to others with a spirit of learning from others.

To develop faith and confidence in solving our problems, and devising ways and means for doing so.

To develop the ability for using simple tools like maps, charts, globe, compass for making learning meaningful.

To acquire the ability to collect, compile, present and interpret different types of information, and to apply and use it

To appreciate the impact of the Physical Environment on the growth and development of the global societies in so far as different types of social development are due to varying kinds of interaction between man and the environment, and not due to any inherent inferiority and superiority of a people or an environment.

To appreciate the problems of contemporary India in terms of Goals and Resources.

To acquire the ability for creating necessary conditions for promoting democratic values among individuals, society and the state.

To work for the creation of a world order based on cooperation, mutual respect and peaceful co-existence.

To develop the abilities for working as a team member.

To acquire the ability to think critically and evaluate the accuracy and dependability of the information for taking decisions.

42.4 Methods of Teaching Social Studies

Some Fundamental Postulates

Social Studies is concerned more with the development of values and attitudes, than with collecting conserving and dispensing information.

The general principles of education assume a special form and direction in teaching Social Studies.

Widening the horizon of the child should be the central goal of teaching Social Studies.

Effective learning takes place when learning experiences are objective-based.

Social studies teaching becomes more vivid illustrative and interesting, when they make use of children's environment and experiences.

Teaching-learning activities become effective devices when they take care of individual differences, interests and potentials of the students.

Some main methods of teaching which can be successfully pressed into service in teaching Social Studies, and particularly so in primary classes, suggested by the book entitled 'Teaching of Social Studies', brought out by the National Council of Educational Research and Training, New Delhi are:

The Observation Method

- Direct experiences are more effective in the process of learning, and are retained for a longer period of time.

- First hand information is a motivating force for further enquiry.
- Immediate surroundings and the community afford many opportunities for observation.
- Observation necessitates well planned and well directed steps and procedure.
- A teacher in the background is much more effective than in the dominant role.

The Discussion Method

- The Discussion Method fosters critical thinking among the pupils and makes them active participants in the learning process.
- Discussion Method in the teaching of Social Studies leads to lasting learning.
- The success of the Discussion Method depends upon the involvement of the maximum number of students.
- Discussion Method generates a healthy rapport between the teacher and the taughts.

Project Method

- Knowledge is best gained when it is an outcome of some purposeful activity enlisting the involvement of pupils.
- Project method amply caters to individual differences, and students learn best when engaged in activities that interest them.
- Productive and creative activities play a very significant role in teaching Social Studies.
- Working in a team and accepting responsibility in a group lead to socialisation of the individual.

Socialised Reaction

The most commonly known and used techniques of socialised reaction are:

- Seminars
- Workshops
- Symposium
- Panel discussion
- Brains trust

Socialised reaction eliminates the limitations of the traditional and formal class-room teaching.

The development of social attributes is possible only through interactions in a large variety of socialised situations.

Socialised reaction secures better teacher pupil relationship in an environment of freedom.

Social reaction requires active participation by all the members of the group in all the activities.

Utilising Community Resources

- Some of the richest instructional resources for the teaching of Social Studies are to be found in the local community.
- The relationship between the school and the community determines to a great extent the quality of educational programmes.
- Utilising community resources provides direct and abiding experiences to learners.

Utilising Current Events

- Current events profoundly reflect the ever changing pattern of the social environment.
- Current events have an inalienable relationship with social issues and problems.
- Current events greatly influence the socio-economic and cultural environment of the community.
- Current events should be described objectively in their realistic background.
- Current events help in bringing a close relationship between the school and the world outside the school.

43

Teaching of History

43.1 The Genesis of History*

History can be regarded as one of the most ancient of the branches of knowledge. The word 'history' derives its origin from a Greek word; it meant 'enquiry' or 'learning by enquiry'. It was assumed that one could and should learn from the experiences of the preceding generations by studying their successes and failures. But in course of time, it became confined to the narratives of the achievement of kings and accounts of battles.

By the 18th century, philosophers began to view history as primarily the study of man in society, and based their political doctrines on their views of history. History then became the study of society as a whole in all its aspects. Changes and growth of societies thus became the subjects of study by historians. In the 19th century, attempts were made to evolve a comprehensive and systematic scheme, which would explain the entire historical development of mankind, and would help in weaving historical events in a logical system of cause and effect. Society as a whole, and the forces and factors leading to its development, became the content of history.

43.2 Some Recent Theories of History

In the later part of the 19th and early years of the 20th century, when science became all-important, history began to be considered as the true science of society, and as such called the "Science of Sciences". [Not only historians, but also political scientists and philosopher then began to study this 'Science of Sciences'.] According to one view, we designate as historians "those scholars who seek to organise the facts that a historian collects, according to the principle of causality."

The term History today is used for that field of study which treats 'History as actuality' or history as a science. It may be defined as an endeavour to reconstruct past events with the help of their remnants and records.

---

* *Source*: 'Teaching of History', NCERT 1970.

The ascertainment of facts that he collects, is the first essential requirement of a historian. The verification of facts, however, presents a serious problem. Remains of the past, that come down to us in the form of archaeological and other physical evidences are in a changed and damaged form. But with the help of modern techniques, we can now detect defects and forgeries. The difficulty is greater when the historian tries to reconstruct the past with the aid of written records, documents, reports, chronicles, etc.

A major difference between the nature of history and other social and physical sciences, arises due to the purposiveness, which in historical events, links effects to causes.

The word should be understood in the sense of a hypothesis or assumption (as in physical sciences), as the starting point of study, as an aid to understanding.

Further information is subsequently collected and the hypothesis is tested in its light.

But no interpretations are ever considered absolutely final. They are not so even in the natural sciences. Constant research to uncover more facts offer new interpretations on the basis of other hypothesis and critical investigation of the work of others will result in the formulation of more correct interpretations.

The means of formulating and examining—hypothesis and developing generalisations, is to inter-relate the facts of historical phenomena into meaningful patterns of cause and effect relationships.

An important question related to causality in history is *the role of incidents and accidents in history*. The view that history is, by and large, a charter of accidents, a series of events determined by chance coincidences, is too superficial to be considered here. The role and significance of accidents in historical phenomena, and their relation with the idea of causality however, do need some consideration.

What has been said of the role of accidents is, generally speaking, true of the role of individuals also. Here we are concerned particularly with the role of great men and how far they have affected the course of history. The great man is historically important because he is an outstanding individual. What is necessary, however, is to treat him as belonging to history and not as some one outside it.

Thus, great-men and their role should be understood in relation to the social and economic forces, how they are the products and agents of those forces, and how far they are the creators of those forces.

It has to be more a study of the society in which he lives, its trends and tendencies, its potentialities of development, and only in the last, a study of the specific role which the great men played in bringing about developments that they are credited with.

Interpretations invariably involve value-judgements. The precise nature of these value-judgements, to be scientific, depends not on one's personal and moral predilections, but on certain objective criteria.

These criteria, to be scientific, cannot be deduced from outside history. They have but to be rooted in the entire content of human history, i.e., in social evolution through the ages. This means that the consideration of social evolution would be the historian's basic criterion.

Acceptance of the idea of progress in history should not, however, be taken to mean that this progress is in an unbroken chain, without reverses, deviations and breaks.

Progress consists in man's increased mastery over environment, and in the accumulation, both of material resources and scientific knowledge. It also implies man's increased control over the social environment and progressive development of human potentialities. In this sense, historical developments and progress go side by side.

History has become one of the most important areas of social sciences. *It has thus travelled a long way, from a story of rulers and their achievements to a scientific study of societies and their evolution.* This new perspective of History is aimed at deepening man's knowledge of the processes of social change. By learning about our social, economic, political and cultural development in the past, we understand our present more accurately.

After these general observations on the nature of history, we can now turn to our own historical writings and their main characteristics. Many chronologies of rulers were produced, for instance, the *Vanshavalis* and the *Puranas*.

There is some evidence of attempts to describe and connect events on the basis of causal relationships also. Kalhana's *Rajatarangini* is an example of such an attempt.

The explanation of this lies perhaps in the concepts that dominated the religious and philosophical thinking of the people in ancient India. The existing social system was sanctified by religion, and hence was considered permanent. The theory of *Karma* which was an important belief in ancient India meant that the consequences of one's actions are determined by the goodness or badness of those actions.

Consequently, there is a dearth of historical writings. *Rajatarangini,* described as a proper historical work is a notable exception. Its author Kalhana seems to have possessed a conception of the proper data or sources of History. He seems to have taken pains to check his facts by consulting ordinances of former kings relating to religious foundations and grants, inscriptions, as well as written records.

When we move on to the second period of Indian history—the medieval period—or to be more specific, the period of the Turks and the Mughals the situation about recording history considerably improves. Hence it may be necessary to mention the highly developed traditions of historical writing that the Turks and the Mughals inherited from the Arabs, who in turn were influenced by Greek historiography.

The main trend in Turkish-Mughal historiography however remains that of the court chronicles. Every ruler in this period had a chronicler who recorded the events of his reign and the reigns of his predecessors. These chroniclers often wrote pure eulogies of the kings under whom they served.

With a careful reading of these works, the attempts of the chroniclers at misrepresentation become obvious, and one is not able to draw a correct picture of the actual situation from them. Generally speaking, the material of medieval historiography is the court and the events connected with it, to the neglect of treatment of society, culture, and economy.

Modern history writing in India is said to begin with the British conquest and the formation of the *Asiatic Societies*. The main purpose was to understand the habits and customs of the people, the knowledge of which was necessary for the purpose of administration. This led to the search of and translating of ancient texts, and to the development of ethnology.

But after 1857, when the British Government took direct charge of Indian administration, the details of imperial policy were worked out for various aspects of political and cultural life.

In subsequent works by English historians, history was deliberately distorted. References to social life were almost completely omitted. Passages referring to tyranny of the kings and conflicts were given prominence. Conflicts, wars, tyranny, bloodshed—this was the picture presented of India before the British conquest. This was done to eulogize the British rule and contrast it with the tyranny of the previous periods. Naturally, the historians who later on worked on the basis of such sources drew conclusions which presented a distorted picture of Indian history.

The next period of modern Indian historiography was the period of the early stages of the rise of Indian nationalism. This resulted in a glorification of the ancient past to fulfil a psychological need, i.e. "the compensation of our sense of political and economic denial". This history was preoccupied with political history again to the detriment of the social and economic facets. The scope of these works was limited to narrating events without much analysis.

An awareness of the objectives that we seek to realise through the teaching of history is necessary. These objectives should be understood in the context of the needs of a developing, secular and socialist democracy. Another important necessity to be kept in view is the question of emotional and national integration, without which our concept of secular and socialist society cannot be realised.

In the first instance; the teaching of history in school should lead to the realisation that *history is the study of the process of social change and development*; that the world of man is not stationary but subject to constant and continuous movement, change and development.

History teaching should therefore help in deepening the pupil's knowledge of the character of the society he lives in. The failures of the past become a warning to him, in tackling the contemporary problems and successes, become a matter of pride and encouragement. History should also promote a deepening of the awareness of social and political weaknesses, so that the necessary conclusions in eliminating those weaknesses may be drawn.

The study of Indian history should arouse in students the feeling of love for his motherland by promoting his understanding of the true national heritage, of how this heritage came about, and of how we have assimilated various races, religions and cultures. It should give due emphasis to the processes of growth and synthesis of our culture, as also unity and diversity of this culture. He should be enabled to realise that *unlike the West, India does not discard and reject the past but assimilates it*.

The pupil, through the teaching of history, should also thus be made familiar with human heritage as a whole.

43.3 Instructional Objectives of History

It is in the context of the above, that the objectives of teaching history have been spelled out as under:

1. To acquire the knowledge of terms, concepts, facts, events, symbols, ideas, problems, trends, personalities, chronologies, generalisations etc. related to the study of History.
2. To develop the understanding of terms, facts, principles, events, trends, etc. related to the study of History and their relationships.
3. To develop the ability of critical and logical thinking.
4. To develop practical skills helpful in the study and understanding of historical phenomena.
5. To develop interest in the study of History.
6. To develop healthy social attitudes.

Objectives and their Specifications

43.3.1 *Objectives: To acquire the knowledge of terms, concepts, facts, events, ideas, problems, trends, personalities, chronologies, generalisations etc. related to the study of History.*

Specifications of the Objective:

To demonstrate the achievement of the above objective, the pupil:

1. recalls facts, terms, concepts, events, etc.
2. recognises facts, terms, concepts, events, etc.

3. shows information on maps, charts, diagrams, etc.
4. reads information presented in various forms.

43.3.2 *Objective: To develop an understanding of terms, facts, principles, events, trends etc. related to the study of History and their relationships.*

Specifications of the Objective:

To demonstrate the achievement of the above objective, the pupil:

1. classifies facts, terms, concepts etc.
2. compares and contrasts events, trends, concepts, etc.
3. illustrates events, trends etc. by citing examples.
4. discriminates between the significant and insignificant, important and less important causes, events, etc.
5. identifies relationship between causes and effects, means and ends, etc.
6. arranges facts, trends etc. in a particular known sequence.
7. detects errors in the statements and rectifies them.
8. summarises information from various sources.
9. interprets maps, charts, extracts etc. from the different sources of History.

43.3.3 *Objective: To develop the ability of critical and logical thinking about history.*

Specifications of the Objective:

To demonstrate the achievement of the above objective, the pupil:

1. identifies the problem.
2. analyses the problem.
3. interprets problems with implications.
4. sets up hypothesis.
5. selects relevant facts, principles, etc.
6. establishes relationships.
7. advances arguments in support of contentions.
8. draws inferences and generalisations.
9. verifies the inferences.
10. predicts.
11. evaluates.

43.3.4 *Objective: To develop practical skills helpful in the study and understanding of historical phenomena.*

Specifications of the Objective:

To demonstrate the achievement of the above objective, the pupil:

1. draws historical maps, charts, diagrams etc.
2. prepares models, time freezes etc.

43.3.5 *Objectives: To develop interest in the study of History.*

Specifications of the Objective:

To demonstrate the achievement of the above objective, the pupil:

1. collects coins of different periods of History and other types of historical material.
2. prepares illustrative materials, aids etc.
3. participates in historical dramas and mock presentations of historical events.
4. visits places of historical interest, archaeological sites, museums and archives.
5. reads historical documents, maps and charts.
6. plays an active role in the activities of the History Association/Club.
7. writes articles on historical and other related topics.

43.3.6 *Objective: To develop healthy social attitudes.*

Specifications of the Objective:

To demonstrate the achievement of the above objective, the pupil:

1. acquires and displays a sense of patriotism.
2. shows respect towards other peoples opinions, ideas, beliefs, and ways of life.
3. reads about other faiths and religions.
4. establishes friendship with pupils of other communities and faiths.
5. practises the spirit of noble ideals.
6. co-operates with others in social and civic activities.
7. appreciates cultural variations.
8. appreciates the contributions made by various civilisations.
9. appreciates the interdependence of nations and peoples.
10. appreciates and supports the need for settling disputes among nations in a peaceful manner.
11. believes in the equality of man irrespective of caste, creed, religion, sex and colour.
12. appreciates the role of UNO, expouses the causes it stands for and endeavours to contribute to them.

43.4 Methods of Teaching History

History is most certainly a ticklish subject to teach, and the framers of curriculum, besides keeping in mind that History is supposed to deal with facts, have also to take into consideration the age of the children and the impressionable minds they have at that age. The selection of content at different levels of education has therefore to be judicious, exercising great care and caution. Young minds need not be introduced to items which may create in them hatred or bigotory. There are certain things, which even though facts, may pollute their thinking at an early age. They may know and learn about them at a later stage when for example, they undertake higher studies or do research on the subject.

Times have changed and so also traditions, but facts of history have to be rationally explained to children without any bias, to enable them to understand the past and the present rationally. This is the solemn duty of the curriculum framers, and more particularly, of the textbook writers and teachers. The facts of History do need a critical analysis for imparting to the students the real meaning and significance of the subject.

Students should be enabled to realise that in writing History, the historian only collects information and analyses it. He has not seen that period or lived through those periods to be an eye witness, but his ideas and ideology do certainly get imbued in his writings. The situation becomes worse because history was not systematically written in the past to be preserved for reference by posterity. The evidences related are not many, and they are these that have become subjects of interpretations by Historians. Though based on the same few sources, these interpretations were made on the basis of their respective backgrounds. Both accident and design worked in imparting different hues to them, and these really have become so-called controversies because all of them are like six blind men, who went to see an elephant. Some hold the tail to take the elephant to be like a rope, others his legs to take it like a pillar and so on. One has, therefore, to be extremely careful in teaching about controversial issues in history where there could be honest differences of opinion. The background of the historians has first to be explained to children before telling them what they said, if that is a subject of controversy. Students should, in these situations, must never be allowed to get waylaid with emotions, but restrained by reason by the teacher.

The teaching of history should be objective and free from any communal, parochial and other prejudices. The perspective of the past should help in understanding the contemporary developments. Independent work by the learners through challenging assignments and project work should be encouraged. Group activities such as organising youth parliament, seminars and discussions should be increasingly used to encourage the learners participation. These exercises would enable them to appreciate that points of view, could be different. The study of newspapers and the use of newspaper clippings in teaching and learning are of particular importance in promoting an understanding of contemporary events and problems.

The controversial issues have but to be introduced at the secondary and the senior secondary stage, and discussions in the class could be held about them. Again, the background of the Historians be brought forth, along with the contexts of the contemporary society of the time, about which the references have been made, besides of course, the times when the historians made their observations. These must all be carefully presented by the teachers. Simple quotations from the writings of the historians will be very inadequate teaching material. At such moments of time, particularly in higher classes, the students may be encouraged to refer to original sources. But again, it will be the onerous duty of the teacher to tell the students about the period of time, the sources available at that time and the mindset of the historian.

In teaching History, one of the prime purposes is to forge national integration and to systematically avoid references which may create chasms between different groups of people of different backgrounds in terms of religious faiths, ideologies, ways of life, customs and traditions. History as taught should not hurt anybody's feelings. What has to be highlighted more are similarities rather than differences, to promote the acceptance of the idea of unity in diversity, as an instrument of cultural enrichment, social cohesion and economic progress.

The methods and techniques of teaching enunciated earlier could be singly and jointly used in teaching History.

44

Teaching of Geography

Geography as such has to be understood in a much wider context than a mere description of continents and countries, land and sea, rivers, plains, deserts, mountains.

44.1 The Concept and Scope of Geography

Geography as a subject of school curriculum is unique in many ways. It is therefore that its concept needs to be clearly understood and appreciated.

What is studied in geography? It is a question which may bother any inquisitive student, even at the elementary stage. Not many school teachers will come forward to answer such a query satisfactorily. This also explains to some extent, the muddle in geographic instruction. The pupil's worry is that all sorts of things—number of planets, eclipses, mountains, forests, deserts, rivers, dresses, customs, and what not under the sky—find a place in a geography course. But, at the same time, these form the topics of a much more comprehensive and deeper study under some other disciplines too. Sometimes it is thought that all this sort of general information should be imparted to pupils, but there is no suitable subject other than geography which can conveniently act as '*omnium gatherum*' at the school stage. What a role to play! Notwithstanding the much matured stature of geography at higher stages of education, even now it continues to show its old ill-defined nature at the school stage and particularly so at the elementary level.

Each subject has its own system of meanings. Important aspects of such a system are a viewpoint, a logic, a clearly defined purpose and a method of enquiry peculiar to itself. "The concept of a discipline implies a subject which has power within itself, its own unique and special contribution which is quite distinct from that of other disciplines." How is it then that we call geography a discipline?

Phenix, calls the instructional facility 'the distinguishing mark of any discipline', which is helped by its three basic qualities: *analytic simplification, synthetic coordination and dynamism*. To put it briefly, in proceeding analytically, the most basic elements are abstracted, thereby reducing the multiplicity of concepts. The abstractions are then synthesised, leading to more comprehensive patterns. These patterns are not static, they grow and modify as and when new abstractions come to the fore. A discipline is thus a living body of knowledge.

Geography as a discipline exhibits these characteristics and distinguishes itself by its peculiar approach to simplifying and synthesising concepts or 'generic structures', whatever they be called. The most fundamental of these may be taken to form its frame-work. Some of them which deserve particular mention are:

(a) Man and Land relationships
(b) Spatial relationships
(c) Cause-effect relationships
(d) Synthesis or whole view
(e) Change or dynamism.

These constitute the core of the methods of teaching geography.

A Study of Man and Land Relationship

Man is, no doubt, the central element in the study of Geography, but only in relation to his environment, for there are several other facets of the study of man which are the subject matter of several other disciplines. Environment is both inorganic and organic, and treating geography as '*organic response to inorganic control*' is a century old concept. The environment is both natural and man-made with man himself being an active agent of change. Kant was interested in geography, in as much as the earth was the 'home of man.' Ritter refers to geography as the study of earth as 'dwelling place of man.' Hartshorne considers "the purpose of geography to read: the study that seeks to provide scientific description of the earth as the world of man." On closer examination, it becomes evident that this man and land relationship works both ways, and is interactive in nature.

This has a variety of implications for geography teachers. At the school stage only the 'hard core' of the subject matter and not its specialities should engage us. For instance, the physical geography by itself can at best be taught as background knowledge.

A Study of Spatial Relationship

Davis calls geography a study of relations. These relations are 'spatial' and 'causal'. The spatial relations have two dimensions—locational and distributional. There is not much difference between the two. Location concerns itself with identification of the place, and distribution, with patterns of such placements. If the place or space is viewed in wider connotation, the distinction ceases altogether.

However, if geography concerned itself with only spatial relations, it could hardly claim a separate identity. Rather, it could form, the regional aspect, of many other disciplines such as zoo-geography, medical geography, etc. All sorts of phenomena have regional or spatial occurrences (where a variety of aspects are taken into account collectively but we also study regions for special aspects just as the distribution of malaria, rainfall, cattle, etc.). The question then arises: When do we call it geography?

Whenever spatial relationship or patterns are studied as part of geography, even for a single aspect, the basic frame remains man-land interaction in its generic form.

A Study of Cause and Effect Relationship

There are phenomena: cultural or otherwise, which are products of man-land relationship, such as an industry, a crop or the like. It may be better to substitute the term environment for inorganic to accommodate the growing scope of modern geography. Causation is seldom one way, especially when it concerns living beings, in which case its interactive character becomes important. Spatial interaction is the essense of geographical studies. It gives rise to such phenomena as movement of goods, migration of people etc. Although spatial relation is in the foreground of the geographical study, the importance of time or temporal relationship can by no means be ignored, especially when the 'why' aspect is being studied.

A Study of Synthesis or Whole View

Irrespective of the character of relationship under study, geography should not be studied in isolation, for variables are interlinked. Hence, interactive and interdependent character of the phenomenon is to be visualised.

The region or regionalisation is the soul of geography. The region is an area of any size, homogeneous in respect of one or more specific criteria. In the context of geography, these criteria flow from the basic premise of Man-Land relationship. It, however, needs to be borne in mind that there can be no perfect system of regions, mainly because Man-Land relationship is interactive, and hence everchanging.

In the interests of a proper 'wholeness', the present alone will not serve the purpose. Historical background, i.e. temporal relationship should, whenever necessary, be explored as a legitimate part of a geographical study. Even a projection into future could be very meaningful.

A Study of Change or Dynamism

The aerial associations and spatial interactions with which geographers are primarily pre-occupied, are always in a state of flux. *There are varying themes of change, evolution, revolution, stagnation, progress; tradition, innovation, retardation, acceleration and such others.*

Change is spiral. Although geography seeks to concentrate on the study of the present, still one of the basic components of its study remains the change, which is because the present is transient.

To sum up, modern geography deals with distribution (where), the causality (why) and the effects (what), concerning the inter-relationship between man and his environment.

44.2 History of Geography

The discussion on the nature of geography will not be complete without a reference to some important current view-points concerning it. This will, in turn, necessitate a *look-back into the past of this discipline.*

The *ancients* began the study of geography, both for practical considerations and intellectual curiosity. Collection of information and reducing it to compact narratives was then a sheer necessity. At the intellectual level, geography helped them in pattern making in mathematics and in astronomy—the two erstwhile prestigious intellectual pursuits. Then came the *middle ages*, characterised by religious dogmatism, invasions, migrations and various acts of violence. Little theoretical progress was made during this period, though compilations of information went unabated. With *Renaissance* in Europe, geography took a new turn with the demand for systematic study of empirically derived knowledge. Mercantilism came in its wake, and the study of geography began with the purpose of furthering immediate economic activities and satisfaction of wander-lust, characteristic of this age.

Growing economic prosperity gave fillip to pursuit of science and humanities. Scholars like Kant, Varenius, Humboldt and Ritter came on the scene, who sought to systematise the study of geography. Geography then received a theoretical base—its philosophy and view-point. By the middle of the 19th century, it not only took a definite shape of its own, but began to bear off-springs such as geology, meteorology, anthropology and oceanography.

Then came the era of great scientific and technological developments. Apart from increasing specialisation in geography, man began to see in himself as the maker of his own destiny. The emphasis began to shift from passive adaptation to positive modification of natural environment. The 'home of man' or the 'story of man' aspects began to get importance. The scientific trend was humanised. The task was facilitated by the emergence of Social Sciences. Geography thereby became both scientific and humane. The methodology grew more and more refined, and the canvas of the subject got widened. Some of the conspicuous new view-points could be identified as below:

(a) Man as a geographical factor
(b) Regional concept in the context of systematic studies
(c) Terrestrial unity and internationalism
(d) Socio-cultural study of the earth
(e) Humanistic view-point

(f) Quantification
(g) Environmental planning

44.3 Instructional Objectives of Geography

In the context of the above paradigms, the objectives of teaching geography could be enunciated as under:

1. To acquire the knowledge (information) of facts, events, terms, concepts, principles, generalisations, hypotheses, problems, methods, trends, symbols, tools, techniques, processes etc. concerning Geography.
2. To develop an understanding of terms, concepts, principles, generalisations, trends, symbols, processes etc. related to the study of Geography.
3. To apply the acquired knowledge in unfamiliar (new) situations.
4. To acquire practical skills related to the study of Geography.
5. To develop interests related to Geography.
6. To develop positive attitudes towards people and environment, both natural and cultural.

Objectives and their Specifications

44.3.1 ***Objective: To acquire the knowledge (information) of facts, events, terms, concepts, principles, generalisations, hypotheses, problems, methods, trends, symbols, tools, techniques, processes etc. concerning Geography.***

Specifications of the Objective:

To demonstrate the achievement of the above objective, the pupil:

1. recalls facts, terms, concepts, principles, processes etc.
2. recognises facts, terms etc.
3. indicates information involving substantive drawing skill on maps, charts, diagrams etc.
4. reads information represented in various forms such as maps, charts, diagrams, graphs, tables etc., which does not require interpretations.

44.3.2 ***Objective: To develop an understanding of terms, concepts, principles, generalisations, trends, symbols, processes etc. related to the study of Geography.***

Specifications of the Objective:

To demonstrate the achievement of the above objective, the pupil:

1. translates information from one form of communication to another.
2. distinguishes (discriminates or differentiates) between different closely related facts, terms etc.
3. compares.

4. contrasts.
5. classifies.
6. arranges facts, statements, articles in a particular sequence—logical, chronological.
7. explains (gives meaning, elucidates or clarifies)
8. summarises (gives the gist of the material read)
9. cites illustrations.
10. detects errors.
11. rectifies errors.
12. identifies relationships (cause and effect, end and means etc.)
13. extrapolates beyond some given data or communication.
14. interpolates simple gaps in data.
15. interprets (gives meaning to) data (information) presented in various forms.

44.3.3 *Objective: To apply the acquired knowledge of Geography in unfamiliar (new) situations.*

Specifications of the Objective:

To demonstrate the achievement of the above objective, the pupil:

1. analyses a particular situation to identify the problem, or to detect the central idea/viewpoint.
2. identifies the underlying and unstated assumptions.
3. selects relevant knowledge of (facts, principles, etc.) to explain new situations or to solve problems.
4. judges adequacy, completeness, reliability, authenticity, relevance, essentiality, verifiability etc. of the data or any other evidence.
5. reorganises (restructures or improvises) the material or communication, showing ingenuity or novelty in approach.
6. establishes relationships not hitherto known to him.
7. formulates hypothesis.
8. verifies (checks the consistency or accuracy of) hypothesis.
9. generalises principles, laws etc.
10. predicts outcomes in a given situation.
11. draws inferences.
12. relates new elements with already learnt organised body of knowledge.
13. states the criterion used in the analysis of a complex body of data or communications.
14. examines or evaluates an issue critically by sifting evidence, using proper criteria and offering interpretations.
15. establishes connection between criterion and judgement.

44.3.4 *Objective: To acquire practical skills related to the study of Geography.*

Specifications of the Objective:

To demonstrate the achievement of the above objective, the pupil:

1. draws maps, charts, diagrams and other such graphical forms to depict geographical information.
2. prepares models, and improvises apparatus, etc.
3. handles instruments, apparatus, etc. efficiently.
4. preserves specimens and other exhibits of geographical interest appropriately.
5. handles and displays various materials of geographical significance.
6. makes observations accurately and objectively.

44.3.5 *Objective: To develop interests related to Geography.*

Specifications of the Objective:

To demonstrate the achievement of the above objective, the pupil:

1. reads literature related to Geography on ones own.
2. collects geographical information from books, newspapers, etc.
3. desires to know about life and activities of people of different regions.
4. participates in the activities of the School Geography Circle/Club.
5. collects articles of geographical interest such as specimen, pictures, etc.
6. advances relevant geographical reasons to explain various human activities and natural phenomena.
7. observes geographical phenomenon keenly.
8. visits places of geographical interest.
9. pursues hobbies related to the study of Geography such as sketching, modelling, photography, etc.

44.3.6 *Objective: To develop positive attitudes towards people and environment, both natural and cultural.*

Specifications of the Objective:

To demonstrate the achievement of the above objective, the pupil:

1. recognises the contribution made by various regions and peoples to the growth of modern civilisation.
2. recognises the significance of interaction between man and his environment.
3. realises the importance of inter-dependence at various levels among states, countries, regions, etc. for better and fuller life.
4. shows fellow-feeling and sympathy for groups of people other than his own group in one's country, or outside.

5. considers local problems in the national context, and national problems in international context.
6. realises the importance of the conservation of natural resources.
7. appreciates the need of population control for better economic planning and prosperity.
8. appreciates the limits to which natural resources can be optimally utilised by man.

44.4 Methods of Teaching Geography

(Like its subject matter, geography uses both adopted and adapted methods and techniques of different disciplines to suit its peculiar requirements.) Uniqueness lies in their permutations and combinations. Some of the broad categories of these methods and techniques are briefly described below:

Regionalisation is an important method in geographical study. It is essentially an inductive approach in which all possible information about spatial distribution, is to be collected and analysed. Common elements in required dimensions are identified, and groupings are made to arrive at regions. It is an analytico-synthetic process, which can either use differentiation or association as procedural approaches. The region is geographer's principal generalisation and a method of study.

Ecological Systematisation (ecosystem): It can be a descriptive name for the sample method. Both man and nature are intrinsic to the character of an area. So intimate, is their interaction that they can only be separated at the peril of inviting the cursed 'dualism' of geography. In this case the interaction and consequent adjustment between man and environment are studied over a small representative area. The result then can be used for drawing conclusions for a larger area.

Historical Method: History and geography are often referred to as twins among social sciences, and more especially so in the school curriculum. Historical method has very illuminating applications in geographical studies. For instance, two regions on the basis of contemporary evidence may appear similar, but their backgrounds may differ, and so will their projection into the future. A casual connection can be usefully demonstrated, tracing the operation of a process through time. Treatment of such topics as industries, settlements and comparative study of regions needs resorting to historical analysis.

Comparative Study: Drawing comparisons is a very important procedural method in geographical studies, especially in dealing with regional and sample studies.

Statistical Methods: Analysis, synthesis and interpretation of quantitative data has an important role to play in the study of geography. Familiarity with statistical devices at a very rudimentary level could be expected, even at the elementary school stage. Beyond the statistical arithmetic, the learner should be made to see real meaning behind the central tendency, variability and correlations. Appreciation of range and probability of occurrence will help mollify the extremes of geographical dualism.

Map Study Method: The map is a very important device in geographical study, whatever the stage of education. It is a fundamental instrument of geographic research. It is essentially a device, but from the way it is employed in analysis and synthesis of geographic phenomena, it can be elevated to the status of a method. It gives precision to a presentation, which in a way may be more meaningful than any reached through words or numbers.

Maps represent geographical phenomena in terms of (i) points, (ii) lines, and (iii) areas. These help both analysis and synthesis of evidence. Differences can be identified in terms of (i) degrees, (ii) number, and (iii) kind and thereby patterns can be discovered. Inferences about accordances and discordances in a real relationship can provide clues for causation. Innumerable are the ways in which this method, device or technique, irrespective of the level of its employment, can be put to use.

Field Study Method: Geography is an exploratory science. Heurism has plenty of scope. 'Go and Look' method is more and more emphasised. Discovering is as important as utilising the findings for a more systematic study, and thereby to weave them into the fabric of a total geographical study more meaningfully and realistically. This is very important for employing this method in a really fruitful way. It is here that the study of the 'home region' becomes important to be employed as a springboard for other geographical studies and methods. 'Home region' is the primary source of geographical realism, a much sought after area in teaching this subject.

Source Method: Its significance is obvious. In brief, it means going to the original data. In involves location of source, identification of required information, collecting, storing and using it. Geographical information is difficult to be catalogued in the mind, or to be known from one single source. All instruction and instructional materials in geography should employ this method gainfully.

To sum up, the subject of geography, like any other recognised discipline, may be taken to be a 'thought system' or rather, an intellectual invention of our highly developed human society. It is a way of thinking, consisting of a set of interconnected and coherent generative propositions peculiar to it.

45

Teaching of Civics/Citizenship Education

Civic sense, is an inherent ingredient of a civilised society, as a determinant of human behaviour.

45.1 The Nature of Civics

Civics permeates the entire life of man and civics education the entire span of education. We learn and practice civics formally and informally directly and indirectly every moment of our lives.

As a *science of social institution habits, customs and manners observed by the members of different political communities, civics education starts from the home and continues thereafter for ever, until the end of ones life.*

The family is the basic unit through which our material, moral, spiritual and recreational needs are met. Although families may differ in size and composition, their basic needs are the same and they also have many common features. Each member of the family has certain privileges as well as responsibilities. Effective family relationship depends upon mutual love, understanding and respect for each other within the family in a spirit of sharing. The family to which we belong does many things for us and each one of us has certain duties towards the other members of the family. Every family has a cultural heritage with customs, traditions, beliefs and faiths. These live variations are the genesis of democracy and the core of national and international social existence.

As we grow in age we observe the varying modes of life and living, modes of transport and local administration (the panchayat, the District Board the Municipal Board) and other administrative manifestations, like the police stations, the post office, the hospitals, educational institutions etc. We also see different places of worship and interest.

We then come to see other facets of administration in regard to basic needs like water and electricity the different modes of transport and administrations in the districts and the state and the country. Our attention is simultaneously drawn to the modern methods of communication and the media. United Nations and its different agencies also then appear on our mental horizons in this context.

All the above constitute the study of Civics which utilises the methods of historians and geographers as aids for understanding the duties and rights of citizenship in a country as also the work of the governmental machinery.

The identified content ought to be a background and exploratory experiences for higher, more elaborate and in-depth study. Such a content would broaden pupils understanding of man and his relationship with the environment by focussing on the civics of people and social institutions.

45.2 The Spectrum of Courses in Civics

A broad outline of the content of courses in Civics is being provided below. The curriculum framers for different levels and classes could use these for developing a graded curriculum of Civics at the school stage.

Local Self-government—Institutions related to this are the primary institutions for training in democracy. The success of these institutions depends on the degree to which each person assumes his responsibility for its proper functioning as local problems can be best understood and better solved by local people.

Community Development—People working in cooperation and by pooling their resources are able to solve their social and economic problems better than what individuals functioning individually can accomplish. The cooperative movement as an embodiment of this spirit imparts self-reliance to people and prompts them to take initiatives in this regard.

Preservation and Protection of Public Property—The money spent on public property is money paid by the people. We should make proper use of public property and try to protect it from damage. Historical monuments are evidences of our heritage and national wealth.

Constitution and the Government—The constitution of a democratic country gives authority to the people and holds that the elected government exists only for the welfare of the people with both fundamental rights and fundamental duties, the performance of which promotes welfare and happiness.

Organisation of the Central and Sate Governments—India is a federation with Central and State Governments. In regard to operating areas of the two there is a central list, a state list and a concurrent list. The real power in both the cases rests with the legislature which are bodies of elected people.

45.3 Instructional Objective of Civics

1. To acquire the knowledge (information) of facts, terms, concepts, conventions, trends, principles, generalisations, assumptions, hypotheses, problems, processes, etc. in Civics.
2. To develop an understanding of facts, terms, concepts, conventions, trends, principles and generalisations, assumptions, hypotheses, problems, processes, etc. in Civics.

3. To apply the acquired knowledge of Civics and its understanding in unfamiliar situations.
4. To acquire practical skills essential for the study of Civics.
5. To develop interest in the subject and problems related to civic and political life of the people of one's country and of those of the world.
6. To develop desirable positive attitudes necessary for developing a broader outlook.

Objectives and their Specifications

45.3.1 ***Objective: To acquire the knowledge (information) of facts, terms, concepts, conventions, principles, generalisations, assumptions, hypotheses, problems, processes etc. in Civics.***

Specifications of the Objective:

To demonstrate the achievement of the above objective, the pupil:

1. recalls facts, terms, concepts, principles, trends, etc.
2. recognises facts, terms, concepts, principles, trends, etc.
3. reads information from various forms of representation data, i.e., maps, charts, diagrams, graphs, etc.

45.3.2 ***Objective: To develop an understanding of facts, terms, concepts, conventions, trends, principles, generalisations, assumptions, hypotheses, problems, processes etc. in Civics.***

Specifications of the Objective:

To demonstrate the achievement of the above objective, the pupil:

1. discriminates.
2. classifies.
3. compares and contrasts.
4. identifies relationships.
5. detects the points of emphasis and the trends of arguments.
6. cites illustrations.
7. detects errors and fallacies and corrects them.
8. explains (analyses or gives meaning or clarifies or elucidates).
9. gives reasons or advances arguments.
10. interprets data presented in different forms.

45.3.3 ***Objective: To apply the acquired knowledge of Civics and its understanding in unfamiliar situations.***

Specifications of the Objective:

To demonstrate the achievement of the above objective, the pupil:

1. analyses the unfamiliar situations or problems, and:
   - finds out what is given and what is required.
   - recalls knowledge relevant to the situation.
   - judges the sufficiency or insufficiency, adequacy or inadequacy of data or any other evidence for solving the problem.

2. establishes relationships.
3. suggests alternative methods for solving a particular problem.
4. selects the most appropriate method to follow.
5. draws inferences and makes generalisations.
6. makes predictions regarding the probable outcome of a given situation.

45.3.4 ***Objective: To acquire practical skills essential for the study of Civics.***

Specifications of the Objective:

To demonstrate the achievement of the above objective, the pupil:

1. draws maps, charts, tables, diagrams, graphs, etc. from given data.
2. translates data from one form of presentation to another.
3. prepares models.

45.3.5 ***Objective: To develop interest in the subject and problems related to Civic and political life of the people of one's country and of those of the world.***

Specifications of the Objective:

To demonstrate the achievement of the above objective, the pupil:

1. voluntarily studies literature related to Civics, and tries to know about the inherent issues and problems.
2. spends leisure in trying to know about civic problems and issues, and exerts in finding solutions to them.
3. closely observes civic and political processes and changes at local, national and international levels.
4. discusses and is able to communicate various aspects of every day civic problems and their implications.
5. enthusiastically participates in excursions, visits and field-trips to places of civic and political activities (e.g. Panchayats, Municipalities, Assemblies, Parliament etc.).
6. enjoys attending and participating in debates, symposiums, discussions on civic and political problems.
7. enjoys writing articles and preparing pamphlets, brochures, etc. on topics related to Civics.
8. enjoys preparing display-materials related to civic and political life and events.
9. enjoys collecting information about other political systems, and facts about other locations, regions and countries.

45.3.6 ***Objective: To develop desirable positive attitudes necessary for developing a broader outlook.***

Specifications of the Objective

To demonstrate the achievement of the above objective, the pupil:

1. respects the views, opinions and problems of others, and displays sympathy and fellow feeling towards them:

- shows tolerance
- controls emotions and displays restraint.
- develops social awareness.

2. is able to examine the present situations in the light of a historical perspective.
3. develops a sense of law-abidingness.
4. assumes responsibility in cooperative and civic activities.
5. judges issues objectively and on their merits.
6. displays abhorrence towards socio-economic malpractices like hoarding, profiteering, black-marketing, smuggling, bribery etc.
7. shows sympathetic understanding of the problems of people belonging to different social, religious, linguistic and cultural groups.
8. realises the importance of the contributions made by the leaders of the nation in different spheres.
9. develops a sense of respect for the National Flag, the National Anthem, the National Emblem and the Constitution of one's own country and those of other countries of the world.
10. develops faith in democratic values.

45.4 Methods of Teaching Civics

The focus in teaching Civics should be on a number of organisations developed by man for satisfying his civic needs. The students should also be enabled to appreciate the effectiveness of these organisations and their direct relationship with the personal responsibility of the individuals in their operations as also the high value and worth in democracies. This appreciation should also be attempted to be extended to the realisation of the fact that progress in any one aspect of political, economic or social facet of the society directly influences progress in the other aspects. In the final analysis it also ought to be brought home to the students that the constitution of the country reflects the basic values of our way of life and outlines the rights and responsibilities of citizenship.

The teaching of Civics ought also to focus on the development of some attitudes like respect for the views, beliefs and vocations of others, willingness to abide by the decisions of the majority, value of the institutions and administrative units working for the welfare of the society, evoking a desire for participation in their operations, appreciation of and respect for the symbols of our natural unity—the constitution, the National Emblems, the National Anthem and the National Days.

The *Prime Minister* and the Chief Ministers of States are responsible to the legislature.

The *Judiciary* (the Supreme Court, The High Courts and other Courts) is the guardian of the constitution and protects the fundamental rights of people.

Our National Symbols—The National symbols signify national unity freedom and ideals. All citizens ought to know their history, significance and the related legends.

India in the Comity of Nations—The United Nations and its various agencies. India's role in the UN and in World Peace as a member of UN.

The emergence of new equations and the establishment of other social, economic, political, cultural organisations of different countries. The purpose of their establishment and India's role in their operations.

45.5 Practical Activities as the Soul of Civics Teaching

Civics is a subject that touches our lives every moment of our existence. It is full of problems and issues and thus *a live subject in our lives.*

Facts will no doubt have to be given by the teacher but after that '*the tongue and the ear method*' loses complete relevance.

Problems related to the course topics, even those that may look trivial could be posed to the students and they may be encouraged to give their own views on that and suggestions for solving them through discussions.

In senior classes even examples of *Court cases and decisions* could be given with advantage. This will give the students more concrete examples of the interpretation of laws.

Visits to Civic Institutions (Panchayat, Municipal Board, District Board) where the officials, may address them will be valuable education. Visits to State Assemblies and the Parliament if possible, will enable them to watch the proceedings and to know things first hand.

Projects both group and individual can be useful teaching learning devices. These may relate to things like:

- transport and communications
- panchayat elections and proceedings
- police stations
- civic amenities
- location of institutions in the area
- major developments in national life and their influence:
    - information technology
    - globlisation
    - liberalisation
    - technologisation of industries
    - India's nuclear policy
    - India and the UN etc. etc.

The teachers of Civics or Citizenship Education could, use their discretion in using the other conventional and unconventional methods of teaching discussed in earlier sections of the book as per the need of the situation.

46

Teaching of Economics

46.1 The Importance of Economics

The importance of economics in the world of today cannot be under-estimated, anywhere. It has also to be recognised that while 'political colonialism' is now a thing of the past, 'economic colonialism' has come to occupy its place with different countries trying hard and competing with one another for reaching the goal.

It all started with industrial revolution for which India had provided the first tool with the 'invention of the wheel' which was fully exploited by the western countries. It marked a new stage in the development of human civilisation by the introduction of machines in industries. Though the Industrial Revolution started in England, its impact was more widespread. It also demonstrated the interrelatedness and interdependence of mankind. Mechanisation of industries and large-scale production also gave birth to a number of problems.

Raw materials in most cases were provided by the not-so-developed countries who received finished products with added cost yielding profits to the industrially advanced nations, thus widening the gap between the developed and the developing nations when the developed countries attempted to capture markets of developing countries.

With inattention to the problems of population growth all the developments in the developing world got diluted. In fact health became their first focus and as they succeeded in controlling child and mother mortality and in increasing longevity, this further aggravated the problem of unbridled population growth and added to the miseries of the developing world.

The developed countries exploited the situation by offering 'Aid' but these gestures were not without strings attached. What was offered in the name of aid, was in fact 'loan', to be repaid with interest. Sometimes the developing countries were even obliged to seek more aid for paying back interest, far from paying the principal. Furthermore when aid was offered it had a substantial proportion assigned to experts deputed by the donor countries as a part of the aid package. This money went back to the developed donor countries and only the remainder could be put to use by the developing countries for developmental purposes.

The debt burden also had the potential of being used as political pressure. The developing countries soon understood the tactics and started asking for the training of their own personnel, but the approaches used by developed countries were not often suitable to the conditions and resources of the developing nations. Thus started the process of marshalling local resources and engineering indigenous approaches for development.

Inspite of this the ocean of developing nations has only islands of developed countries and dependence on the latter for a host of things remains.

Thus economics has come to occupy the centre stage in the world that is evolving. The disparities are great and will take time to be bridged inspite of the pace of industrialisation in the developing world that is picking up.

The concept of liberalisation and globalisation too is picking up fast and economics is one of its important cornerstones in this respact. However, it deserves to be clearly and unambiguously appreciated that *globalisation is not to be conceived as related to economic facets alone and also that if has a built in component of reciprocity and is not a one way traffic.*

The study of economics ought to acquaint students with the contemporary economic problems and the efforts being made nationally and internationally to solve them. They should also be enabled to understand the concept of economic interdependence of nations and the physical and human resources of the country and their optimum utilisation in the economic reconstruction of the country.

46.2 Instructional Objectives of Economics

In the context of the above, the instructional objectives of economics could be listed as under :

1. To acquire the knowledge (information) of facts, terms, concepts, conventions, trends, principles, generalisations, assumptions, hypotheses, problems, processes, etc. in Economics.
2. To develop an understanding of facts, terms, concepts, conventions, trends, principles, generalisations, assumptions, hypotheses, problems, processes, etc. in Economics.
3. To apply the acquired knowledge of Economics and its understanding in unfamiliar situations.
4. To acquire practical skills essential for the study of Economics.
5. To develop interest in the subject and problems related to economic life of the people of one's own country and of those of other countries of the world.
6. To develop desirable positive attitudes necessary for developing a broader outlook.

Objectives and their Specification

46.2.1 ***Objective: To acquire the knowledge (information) of facts, terms, concepts, conventions, trends, principles, generalisations, assumptions, hypotheses, problems, processes, etc. in Economics.***

Specifications of the Objective:

To demonstrate the achievement of the above objective, the pupil:

1. recalls facts, terms, concepts, principles, trends, etc.
2. recognises facts, terms, concepts, principles, trends, etc.
3. reads information from various forms of presentation of data, i.e. maps, charts, tables, diagrams, graphs, etc.

46.2.2 ***Objective: To develop an understanding of facts, terms, concepts, conventions, trends, principles, generalisations, assumptions, hypotheses, problems, processes, etc. in Economics.***

Specifications of the Objective:

To demonstrate the achievement of the above objective, the pupil:

1. discriminates.
2. classifies.
3. compares and contrasts.
4. identifies relationships.
5. locates points of emphasis and the trends of arguments.
6. cites illustrations.
7. detects errors and fallacies and rectifies them.
8. explains (analyses or gives meaning or clarifies or elucidates.)
9. gives reasons and/or advances arguments.
10. interprets data presented in different forms.

46.2.3 ***Objective: To apply the acquired knowledge of Economics and its understanding in unfamiliar situations.***

Specifications of the Objective:

To demonstrate the achievement of the above objective, the pupil:

1. analyses the unfamiliar situation or problem.
   - 1.1 finds out what is given and what is required.
   - 1.2 recalls knowledge relevant to the situation.
   - 1.3 judges sufficiency or insufficiency, appropriateness and unappropriateness of data, or any other evidence for solving the problem.
2. establishes relationships.
3. suggests alternative methods for solving a problem.
4. draws inferences and makes generalisations.
5. makes predictions regarding the probable outcome of a given situation.

46.2.4 *Objective: To acquire practical skills essential for the study of Economics.*

Specifications of the Objective:

To demonstrate the achievement of the above objective, the pupil:

1. draws maps, charts, tables, diagrams, graphs, etc. from the given data.
2. translates data from one form of presentation to another and interprets it.
3. prepares models.

46.2.5 *Objective: To develop interest in the subject and problems related to economic life of the people of one's own country and of those of other countries of the world.*

Specifications of the Objective:

To demonstrate the achievement of the above objective, the pupil:

1. voluntarily studies literature related to Economics and tries to know about the inherent economic issues and problems.
2. spends leisure in trying to know about economic problems and issues and works for finding solutions to them.
3. closely observes economic processes and changes at local, national and international levels.
4. discusses and is able to communicate various aspects of everyday economic problems and their implications.
5. enthusiastically participates in excursions, visits and field-trips to places of economic activity (farms, factories, fairs, etc.)
6. collects information about other economic systems and facts about the economy of other localities, regions and countries.

46.2.6 *Objective: To develop desirable positive attitudes necessary for developing a broader outlook.*

Specifications of the Objective:

To demonstrate the achievement of the above objective, the pupil:

1. respects the views, opinions and problems of others and displays sympathy and fellow feeling towards them.
   - 1.1 shows tolerance.
   - 1.2 controls emotions and displays restraint.
   - 1.3 discusses issues of disagreement with others impartially.
2. unhesitatingly mixes with people of different economic strata.
3. judges issues objectively and on their merits.
4. assumes responsibility in co-operative ventures.
5. displays abhorrence towards:
   - 5.1 socio-economic malpractices like hoarding, profiteering, black-marketing, evasion of taxes, smuggling, etc.
   - 5.2 wasteful, showful and uneconomic expenditure.

6. realises the importance of, and respects man's potential and his contribution to national economic development.

46.3 Methods of Teaching Economics

In the context of the changing world order it is urgent that we reorient our courses in Economics to prepare students for meeting the emerging challenges of becoming a developed country by 2020 as envisaged.

This will need a study of the Indian Economic institutions, the shrinking public sector and the growing private sector, the enlarged concepts of primary, secondary and tertiary occupations with their changing priorities, the nature of economic stage, the constituents of social and economic infrastructure, the strides in economic regeneration in the field of agriculture, industry, information technology including the current status and future prospects of foreign trade and foreign exchange reserves, foreign investments in India and Indian investments abroad.

All these will need to be studied in terms of ending the eras of shortages and beginning of the phases of affluence.

To teach all thus successfully we will need to conceive and implement strategies for moving beyond textbooks and institutions, for learning the basics of economics. The newspapers, the business reports on the T.V., the study and interpretation of the market indices for different commodities, and so on with have to be the main sources of information. In this process the teacher too will become a co-student with his students in the quest of new knowledge for keeping updated and to remain relevant.

The teacher, however, will never become redundant but his role will certainly change from being a dispenser of information to becoming a guide. He will thus become an important agent for *transforming students from being objects of education to becoming subjects of education.*

He will remain relevant as one, for providing clarifications to the doubts and apprehension of the students.

Participatory learning with sharing of responsibilities for exploring the universe of economics will need to replace individual learning. This will be a powerful instrument of enrichment of learning, because of the sharing of learning labour enabling indepth explorations by way of sharing the exploits.

Project work and surveys will therefore need to occupy the centre-stage. These will enlighten students about the purposefulness of their learning adventures and make internalisation of learning quicker and more abiding.

Classroom discussions will replace lectures in a very large measure, after the students would have explored and studied the themes on their own. Some explanations by the teachers will still survive almost perpetually.

47

Teaching of Commerce

Commerce is neither a science nor an art, but an enterprise filled craft, moving through the compounded mazes of economics and sociology and displaying ever-changing kaleidoscopic variety.

Commerce is also a mother of so many new subjects of study like Business Management, Commercial Economics, etc. The subjects of Commerce and Business and Financial Management, Accounting, Book-keeping have quite a lot of overlap among themselves and with other foundational subjects like Economics. In fact all Business and Commerce and trade have economics at their root. The traditional boundaries of these subjects have also become fragile and flexible. Subjects in this segment have, in fact, enriched themselves through the elements of other subjects. Statistics on the other hand has come to be the through fertilisation with common element of these subjects, enabling validation of inferences and for making predictions. The degree of accuracy attained through statistics becomes the core of all activities related to business and commerce which whet entrepreneurship with particular reference to risk taking. Type writing which in the good old days used to be one of the crucial first steps of commerce courses has with computerisation permeated all the subjects.

Even many other areas like education which were considered to be philanthropic are also now becoming business propositions and items of trade and business. Teaching, which used to be taken as a vocation has also now become a profession and teachers have come to be treated at par with factory workers, working for money and not for performing a duty entrusted to them by God, for the benefit of humanity as a selfless social service and a welfare activity.

Globalisation too has been greatly responsible for a host of emerging attitudes of the mind impelled by materialism, consumerism, pragmatism leaving idealism far behind in the race with little hope of catching up for raising its head. Every facet of life is gradually getting converted and transformed into becoming commercial.

47.1 Objectives of Teaching Commerce

The subjects of the Commerce stream have essentially a practical bias where the possession of just knowledge or information has no more remained adequate. What is really required now is the use of the facts, terms, concepts, principles, procedures in life situations. Acquaintance with the formats and proformas is again not enough and what is required is the ability to accurately fill them in, or to detect and correct errors in the formats or the entries made therein. Identification of shortfalls in information available or entered is yet another ability desired to be acquired.

Apart from these the development of interest in the job and desirable attitudes for executing them too are necessary to be acquired.

Among the other competencies, those that acquire the focal position are identification of relationships between cause and effect, analysis of problems, ability to make predictions, conduct of sample surveys, audit of accounts for discovering shortfalls, besides, of course, the procedures for the maintenance of accounts. By way of examples, the instructional objectives of elements of Banking and of Book Keeping are being presented hereunder.

The specifications of each of the objectives in the two areas spell out the activities which a student will be able to undertake to demonstrate to us that the student has realised a particular objective. These specification, are also tangible elements of each objective which could become the bases for designing evaluation practices and tools.

The greatest merit of such an enunciation is the diagnostic purpose that it serves. The sub-objectives (specifications) also enable us to test them and to discover the kind and degree of pupil growth that may have occurred as an outcome of the instructional programme and to identify those aspects of content and abilities where reinforcements are called for, for improving the level of attainments.

47.2 Instructional Objectives of Elements of Banking

1. To acquire the knowledge of facts, terms, concepts, principles, trends, etc. in Money and Banking.
2. To develop the understanding of facts, terms, concepts, principles, etc. in Money and Banking.
3. To develop the ability to apply the knowledge of facts, concepts, principles, etc. in Money and Banking in unfamiliar situations.
4. To develop the practical skills related to the elementary banking functions.
5. To develop desirable interests in banking procedures and currency functions.
6. To develop healthy attitudes expected of a good banker.

47.3 Objectives and Their Specifications

47.3.1. Objective: To acquire the knowledge of facts, terms, concepts, principles, trends, etc. in Money and Banking.

Specifications of the Objective

To demonstrate the achievement of the above objective, the student:

1.1 recalls facts, concepts, etc. in Money and Banking.

1.2 recognises facts, concepts, principles and proformas, etc. in Elements of Banking.

1.3 fills up and uses various proformas and banking documents.

47.3.2. Objective: To develop the understanding of facts, terms, concepts, etc. related to Money and Banking.

Specifications of the Objective

To demonstrate the achievement of the above objective, the student:

2.1 distinguishes between relevant and irrelevant, essential and incidental data.

2.2 discriminates between different facts, concepts, etc. in Money and Banking.

2.3 classifies.

2.4 compares and contrasts.

2.5 cites illustrations.

2.6 detects errors and rectifies them.

2.7 identifies relationships between cause and effect.

2.8 interprets data presented in various forms.

47.3.3. Objective: To develop the ability to apply the knowledge of facts, concepts, etc. in Money and Banking in unfamiliar situations.

Specifications of the Objective

To demonstrate the achievement of the above objective, the student:

3.1 analyses a new problem to identify the issues involved in it.

3.2 selects facts relevant to a new situation.

3.3 establishes relevant relationship between different facts, concepts, etc.

3.4 judges the adequacy of data, arguments, etc.

3.5 draws inferences and generalisations.

3.6 predicts events, trends, etc.

47.3.4. Objective: To develop the practical skills related to the elementary banking functions.

Specifications of the Objective

To demonstrate the achievement of the above objective, the student:

4.1 draws cheques, B/Es, Hundis, etc. neatly and accurately.

4.2 prepares various proformas neatly and correctly.

4.3 collects relevant information, preserves and appropriately presents it.

4.4 conducts simple Banking surveys.

47.3.5. Objective: To develop desirable interests in banking procedures and currency functions.

Specifications of the Objective

To demonstrate the achievement of the above objective, the student voluntarily:

5.1 reads periodicals, related books, newspapers, etc. giving information about developments in banking.

5.2 collects specimens, pictures, charts, data and other such materials related to areas of his interest in banking and currency.

5.3 discusses problems related to banking and currency with his colleagues, teachers and parents.

5.4 participates in banking transactions in and outside the school.

5.5 visits places of banking operations.

5.6 prepares exhibits related to the subject matter of Elements of Banking for display.

5.7 maintains and operates a bank account.

47.3.6. Objective: To develop healthy attitudes expected of a good Banker.

Specifications of the Objective

To demonstrate the achievement of the above objective, the student:

6.1 assumes responsibility.

6.2 is open to new ideas.

6.3 behaves courteously and politely.

6.4 respects law.

6.5 develops thrifty habits.

47.4 Instructional Objectives of Book-Keeping

1. To acquire the knowledge of facts, concepts, terms, principles and procedures, forms and statements related to Book-keeping.
2. To develop an understanding of facts, concepts, terms, principles and procedures, forms and statements related to Book-keeping.
3. To apply the acquired knowledge and understanding of concepts and principles of Book-keeping in new situations.
4. To acquire the competencies of maintaining and auditing books of accounts and presentation of Book-keeping data properly.
5. To develop desirable interests in Book-keeping and in the acquisition of further knowledge of Book-keeping and accountancy.
6. To develop positive attitudes towards Book-keeping practices, and related aspects.

47.5 Objectives and Their Specifications

47.5.1. Objective: To acquire the knowledge of facts, concepts, terms, principles and procedures, forms and statements used in Book-keeping.

Specifications of tire Objective

To demonstrate the achievement of the above objective, the student:

1.1 recalls items constituting different forms.

1.2 recognises items in various proformas.

1.3 reproduces, principles and concepts, etc. in Book-keeping as mentioned above.

47.5.2. Objective: To develop an understanding of facts, concepts, terms, principles and procedures, forms and statements related to Book-keeping.

Specifications of tire Objective

To demonstrate the achievement of the above objective, the student:

2.1 distinguishes between facts, terms, etc.

2.2 discriminates between various forms and proformas.

2.3 classifies facts related to various forms and proformas.

2.4 compares and contrasts.

2.5 gives examples.

2.6 identifies relationships.

2.7 arranges steps in proper sequence.

2.8 gives reasons for the occurrence of problems related to Book-keeping.

2.9 interprets data.

2.10 locates errors and rectifies them.

47.5.3. Objective: To apply the acquired knowledge and understanding of concepts and principles of Book-keeping in unfamiliar situations.

Specifications of the Objective

To demonstrate the achievement of the above objective, the student:

3.1 analyses the given situations and problems.

3.2 selects facts, relevant to the given problem.

3.3 judges adequacy of data for studying a particular situation.

3.4 establishes relationships.

3.5 suggests innovations for improving procedures.

3.6 formulates hypothesis and verifies them.

3.7 draws inferences.

3.8 predicts probabilities in a given set of situations.

47.5.4. Objective: To acquire necessary competencies for maintaining Books of Accounts and presentation of Book-keeping data properly.

Specifications of the Objective

To demonstrate the achievement of the above objective, the student

4.1 calculates and computes quickly and correctly

4.2 handles and operates computers

4.3 fills in proformas, statements and accounts correctly, proportionately and neatly.

4.4 writes entries and figures in the appropriate manner.
4.5 writes in a good and legible hand.
4.6 preserves and maintains the Books of Accounts properly.
4.7 learns to use computers in Book-keeping and accountancy.

47.5.5. Objective: To develop desirable interests in Book-keeping and in the acquisition of further knowledge of Book-keeping and Accountancy.

Specifications of the Objective

To demonstrate the achievement of the above objective, the student voluntarily:

5.1 collects information about new developments in accounting systems.
5.2 reads latest literature on Book-keeping and accounting.
5.3 studies final accounts and statements published by different business concerns, corporations, etc.

47.5.6. Objective: To develop positive attitudes towards Book-keeping practices.

Specifications of the Objective

To demonstrate the achievement of the above objective, the student:

6.1 shows receptivity to scientific and modern ideas and tries them out.
6.2 assumes responsibility in assigned tasks and volunteers to do more.
6.3 acquires integrity and honesty of purpose.
6.4 respects and follows laws and rules relating to Accountancy.
6.5 develops a habit of hard work and perseverance.

47.6 Methods of Teaching Commerce

By and large the branches of commerce called subjects of study in commerce, follow almost similar approaches in teaching and learning. The main of these are enunciated below:

Theoretical Orientation about the facts, terms, concepts, principles, procedures, trends etc. of the concerned subjects. This would imply acquisition of knowledge, about the fundamentals, consisting of basic information required to be used in different operations. The student will need to possess it, recollect the facets relevant to specific situations at the points of their use.

Demonstration of the details related to different operations by the teacher step-by-step, in the required sequence while sequentially these demonstrations will be graded leading the students from easy to difficult, simple to complex, each demonstration will need to be followed up by related practical work.

Guided operations will be the next natural step where the students will be required to execute the tasks under direct supervision of the teachers. The teachers will observe the students in working situations and undertake on the spot correction of mistakes. In case a particular mistake is committed by many students, the teacher would take up these for discussion and remediation.

Independent work could now be given to the students. These exercises again will be graded from small to big and simple to complicated. Competencies could first be taken up one by one, for being developed and evaluated and then in clusters. This independent work will prove to be helpful in developing confidence in the students about the execution of jobs displaying competencies of different degree of complexities.

Comprehensive exercises of different levels of complexity could now be given to the students. The student will naturally be required to draw upon the knowledge and understanding of the content and its application in unfamiliar situations he may be required to face. In the beginning, these would be hypothetical. Subsequently, he may be posed with actual situations of life. These comprehensive exercises, will require different themes of content and different competencies for executing them. The student will thus be required to be selective in cutting out those aspects of subject matter and those facets of abilities out of his treasure of possessions. This matching of requirements of the two sides will by no means be an easy job. The students will need to use their discretion and other abilities in this regard.

Evaluation of content and competencies will be next step/stage to confirm the degree of their acquisition by the students. This assessment could also be then used for purposes of certification in terms of classification of examinees into different categories based on the levels of competencies they possess. This evaluation will need to be in all the three domains of development – cognitive, affective and psycho-motor – using a variety of conventional and unconventional techniques and tools of evaluation. This evaluation will thus cover the capabilities of students in both scholastic and co-scholastic aspects also covering personal and social qualities often referred to as soft skills, interests, attitudes and proficiency in outdoor activities. An attempt will thus be made to cover the total personality of the students, to as great an extent as possible. This evaluation is, therefore, likely to prove helpful in better predicting the potential for success in life.

Conclusion

With such an evaluation outcomes of grading, classification and certification of students and the bench-marking of their current abilities and future potential, the student could move to life situations with confidence and success.

48

Teaching of Integrated Science

The subjects called science are treated in two ways—in an integrated fashion upto the Secondary Stage and as disciplines in stages commencing with the Senior Secondary Stage. Both these patterns of treatment are therefore being attempted.

48.1 The Nature and Scope of Integrated Science

It is an admitted fact that science for all is basic to any modern curriculum. It therefore must be taught in a way that reflects the nature and structure of science

Science Defined

The words 'science' and 'scientific' have become so popular in all walks of life that science is considered the hallmark of progress, and a prominent theme of the present age. Science is regarded as an area of study reflecting organised concepts, principles and theories or systematised knowledge. Science is also regarded as an activity which forms the basis of acquiring and refining knowledge. The former is the *static view* of science and refers to the content or the subject-matter of science. The latter is the *dynamic view* of science and refers to the process aspect or the methods of the scientists and their attitudes towards work, which are commonly called scientific methods and scientific attitudes aimed at enquiry.

Science does not deal with value judgements. It is concerned only with adducing the evidence. Thus "What ought or ought not to be done", is beyond the boundaries of science. Likewise, science cannot prove or disprove certain beliefs, as they are based on certain notions and values which science does not handle. Truth, value and purpose are the words which science does not contain within its fold. Science advances and attempts to explain the mysteries of nature through the use of reliable tools and the scientific method.

Science and the Scientific Method

The scientific method has become so common in parlance that its use is sometimes abused. In a wider context, the meaning of science is derived from the scope of the scientific method.

The scientific method involves the following steps in solving problems:

(a) Identifying and defining the problem.
(b) Collecting relevant data and information regarding the problem.
(c) Formulating tentative hypotheses.
(d) Observation or conduct of experiments to test hypotheses.
(e) Drawing inferences or conclusions.
(f) Accepting or rejecting hypotheses on the basis of findings.
(g) Verifying facts by applying the generalisations drawn to new situations.

Tools of Science

The scientific method uses tools of science like microscope, telescope, barometer etc., which help in acquiring knowledge of science. Indeed, much of the expanding knowledge of science is due to the development and refinement of tools used in the laboratories. But for the invention of certain instruments of science, many discoveries in the field of science, would have remained only a dream.

48.2 Nature and Characteristics of Science

48.2.1 *Science is Empirical*

Every idea in science is to be checked and verified before it is accepted. According to **Conant**, empiricism is a 'cut and dry' approach. It is a common sense approach. Direct observations and experiments are used for verification. Objective standard is the touchstone of scientific truth, and therefore, every idea must be subjected to test to see if it works.

48.2.2 *Hypothesis is the Intellectual Tool of Scientific Investigation*

It is on the basis of a hypothesis that investigations are carried out to see whether suppositions made in advance by way of suggested answers, are correct or not. Formulation of a good hypothesis depends on one's knowledge of the subject area, past experience and experience of other persons engaged in related works. This helps to reduce the number of hunches from among the numerous ones that can be framed.

Hypotheses are the result of hunches, intuition and sometimes lucky incidents. The solution to those hypotheses are sought in the form of 'yes' or 'no' as far as possible, rather than 'may be', so that the hypothesis is either accepted or rejected, on the basis of evidences obtained. However, most of the solutions are initially in a 'may be' form. When they yield 'yes' or 'no' form, such discoveries become milestones in science.

48.2.3 *Controlled Experimentation is Basic to all Scientific Investigations*

In order to have scientific investigations, control is important. Whether the observed change in a phenomenon is actually due to a particular variable, can be known only when control is applied on all other possible factors affecting the change. The use of the investigatory approach in developing scientific concepts, and the inclusion of projects in review exercises can be taken advantage of for the purpose.

48.2.4 *Science is Cumulative in Nature*

Science is not concerned with the discovery of everything. It can start from where the previous workers left. The students should depend on books and other sources for collecting relevant knowledge, which they can start applying in the new situations. *Michael Faraday's* discovery regarding the use of magnets to generate electricity, is a good example to illustrate how his discovery was dependent upon the work of *Volta*, *Oersted*, *Arago* and *Ampere*.

48.2.5 *Ideas and Achievements of Science are Expressed as Precisely as Possible*

Precise expression, renders communication better understood and facilitates comprehension. Children should get this experience in discussing their ideas by using precise statements and reporting data quantitatively as far as possible.

48.2.6 *Science Stresses the Narrative of Inquiry rather than the Rhetoric of Conclusions*

This is the most important characteristic of science which needs to be emphasised. This aims at supporting the idea that scientific knowledge, is not just reporting of observatrions made, or that science deals with unalterable truth. Science changes with the advance of knowledge, and is thus never complete. Emphasis in science should be on the narrative of inquiry, rather than on conclusion. It is, therefore, essential that the investigatory approach may be used to acquaint the students with various processes of science used by scientists to discover new knowledge.

48.2.7 *Science deals with Truths which are not Absolute, but are Subject to Change*

Facts of science are indisputable, but the theories are always subject to change. The ever changing nature of science must be brought home to the students through science textbooks and the instructional programmes. They should be able to know, what is certain and what is uncertain, or only speculation.

Scientific information is rearranged and reorientated consistently. Therefore, the content and process of science education should not only show the patterns of success, but also the blunders and blind alleys where science takes us sometimes. The tentative nature of science, in the form of temporary or conditional truths, rather than absolute truths, needs to be appreciated. That scientific conclusions can be challenged, and are subject to modifications, should be appropriately appreciated in this context.

48.3 Correlational and Exact Sciences

As pointed out earlier, Science connotes a group of subjects like Physics, Chemistry, Biology, Geology, Astronomy, etc. Among these Biological Sciences are comparatively less exact than the physical sciences. However, advances in Genetics and Bio-technology are tending to make this too, more exact than what it used to be. Another feature of these sciences is the inductive generalisations which mainly summarise or describe, rather than predict. (As such lack of basic explanation does not satisfy the investigators.) Physics and Chemistry are more exact sciences because they have developed the explanatory system, which is helpful in making predictions. Emphasis on inductive generalisations in case of biological and related sciences and on deductive system of explanation in case of other physical sciences, should be reflected in the content and teaching of Sciences.

48.3.1 *Structure of Science*

The structure of science is based on two assumptions. *Firstly*, that all phenomena in the universe can be explained in a logical or a rational way. *Secondly*, that every idea can be empirically tested to see whether it is in accordance with the evidences we get on trying it out. On the basis of these two assumptions, inquiry through various processes like observation, measurement, classification, experimentation, hypothesis formulation are made and generalisations arrived at. It is these generalisations, themes, conceptual schemes or major ideas, that form the structure of science.

Generalisations are broad statements that represent the major ideas in science. They help to explain a number of phenomena or details, and serve as tools for further investigation. Such generalisations represent a system of facts, concepts and principles, which can be organised into sound learning sequences from simple to complex. Such generalisations are the pillars of the structure of science and, are regarded as the focal points for curriculum construction.

48.3.2 *Processes of Science*

The process-approach in teaching science is becoming more popular these days. This does not, however, mean a corresponding de-emphasis of content. According to *Gagne* (1966), the word 'process' corresponds to what scientists do, or the 'processes' that they carry out. For example, process may also be considered as the way of processing the information and may be taken as the operation of intellectual skills. Processes of science are, therefore, the intellectual tools of the scientists for exploring the scientific, including natural, phenomena.

The development of intellectual skills may vary from the concrete and specific to the increasingly abstract and general (Piaget's work). According to this approach there is a progressive intellectual development within each process category. There is increase in the complexity of the processes as the development proceeds. Inferring, for example, partakes of prior development of skills in observing, classifying and measuring. The interrelation of different processes leads to certain integrated processes like experimentation.

The basic and integrated processes of science which should be reflected in the teaching of science are *observing, classifying, using numbers, measuring, using space-time relationship, predicting, inferring, defining operationally, formulating hypotheses, interpreting data, controlling variables and experimenting*. All these processes which represent the sequence of intellectual development do, however, need to be defined. The different behaviours are represented in hierarchies which can be related to the learning hierarchies as described by *Gagne* (1966).

48.3.3 *A Case for an Integrated Science Course*

A course like General Science, Elementary Science or Natural Science, which is prescribed as a compulsory core-subject in many of the curricula of different states is an example of *an integrated course in science*. Though there are various ways in which integration could be sought, yet all the courses initially aim at providing experiences from different areas of the pupil's natural environment in a unified way. A course of integrated science emphasises observation and logical thinking and involves the scientific method. The extent of integration would depend on the age of pupils, the type of institution and the local conditions.

The unified approach of teaching science, too, can be achieved in different ways. We may make the conceptual scheme as the basis for designing a course around broad themes or big ideas for science. We may adopt *an environmental approach* where issues of social relevance or utility may become the starting points, e.g., problems of nutrition and health, conservation of resources, etc. We may adopt the *enquiry approach* in which problem-solving activities become the unifying element. The *process-approach* can also be used for designing an integrated science course. In this case the focus is on training students in the processes of science and scientific phenomenon as a coherent whole rather than the content of a particular discipline.

From another angle, integration could be thought of, as a multi-track approach where different subject-areas like Physics, Chemistry, Biology, Astronomy, Geology etc., can be taught simultaneously in an integrated manner or through a disciplinary approach with increasing order of complexity from one stage or grade to the other. Alternatively, different subjects may be taught at different grade-levels, and the subject is discussed more intensively at each next higher level. Still another approach is to identify different areas like conservation of matter and energy, weather, food etc., in which case, the relevant subject-matter from different disciplines is brought to bear on such themes.

48.4 Concept and Place of Science and Technology in School Curriculum*

Science and Technology

Science is the creative response to the curiosity and capacity to wonder, present in every human being. Learning of science in schools augments the spirit of enquiry, creativity and objectivity, alongwith aesthetic sensibility. It aims to develop well-defined abilities of knowing, doing and being. It also nurtures the ability to explore and seek solution of the problems related to environment and daily life situations, and to question the existing beliefs, prejudices and practices in society. Science concerns itself with the fundamental knowledge of universe, world and its environment. Technology deals with numerous ways and means of pressing science into the service of mankind, thus enhancing and improving the quality of human life. Learning of science in general education up to secondary stage, therefore, needs to be replaced by learning of science and technology involving a *shift of focus and emphasis from teaching the evolution or history of science to its applications* in view of the strong organic linkages between the two. Scientific pursuits have primarily attempted to comprehend the physical world and the technological initiatives that have tended to manipulate and control the same. Science is universal, and its principles and laws can be verified anywhere. Technology in this context takes appropriate shapes, depending upon various factors including economic, geographical, social and political conditions. The twenty-first century citizens, will have to acquire the basics of scientific and technological literacy. The learners have to understand how basic scientific principles are applied in finding solutions to problems in the field of agriculture, weather, energy, health and nutrition, industry, defence, information processing and other areas of human concern. It would help them discover the relationship between science and technology in these areas, besides acquiring problem-solving and decision-making skills.

Science should be treated as one of the curricular areas, that play a decisive role, in equipping the learner for understanding, interpreting and dealing with, various things and phenomena around him/her in a more scientific way. Education in science should aim at developing well defined abilities in cognitive, affective and psychomotor domains, such as spirit of inquiry, creativity, objectivity, the courage to question and aesthetic sensibility. Programmes in science education should be designed so as to enable the learner to acquire problems solving and decision-making competencies, and to discover the relationship of science with health, agriculture, industry and other aspects of daily life.

Science should help in reducing obscurantism and all sorts of prejudices based on sex, caste, religion, language or region. Thus by emphasising a rational

---

* *Source*: National Curriculum Framework for School Education, 2000, NCERT, New Delhi.

approach, science should help the development of a democratic, secular and socialist state.

All disciplines are now gradually becoming scientific. The method of observation, of making symbolic, graphical or linguistic models, of designing experiments, of applying reason as well as imagination, to draw conclusions from data to formulate theories, the method of keeping an objective view while theories are tested, is a method which pervades every discipline but more rigorously so in the sciences. The facts of today may not be the facts of tomorrow, and theories may also undergo change, but there can be no going away from the method of science.

48.5 Methods of Teaching Integrated Science at Different Stages

Science operates through its processes. Consequently, teaching and learning of science needs to be characterised by focussed emphasis on processes, i.e. experimentation, taking observations, collection of data, classification, analysis, making hypothesis, drawing inferences, and objectively arriving at conclusions for discovering truths. The process skills so acquired would help in developing attitudes and values that constitute the spirit of scientific temper. Science can be learned better in familiar environments than in alien and contrived situations.

An important purpose of science and technology teaching in general education up to secondary stage, is to familiarise the learner with various dimensions of scientific and technological literacy. These would include—understanding the nature of science; ability to properly apply appropriate scientific concepts and their technological applications; capacity to understand values that underlie science and technology; willingness to understand and appreciate the joint enterprise of science, technology and society, ability to develop rich and satisfying views of the universe and to continue science and technology education throughout life. This would involve the development of certain manipulative skills which are required in day-to-day life situations. In addition to the support available to develop these skills within and outside the laboratories, it would be imperative to make use of tools of information technology such as computers and multimedia packages.

Science and technology education should have something of value to offer to all students. In the Indian context, it could be strongly pleaded that rural and tribal oriented technology ought also be made an important part of the educational package and its connectivity will have to be ensured. Science must cut across traditional subject boundaries and open itself to issues such as gender, culture, language, poverty, impairment, future occupation and environment and observance of the small family norm. It is also necessary to familiarise children with Indian traditions of scientific and technological learning, and contributions of Indian scientists, both in the past and the present.

The achievement of India in various fields through scientific and technological enterprises, would develop and nurture self-confidence and self-assurance amongst the learners. All these issues should become integral aspects of science curriculum.

It is expected that a pupil studying science for ten years will acquire observational and analytical skills for self-regulation, ability to use tools, apparatus and equipment appropriate to his/her immediate and future needs; ability to identify factors operating in his/her system and understand their causal relationships; collect, classify, interpret data and make reasonable inferences. He/she will also understand the basic scientific concepts, laws and principles, and apply them in solving problems.

Thus, there are three aspects of the study of physical and natural environment under science education. The pupil has *firstly* to learn about the flora and fauna, natural resources, sources of energy, etc. *Secondly*, the learning here should take place to a great extent, through the learner's physical and natural environment, implying thereby systematic observation and exploration of the environment by applying scientific procedures of study. *Thirdly*, learning should be for the physical and natural environment, meaning thereby that it should be aimed at the development of a genuine concern, sensitivity and ability necessary for the preservation and protection of physical and natural resources. It is desirable at this point, to briefly deliberate upon the genesis of science and technology education at different stages of education.

48.5.1 *Pre-Primary Stage*

Though pre-primary education does not aim at imparting formal instruction in any of the school curricular areas, a number of activities like gardening, water, play with different materials, maintaining pets, going on nature walks, maintaining a science corner etc., provided at that stage, help in developing science concepts related to plant and animal life, solids, liquids and gases, temperature, light and sound, work and energy, chemical changes, etc. through exploration, experimentation, assimilation and application.

48.5.2 *Lower Primary Stage*

Science forms an integral part of learning at the primary stage, mainly in the form of Environmental Studies. Essentially, it has to be learnt mainly through concrete situations related to immediate environment during the first two years. The focus would be on sharpening senses of the learners and encouraging them to discover, observe and explore their environment and surroundings. This will lead to enrichment of the experiences, mostly on their own, and supplemented by the teacher. The experiences and activities can be gradually structured during the remaining three years of primary education where Environmental Studies is to be introduced. The focus would, however, remain on objects, events, natural phenomena and learner's environment. Children would continue to learn to observe, explore and identify occurrences in their environment. This would also lead to stimulation of curiosity, which would further lead to formulation of several questions in the mind of the learners. Teacher could utilise this as a major input in the learning process by further encouraging children to collect information and wherever possible, attempt to classify the same. The process of searching for answers independently and in groups, can begin at this stage. Skills of estimation and measurement can also be attempted to be developed.

At the primary stage, science will form an integral part of Environmental Studies. In Classes I and II, a child learns mainly through concrete situations mainly related to his immediate environment. The major thrust of science education under environmental studies in Classes I and II, therefore, should not be to impart information to the children, but to sharpen their senses, by encouraging them to observe and explore their environment, and to enrich their experiences related to different aspects of their immediate environment. This should involve informal and unstructured reactions to their environment which, during Classes III to V, should gradually be made more structured by systematically exposing the children to a variety of objects, events and phenomena in the environment. Thus, towards the later years of primary education, the child should be helped to discover and understand scientific facts, concepts, principles and processes underlying various phenomena around them. In this process, the child should be encouraged to systematically observe and explore things and occurrences in his/her environment, formulate precise questions related to them, record and classify the observations systematically, collect information based on concrete experiences, analyse it and draw conclusions, including those related to cause and effect relationships discovered through simple experimental, acivities and demonstrations. S/he should also be able to identify the resources in the locality and use them properly. To make his/her observations precise, s/he must develop skills of measuring length, area, volume, time, temperature, etc. Science education at this stage should promote in children, attitudes and values like objectivity, open mindedness, perseverance, precision, and concern for maintenance and improvement of environment.

48.5.3 *Upper Primary Stage (Classes VI–VIII)*

Children at this stage begin to recognise the relationship of science and technology with human enterprises. The process has to be further strengthened and concretised. The learner is better equipped to understand the processes that underlie simple scientific activities, and to visualise their use in solving problems and taking decisions. They also begin to appreciate the cause-effect and structure-function relationships. Environment should continue to be a major source of learning, and the students should try to understand the changes taking place all around. They would also gain an understanding of the living world, balance in nature and the role of air, water and energy. Due emphasis should be given to the conservation of natural resources. Elementary understanding of some basic principles of science relating to matter, materials and energy can be introduced at this stage. Familiarity with life processes, health, nutrition and diseases, soils and agricultural practices and the continuous process of adaptation for advancement, would also be included.

Instead of loading the students with scientific information, efforts should be made to help them to learn *key concepts* which cut across different disciplines of science. This would generate curiosity, and would enhance awareness and understanding. The learner can also thus be encouraged to improvise simple equipments and design experiments using local resources to understand scientific concepts and seek explanation of some of the natural phenomena. They can also be made aware of some of the local and global concerns and the need to be constantly made aware of these, particularly in areas like drinking water, environment, health, nutrition and family welfare and others alongwith their direct and indirect linkages.

At the upper primary stage, the learner is expected to consolidate and strengthen the abilities acquired at the primary stage. In addition, the objective should be to develop an understanding of the nature of scientific knowledge, and certain physical, chemical and biological principles and their relationships and their operation in nature as well as in daily life. The learner should be helped in developing the capability of using the processes of science in solving problems, making decisions and furthering his own understanding of the universe. The pupil should be enabled to develop skills of manipulating simple science equipment and designing of simple experiments to seek explanations of natural phenomena. Science education at this stage should help the learner to develop an understanding and appreciation of the joint enterprises of science and technology, and the inter-relationship of these with other facets of society.

48.5.4 *Secondary and Senior Secondary Stage*

These stages are terminal after which a majority of the learners enter the world of the work. Scientific attitudes and skills developed at this stage would become foundations for further growth. They need to be exposed to the nature and the structure of science, and the support it provides to the technological developments. At this stage, learning of science would continue to be built around natural and social elements of environment. Focus would continue to be on understanding of concepts, of applications in the areas of matter and its properties, energy, relationship of various physical processes and the technological applications of principles of science. The biological sciences will deal with living organisms, their organisation and life processes. An integrated approach to science and technology leading to their application in areas like health and nutrition, industry, agriculture and animal husbandry and allied areas, would establish linkages of science to societal aspirations. Science, technology, society and environment would coalesce in teaching and learning of science at this stage.

Practical activities incorporated in the educational programme to be chosen should have relevance for future life, in terms of acquisition of skills and values. The learners need to be encouraged to work, both individually as well as in the groups. Critical, creative and generative thinking has to be developed. Improvisation should be encouraged, but designing would also need to be provided for, as a component in exploration. Flexibility in experimentation too needs to be widely promoted. Teachers could help the learners devise appropriate experimentation and activities within the school and also outside school, involving immediate environment such as farms, factories, industries and community.

The content of science should be organised on the basis of two guidelines, namely, *contemporary science and learning ability of the learner*. It should reflect that science is a continuing human endeavour, and that it is international in character and method. The topics should be presented sequentially and hierarchically on the basis of complexity, from concrete to abstract.

Science, by its very nature, should provide sufficient scope for directly contributing to important core components and related values like equality of sexes, protection of environment, observance and small family norm, and inculcation of scientific temper.

49

Teaching of Physics

49.1 The Concept of Physics

PSSC Physics in its introduction cites the example of the natural phenomenon like lightening and thunder, the eclipses earlier thought to be the periods of the illness of the sun, to state that "Physics enables us to answer such questions. It gives us the power to predict and design, to understand and to adventure into the unknown. From what we learn in physics, new things are made. With new answers in physics new questions are always arising. Many of these questions would never have been asked of physics itself had not been put to use."

Subsequently the mathematical branch of physics called 'mechanics' was developed for answering many unanswered questions like those about the complex motions of the heavenly bodies. Physics continues to grow like a building under construction enabling us to enlarge our horizons.

Physics uses mathematics as a tool which is clear and flexible as its eyes, ears and hands. These both are now becoming more complex.

"Physics lies behind the gadgets that create new jobs and behind the new problems every citizen has to face. In studying this growing subject, one of the most significant in the history of man, you will have a chance to nourish that curiosity about the world which makes us humans so sharply different from other animals. It generates that wonderful feeling of *wanting to know* which can be a deep satisfaction throughout a whole life time."

The most significant of these tools are built into our own bodies called senses, which help us collect information—sight, hearing, touch, smell and taste. We all have however to train ourselves to use them.

The basic notions of physics comprise time and space and their combinations in what we call motion and matter.

49.2 Instructional Objectives of Physics

1. To acquire the knowledge of terms, facts, concepts, definitions, fundamental laws, principles and processes in the field of Physics.

2. To develop an understanding of terms, facts, concepts, definitions, fundamental laws, principles and processes in the field of Physics.
3. To apply the knowledge and understanding of Physics in unfamiliar situations.
4. To develop skills related to (a) the practical aspects of handling apparatus, recording observations and (b) drawing diagrams, graphs, etc.
5. To appreciate the contributions of Physics to scientific and technological developments and human happiness.
6. To develop interest in the world of Physical Sciences.
7. To develop scientific attitude through the study of Physical Sciences.

Objectives and their Specifications

49.2.1 ***Objective: To acquire the knowledge of terms, facts, concepts, definitions, fundamental laws, principles and processes in the field of Physics.***

Specifications of the Objective:

To demonstrate the achievement of the above objective, the pupil:

1. recalls terms, facts, concepts etc. in Physics.
2. recognises terms, facts, concepts etc. in Physics.

49.2.2 ***Objective: To develop an understanding of terms, facts, concepts, definitions, fundamental laws, principles and processes in the field of Physics.***

Specifications of the Objective:

To demonstrate the achievement of the above objective, the pupil:

1. gives illustrations of principles.
2. locates errors in the given statements, arrangements etc. and rectifies the same.
3. sees relationship between cause and effect.
4. classifies data and phenomenon as per criteria.
5. translates verbal statements into symbolic ones and vice versa.
6. verifies facts, principles etc.
7. distinguishes between related concepts.
8. gives explanations of the familiar phenomenon.
9. solves numerical problems involving physical principles.

49.2.3 ***Objective: To apply the knowledge and understanding of Physics in unfamiliar situations.***

Specifications of the Objective:

To demonstrate the achievement of the above objective, the pupil:

1. analyses the situation or the problem.

2. formulates hypotheses.
3. devises experiments to test hypotheses.
4. establishes relationship between cause and effect, the known and the unknown.
5. makes certain predictions.
6. verifies predictions.

49.2.4 *Objective: To develop skills related to (a) the practical aspects of handling apparatus, recording observations and (b) drawing diagrams, graphs, etc.*

Specifications of the Objective:

To demonstrate the achievement of the above objective, the pupil:

A. *Manipulative Skills*

1. checks the working condition of apparatus and equipment before use.
2. rectifies faults in apparatus if possible, under laboratory conditions.
3. sketches the arrangements of apparatus at the outset.
4. sets up the apparatus in a planned manner.
5. uses equipments with the realisation of their limitations and with proper precautions.
6. records relevant readings accurately and systematically at appropriate time.
7. performs experiments with reasonable speed, neatness and accuracy following the stipulated steps in sequence.
8. improvises instruments for various purposes.
9. carries out simple original projects.

B. *Drawing Skills*

10. draws neat sketches and diagrams to scale.
11. draws diagrams according to the actual arrangement of the apparatus.
12. selects proper scales for graphs.
13. draws neat free-hand diagrams, graphs etc.
14. records and presents data in tables, charts, graphs etc.
15. lables the parts of a diagram accurately.

49.2.5 *Objective: To appreciate the contributions of Physics to scientific and technological developments and human happiness.*

Specifications of the Objective

To demonstrate the achievement of the above objective, the pupil:

1. follows and adjusts to the impact of Physics on society and the individual.
2. derives pleasure in understanding the scientific advances in interplanetary travels, astronomy, electronics etc.

3. realises that more inventions and discoveries are possible.
4. shows respect and admiration for the contributions of great scientists.
5. manifests a spirit of scientific enquiry.

49.2.6 *Objective: To develop interest in the world of Physical Sciences.*

Specifications of the Objective:

To demonstrate the achievement of the above objective, the pupil:

1. puts questions in scientific discussions.
2. reads scientific literature and biographies of prominent scientists.
3. pursues scientific hobbies to utilise leisure.
4. takes part in science talks and debates voluntarily.
5. visits places of scientific interest on his own.
6. organises and actively participates in Science Club activities.
7. contributes articles on topics of scientific interest.
8. observes and studies natural and man-made surroundings keenly.

49.2.7 *Objective: To develop a scientific attitude through the study of physical sciences.*

Specifications of the Objective:

To demonstrate the achievement of the above objective, the pupil:

1. respects the teacher of Physics.
2. records and interprets his observations honestly.
3. bases his judgment on verified facts and not just on opinion.
4. is willing to consider new ideas and discoveries.
5. is prepared to reconsider his own judgement in the light of newly available facts.
6. develops independent thinking.
7. pursues his activities with precision and consistency, undaunted by failures.
8. shows a spirit of team work, self-help and self-reliance.
9. realises the dangers in the misuse of scientific knowledge.

49.3 Methods of Teaching Physics

The nature of physics lends itself to a variety of instructional approaches. The study of physics invariably leads to the development of a scientific attitude, an interest in the environment and a critical observational eye.

Physics consists of both theory and practice and needs activities in the classroom, the laboratory and the environment as such.

Physics makes individuals feel indebted to scientists, discoverers, inventors and technologists through the fruits of whose contributions our life has been made worthy of living in comfort. This realisation also evokes in them an urge to explore and experiment for following the footprints of such people.

Teaching of Physics, needs special settings, which have but to be made available to the students by the teacher and the school. Concrete guidance about handling the tools is also necessary for effectively utilising the opportunities provided.

49.3.1 *Giving and Evoking Examples*

The theory part of physics often proves to be difficult to the students. This is because the fundamentals are often treated theoretically and these abound in abstractions. The most important thing to be done by the teacher is to give as many illustrations as possible from the practical applications of theory. The students may then be evoked to give additional examples of the theoretical phenomenon. They could even be encouraged to develop/coin hypothetical situations for exemplifying the facts or phenomenon or theories.

The students ought to have adequate opportunities for consolidating their learning through activities like the detection and correction of errors in experiments, setting up of apparatus, collection of necessary material for experimentation. A checklist for items to be observed is also a part of this preparation.

49.3.2 *Aiding Self-Drawn Conclusions*

The students after study and/or experimentation should also be encouraged to identify and/or establish cause and effect and other relationships and to draw their own conclusions for verifying the things learnt. This ought to be done through indirect help and guidance. These self-drawn inferences will be the personal treasures of the students and impart to them a sense of self-assurance and confidence in picking up other challenges.

49.3.3 *Verification of Facts and Principles*

When the students acquire clarity about the aforesaid conclusions related to relationships they should be encouraged to develop distinguishing criteria for purposes of classifying facts, terms, concepts, phenomenon. This could be followed by exercises on translating symbols into verbal statements and vice versa. Finally this could become a stepping stone for verifying facts and principles.

49.3.4 *Drawing and Verifying Self-drawn Conclusions*

As students proceed with their studies and the consequent acquisition of competencies, further exercises could be given to analyse familiar and unfamiliar problems and phenomenon enabling them to frame and verify hypothesis on their own. On this basis they may be prompted to make some predictions and even subsequently to verify the predictions they may themselves made earlier.

49.3.5 *Acquiring Experimental Skills*

Experimentation is the crux of learning in Physics. It is, therefore, necessary that the students learning Physics ought to acquire *manipulative skills* related to the handling of apparatus on the basis of the knowledge of theory. The students may first be given a demonstration supplemented by explanations. The students may then draw a sketch of the arrangement of the apparatus for the experiment, check the working condition of the apparatus, detect and correct faults if necessary, set up the apparatus, conduct the experiment with reasonable speed taking all the required steps and precautions, record the fundings/readings, analyse them and derive inferences. Finally, the student may move on to conceive, plan and execute, experiments on his own, as a demonstration of the acquisition of knowledge, skills and motivation for further adding to his knowledge.

49.3.6 *Learning Drawing Skills*

The students would, in the methodical process of learning would naturally as a matter of necessity, learn to draw sketches and diagrams. He may also draw graphs to scale as required. He may also acquire the skill of devising and developing tables, as per need for recording readings and data, labelling apparatus and other items in the sketches and diagrams would also need to be done.

The students should thus be enabled to inculcate a spirit of enquiry, a habit of carefully and critically examining different types of phenomenon, an appreciation of the benefits of physics and above all a belief that more discoveries and inventions are possible.

Apart from the above described content-specific methodologies, the teachers could use any other conventional and unconventional ones described earlier in the earlier section of the book.

50

Teaching of Chemistry

50.1 The Concept of Chemistry

Chemistry is an experimental science, related to a wide variety of human activities. Chemistry is concerned with the structure, properties, reactions and energy effects associated with substances. Bio-chemistry and nuclear chemistry are also its parts with Genetics and Bio-technology the latest additions to its fold.

Chemistry has wider and varied applications in life. At the school stage what is aimed at is only to provide glimpses of some of these and not a mastery over them.

Chemistry harnesses *observation* as an important approach to learning which implies sample sensory responses. Senses in subsequent advanced operations are attempted to be augmented and sharpened through sophisticated instruments.

Observation instills concentration and both qualitative and quantitative observation are used in the study of Chemistry and its experimental pursuits. The quantitative observation is also often subjected to mathematical analysis for discovering similarities and differences and for purposes of classification of different facts and phenomenon.

As a part of the pursuits related to Chemistry both qualitative and quantitative relationships are derived. These infact are the manifestations that observations assume in a direct or an indirect manner. It is on the basis of such evidences and inferences that these relationships are interpreted in terms of significance and implications for drawing more meaning from observations.

Even observing such a simple thing as a lighted candle the students are enabled to identify, the three zones of its flame—the *innermost zone* which is dark consisting of unburnt hydro-carbons, the *middle zone* which is yellow in colour and consists of solid carbon particles produced by incomplete combustion of hydro-carbons and the *outermost zone* which is pale-blue because the abundance of oxygen allows complete combustion of hydro-carbons.

50.2 Instructional Objectives of Chemistry

In the context of the above, the instructional objectives could be listed as under:

1. To acquire the knowledge of terms, concepts, processes, techniques and principles relating to the subject of Chemistry.
2. To develop the ability to understand terms, concepts, facts, processes, techniques and principles of Chemistry.
3. To develop the ability to apply the knowledge of concepts and principles of Chemistry in new or unfamiliar situations.
4. To develop skills required in Chemistry, such as manipulative skills in the proper handling of apparatus and chemicals.
5. To develop the power of appreciation of the achievements in Chemistry and its role in nature and society.
6. To develop interest in pursuits related to Chemistry.
7. To develop a scientific attitude towards phenomenon related to Chemistry.

Objectives and their Specifications

50.2.1 *Objective: To acquire the knowledge of terms, concepts, processes, techniques and principles relating to the subject of Chemistry.*

Specifications of the Objective:

To demonstrate the achievement of the above objective, the pupil:

1. recalls terms, concepts, facts, principles and processes in Chemistry.
2. recognises the terms, concepts etc. of Chemistry.

50.2.2 *Objective: To develop the ability to understand terms, concepts, facts, processes, techniques and principles of Chemistry.*

Specifications of the Objective:

To demonstrate the achievement of the above objective, the pupil:

1. illustrates terms, concepts and principles by citing examples.
2. expresses the same fact in different ways, by way of explanation.
3. locates errors in known situations and corrects them.
4. compares and contrasts, or finds similarities and dissimilarities between related terms, concepts phenomenon etc.
5. classifies substances and facts.
6. discriminates between allied substances, concepts etc.
7. identifies relationships, performs simple chemical calculations by substituting formulae.
8. extrapolates from known information.
9. translates symbolic statements into verbal statements and vice versa.

50.2.3 *Objective: To develop the ability to apply the knowledge of concepts and principles of Chemistry in new or unfamiliar situations.*

Specifications of the Objective:

To demonstrate the achievement of the above objective, the pupil:

1. analyses situations and problems.
2. formulates hypotheses on the basis of observations of given data.
3. selects appropriate methods and materials for testing a hypothesis.
4. establishes relationships for solving numerical problems involving novel situations.
5. gives reasons for happenings, reactions etc.
6. draws inferences, conclusions and generalisations.
7. predicts results on the basis of known facts.

50.2.4 *Objective: To develop skills required in Chemistry such as manipulative skills in the proper handling of apparatus and chemicals.*

Specifications of the Objective:

To demonstrate the achievement of the above objective, the pupil:

1. fits up apparatus for different experiments.
2. cleans the apparatus.
3. puts articles in proper order and place.
4. measures volume, weight and temperature etc. accurately.
5. follows the correct sequence in performing experiments.
6. takes necessary precautions.
7. draws neat and proportionate diagrams.
8. develops the power of observation, and records relevant data accurately and systematically on the spot.
9. makes graphs, charts and such other material from given data.

50.2.5 *Objective: To develop the power of appreciation of the developments in Chemistry and its role in nature and society.*

Specifications of the Objective:

To demonstrate the achievement of the above objective, the pupil:

1. shows thrill and excitement at the discoveries in Chemistry and chemical processes occurring in nature.
2. feels satisfaction in collecting and exhibiting pictures of renowned chemists, chemical activities and cuttings about developments in Chemistry.
3. enjoys spectacular and colourful experiments such as colour changes, crystal development etc.
4. shows thrill and excitement in declaring his own experimental achievements, as well as those of others.

5. reads with interest about the achievements and sacrifices of great chemists.

50.2.6 *Objective: To develop interest in chemical pursuits.*

Specifications of the Objective:

To demonstrate the achievement of the above objective, the pupil:

1. collects specimens of materials such as minerals.
2. reads with satisfaction, allied literature from books and journals on his own.
3. performs experiments in his spare time.
4. engages himself in Chemistry related hobbies for utilising leisure.
5. visits places of interest in the area of Chemistry such as factories, science clubs, museums, exhibitions, etc.
6. voluntarily takes part in debates, lectures, paper readings, etc. on topics of Chemistry.

50.2.7 *Objective: To develop a scientific attitude towards phenomenon related to Chemistry.*

Specifications of the Objective:

To demonstrate the achievement of the above objective, the pupil:

1. does not accept or reject anything without valid reasons.
2. a displays keen desire to know how and why of anything that happens.
3. is prepared to face hazards in his investigations.
4. admits his mistakes unhesitatingly.
5. suspends judgement till it is repeatedly confirmed.
6. is unbiased in his approach to problems.
7. does not ignore any detail even if it is of no direct relevance to the work in hand.
8. reports the results faithfully.

50.3 The Focus in the Teaching of Chemistry

The variety of themes with striking differences call for some pin pointed specificity about suggestions for teaching them and this is what is attempted in respect of the main of them. The idea source consulted in the present regard is the Teachers Guide for Chemistry prepared by the Chemical Education Material Study of the United States of America, the Indian edition of which was published by the National Council of Educational Research and Training, New Delhi in 1964.

Students of Chemistry ought to be provided with support by way of guidance on theory consisting of fundamental concepts to be developed and utilised. It is also advisable that concepts in descriptive Chemistry are used repeatedly so that they get internalised and can be subsequently used in a casual manner for proceeding on, to more complex ideas. Questions posed to students should stimulate thinking and not assigned merely as written work. All these tasks should be appended by suggestions for further work.

After such a theoretical orientation the students be led to the laboratory to verify the ideas to whatever extent that may be possible. The point desired to be made is that practical work in the laboratory ought to go on side-by-side with theoretical discussions and not one after the other. While being sent to the laboratory, students ought to be acquainted about the precautions related to the dangers of mishandling even common chemicals and equipment. Some of the main of these could be:

1. Undertake a thorough theoretical and practical preparation for the experiment and follow all precautions.
2. Not to touch chemicals with hand unless directed.
3. Wash away any spilled chemical.
4. Never taste a chemical.
5. Double check the label on the bottle.
6. Wear goggles/apron/gloves while doing experiments whenever advised.
7. Do not put back unused chemicals into the bottles.
8. Report the minutest of accidents.
9. Wash hands before leaving the laboratory.

Some suggestions, for tackling some specific topics in Chemistry are being listed below by way of examples:

Use structural information and molecular models for introducing major topics, like:

- liquid vapour equilibrium
- properties of solutions
- the electrical nature of water
- kinds of solids

While taking up the structure of the atoms and the periodic table introduce:

- Alkalies
- Halogens
- Hydrogen a family by itself
- The third row elements

While dealing with energy effects and chemical reaction introduce ideas like:

- energy changes are integral part of chemical reactions.
- discovery of the additive relation and its substantiation.

In teaching chemical reactions focus on:

- the different rates at which reactions occur.
- the role of catalysts in changing reaction rates.

While dealing with equilibrium chemical reactions focus on:

- dynamic nature of chemical reactions.
- factors determining chemical equilibrium.

While dealing with solubility equilibrium do discuss:

- individual character of ions
- application of equilibrium law to practical problems.

When taking up acids and bases discuss:

- equilibrium as applied to acids and bases.
- equilibrium constant as a qualitative measure in the treatment of acid strength.

While dealing with Oxidation-Reduction reactions take up:

- definitions of oxidation, reduction, anion, cation, anode, cathode.
- difference between the convention model and experimental fact.

When dealing with electrons and the periodic table take up:

- explanation of the periodic table in terms of hydrogen atom spectrum.
- electrons configuration of atom.
- chemical trends in the periodic table.

While discussing molecules in the gas phase do take up:

- chemical bonding
- stability of molecules as compared to atom
- possible number of bonds in the first three rows
- bond angles displayed by a given atom
- possibility of a polar character between two atoms
- symmetry and zero electric dipole
- formation of multiple bonds

When teaching bonding in solids and liquids do not miss to discuss:

- molecular solids, network solids as bases for—
  - valence orbital occupancy
  - ionisation energy
  - electron sharing by nuclei

While dealing with the Chemistry of carbon compounds it is enriching to take up:

- inorganic compounds as chemistry deals more with ionic substances than with non-ionised compounds
- number of carbon compounds is enormous and their behaviour is different from inorganic compounds

While dealing with Halogens, highlight:

- similarities and differences displayed by these elements
- shift from principles to descriptive facets of chemistry

While teaching alkaline earths:

- integrate the things learnt for still different groups of elements

While dealing with Bio-chemistry which is often taken to be mystical and beyond mathematical models to capture, highlight:

- how molecular composition and reaction energy effects and how molecular structure finds applications in bio-chemical substances.

While dealing with the Chemistry of the earth planets and stars do highlight that:

- planetary chemistry and geo-chemistry undergo only a very slow snail pace process spread over millions of years .

The above description has been specially included in the present discussion because the prescribed syllabi sometimes do not include them and the teachers while teaching different themes (religiously following the syllabus) miss valuable opportunities of introducing themes quite early at some points, which may otherwise take much longer and may not also be that easy at that stage.

50.4 Methods of Teaching Chemistry

So far the methods of teaching are concerned those related to Chemistry are almost the same as in other science subjects viz.:

- discussion
- demonstration
- experimentation/exploration
- analysis of results
- verification of hypotheses
- mathematical calculation and derivation of conclusions.

The contents of the whole section on conventional and unconventional methodologies of teaching and learning could be selected and used as per need.

51

Teaching of Biology

51.1 The Nature of Biology

The origin of Biology is usually traced to ancient Greece, though paintings and sculptures of animals existed even earlier. Human need for food led man to discover edible plants and to hunt animals.

In the present times we find many *subjects which have links and/or origins in Biology* like Anatomy, Physiology, Ecology, Entomology, Malacology, Virology, Genetics, Cellular Biology, Pathology, Space Biology, Radiation Biology etc. etc. These manifestations by themselves easily give the idea of the vastness of the subject of Biology.

Some of the modern day *applications of Biology*, in medicine, agriculture, horticulture entomology, eugenics, reflect the need-based characteristic of biology. These branches have indeed tended to link ancient and modern biology.

Biology has also developed and evolved through *biological technology* like the inventions of the microscope. The links established with Physics and Chemistry are also examples of such an evolution where Biology often merges with these subjects.

Biology is the science of life which enables us to travel in the domains of living organisms. It has grown out of its narrow concept as a handmaid of Physics and Chemistry to become an independent discipline only during the later part of the twentieth century.

The book Preparation and Evaluation of Textbooks in Biology brought out by the National Council of Educational Research and Training, New Delhi in 1972 has given special significance of Biology which is a useful background to the teaching and learning of Biology. These aspects are summarised hereunder.

Biology attempts to explain the *social behaviour of man* in two ways. *Firstly*, man is enabled to understand himself better as a biological organism *and secondly,* it helps man to appreciate being a part of a social organism like other plants and animals. He is also a part of the social milieu continuously adjusting to the needs of the community.

Biology is also directly related to human needs of food clothing and shelter and also provides solution to human problems of health, conservation of life, population control etc.

Biology is also a *means to understanding* and *controlling life* with Biology, Zoology and Human Physiology as its manifestations. It helps to explain not only various forms of life but also their relationship with one another. It also helps to clarify how the natural phenomenon could be exploited for human advantage like evolving high yielding crops, improved varieties of fruits and vegetables, better breed of cattle, preventive and curative measures for diseases and so on. Biology also explains the development of complex breeds of plants as also human beings from simple organisms like microbes. The above are just a few examples to present the idea of the Biological control of life in its various aspects.

Biology is also free of dogmas—All issues in Biology never stand fully resolved. Its conclusions are not unalterable truths or absolute truths. They are only temporary truths and liable to change. Biology admits open mindedness and a suspended judgement. *Richard S. Young* in his book 'Extra Terrestrial Biology' (Holt Renchart and Winston, Inc. 1966) states that "Biology is the only natural science which has no universal laws and principles."

Biology enables us to *understand ourselves into our biological environment*—Man can be understood more accurately by the study of other living organisms. It shakes ourselves free from isolationism. We have the *paradox of man APART from nature and man as PART of nature.* Man as a part of nature also distinguishes himself from the other elements of nature on the basis of his uniqueness. He is a part of the web of knowledge and can be understood only as a part of this web.

Biology is also a correlational science—Different sciences involve observation and speculation followed by data collection, comparison and correlation. Biological sciences are characterised by procedures of correlational sciences with a thrust towards exact or theoretical sciences Biology is a more descriptive or correlative science, than an exact science because *its general statements do not consist of any theoretical system of explanations but are inductive generalisations.*

Biology has evolved into an investigation of the dynamics of living systems through different levels of organisation molecule, organelle, cell, organ, individual, population and biome. With molecular level as its base, Biology exhibits a hierarchy in its composition, leading to more and more complex levels in the form of an inverted pyramid. The comparatively recent shift from descriptive to experimental stage in Biology has also now come to be reflected in the instructional material in Biology.

Biology is also an empirical Science which attempts to explain biological phenomenon on the basis of observations and experiments. It aims at discovering truths and motivating those that pursue its study for seeking them. Biology seeks to find evidences about living organisms by using the scientific method of enquiry. These facts represent the process and product of the investigations. Spirit of enquiry and the method of enquiry are the two basic sources of getting knowledge of Biology.

Product and process are both integral to Biology—The product aspect consists of facts, terms, principles. The process represents the ways in which biologists work—defining a problem locating and analysing information, formulating, experimenting and observing to verify the hypothesis Biology also concerns itself with the manner in which students, teachers and researchers react to different situations which in fact is a matter of scientific attitudes like those of objectivity, open mindedness intellectual honesty, curiosity etc.

The methods of Biology do not display absolute congruency with those of other sciences, as scientific methods cannot help us in making value judgements. It is not a normative subject as it cannot give any idea of what is good and what is bad.

Scientific method cannot also reveal purposes or reflect human values. But the future of Biology, however, depends on the bed rock of the scientific method rather than values. It also leans heavily on scientific tools in modern themes for enriching itself.

New disciplinary manifestations of Biology which were not known earlier have come to be known now. Enzymology, bio-chemistry and immunology are examples. Certain other subjects which revealed themselves when *molecular* researches were made are Cell Biology, Plant Physiology and Animal Physiology. Investigations at the level of the *cells* also gave rise to disciplines like protozology microbiology and bacteriology. Investigations at the level of *organ* led to disciplines like analogy and histology. Investigations at the *species* level led to the emergence of subjects like Evolution and Paleontology. When investigations at the level of *community* were made, disciplines like ecology, population genetics, epidemiology came into prominence.

51.2 Instructional Objectives of Biology

In the context of the above, the instructional objectives of Biology could be listed as under :

1. To acquire the knowledge of biological terms, facts, concepts, principles, formulae etc.
2. To develop an understanding of biological terms, facts, concepts, principles, processes etc.
3. To develop the ability to apply the knowledge of Biology in unfamiliar situations.

4. To develop experimental skills required in Biology practicals.
5. To develop the ability to appreciate biological phenomena in nature, and the contribution of Biology to human welfare.
6. To develop interest in plants and animals and in their respective environments.
7. To develop scientific attitudes towards biological phenomena.

Objectives and their Specifications

51.2.1 ***Objective: To acquire the knowledge of biological terms, facts, concepts, principles, formulae etc.***

Specifications of the Objective:

To demonstrate the achievement of the above objective, the pupil:

1. recalls biological terms, facts, concepts, principles and processes.
2. recognises biological terms, facts, concepts, specimens, principles and apparatus.

51.2.2 ***Objective: To develop an understanding of biological terms, facts, concepts, principles, processes etc.***

Specifications of the Objective:

To demonstrate the achievement of the above objective, the pupil:

1. translates tables, floral diagrams, floral formulae etc. from one form of presentation to another.
2. interprets charts, graphs, data, etc.
3. illustrates given biological phenomenon.
4. detects errors in faulty statements, diagrams, and rectifies them.
5. identifies relationship between various facts, concepts, processes etc.
6. compares biological facts, concepts, processes etc.
7. discriminates between closely related concepts, principles, processes, etc.
8. explains biological concepts, principles, processes etc.

51.2.3 ***Objective: To develop the ability to apply the knowledge of Biology in unfamiliar situations.***

Specifications of the Objective:

To demonstrate the achievement of the above objective, the pupil:

1. analyses the given data or the problems.
2. sifts the relevant data for the purpose.
3. makes hypothesis, based on observations and/or given data.
4. selects appropriate methods and materials for a given purpose.

5. establishes relationship between cause and effect.
6. explains biological phenomenon with reasons.
7. draws inferences and conclusions from the observed facts.
8. predicts biological phenomenon from the given data.

51.2.4 *Objective: To develop the experimental skills required in Biology Practicals.*

Specifications of the Objective:

1. To demonstrate the achievement of the above objective, the pupil in regard to: Manipulative Skills :
   1.1 arranges apparatus systematically.
   1.2 handles apparatus and instruments properly.
   1.3 maintains the apparatus and instruments in order.
   1.4 improvises apparatus and models.
   1.5 manipulates apparatus and instruments at reasonable speed.
2. To demonstrate the achievement of the above objective, the pupil in regard to: Dissection Skills :
   2.1 selects appropriate specimens for the given purpose.
   2.2 kills the animal by using appropriate methods.
   2.3 places the specimen in the right perspective.
   2.4 fixes up the specimen properly for dissection.
   2.5 handles the instruments with precision to dissect the specimen.
   2.6 exposes the desired parts properly without damages.
   2.7 displays the required parts of the specimen by flag labels.
   2.8 separates and removes the desired parts of the specimen for detailed examination without any damage.
3. To demonstrate the achievement of the above objective, the pupil in regard to: Observational Skills :
   3.1 notices the relevant details in the specimen carefully.
   3.2 reads the instruments correctly.
   3.3 discriminates between closely related structures, parts, phenomena and specimens accurately.
   3.4 locates the desired parts exactly.
   3.5 detects errors in the experimental set-up and procedures.
4. To demonstrate the achievement of the above objective, the pupil in regard to: Drawing Skills :
   4.1 represents the desired parts and structures faithfully.
   4.2 makes diagrams with a sense of proportion.
   4.3 labels diagrams neatly, methodically and correctly.
   4.4 draws sketches and diagrams at a reasonable speed.

5. To demonstrate the achievement of the above objective, the pupil in regard to: Collecting, Mounting and Preserving Skills:
   - 5.1 locates the right habitat for a particular specimen.
   - 5.2 selects the appropriate instruments for collection of specimens.
   - 5.3 gathers the required specimens at the appropriate time.
   - 5.4 uses the relevant material to count the specimens.
   - 5.5 selects the proper method of preservation.
   - 5.6 uses the appropriate preservatives for different specimens.
   - 5.7 arranges the material in systematic order.
6. To demonstrate the achievement of the above objective, the pupil in regard to: Skills in Locating Biological Information:
   - 6.1 taps different sources of biological information carefully.
   - 6.2 uses the index card in the library properly to get the desired information.
   - 6.3 studies the table of contents and index correctly to locate and collect the required information.
   - 6.4 sifts the relevant material for the purpose efficiently.
   - 6.5 accurately refers to the relevant bibliographies for further reading.

51.2.5 ***Objective: To develop the ability to appreciate biological phenomena in nature, and the contribution of Biology to human welfare.***

Specifications of the Objective:

To demonstrate the achievement of the above objective, the pupil:

1. understands the impact of Biology in daily life.
2. uses scientific methods in solving biological problems.
3. realises the need for investigation of biological problems through cooperative and selfless efforts for tackling the problems.
4. signifies the role of the tools of Biology in unfolding the mysteries of science.
5. admires life and work of biologists.
6. explains interdependence of organism and environments and among organisms themselves.
7. expresses thrill, joy and excitement at new achievements in Biology, and shares the same with others.

51.2.6 ***Objective: To develop interest in plants and animals and in their respective environments.***

Specifications of the Objective:

To demonstrate the achievement of the above objective, the pupil:

1. collects, mounts and preserves plants and animals on his own.

2. enjoys observing the behaviour of plants and animals.
3. participates in the activities of the Biology Club voluntarily.
4. contributes biological material for school and other magazines voluntarily.
5. reads extra books and journals on Biology and biographies of biologists.
6. visits botanical gardens, zoos, museums and forests on his own for getting additional information about plants and animals.
7. improvises biological apparatus and models in spare time.

51.2.7 *Objective: To develop scientific attitudes towards biological phenomena.*

Specifications of the Objective:

To demonstrate the achievement of the above objective, the pupil:

1. shows inquisitiveness about knowing biological phenomena.
2. shows willingness to consider new interpretation of biological data.
3. develops intellectual honesty in expressing and recording biological data.
4. believes in cause and effect relationship in biological data.
5. does not accept or reject views and conclusions without valid reasons or verification.
6. suspends judgement in the absence of proper and adequate evidence.
7. shows perseverance in accomplishing various biological tasks.

51.3 Methods of Teaching Biology

The content of a subject becomes the basic subject-matter of teaching. *J.J. Schwals* in his book 'Biology Teachers Handbook' (John Wiley and Sons Inc., New York, 1963, pp. 30-42) has indicated some themes which ought to be emphasised in the teaching of Biology at the upper primary and the secondary stages. The titles of these are reproduced below:

- Change of living things through time
- Conversely of type and unity of pattern
- Genetic continuity of life
- The complementarity of organism and environment
- Biological roots of behaviour
- Complementarity of structure and function
- Regulation of homeostasis
- Science as enquiry
- The history of Biological concepts

While the structure of the subject, the conceptual framework and the entire gamut of Being-Becoming-Behaviour are no doubt important, the learner holds the supreme and the central position in the game of education.

The child comes to school with a specific background in the family and the neighbourhood, possesses a set of abilities, skills, interests and aptitudes which make him a unique individual. Thus *even when a class is exposed to the same learning experience, each student comes to be a unique learner.*

Objectives of teaching in this context do not have any status of their own. They give out to each individual learner a different implication about *what he would be* as compared to *what he is,* as a result of the learning intake. The learning process in fact sets in an evolutionary trend in the learner enhancing his competencies and capacity as a learner.

Science as a whole including Biology, involves not only acquisition of abilities and proficiencies but also of the methods and attitudes scientists use for gaining new knowledge. These aspects are designated as the *product* and *process* of learning. The product basically consists of facts, figures, principles. The process relates to scientific methods and the applications of the different disciplines for improving our lives.

Biologists in different situations do different things observing a flower and an animal grow. Some processes and skills involved in such exercises could be listed as under:

Observation	Experimentation
Classification	Analysis and interpretation
Measurement	Prediction
Communication	

The teacher's role in this context is that of *a manager of learning operations*. The enquiry oriented activities presented should be interesting yet challenging.

In the first orientation of the learning situation, the teacher is the focus of all the activities like dispensing of factual information, explanation, demonstration etc. Pupil's activities take the form of group work with specific tasks/inquiries/investigation, assigned by the teachers who offer guidance and assistance through their interventions where necessary or where requested. The teacher then coordinates the work of the different groups. Pupils could then in the next stage be encouraged to work independently on different assignments.

In the above sequence the teacher is busy in the beginning explaining and demonstrating, then he becomes comparatively free observing and guiding the groups or individuals. The individually pursued activities offer an opportunity for knowing about the depth and dimensions of the acquisitions of students in terms of knowledge and skills. Evaluation at this juncture helps in validating the effectiveness of the instructional inputs and methodology through regular feedback.

Willard J. Jacobson in his book "The New Elementary School Science" lists four goals of learning as:

- The building of a world view

- The understanding of the conceptual structure
- The skills in using key processes
- The appreciation of the benefits of science

Jacobson has also enunciated the following devices for keeping a record of the progress made by students in respect of their growth:

- Anecdotal Records
- Observational check-lists
- Writings of students
- Reactions to demonstrations and experiments
- Number and kind of questions asked by students
- Tests

All these are, however, to be used for further improving the competencies of students and the pace of their learning.

51.4 The Focal Points in Teaching of Biology

The teacher of Biology apart from developing functional understanding of the subject in the students should also: *Firstly* attempt to develop scientific attitudes among pupils. *Secondly* the students should not only get an idea of the product of Biology but also its processes. *Thirdly* while giving an idea about the tools and techniques of Biology, the corresponding method, normally used by biologists for purposes of investigations ought to be highlighted. *Fourthly* the social aspects of Biology about how it helps as a socialising agent in developing certain attitudinal values and how the impact of Biology has changed our daily lives, ought to be brought to the forefront. *Fifthly* the idea of conceptual schemes of Biology is also essential to be imparted for giving an idea about the gestalt of the subject. *Sixthly* an objective presentation of facts is essential for establishing the basis for understanding the biological problems related to human welfare and well-being.

51.5 Realising the Objectives of Teaching Biology

It is not just desirable but imperative that all the objectives of teaching Biology are kept in mind while treating different themes. The following could be specially mentioned in this regard as the action points for the teacher.

Develop a functional understanding of biological concepts—To build the desired concepts, learning the operational meaning of technical terms with exactness and acquaintance with reliable sources of information are necessary for developing functional understanding for which concrete efforts deserve to be made.

Develop problem solving skills in Biology—In this context the problems posed should be real for which no textbook answers may be immediately available. The students may be required, for example, to draw inferences and generalisations. The learner should be put in such a situation as requires him to apply the generalisation drawn, to an unfamiliar unique situation. The situations so posed may lead to a number of problems out of which the pupils may be made to sense the significant ones, isolate the major idea, recognise valid evidences, formulate tentative hypothesis, test hypothesis and draw conclusions. Adoption of a complete sequence may not be necessary as there abilities cannot be developed independently.

Develop appreciation for Biological phenomenon—This aspect is often neglected. In this context emphasis may be laid on things like the potential of Biology in providing food, shelter and clothing to human beings, its significance in conserving life, place of man in biological environments application of biology in raising the standards of living, adventures of biologists and the like, ought to be highlighted.

Develop interest in Biology—Development of interests is both a means and ends. The *ends* may create motivations for deep and abiding interest. Means act as a vehicle for understanding. The applications of biological principles in daily life and in understanding and solving problems related to life ought to be focussed upon.

Develop scientific attitudes towards biological phenomenon—The study of Biology should enable the students to inculcate open-mindedness, intellectual honesty, suspended judgement, freedom from bias and an understanding and appreciation of cause and effect relationships. Quoting research findings for dispelling superstition and unfounded beliefs, highlighting inadequacies of data and limitations of conclusions, could be some concrete suggestions in this regard.

Psychology of Learning to be the Basis for Teaching—Efforts in this regard should be made to present the numerous facts and phenomenon related to Biology in a condensed form, in the name of concepts and principles. Psychologically sound and appropriate conditions that facilitate learning ought to be created. Some hints in this regard are being listed below:

Provide subject matter for which the learner is ready for disallowing any dissatisfaction or frustration. This will be dependent on the maturity level of the student and for being satisfying, it will also need to be founded on previous knowledge.

Sensory contact, contrived material and oral or printed words are the three main tools leading to learning.

We should also proceed from simple to complex. Grading of concepts and their proper placement is essential for the purpose. The sophistication needed for different classes ought also to be kept in mind in this regard.

Motivate students to promote learning—Motivation is the soul of learning. Motivation of pupils is Trapped when the presentation is meaningful to them. Students ought, therefore, be first exposed to familiar material before proceeding on to unfamiliar material. Academic and experiential background are therefore essential foundations for building the instructional structure upon, at each stage.

Furthermore the presentation of functional aspects should precede the structural aspects. When functions are understood, it is easier for the students to reconstruct the forgotten structures in relation to different functions.

Specific information should be preceded by inclusive principles. This helps in anchoring the more easily forgettable specifies, which in turn are again subsumed under the major concepts and generalisations.

It also needs to be remembered that *things learnt last longer if there is reinforcement through recurrent experiences.*

Furthermore pupils are more interested in observing and understanding facts rather than accepting generalisations to begin with. The axiom 'observation to reasoning' can therefore be applied with profit.

Learning of a more permanent nature is also more easily transferred to more complex and more varied new situations. Transfer of learning is also then faster and more effective. These aspects do need to be taken care of.

51.6 Ensuring Effective Communication of Subject-Matter

Verbal communications are effective if the learner comprehends them. The ease and economy, with which the instructional material is comprehended by the learner determines the degree of appropriateness of the verbal communication.

Use of appropriate mode of communication—Different modes of communication are applicable in different types of content, depending upon their suitability in a particular context.

Description, narration, explanation are the main modes, but their choice in different situations has to be apt and appropriate—a decision which the teacher can best make in respect of his familiarity with the group/class he may be teaching.

Use of technical terminology of biological science—Use of appropriate terms is essential for explaining biological phenomenon. Whenever new terms are introduced they must be appropriately explained with concrete examples as far as possible. Precaution of course, is to be taken for not using technical terminology indiscriminately as that confuses students.

Be consistent in making presentations—This enhances the acceptance of the presentation by the students due to familiarity and also helps in better consolidation of the context.

Assure coherence—Proper sequencing is the key to learning and this ought to be maintained.

Prompt response to classifications sought—The teacher should ask students to ask questions whenever they occur to them so as to nip confusions in the bud.

51.7 Use Appropriate Illustrations Appropriately

Some basic principles and pre-requisites to be followed in using appropriate illustrations in an appropriate manner by the teacher are as under:

- to determine in advance where to use illustrations and design them.
- to determine the suitability of different forms of illustrations, diagrams, graphs, pictures, photographs etc.
- to identify the specific purpose for which the illustration is to be used—for explaining a concept, for describing a biological fact, for interpreting a particular biological phenomenon or for purposes of drawing generalisation. Such a clarity will enable the teacher to design and/or use suitable illustrations.

In fact, illustrations are the soul of subjects like Biology and Geography and ought to be abundantly used for leading teaching to learning.

52

Teaching of Home Science

The original concept of Home Science has of late undergone an unprecedented change with each of its aspects having acquired a professional connotation driven towards commercialisation.

52.1 The Scope of Home Science

Rajammal P. Devadas enunciates the scope and contributions of the different components of Home Science. An adapted version of the same is presented hereunder.

In the area of spiritual values

Pupils studying Home Science will be:

1. performing fundamental duties enshrined in the constitution
2. contributing their best willingly and happily for national progress.
3. living in harmony with all people.
4. developing community spirit and eagerness to do social service.
5. leading an orderly and disciplined life.

In the area of child care and development

Home Science alerts pupils to the importance of keeping children healthy, happy and secure by:

1. taking care of younger children in the home when their mothers are away.
2. helping children develop self-reliance.
3. keeping children constructively occupied when their parents are busy.
4. helping in crèches established for working women.
5. helping in Balwadis.

In the area of food and nutrition

Home Science education can help pupils to produce more food and utilise food effectively by:

1. understanding the principles of nutrition and good eating habits, so that optimum health and growth is achieved.

2. selection and use of protective foods which are rich in nutrients, and at the same time in expensive for being within reach of all, such as leafy green vegetables, high lysine maize, ragi and many others. This will ensure good health with no additional expenditure on tonics and drugs.
3. use of inexpensive food supplements.
4. use of proper methods of cooking, which conserve the nutrition value of food.
5. sensitivity to over-eating and thus promote better health.
6. using every centimeter of space available, for raising kitchen gardens to help increase food production.
7. propagating the principles of good nutrition in the community.
8. evaluation of food habits born out of traditional practices.

In the area of home management

Home Science helps pupils recognise how good management in the home, making full use of their resources and abilities can be valuable for the nation by:

1. spending every paisa wisely.
2. teaching that saving is investment for future spending, and therefore should be voluntary and spontaneous.
3. spending time fruitfully so that maximum work can be accomplished in minimum time.
4. spending time productively.
5. using time efficiently to release adults from their household responsibilities for more urgent and fruitful tasks.
6. spending energy profitably.
7. taking care of personal property as well as school's property to save expenditure on repair and replacements.
8. investing time and effort for social service activities.
9. practising economy in the use of electricity and other fuels, water and other utilities.

In the area of housing

Home Science impresses upon pupils the relation between adequate housing to good health and comfort by:

1. understanding the requirements of good housing.
2. maintaining cleanliness in the house and surroundings.
3. avoiding accumulating unnecessary articles in the house and surroundings.
4. avoiding extravagance in the use of space.

In the area of textiles and clothing

Home Science helps pupils in understanding the principles and practices important in the selection, care and repair of textiles and clothing by:

1. having the minimum amount of comfortable essential clothing, regardless of fashions and notions.
2. washing clothes properly.
3. making clothes attractive.
4. storing clothes so that they give full service.
5. mending clothes promptly to extend their usefulness.

Integrating influence of Home Science

Consideration of various aspects of Home Science emphasises how closely they need to be interrelated to help pupils with their home and family problems. For example, providing food for the family is not just a problem of food and nutrition, but also involves problems of child development in regard to children. In the same way, other family problems cut across several areas of Home Science.

Family living has spiritual, physiological and psychological dimensions. Harmony, comfort, health, economy, beauty and conveniences contribute to the wellbeing of the family. The study of Home Science has, therefore, a wide appeal to pupils who are the future parents, citizens and leaders. It is necessary to include Home Science as one of the core subjects in schools for both boys and girls.

Teachers of Home Science face tremendous challenges as they attempt to develop the kinds of programmes that will meet the needs of their pupils. Theirs is the most rewarding vocation, since they assist pupils to cope with, and meet the demands of home and family living today.

52.2 Instructional Objectives of Home Science

In the context of the above the instructional objectives of Home Science could be stated as under:

1. To acquire the knowledge of terms, facts, concepts and principles required for setting up and managing better homes, providing good health and convenience at minimum expense.
2. To develop an understanding of:
   - 2.1 the principles and procedures of setting the home better.
   - 2.2 the factors and principles that provide good health.
   - 2.3 the principles for convenient arrangement for providing comfort.
   - 2.4 intelligent use of money to provide necessities and comforts.
3. To apply knowledge and understanding of the principles for carrying out the following tasks within ones budget:
   - 3.1 selecting a proper house.
   - 3.2 setting up the home conveniently.

   3.3 providing balanced food for the members of the family and
   3.4 providing suitable clothing.
4. To acquire the competencies related to:
   4.1 the setting up of rooms attractively and conveniently for providing comfort.
   4.2 preparing menus and cooking the food for the family.
   4.3 repairing and stitching clothes for the family.
   4.4 taking care of the health of the members of the family.
   4.5 purchasing goods and dealing with monetary transactions according to needs and budget, and
   4.6 maintaining necessary records.
5. To develop interest in hobbies for fruitfully and pleasurably spending leisure time.
6. To develop scientific attitudes towards health, hygiene and food-habits by working towards the removal of superstitions and undesirable customs.
7. To develop the ability to appreciate beauty in interior and exterior decoration, colour schemes, presentation serving of food, designs of garments and designs of furniture and equipments.

Objectives and their Specifications

52.2.1 ***Objective: To acquire the knowledge of terms, facts, concepts and principles required for setting up and managing better homes, providing good health and convenience at minimum expense.***

Specifications of the Objective:

To demonstrate the achievement of the above objective, the pupil:

1. recalls necessary information.
2. recognises needs of different categories of people.

52.2.2 ***Objective: To develop an understanding of (a) the principles and procedures of setting up the home better, (b) the factors and principles that provide good health, (c) the principles for convenient arrangement for providing comfort and (d) an intelligent use of money to provide necessities and comforts.***

Specifications of the Objective:

To demonstrate the achievement of the above objective, the pupil:

1. identifies the needs of different types of homes, and the means of satisfying them in the best possible manner within the budget.
2. compares and contrasts information.
3. classifies.

4. discriminates between different types of homes.
5. sees relationships.

52.2.3 ***Objective: To apply knowledge and understanding of the principles for carrying out the following tasks within one's budget: (i) selecting a proper house, (ii) setting up the home for conveniently, (iii) providing balanced food for the members of the family and (iv) providing suitable clothing.***

Specifications of the Objective:

To demonstrate the achievement of the above objective, the pupil:

1. plans and makes suggestions.
2. selects appropriate items for the home.
3. identifies past mistakes in home management and rectifies them.
4. analyses investments and gains.
5. generalises about principles to be followed in home management.
6. predicts results of efforts made.

52.2.4 ***Objective: To acquire the competencies related to (a) the setting up of rooms attractively and conveniently for providing comfort, (b) preparing menus and cooking the food for the family, (c) repairing and stitching clothes for the family wherever needed, (d) taking care of the health of the members of the family, (e) purchasing goods and dealing with monetary transactions according to needs and budget and (f) maintaining necessary records of expenditure and family income.***

Specifications of the Objective:

To demonstrate the achievement of the above objective, the pupil:

1. cleans and sets the rooms.
2. arranges rooms and work areas.
3. cooks and serves food.
4. uses appropriate tools and equipments.
5. designs and prepares appropriate garments of required.
6. takes care of the repair and storage of clothing and linen.
7. prepares budgets and makes necessary purchases accordingly.
8. maintains necessary accounts and records.
9. renders first aid when required, and takes care of the sick.
10. takes care of the children.
11. entertains guests and visitors.

52.2.5 ***Objective: To develop an interest in hobbies for fruitfully and pleasurably spending leisure time.***

Specifications of the Objective:

To demonstrate the achievement of the above objective, the pupil: organises work for engaging oneself in hobbies, such as collection, reading and writing, painting, decoration, stitching and needle-work; trying out new recipies, clay modelling, toy making, community (social) service etc.

52.2.6 ***Objective: To develop scientific attitudes towards health, hygiene and food-habits by working towards the removal of superstitions and undesirable customs.***

Specifications of the Objective:

To demonstrate the achievement of the above objective, the pupil:

1. shows open-mindedness and accepts facts with reason.
2. does not believe in superstitions.
3. cultivates healthy habits (health promotion).

52.2.7 ***Objective: To develop the ability to appreciate beauty in interior and exterior decoration, colour schemes, presentation and serving of food, designs of garments and designs of furniture and equipments.***

Specifications of the Objective:

To demonstrate the achievement of the above objective, the pupil:

1. decorates the home with simple artistic things.
2. selects designs in cloth and clothing to suit places and persons.
3. makes plain and simple articles attractive.
4. serves food attractively.
5. chooses the right style in dress to improve personal looks.

52.3 Methods of Teaching Home Science

Though Home Science does have a theoretical foundation, its operations are by and large operational, as the above described scope of Home Science portrays.

The teaching of Home Science, therefore, follows the following basic steps.

Theoretical Discussion is a natural first, because the theoretical concepts and constructs lay the foundation of all future steps. They enable students to make the practical operations scientific, by communicating to the learners as to 'why' a particular thing is being done. Such justifications, besides being enlightening, impart confidence to the students about doing the right things in the right way. This, however, does not preclude exploration and experimentation for coming out with original ideas. They only provide general guidelines. For example, the student may use any dress material or design any design, but whatever he/she prepares, has to fit the given chest or waist size.

Demonstration is the next step, and the teacher actually teaches by following the rules of the game and the sequence of the steps of demonstration. In this process the basic principles guiding each step too are once again explained. These theoretical references illuminate practice and make learning abiding. The ingredients/raw materials too, are introduced to the students along with possible alternatives to encourage them to experiment later. Students are also told about economy in the use of material, and ways of avoiding wastage. Highlighting of cautions and precautions constitutes an important part of demonstration. They are always made to focus on the outcomes of their efforts and the characteristics they should endeavour to impart to them, and those they should not, are also highlighted through emphasis on do's and don'ts. They have also to be enabled to understand that the 'senses' are the sole index for judging a product, besides of course utility.

There are however, situations where no standard rules and principles apply, where the situations are always singularly unique, where originality is the key-word, where aesthetic sense is the permeating ethos, where ingenuity is the soul of all ventures, and where past experiences too play only a marginal role. These are settings of interior design. Demonstration in such situations changes with each setting, and it could thus take a variety of forms. Each setting could be photographed, and these photographs discussed in class and ideas elicited from the students about the merits and shortfalls of each exercise. Even in actual practice, the interior designers work by trial and error, for putting up alternative specimens, out of which they choose the best, which they and their clients decide on.

Demonstration, apart from everything else, is a great confidence booster, in so far as it proves that what the books state and what the teacher says are not just flights of imagination, but something which is feasible, applicable as also adaptable, and above all something that they also can do.

Supervised Work

After the students have acquired the theoretical background and observed the operations, they are now asked to repeat what they observed. All facilities, equipment, apparatus and materials are made available to them. They do not have to prepare an inventory of the things required nor are they expected to check up the availability of the requirements through a checklist. All items of equipment and apparatus already stand checked up to ensure that they are all usable and in working condition. They are just there, ready to use. They only have to know what is what, and recall the manner in which the teacher had used them in the course of the demonstration.

Sometimes, the teacher also executes the exercise side by side and step by step.

The teacher also, after distinct steps, goes round to observe that the students are doing the job appropriately. During these rounds, be checks that:

- the basic theoretical principles are being followed.
- the correct tools and implements are being used.
- the required sequence of operations is being observed.

- the tools and implements are appropriately used.
- the tools and implements are being placed in an aesthetic, orderly fashion for being easily picked up, whenever needed.
- the required material is being appropriately used and in appropriate quantities.
- wastage is being contained through all possible measures.
- necessary precautions are being taken for avoiding accidents.
- the senses qualify the outcome or the product etc. etc.

Any student who specially needs some special help is provided the same on the spot.

Discussion of the common shortfalls is an essential concluding part of the supervised work. It serves both as a diagnostic and a corrective measure.

Independent work

The learners are then to be given an opportunity for working independently on their own, as per the tasks assigned by the teacher. These tasks could first be small parts/steps, and subsequently, the total operations related to the task. Finally the learner assumes greater responsibility in regard to planning, execution and marshalling of needs. Peer evaluation of the product or outcome is an essential step of evaluation, before it is evaluated for all types of tasks.

The objectives of teaching Home Science will be of great help in preparing evaluation proformas for different types of tasks and operations. While being tools for formal evaluation by the teacher, they will also be a useful self-evaluation devices for the learner.

Drill

Repeated practice on the same item by the learner is of great help in consolidating learning, and making it a permanent asset of the learner. This also imparts precise familiarity with do's and don'ts, as experience is the greatest teacher. Drill enables students to learn by trial and error and is a valuable exercise in learning by doing, in which situation s/he learns from his own mistakes. Drill also provides an opportunity for experimentation and innovation, which gives learners a sense of achievement and satisfaction.

The innovations tried by the learners should invariably be shared with the entire class. Besides learning from the experience of peers, these sharing sessions would also be motivating for others to try new ideas and processes.

Autonomous work

After all these steps, the learner ought to be given the opportunity for being autonomous, where he takes full responsibility for all tasks and operations. S/he selects the tasks, decides on the steps of his action plan, chooses the material to be used and decides on how to use it, designs his own design and above all, *lavishly uses his imagination* in everything, to bring out a product which s/he may call his own in all respects.

Autonomous work allows full play to creativity, originality and the application of aesthetic sense. The learner learns to economise on money, material and time in executing the task and his natural saving instinct comes into play as s/he learns to make the best of what s/he has by exercising to the full, the maxim of waste nothing.

With the acquisition of the abilities for working autonomously, s/he starts looking beyond the formal educational settings and eyes for professionalising the acquired competencies. This is because Home Science has now become the starting point of a host of new professions like different branches of Hotel Management.

Internship in Business and Industry

This is now a confirmed pre-requisite for almost all learners of Home Science, irrespective of gender. S/he also now makes an initial choice of the professional line s/he desires to pursue as a vocation. The learner may make mid-course changes if s/he feels like, according to his interest and aptitude.

The internship period is a crucial period for the beginning of a professional life. Quite often, students are even picked up by the establishments for being offered jobs right at this time. The offer of a job is invariably an enticing proposition for any trainee, because earning money is everybody's ambition. Normally, the process of job-hopping commences until one finds a professional niche for himself/herself.

It is during the internship period that a student steps into a business setting where he has to put in his best for a professional ascent to be noticed.

This is also a time for brushing up his theoretical knowledge and applying it in real life situations. *It is no more learning for learning sake, but working for earning sake.* The stakes, therefore, are much higher here.

Entering the world of work

As mentioned in passing earlier, this is the final destination, one aspires to reach where he is face to face with life. *Everything is real and nothing imaginary. It is all practice, no theory. It is all work and little leisure. S/he has no qualifying examination to clear, or any certificate to earn. He has to prove his mettle, demonstrate his potentials and display his abilities, and everything has to sell.*

He has to work with others as a team, and yet retain his/her individuality. *There is cooperation for strength, and competition for excellence.* S/he has to learn to live with both. Efficiency on the job is all that counts, and s/he has no alternative but to acquire that for sheer survival.

S/he has to also realise that he is constantly under watch, not just for his/her competencies, but more so for personal and social qualities of adjustment with people and situations, displaying deligence, sincerity, patience, tolerance and the like. S/he should always be willing to accept mistakes and never attempt to rationalise them. S/He should also then try to make amends and ensure that the mistakes are not repeated. *Committing a mistake is condonable, but repeating it is a sin, which also sometimes becomes unpardonable and even punishable in business enterprises.*

The supervisors also unmistakably distinguish between instances of flattery and of genuine appreciation, of show off and earnest work. The functionary ought not just know, but understand this in his/her own interest. It is also desirable to keep oneself detatched from personal matters of other co-workers except in emergencies, when s/he must come forward to help as a humantarian gesture.

It is also not desirable to look for business secrets until the bosses start reposing confidence to share them on their own. Again, these have not to be spoken about openly, and kept well guarded.

Loose statements travel faster than anything else, and they always reach the destinations they are not meant to reach. One should also, therefore, desist from any derogatory statements against anybody in the organisation. One should rather identify the good points to praise people about them.

Conclusion

These are not just the steps of learning, but the landmarks in the life cycle of learning, which deserve to be taken cognisance of.

53

Teaching of Art

53.1 Art in Life and in Education

Perhaps the feeling for art is as old as the development of speech, which is also one of the basic ways of self-expression. Art is another channel through which the individual can express himself, his nascent ideas and feelings, his joy in living, his sorrows and trials.

It can, therefore, be safely presumed that 'instinct' for art and beauty has been part of man's heritage from the very beginning.

Place of Art in Life

In all the great civilisations of the world—in fact in all civilisations, great or small—art has been woven into the life of the people, sophisticated or unsophisticated, educated or illiterate, advanced or backward.

At the same time, it is necessary to realise that conditions of stress and strain of unprecedented magnitude have been created in contemporary civilisations, which make the role of art in life even more important than what it has been in the past.

The present day man, however, is ceasing to be a creator who experiences the thrill of creative activity. He is increasingly becoming a helpless adjunct of the machines that he operates. This leaves large areas of his interests and emotions uncared for and create a sense of conscious or unconscious frustration and resentment in him.

It is, however, a matter of some surprise and gratification that art still survives in its rudiments in our economically backward villages and towns, and finds expression at religious functions or seasonal festivals.

The kind of pleasure that they find in some of the modern media, like radio, television, films, etc. cannot fill in this gap. These media, therefore, instead of engaging their creative hands, minds or emotions, present an endless variety of programmes which appeal to their sensationalism and dull their imagination and finer sensibilities.

Place of Art in Education

This analysis helps us in placing art in its proper perspective and focus in the education of the child and the adolescent. Any education, which ignores art or confines it to a small proportion of children and youth, or makes it so dull or so sophisticated that they are unable to enjoy it, cannot be regarded as a liberating influence in their life. Secondly, as this 'instinct for art' is acquired by the children from the outset, there is no stage of education at which it can be dispensed with. Art must, therefore, find a place of due honour in our syllabi in pre-primary, primary and secondary schools. While contents and techniques will deepen and broaden, and respect for form and sophistication will find an increasingly prominent place in higher classes, the basic sense of spontaneity, self-expression and joy should never be allowed to disappear or recede into the background. The young art student, like the great artist, is anxious to find an outlet for 'making the inner outer', and doing so as effectively and beautifully as possible. This is something about which most of our 'art teachers'—if they can be so described—are not usually bothered. The training of teachers should be obviously so patterned that this essential element in art education is assimilated into their being. Every child will not necessarily be a painter or a sculptor or a clay modeller or a dancer or a musician or a maker of beautiful things out of waste materials, etc., but he will at least be able to find a congenial medium of self-expression in one or more than one of these forms. To learn to enjoy beauty, without necessarily being able to assign reasons, which will satisfy the sophisticated art critics, is a gift of great value, and for this purpose, some experience of creation, which may not necessarily produce art works of any high significance, is of great help.

In order to form and promote the aesthetic tastes of children, it is necessary that something drastic should be done to retrieve their total environment from being arid deserts with no art, no sense of beauty, no style.

There are, however, great treasures of beauty, which both nature and art have scattered all about us, but somehow many of us have lost the capacity to draw joy and inspiration from these resources.

It is necessary not merely in the interest of education, but in the interest of the emotional and aesthetic health of the people at large, that present conditions should be altered and the touch of beauty brought to bear on all that we do and make, and where we live and work and play. There are numerous such things that need to be done and can be done, if only we have the vision and sigleness of purpose. It is only when the younger generation has a chance to live and breathe and grow in such simple but artistic environment, where it can assimilate the beauty in nature and art almost unconsciously from the outset. It is to such a view of art education that it is desired to invite the attention and interest of all those who are wedded to a better vision of life and of education.

53.2 Instructional Objectives of Drawing and Painting

In the context of the aforesaid concept of Art, the following instructional objectives of drawing and painting as manifestations of Art could be listed:

1. To acquire the knowledge of artistic terms, facts, concepts, theories, principles and laws in Drawing and Painting, viz. imagination, creativity, expression, observation, aesthetic sense, organisation, interest in life and cultural heritage.
2. To develop an understanding of artistic terms, facts, concepts, theories, principles and laws, and the use of various materials and media in Drawing and Painting.
3. To apply the artistic knowledge and creative imagination in various unfamiliar situations.
4. To acquire skills in
   - Observation
   - Handling tools and
   - Drawing illustrations
5. To develop interest in the world of art.
6. To develop artistic attitudes, values and qualities through the pursuit of Drawing and Painting.
7. To appreciate the contributions of Drawing and Painting to human life and happiness.

Objectives and their Specifications

53.2.1 ***To acquire the knowledge of artistic terms, facts, concepts, theories, principles and laws in Drawing and Painting, viz., imaginations, creativity, expression, observation, aesthetic sense, organisation, interest in life and cultural heritage.***

Specifications of the Objective:

To demonstrate the achievement of the above objective, the pupil:

1. recalls terms, facts, concepts etc.
2. recognises materials, instruments, devices etc. used in Drawing and Painting.

53.2.2 ***To develop an understanding of artistic terms, facts, concepts, theories, principles and laws, and the use of various materials and media in Drawing and Painting.***

Specifications of the Objective

To demonstrate the achievement of the above objective, the pupil:

1. sees relationship between form and space.
2. organises and distinguishes between the related aspects.
3. finds balance, rhythm and force in lines.

4. distinguishes between two-dimensional and three-dimensional objects in drawing.
5. understands perspective and its related terms.
6. understands ways of creating varied forms through various media.

53.2.3 ***To apply the artistic knowledge and creative imagination in various unfamiliar situations.***

Specifications of the Objective:

To demonstrate the achievement of the above objective, the pupil:

1. analyses a particular situation in relation to form, space and time.
2. equips oneself with the resources at hand to face particular situations.
3. applies the principles according to situations.
4. gives concrete shape in line or colour to one's concepts and ideas.
5. applies different means of judging forms in relation to perception.
6. harnesses the creative power.
7. distinguishes between two-dimensional and three-dimensional drawings and paintings by drawing forms of plane and solid figures.
8. establishes relationship between forms and objects.
9. selects tools and procedures for purposeful creations.
10. transforms natural perception into visual forms.
11. applies aesthetic knowledge to one's creations.
12. applies colour schemes appropriate to the situations.

53.2.4 ***To acquire skills in (1) Observation (2) Handling tools and (3) Drawing illustrations.***

Specifications of the Objective:

To demonstrate the acquisition of the *competencies of observation*, the pupil:

- observes with purpose.
- observes relevant details in forms and colours.
- observes the effect of significant forms in perspective.
- summarises observations leading to generalisations.
- represents observations by drawing figures in line, colour etc.
- appreciates the efforts of observation.

To demonstrate the acquisition of the *competencies in handling tools*, the pupil:

- checks equipment and tools to see whether they are workable.
- corrects the possible shortcomings under classroom situations.
- selects and handles tools related to a particular medium.
- compares variation and gradation of colours, tone, tints etc.
- handles transparent and tempra colours and related tools in appropriate manner.

- ➢ demonstrates skilful craftmanship through his creations.
- ➢ skilfully uses the eraser etc.
- ➢ applies skill in handing pencils of various grades.
- ➢ selects various textures of paper or canvas according to needs.

To demonstrate the acquisition of the *competencies in drawing illustrations,* the pupil:

- ➢ draws sketches of imaginary forms according to actual arrangement.
- ➢ draws sketches with reasonable accuracy and speed.
- ➢ uses appropriate techniques and tools in drawing sketches.
- ➢ balances the form in relation to space.
- ➢ skilfully uses the colours in illustrations.
- ➢ applies the laws of rhythm, symmetry, contrast etc.
- ➢ designs skilfully for specific purposes.
- ➢ develops an artistic sense in patterns and design.
- ➢ exhibits aesthetic sensibility in skilful drawings.

53.2.5 *To develop interest in the world of art.*

Specifications of the Objective:

To demonstrate the achievement of the above objective, the pupil voluntarily:

1. reads art literature.
2. looks at various styles of pictures, paintings, sketches, pieces of art with attention and appreciation.
3. collects specimens of artistic creations.
4. takes up art hobbies.
5. takes part in activities like art exhibitions.
6. visits places of artistic interest.
7. helps in the maintenance of the school museum.
8. selects art projects and works upon them.
9. organises and actively participates in the activities of Art Association.
10. collects reproductions of notable artists of different ages.
11. prepares picture albums.
12. taps resource for the development of artistic sensibility.

53.2.6 *To develop artistic attitudes, values and qualities through the study of Drawing and Painting.*

Specifications of the Objective:

To demonstrate the achievement of the above objective, the pupil:

1. is clear and precise in his presentation of art activities.
2. bases his judgement on visual facts.
3. is willing to consider the new ideas and to explore new possibilities.
4. reacts favourably to efforts made for using art for human welfare.

5. is prepared to review his own decision.
6. derives aesthetic satisfaction from one's artistic creations.
7. develops a creative faculty.
8. shows the spirit of team work, self-help, self-confidence.
9. uses art material appropriately.
10. makes the best use of available waste material.
11. believes that experimentation can bring in a new world of creation.

53.2.7 *To appreciate the contributions of Drawing and Painting to human life and happiness.*

Specifications of the Objective:

To demonstrate the achievement of the above objective, the pupil:

1. realises the importance of art in human progress and happiness.
2. derives pleasure in understanding the advances in art in different fields of learning.
3. expresses joy, excitement, thrill at new significant artistic achievements.
4. shows eagerness to share and convey one's joy and thrill to others.
5. shows respect to and admiration of great artists and their works.
6. observes and takes delight in the understanding of the various forms of beauty in his environment.
7. appreciates various art styles.
8. enjoys new trends in art and painting.
9. appreciates the heritage of art.

53.3 Methods of Art Education

To explore, to discover, to express and to create have been the basic urges that have helped growth in man, and through the full utilisation of these faculties, man has come to be what he is today. It should be the business of art education, to make the child sensitive to the world around, both organic and inorganic, and release the creative forces of curiosity and adventure, exploration and imagination, discovery and expression, so that the child experiences living more intensely. In this way, his experience becomes more purposeful and satisfying.

To promote creativity, we must encourage curiosity, thinking, dreaming, imagining. We must re-examine our adult systems of approval and disapproval, must encourage children to daub, to dream. It is the responsibility of the teacher to encourage, to give freedom, to swing the gates wide open, wherever the child's mind wants to explore to make contacts, to know, and to allow the free expression of creativity. What is important in this context is the germination of ideas in children which motivate them to think and act in the way they choose.

Any attempt to limit this field with pre-conceived notions on what direction you want the child to take, whether 'traditional' or 'modern', is really limiting, and making this act of idea germination impossible.

Any adherence to dogmas and pre-conceived notions presents many handicaps, the worst of which is that *style becomes more important than structure.* Thus, the chief obstacle springs from our static concept of beauty and our belief that the work of art teaching, is to help the development of such beauty, *our adherence to the traditions which we have not fully understood is a burden of this otherwise valuable heritage.* The present art teaching in our schools is based on the tacit concept that the ideas of beauty can be established once for all—thus making it a static phenomenon. The present age is offering a new challenge to the creation of beauty, which consists of an individual search and effort. It is not necessary, at least for a student, to belong to a particular school. *What is essential is the capacity to see colour as colour, to hear sound as sound, to react fully and spontaneously to life around us.* Therefore, the teaching of art in our schools must strip itself of all clichés, stereotyped directions and attempts to mould the mind of a child. What is really important is intensive and active attention to his environment; it is in this field that creation takes place. It is this field in which germination and flowering of imagination take place.

It may be stressed once again that in the teaching of art in school, it is not important to attempt to create a great painter or a sculptor or an actor. But what is significant is to *enhance the capacity of the child to participate in this art experience.* This is far more important, and every school-going child must be given the benefit of this fruitful activity.

Art education would basically consist of providing opportunities and offering motivation to children on participating in them. These are attempted to be listed below in respect of different stages of education in terms of some action points.

It needs to be appreciated that *art experience is a universal experience,* and that art education must be provided at all stages of education as an integral part of the general education programme. The specific tasks which the teachers of different stages of education are expected to do can be spelt out as under:

Primary Stage: Age-group 6 to 11 years.

1. To provide children the opportunities for expressing freely their feeling, thoughts and sentiments.
2. To help children to observe, explore, invent i.e. to develop in them powers of visualisation, imagination and aesthetic sensibilities.
3. To provide opportunity for developing creative powers and experimentation.
4. To provide opportunities for manipulation, exploration and experimentation with media and materials.
5. To develop appreciation of visual experimentation and respect for creative work of others.

Upper Primary/Middle: Age-group 12 to 14 years.

1. To develop 'design consciousness' in children, which enables them

to improve their personal appearance, their homes, their surroundings, their school and their community.

2. To help them in their all-round individual and social growth, enlarging their educational horizons and enriching their lives.
3. To discover and nurture in them competencies related to art, which are of value to them in any creative work they undertake.
4. To contribute generously to their intellectual, spiritual and aesthetic growth, i.e. fostering growth and development of the creative, spiritual, appreciative and aesthetic qualities, abilities and potentialities.
5. To offer to children a deep and lasting enjoyment of art that will persist in their adult life.

Secondary and Senior Secondary Stages: Age-group 15 to 18 years. (in general and also in the elective courses).

1. To provide opportunities for creative expression.
2. To develop sensitivity to, and appreciation of art.
3. To develop the fundamentals and techniques which will provide the means of better art expression.
4. To develop a satisfying vocational interest.
5. To identify talented children and provide counselling, where possible, in the choice of an art related vocation.
6. To provide a gradual transition form pre-adolescent art training to art education, suited to the needs and interests of the adolescent.
7. To develop a genuine relationship between contemporary art and daily living.
8. To help in the development of a well-integrated personality.

In the light of the above, we need to select suitable art activities for our school children. The following questions would need to be studied before selecting art activities for them:

1. Is the project activity within the experience level of the children?
2. Does the proposed activity permit sufficient variety of interpretation to satisfy each child's needs?
3. Are the materials and tools of expressing suited to the manipulative and mental capabilities of the children?
4. Is the objective of the proposed activity worthwhile in terms of healthy growth of the children?
5. Will the proposed activity lead to further self-development of the children?
6. What stimulation will best evoke expression on the part of the children?

54

Teaching of Computer Science

Though a comparatively new subject in the school curriculum, Computer Science has come to be a very widely pursued course today.

The courses broadly cover the role of computers in Information Technology, the use of computer hardware in producing educational documents and in other educational processes, as also the use of internet for enriched self-learning, evaluation of software for school subjects and of the use of computers in education.

54.1 Instructional Objectives of Computer Science

1. To acquire the knowledge of facts, terms, symbols, concepts, principles, trends, definitions, processes, functions and languages in the field of Computer Science.
2. To develop an understanding of facts, terms, symbols, concepts, principles, trends, definitions, processes, functions and languages in the field of Computer Sciences.
3. To apply the knowledge and understanding of Computer Science in unfamiliar/new situations.
4. To develop an interest in the range of Computer applications.
5. To develop a scientific attitude through the study of Computer Science.
6. To acquire appropriate skills in handling hardware and developing software and other related materials.

Objectives and their Specifications

54.1.1 ***Objective: To acquire the knowledge of facts, terms, symbols, concepts, principles, trends, definitions, processes, functions and languages in the field of Computer Science.***

Specifications of the Objective:

To demonstrate the achievement of the above objective, the student:

1. Recalls with ease the facts, terms, symbols, definitions etc. in Computer Science.

2. Observes a computer system from inside and sees for oneself the architectural arrangements of the hardware.
3. Recognises the hardware and software components.
4. Reproduces with confidence (processes, syntax of languages, concepts etc.)

54.1.2 ***Objective: To develop an understanding of facts, terms, symbols, concepts, principles, trends, definitions, processes, functions and languages in the field of Computer Science.***

Specifications of the Objective:

To demonstrate the achievement of the above objective, the student:

1. Discriminates between closely related concepts.
2. Classifies items as per criteria.
3. Identifies relationships among the given data.
4. Translates verbal statements into symbolic representation (flow chart—pseudocodes—syntically correct programmes)
5. Gives illustrations.
6. Locates errors and rectifies the same.
7. Handles with dexterity the accessible hardware and software resources.
8. Displays rationality in work.
9. Displays computational proficiency.

54.1.3 ***Objective: To apply the knowledge and understanding of Computer Science in unfamiliar/new situations.***

Specifications of the Objective:

To demonstrate the achievement of the above objective, the student:

1. Studies and analyses the situation or the problem.
2. Finds out the adequacy, superfluity, relevance/irrelevance of data for a given situation.
3. Establishes relationship among the available data.
4. Suggests resource-friendly ways of tackling problems.
5. Substantiates his reasoning with comprehensible inputs.
6. Verifies facts, principles etc., i.e., finds out the validity or invalidity of the facts in today's context.
7. Introduces innovations and originality in the programmes that he/she is exposed to, or writes himself/herself.
8. Expresses in one's own way the ideas acquired through a computer language.
9. Knows thoroughly the syntax, limitations and highlights of a computer language.

10. Fully realises and anticipates the possible problems and context before selecting a solution in the selected language.
11. Identifies short-cuts and alternative approaches of solving problems.

54.1.4 *Objective: To develop an interest in the range of Computer applications.*

Specifications of the Objective:

To demonstrate the achievement of the above objective, the student:

1. Reads literature specially magazines on computers to constantly update himself/herself on advances in Information Technology.
2. Attempts writing articles on computers/computing for journals.
3. Pursues hobbies (related to computers) to utilise leisure.
4. Visits exhibitions, attends seminars where major theme/emphasis is on computers and encourages fellow students as well to do so.
5. Organises and actively participates in Computer Club activities.
6. Does additional study on computers.
7. Brings to the teacher additional problems not related to the syllabus.
8. Debates voluntarily and takes part in talks pertaining to Computer science.
9. Explores the Internet and WWW.

54.1.5 *Objective: To develop a scientific attitude through the study of Computer Science.*

Specifications of the Objective:

To demonstrate the achievement of the above objective, the student:

1. Follows and adjusts to the impact of computers on society and individuals.
2. Derives pleasure in understanding the world-wide technological advances made in the field of computers.
3. Appreciates the role of computers in solving problems of other branches of study (e.g., sciences, commercial applications, business problems etc.)
4. Appreciates qualities related to computers (e.g., speed, brevity, repetition of routine jobs without mistakes, exactness, memory etc.)
5. Shows respect and admiration for the contribution of great computer scientists.
6. Manifests an inquisitive spirit—one of enquiry with no reservations.
7. Examines all aspects of a problem and accepts a proposition only when logically proved.
8. Points out errors if convinced.
9. Is willing to consider new ideas and discoveries.
10. Bases his/her recommendations to the solution of a problem on verified facts.

11. Is prepared to reconsider his/her recommendations in the light of newly available facts.
12. Accepts ones errors without hesitation.
13. Respects the opinion of others.
14. Realises the dangers in the misuse of hardware and software resources and knowledge VIRUSES.

54.1.6 *Objective: To acquire appropriate skills in handling Hardware and Developing Software and other related materials.*

Specifications of the Objective:

To demonstrate the achievement of the above objective, the student:

1. Uses hardware and software resources within their limitations and with proper precautions.
2. Can crack any problem with simple, logical and hierarchical steps.
3. Can accurately carry out oral calculations with ease and speed.
4. Can accurately carry out written calculations with ease and speed.
5. Can write simple programmes for computations requiring multiple operations.
6. Knows the highlights, merits and the shortcomings of the various computer languages at his disposal.
7. Can judge and suggest which language is best suited for tackling a problem and substantiate it with proper reasoning.
8. Can easily start, use and switch off a computer system.
9. Can work easily and without hurdles in his/her operating environment (DOS, UNIX, WINDOWS etc.)
10. Constantly endeavours to update his knowledge and skills related to new generation computers and explores new possibilities of doing things.

The newness of the subject in the school curriculum prompts the presentation of the course content, in broad terms as that would help a better appreciation of the methodology of instruction which is based on both content and objectives. It can also prove helpful in designing curriculum.

54.2 An Illustrative Outline of a Course on Computer Education & Information Technology for the Secondary Stage

Unit I: An Introduction to Computers

(a) Concept of computer and computer system and its characteristics and capabilities.

(b) History of Computer Development and special features of the new generation of Computers.

(c) Classification of Computers based on : size, purpose and type of data processed.
(d) Concepts of major elements in a computer system : Hardware– input–process–output (block diagram). Software–systems and software application.
(e) Concept of Information Technology and the Role of Computers in Information Technology.

Unit II: Computer Hardware Functions & Applications (Input, Process & Output Devices)

(a) Input Devices – (i) Terminals and Dedicated Data Entry Systems (ii) Direct Data Entry Devices, (iii) Voice Input Devices, (iv) Pointing Devices.
(b) Storage Devices – (i) Primary Storage Devices, (ii) Secondary Storage Devices.
(c) Central Processing Unit : (i) Control Unit, (ii) Arithmetic/Logic Unit, (iii) Memory Unit.
(d) Output Devices (i) Hard Copy Devices and (ii) Soft Copy Devices.

Unit III: Computer Software

(a) Computer Software and its types.
(b) Types of Operating System.
(c) MS-DOS – Commands and Working with DOS.
(d) Compilers, Interpreters and Translators (in brief).
(e) Programming Languages—Syntax, Semantics and Concept of Higher Level Languages: BASIC, FORTRAN, PASCAL, COBOL, LISP, C AND LOGO (In brief).

Unit IV: Application Software for Education

(a) Features of Microsoft Windows – 95/98/2000 (or whichever is available).
(b) Features of M.S.-Office 97 (or whichever version of M.S.-Office is available.
(c) Readymade Packages for teaching school subjects.

Unit V: Use of Computers and Multimedia in Education

(a) Use of Computers and Multimedia in teaching-learning process.
(b) Use of Computers in Office Management.
(c) Use of Computers for Examination.
(d) Internet-Genesis, Software and Hardware requirement for Internet, Surfing, Educational Websites, Uses of Internet.
(e) Effects of Use of Computers in Education—on students, teachers and processes of Education.

The course related practical work could consist of one or more of the following activities:

1. Preparation of an Educational Document with the help of a readymade package.
2. Preparation and presentation of Educational Slides with the help of MS-Power Point.
3. Preparation and use of any Computer Graphics in Education.
4. Preparation of report applying statistical analysis by Using MS-Excel.

Aids to Instruction

- A computer unit (as hardware)
- Software related to the course
- Computer stationery

54.3 Methods of Teaching Computer Science

The methodology of instruction in computer science, broadly corresponds to that of any practical subject and involves the following main steps:

Theoretical Orientation

1. Enunciation of the theoretical foundations in terms of definitions processes functions and computer languages;
2. Introduction to Hardware, its technical structure and uses as also its handling.
3. Applications of computers.
4. Development of softwares and other related materials.
5. Demonstration with exemplary situations/material.
6. Practical work
   - 6.1 Teacher-assisted Practice
   - 6.2 Drill with repeated familiar exercises
   - 6.3 Experience with unfamiliar situations and material
   - 6.4 Self-initiated programmes and applications
   - 6.5 Adaptations of different techniques.

Elements of the conventional and unconventional methodologies discussed earlier could be identified as per the needs of the situation and pressed into service.

55

Teaching of the Physical Education

Somehow inspite of its accepted importance, Physical Education has come to be one of the most neglected subjects of the curriculum. The lack of playgrounds and instructors largely account for this phenomenon.

55.1 Purpose of the Programme

The age old saying "A sound mind in a sound body" has a perpetual relevance. By itself it is enough to highlight the relevance and importance of Physical and Health Education as an integral part of all educational programmes.

Activities related to Physical Education are, in fact, positive inputs for the development of multiuse proficiencies, neuro-muscular skills, values and attitudes, which have great potential for success in life. Activities like rhythmic, expressive movements, dance, mass-drill, specially flag salutation and singing of the National Anthem, do certainly go a long way in strengthening national cohesion and integration.

55.2 Objectives of Physical Education

The main objectives of Physical and Health Education Programmes are:

- to develop the concept of good health, physical fitness, grace and poise
- to develop healthy habits relating to sleep, food, exercise and hygiene
- to develop neuro-muscular coordination (bodily skills)
- to develop attitudes and values of cooperation, sportsmanliness, fair play and team spirit
- to develop traits of character such as discipline, courage, respect and self-confidence and a sense of responsibility
- to develop the ability for making an enjoyable use of leisure
- to promote talent in sports and to achieve international standards.

55.3 Activities at Different Stages of Education

Before proceeding further it appears desirable to survey different possible activities related to Physical Education at different stages of school education

55.4 Activities at the Pre-Primary and Primary Stages

A variety of activities can be provided at this stage and the teacher will need to select and provide them on the basis of age and health status of the children. Local conditions and available facilities could also be important criteria for selecting the activities. Some of these are listed below.

Free Movements

Movements like walking, running, jumping, throwing are a part of movement education. With the help of some improvised gadgets like hoops, old tyres, old boxes, old chairs, obstacles (prepared or existing) could be used.

These activities contribute to poise and coordination.

Rhythmic

Dance and action songs come under this category. Examples of such activities are group dance, action songs, flag drill etc.

At this stage various stimuli for dancing are provided by audio-stimuli like mouth sounds, clapping, drums and also visual stimuli like demonstration, community songs and other poems and songs selected from language readers.

These activities help develop an agile body, balance and physical poise, graceful movements, a sense of rhythm and above all they yield joy and satisfaction.

Imitation, Story Plays and Mimetic

Movement Education provides many opportunities for children to imitate what they see in the environment. Activities in this area can easily be integrated with language and environmental studies.

Examples of imitation exercises could represent human beings or animals.

These activities help develop creative self-expression, formation of concepts regarding form, size etc., ability for expression through modes other than the word of mouth and of course they yield joy and fun.

Small Area Games

These are simple games played within a small area involving running, chasing, dodging etc. Students could play these individually in pairs or in groups. Examples of such games are Lion in the well, Follow the leader, Thief and the Policeman, etc. Such games provide exercise to various muscles, help develop physical strength and neuro-muscular coordination, foster a sense of cooperation and quite naturally provide fun and enjoyment.

Gymnastics

Physical activities of this type should be so selected that the children of the age-group in question are able to perform without any special equipment.

Activities in this area could include, items like rabbit jumping, developing the postures of standing, sitting, lifting bending and stretching, forward, backward roll, monkey walk, cart wheel, wheel-barrow, shoulder roll, balance walk etc.

Gymnastic activities help establish body control and neuro-muscular coordination skills. They also impart strength, suppleness and balance to the body.

Simple Combatives

Simple combatives like pushing, pulling, toppling help children in sublimating their aggressive drives and desires.

Examples of these activities are drake fight, cock fight, lame duck fight, hand wrestle, pushing off the bench or the stool, stepping on the toes, knee slap etc.

These activities help children to know about their strength in relation to others and help develop courage and self-confidence.

Callisthenics

These are exercises without apparatus. They involve continuous movement of the head, arms, trunk, legs without any rigid positions being held and have to be done in a formal prescribed manner for a sufficiently long time. These are normally 6 to 8 exercises of 2 to 4 counts. They should be planned for the exercise of the whole body with big muscle movements stressed.

Callisthenics help develop coordination of bodily movements leading to the growth and development of the body and better postures.

Athletics

Athletics have an important place in physical education.

A healthy competition can be fostered through these activities because achievements can be measured and tested objectively where even an individual can compete with himself.

Activities in this area could include Short Sprints (25 M), Hopping (25-50 M), Endurance (200 M), Throwing cricket ball or football, Jumping for distance and height.

Athletic activities help develop fundamental motor skills, contribute to physical fitness and open up avenues for competition.

Games

Even though playground faculties and coaches or instructors are not available in many schools, an exposure to games, even in a limited way will help children to develop interest in them at an early age.

With this in view children may be offered opportunities for playing "lead-up" games leading them finally to major games, where they may encouraged to learn and practice a few fundamental skills and finally to play the games in the modified simple form.

Games help children to develop the ability to participate in vigorous activities, to learn new skills, to cultivate an interest in games and to derive fun and enjoyment.

Yogic Exercises

Yoga is an Indian contribution to the field of Health Education. Yogic asanas have to be performed in a calm atmosphere. They produce desirable effects on the body and the mind and offer excellent carry over activities.

Yoga helps, develop the ability to concentrate, has a carry over effect for later life and contributes to physical fitness and is now being increasingly used for therapeutic purposes in a number of ailments.

Asanas in which students could be trained at this stage are Swastikasana, Ardhpadmasana (Veerasana), Bhujangasana, Ardhshala–bhasana, Utkatasana, Tandasana, Vrikshasana, Naukasana, Padahastasana, Shavasana.

Drill and Marching

Drill and Marching are to be introduced at this stage as a compulsory activity.

These activities enable the class/group to develop uniformity in orderly movements, a sense of discipline and enables the formation of a habit for maintaining good posture besides leading to proper and effective control of the body.

Swimming

Very few schools have swimming pools. However, whenever, natural facilities like a river, a sea, a pond is available nearby, swimming could be made a core programme under the supervision of coaches. Children ought to be encouraged and guided to get over the fear of water through water confidence drill consisting (step-by-step) of:

- Walking in waist deep water.
- Jumping on the spot back and forth and opening the eyes in the water.
- Practice of aquatic breathing with the face above the water level, breathing in through the mouth and breathing out through the nose.
- Floating with the support of a partner-holding the partner's waist and body stretched in a horizontal position.

The basic skill to be acquired for all the strokes should be body position (horizontal), leg action, arm action, breathing, coordination.

Swimming leads to the removal of the fear of water, helps develop confidence and gives fun and pleasure.

55.5 Activities at the Upper Primary Stage

This stage relates to children in the 11+ to 14+ age-group and is a period of accelerated growth. In this period, group affinity becomes pronounced and children display loyalty to the team, class, house or school. Girls start taking interest in social and rhythmic activities. Team games, competitive sports, developmental exercises and rhythmic exercises come to be appealing to both boys and girls. The main areas of Physical Education at this stage are:

Callisthenics

These may consists of say two exercise tables consisting of six to eight exercises in each, of four counts arranged in a sequence—rhythmic jump, Arm and Shoulder, Leg and balance, Trunk bending and twisting, agility and coordination — could be performed by the students.

Athletics

General physical fitness exercise in circle/open, order/scattered formation.

Principles of Sprints and techniques of performance (fixing of starting blocks, getting off the block, stride length - body position and finish).

Principles of Jumps

- Broad jumps — warming up and agility exercises, approach run, take off flight and landing.
- High jumps — warming up and agility exercises, approach run take off, bar clearance and landing.

Principles of Throws

- Shot put — warming up exercises, hold, placement, initial stance, glide delivery stance, delivery action and reverse.
- Javelin — warming up exercises, hold and placement, carry, pegging, withdrawal of the javelin, delivery stance, delivery action and reverse.

Minor Games

- Luggage van
- Poison circle
- Pinch-ho
- Touch and go
- Dodge and mark
- Jump and shot
- Form threes
- Bombardment

Relays

- Over and under relay
- Human obstacle
- Crab relay
- Siamese twins
- Sedan chair relay
- Horse and the rider
- All up relay
- Jump the stick

- Chariot relay
- Lateral ball-pass relay

Major Games

Opportunities ought to be provided for learning and practising the skills and playing the games with suitable modification with regard to the size of the field and the number of players. Participation of all and not a selected few is to be given attention.

Hockey

- Brief introduction to the game
- Hitting it
- Dribbling
- Striking
- Pushing
- Passing between the players

Cricket

- Introduction —playing rules
- Tennis-ball cricket (in the beginning)
- General conditioning
- Fundamentals of batting
- Fundamentals of fielding
- Pitch practice

Kho Kho

- Introduction — playing rules
- Brief understanding of the game
- General conditioning
- Fundamentals of running fast
- Fundamentals of chasing

Basket ball

- Introduction — playing rules
- Dribble relay
- Ball pass — relay, chest pass, two hands over head pass, bounce pass, hook pass
- Dribbling — single hand, alternate hand, dribble and shot.

Volley ball

- Introduction and rules of the game
- Serving
- Receiving
- Setting —set pass
- Smashing

Hand ball

- Introduction and rules of the game
- Throwing
- Catching
- Passing
- Goal keeping

Kabaddi

- Whip tag Kabaddi
- Knocking down the club
- Cant — side kick, safe raiding, jumping and catching leg or hands.

Rhythmic Activities

- Movement coordination with rhythm
- Dancing
- Jumping
- Skipping
- Swinging
- Running and leaping
- Square walking circle walking

Lezium

- Ghati, lezium — Eight strokes
- Kadam Tal, Aage paon
- Kadam Pavitra, Pavitra Baithak
- Phirke (ardh chakra), Paon charka
- Poorna charka

Physical Education Dances

- On spot stepping movement with rhythm
- On spot stepping combined with hand movements
- On spot stepping, hand movements and bending side-wards, shifting weights
- Stepping and moving to right and left
- Stepping forward, backward, sideward with hand movements
- Movements of turning and bending body with grace and poise
- Balancing and shifting weight with hand movements
- Stepping and moving in diagonal directions
- Moving with shoulder, neck, eyes, hands and finger gestures
- Skipping and jumping with turning in different directions
- Movements and gestures to express the characteristics of birds and animals.
- Balancing in bending and twisting movements to imitate historical and mythological characters.

- Combinations of various movements to form a group dance or dance drama.
- A local dance or folk dance or tribal dance.

Gymnastics

With bodily and physiological developments among the children of different sexes, gymnastic exercises have also to be varied to suit them. In both the cases, however, skills learnt previously could be repeated with advantage. The following exercises could be added to these:

- Mat work or ground work
- Parallel Bars
- Vaulting Box
  Broad Horse
  Long Horse
- Malkhamb
  Pavitra salami, Sadhi udi, Khanda udi, Kamani udi, Do hathi udi, Bagali udi.
  Dands and Baithaks

Yogic Exercises/Practices

To build upon the Asanas already learnt in previous classes, the following Asanas could be added:

- Halasana
- Ardh-mastyendrasana
- Pashchimothasana
- Gomnkhasana (Baddha Hasta)
- Bhaddrasana
- Tolasaha
- Udaiyana Bandha
- Agrusana
- Shavasana

Combative

- *Wrestling (for boys)*
  Stance — diagonal and square
  Simple holds for "go behind"
  Counters for the above
  Primary holds
  Exercises for developing strength, stamina and agility
- *Daggar fight (Jambia) — Indian art of self-defence*
  Basic positions
  Strokes and Defence
- *Judo*
  Natural postures, self-defence postures

Breaking and disturbing balance or posture (Kuzushi)
Techniques of advance and retreat movements (Shintai)
Techniques of break-fall (Ukerni)
Methods of taking hold (Kummi-kata)

Swimming

Apart from its valuable uses in times of emergency, swimming is a pleasurable and healthful pursuit and everybody who has once learnt it does not normally let an opportunity go by.

While the skills learnt earlier could be consolidated through repetition, the following could be usefully added to the scheme of instruction at this stage.

- Propelling forward using the leg action only, using the arm action only.
- Learning of the starting and turning techniques.
- Covering longer distances — 400 to 500 metres.
- Simple jumping with feet first, entry.

55.6 Activities at the Secondary and Senior Secondary Stages

Physical Education until the Secondary stage is a part of the compulsory curriculum.

The dominant interest at this stage is to participate in competitions and every possible opportunity should be provided for the same.

Some basic principles, which could prove to be beneficial in learning and practising the skills related to different activities are listed below:

- No activity may be conducted without proper warming up.
- Rules of the games may be taught in the game situation.
- In major games, half of the time may be spent in practising the game.
- Students be exposed to competition to enable them to evaluate their performance and proficiency.

The main activities which could be focussed upon at this stage for providing facilities and offering opportunities for participation to the students are enumerated and briefly described below:

Athletics

- 200 M and 400 M run sprints
- Distance running
  (800 M to 1500 M for boys and 800 M for girls)
- Jumps
  Triple jump
  Approach run, take off and landing for hop, step and jump
  Mid-air action
  Landing

- Throws
  Hammer and discus throws
  Hold, spinning, initial stand and preliminary swing turn, delivery stance, delivery and reverse.
- Hurdles
  Warming up exercises
  Running over sticks
  Lead kg action (with and without hurdles)
  Rear leg action
  Full action
- Consolidation exercises
  Specialisation exercises in sprints, endurance runs, jumps and throws.

Major games (Some higher skills and proficiencies)

- Badminton (shuttle cock)
  Serving, Receiving, Returning — Smash, pushing/chapping float.
- Basket ball
  Passing, Shooting, Drilling, Pivoting, Faking techniques, Passing techniques, Offensive and defensive techniques.
  Positional play
  Training for endurance
- Cricket
  Batting
  Bowling
  Wicket-keeping
  Fielding
  Offensive and defensive techniques
  Practice matches
  Endurance training
- Football
  Kicking and trapping
  Heading
  Ball tackling
  Goal keeping
  Offensive and defensive techniques
  Training — pressure training and interval training
- Handball
  Passing, shooting, goal keeping, blocking, carrying, catch and run, positional play, offensive and defensive tactics
- Hockey
  Passing for speed, direction and timing, hitting, pushing, dribbling, goal shooting, goal keeping, offensive and defensive techniques
  Endurance training

- Kabaddi
  Cant, fast raiding, back-kick, feinting, jumping, movements of arms and shoulders, catching, trapping, breathing practice
- Kho Kho
  Pole drive
  Playing around the pole
  Single and double chain dodging
  Positional play
- Volley ball
  Passing — upper and under hand, both hands, one hand, jump and pass.
  Smashing — round arm and twist smashing.
  Defence — single and double block.
  Offensive and defensive techniques

Gymnastics (for Boys)

- Floor exercises — combination of different exercises to form a series evolved by the teacher
- Parallel bars
  Single march, double march, double march with bend arms.
  Bent arm swinging, forward clearing, single bar to the rear.
  Swinging forward and backward, bending arm at every forward swing.
  Lion's crawl
  Screwing to rest on both the bars.
- Horizontal bars
  Swing forward and backward
  Pull-ups
  Upward swing and dismount
  Swinging to mount and dismount
  Swinging, changing hands to face opposite direction.
- Vaulting bar
  Broad horse — shoulder spring
  Long horse — horizontal stride and between vault, cats sprints and jump off.
  Wolf vault — one leg between and the other straight
  Oblique back vault (single take-off)
  Side vault
- Malkhamb
  Sidhi, Tedhi
  Bagali darsang
  Bagali, Tedhi darsang
  Khanda darsang

Simple balance
Simple pyramids
Dand and Baithak

Gymnastics for Girls

- Mat Work
- Beam Work
- Vaulting Bar
- Long Horse
- Floor Exercises: A combination of dance movement exercises on the mat, to be evolved by the teacher.
- Surya Namaskar/Abhtang

Yogic Exercises

- Ugrasan
- Dhanurekshasan
- Singhasana
- Uttanmandukasana
- Kukutasan
- Shavasan
- Shirshasana
- Shalabhasana
- Bakasana
- Mayurasana
- Ullankurmasana
- Anuloma viloma

Combative

- Wrestling
  Simple holds
  Pinning holds
- Dagger fight (Jambia) with collapsible plastic or wooden daggers.
  Side stroke
  Chest stroke
  Stroke on any part of the body and defence
  Fight after dagger release
  Demonstration fights
- Judo: Selected standing throws (tachiwaza) of hand technique (tewasa)
  Floating drop (ukiotoshi)
  Shoulder throw (seoinase)
  Body drop (taioloshi)
  Shoulder drop (seaiotoshi)
  Shoulder wheel (kataguruma)

Belt drop (obiotoshi)
Outer winding throw (sotomakikomi)

- Selected throws (tachiwaza) of lion or waist techniques (koshiwaza)
  Floating lion or waist (Ukigoshi)
  Sweeping lion (Haraigoshi)
  Lift pull lion (Tsurikomigoshi)
  Spring waist or lion (Hanegoshi)
  Major lion (Ogoshi)
  Rear lion (Ushirogoshi)
  Lion wheel (Koshiguruma)
  Lifting hip throw (Tsurigoshi)
  Transition lion (Utsurigoshi)

Swimming

- Elementary back stroke and breast stroke
- Covering distances using leg kick only in elementary back stroke
- Treading water
- Horizontal and vertical floating
- Under water swimming
- Surface diving
- Skills in all the four strokes
- Release from victim
- Simple ways of saving using towel, rope, rubber tubes etc.

55.7 Minimum Equipment for Physical Education Programmes

- Football
  Footballs and goal posts
- Hockey
  Hockey sticks, hockey balls and goal posts and shin guards
- Basketball
  Basketball, uprights with boards and rings
- Volleyball
  Volleyballs, posts and nets
- Cricket
  Bats, cricket balls, stumps, helmets, abdominal guards and hand gloves
- Throw ball
  Throw balls, posts and nets
- Kho Kho
  Posts
- Badminton
  Posts, nets, rackets, shuttle-cocks (or balls)
- Tenicoit
  Posts, nets, rings

- Soft ball
  Bats, balls, hand gloves
- Athletics
  Shots, javelins, discus, hammer, jumping boards and uprights for jumps
- Gymnastics
  Parallel bars, horizontal bars, roman rings, vaulting horse, climbing ropes, beam, ladders and mats
- Wrestling/Boxing/Judo
  Mattresses and boxing gloves
- Other accessories
  Measuring tapes, ropes, stop watches and whistles

The above are the bare minimum requirements. Continuous upgradation and sophistication of equipment is necessary and ought to be provided for.

55.8 Stages in Acquiring Psycho-Motor Competencies

The teaching of Physical Education follows the basic principles of learning psycho-motor skills. The natural steps in the learning process, therefore, follow the taxonomy of the psychomotor domain of development.

The Taxonomy of the psychomotor domain enunciated by R.H. Dave could be cited with advantage at this point, even though it has been given earlier as part of the chapter on objectives.

Psycho-motor Domain—Dave's model

The Psycho-motor Domain concerns itself with levels of attainment on neuro-muscular coordination. As the level of coordination goes up, the action becomes more refined, speedy and automatic. In this case five broad categories have been identified as given below:

1.0 Imitation
  1.1 Impulsion
  1.2 Overt repetition
2.0 Manipulation
  2.1 Following direction
  2.2 Selection
  2.3 Fixation
3.0. Precision
  3.1 Reproduction
  3.2 Control
4.0 Articulation
  4.1 Sequence
  4.2 Harmony
5.0 Naturalisation
  5.1 Automatism
  5.2 Interiorisation

Imitation accounts for the lowest level of psycho-motor behaviour. It starts as an inner push or impulse. It is represented by "Covert inner rehearsal of the muscular system" which may be taken to be more of an action at the mental level. Soon it may grow into an overt act with capacity to repeat the performance with very rudimentary coordination.

Manipulation is the next higher level of psycho-motor behaviour. It involves following directions, selecting certain actions in preference to others and acting accordingly. It marks the beginning of the fixation of operation and the end of initial fumbling in the manipulative actions.

Precision is the third category and is reached when reproduction of operations is carried out with speed and refinement, giving the learner the ability to control (increase, decrease or modify) his action in response to requirements.

Articulation which is the fourth category, can be said to have been attained when the learner is able to handle a number of actions in unison, keeping in view their sequence and rhythm. It involves coordination in action, i.e. right sequence in right proportion of time or at the right moment.

Naturalisation is the final stage which is the equivalent of perfect habituation ranging from automatisation to routinisation. At this level the performer does not expend any psychic energy in carrying out an operation. His actions are more or less mechanical and without any conscious thinking or planning, i.e. a mere reflex action.

The classification of objectives of the psycho-motor domain may not interest in its entirety the teachers of all subjects but in such curricular areas as writing, speech, driving, crafts, etc., it will find a very wide application. Unlike Cognitive and Affective domains the transfer value of an objective in the psycho-motor domain from one context to another may not be quite so pervasive.

55.9 The Methods of Teaching Physical Education

The steps of teaching and learning the competencies related to different activities of Physical Education, follow almost the same process. The main steps of learning, in this regard, are:

1. An understanding of the fundamental rules about the particular game, sport, activity. These have to be stated by the Physical Instructor/ Teacher in the very beginning examples will be an important part of imparting knowledge about these. The examples will not just be oral or written, but more so practical.
2. Demonstration has but to be the next step. These demonstrations could be both full length and sectoral. As parts are better understood if presented as parts of the whole, it is better to give a full length complete, coherent demonstration of all the steps in the required

sequence. Parts or segments could then be taken up individually for being explained with action.

3. Guided Practice is the initial first step of learning. This has, but to start in parts. Acquiring mastery over parts will automatically ensure mastery of the whole exercise. Individual attention of the teacher will be an essential prerequisite at this stage. The teacher will have to be near the learner particularly where children could hurt themselves. Step-by-step guidance with physical support wherever will be required. This will pave the way for learning and success in different operations. Each little success, will be reassuring to the student and impart confidence to him in performing better and better in subsequent attempts. Finally, the student will become confident of performing independently and in improving upon the quality of his own performance.
3. Independent Practice will in course of time become an automatic affair. Where a student will be constantly trying for excellence. The emulation of others will be a great motivation for the student who in this process will become his own rival.
4. Performance in life situations when a student may perform individually or as part of a team in matches, tournaments, etc. will give the student an opportunity of manipulating his own competencies for meeting unfamiliar situations. These will bring forth his ingenuity, creativity and innovativeness while in some events like races where the students solo performance will be taken into account in measurable terms, in other situations, the assessments of quality will only be qualitative.
5. Guidance for further improvement will become possible only through critical monitoring of performance and remediation of shortfalls. A rapport between the teacher and the taught will be necessary for the realisation of excellence passing through the stages of ennoblement and empowerment.

   Whetting of interests and germination of desirable attitudes will be an important component of such guidance.
6. Drill is the most important pre-requisite for attaining excellence. Regularity in practice is necessary for not just improving one's level of performance, but more so, for retaining the gains made. The losses incurred are faster and greater than the gains made. One has, therefore, to be conscious about the vital facet.

56

Teaching of Music

The chapter is based on information and extracts from the prescribed syllabi of Secondary and Senior Secondary Examination of different Board of School Education in India

Music, Dance, Drama Constitute performing Acts. Very title has been documented about the transaction of curriculum in this area though its context stands elaborately deleted.

56.1 Aims of Performing Arts

The aims of performing Arts could be enunciated as under:

56.1.1. To develop a perceptive, sensitive and critical response to music, dance and drama in its historical and cultural contexts.

56.1.2. To stimulate and develop an appreciation and enjoyment f music, dance and dram through active involvement.

56.1.3. To balance the demands of disciplined skills and challenging standards n an environment of emotional, aesthetic, imaginative and creative development.

56.1.4. To develop performing skills, and so encourage a participation in the wide range of performance activities likely to be found in the school and community.

56.1.5. To develop a co-operative attitude through the organization and participation associated with music, dance and drama.

56.1.6. To provide an appropriate body of knowledge with understanding, and to develop appropriate skills as a basis for further study or leisure or both.

56.2 Components of Hindustani Vocal Music

The syllabus of the Indian School Certificate Examinations of 2009 given the following.

56.2.1. *Musical Sound*: Nad, Shruti, Swar, Saptak (Mandra, Madhya, Tar) That, Rag, Jati.

Production, Transmission and reception of Sounds. Volume, Pitch, and Timbre.

Relation between frequency and length of wire vis-à-vis wire tension.

56.2.2. *Swars*: Tivra, Komal, Shudha, Prakrat, Vikrit Vadi, Samvadi, Anuvadi, Vivadi, Varja Vakra, Grah, Ansh, Nayas Swaras.

56.2.3. *Types of Ragas*: Odava, Shadava, Sampoorna, Ashraya, Janak, Jaya, Purva, Uttar, Sandi-Prakash, Shudha, Chhayalag, Sankirana.

56.2.4. *Varna*: Sthayi, Arohi, Avrohi and Sanchari.

56.2.5. *Alankar*: Plate, Aroha, Avroha.

56.2.6. *Tal*: Mata, Sam, Tali, Khali, Bhag, Vibhag, Theka, Avartan, Dugun, Chaugun.

56.2.7. *Form of Composition*: Khyal (Vilambit, Drut Khyal), Lakshan Geet, Sargam and their division into Sthayee Antara, Sanchari, and Abhog.

Dhrupad, Dhamar and their division in to Sathai, Antra, Alap, Tan, Meend, Andolan, Gamak, Kan.

56.2.8. Sangeet:

- Two systems of Indian classical music.
- Division of twenty two shruties among seven notes.
- Formation of "That" out of Saptak.
- Classification of Ragas among "Thats".
- Relationship between Vadi Swar and time of Raga.
- Time Table of Raga.

56.2.9. Laya: Drut, Vilambit and Madhya Laya.

56.2.10. Complete Theory of the Following Ragas with:

- Special reference to Vivadi their notes, Aroh, Avroh, Pakar Vadi, Samvadi Vivadi time etc. with special emphasis on their Chalan, Ansh and Nyas Swaras.
  (i) Rag Asawari (ii) Rag Khamaj (iii) Rag Kafi (iv) Rag Bhairavi. (v) Rag Yamn (vi) Rag Bhoopali (vii) Rag Bilawal (viii) Rag Bhairawa.
- General Knowledge of the following Ragas:
  (i) Rag Bageshwari, (ii) Rag Malkauns (iii) Rag Brindabani Sarang. (iv) Rag Desh.
- Notation of the following Talas with their Thekas, Tali, Khali, Shioahag in Dugun and Chaugun Laya:
  (i) Teen Tal (ii) Dadva, (iii) Roopak (iv) Ektal (v) Chartal (vii) Tivra Tal (vii) Zhaptal (viii) Kahrva.
- Notation of note combinations, "Khyal" with Alap and Tan (Any Indian system of notation can be adopted).

- Identification of Ragas by written note-combination.
- Comparison and contrast between Ragas.
- Brief History of Indian Music.
- Contribution of the following musicians:
  (i) Tansen (ii) Amir Khusroo (iii) Vishnu Narayan Bhatkhande (iv) Vishnu Diganmbar Puluskar (v) Kesar Bai Kelkar (vi Khalifa Nathu Khan (vii) Biroo Mishra (viii) Adarang, (ix) Fiyaz Khan, (x) Bade Ghulam Ali Khan (xi) Dagar Brothers. (xii) Inayat Khan (xiii) Allaudin Khan.)
- Essay of general or topical interest on music and allied subject.

56.2.11 Practical

- Demonstration of the following Ragas by singing "Khyal" with Alap, Bol alap, Sargam and Tans:
  (i) Rag Asawari (ii) Rag Khamaj (iii) Rag Kafi (iv) Rag Bhairvi. (v) Rag Bilawal (vi) Rag Yaman (vii) Rag Bhoopali
- Swar Vistar in the following additional Ragas:
  (i) Rag Bageshwari (ii) Rag Malkauns. (iii) Rag Desh
- One "Dhrupad" Bilambit Khyal in any of the Ragas in Paragraph 1.
- Identification and production of all the twelve notes individually or jointly in small combinations with definite Matras of each.
- Use of grace notes, Khatka, Murki, Sparsh.
- Identification of all the Ragas by listening to their main Alaps.
- Singing of Ten Alankaras.
- Recitation of the following Talas in Dugun and Chaugun Laya: showing various divisions by Tali Khali and Bhari by hand beats.
- Practice of singing self-made Alaps by quick changeover from one Raga to another in a sequence of at least two Ragas.
- Practice of rendering Dugun, Chaugun by Swaras, numericals or syllables.

56.3 Instrumental Music

56.3.1

- Musical Sound: Nad, Shruti, Swar, Septak (Mandra, Madhya - Tar) That, Rag, Jati.
- Swaras: Tivra, Komal, Shuddha, Prakrat, Vikrit, Vadi, Samvadi, Vivadi, Vakra, Varjya, Grah, Ansh, Nayas.
- Types of Ragas: Odava, Shadava, Sampoorna, Ashraya, Janak, Janya.

- Varna: Sthayee, Arohi, Avrohi and Sanchari.
- Alankaras : Palte, Aroha, Avroha.
- Tal, Matra, Sam, Tali, Khali, Bhag, Vinhag, Theka, Avartan, Dugun, Chaugun.
- Sangeet:
  (i) Two main systems.
  (ii) Division of twenty-two shruties among seven notes.
  (iii) Placement of Swaras on specific shruties.
  (iv) Formation of "That" out of Saptak.
  (v) Classification of Ragas among "Thats".
  (vi) Relationship between vaid and time of Ragas.
  (vii) Time of Ragas.

56.4 Carnatic Music

56.4.1 Complete theory of the following Ragas with special reference to their notes: Aroh, Avroh, Pakad, Vadi, Samvadi, Vivadi time etc. and specific emphasis on their chalan, Ansh and Nayas Swaras.
(i) Rag Yaman
(ii) Rag Bhoopali
(iii) Rag Bhairva
(iv) Rag Bilawal

56.4.2 General Knowledge of the following additional Ragas:
(i) Brindabani Sarang.
(ii) Rag Desh

- Notation of the following Talas with their thekas, Tali, Khali, Vibhag in Dugun and Chaugun Laya:
  (i) Teen Tal (ii) Dadra (iii) Rupak (iv) Ektal.
- Notation of note combination with Gat and Alap Tora and Jhala.
- Contribution of the following Musicians:
  (i) Tansen (ii) Amir Khusroo (iii) Vishnu Narayan Bhatkhande (iv) Vishnu Digambur Puluskar (v) Kesar bai Kelkar (vi) Khalifa Nathu Khan (vii) Biroo Mishra.
- Essay of general topical interest on Music and allied subjects.
- Manner of holding the instrument while playing it.
- Explanation/Definition of the following Bols:
  (i) Akarsh (ii) Apkarsh Bols.
  Gat Razakhani - Maseet Khanj
- Description of various pats of musical instruments.
- Classification of Indian musical instruments:
  (i) Tat (ii) Vitat (iii) Sushir (iv) Avnada.

56.4.3. Raga classification in Carnatic Music. The scheme of the 72 Melakartas. The names of the 12 chakras Katapayadi Formula and its application.

56.4.4. Lakshanas of the following 24 ragas:

- Todi
- Saveri
- Chakravakam
- Bhairavi
- Anandha Bhairavi
- Karaharapriya
- Shri Ranjani
- Ritigoula
- Mukhari
- Harikambhoji
- Natakuranji
- Medaragoula
- Sahana
- Kambhoji
- Yadukulakambhoji
- Sankarabharana
- hamsadhwani
- Begada
- Atana
- Nata
- Purvakalyani
- Shanmukhapriya
- Kalyani
- Saranga

56.4.5. Manodharma Sangita and its Forms: Paddati in developing rage alpana and Kapana Svaras.

56.4.6. Dasavida gamakas (Ten gamakas).

56.4.7. The scheme of the 35 Talas. Chapu tala and its varieties. Desadi and Madyadi talas, Kriya, Anga. Laya, Gati, Matra (a detailed knowledge of two/five pranas) shadhangas.

56.4.8. Musical forms and their association. An advanced knowledge of the following musical forms:

1. Gita
2. Tana Verma
3. Padavarna
4. Kriti
4. Ragamalika
6. Padam
7. Javali
8. Tillana

56.4.9. History of Carnatic Music with special reference to the following composers and theorists including their biographies and their contributions to Carnatic Music. 10 out of 20 must be known.

- Jayadeva
- Muthuswami Dikshitar
- Purandaradas
- Syama Sastri
- Ramamatya
- Arunachalam Kavirayar
- Somanatha
- Gopalkrishna Gharat
- Narayan Tirtha
- Svati Tirunal
- Bhadrachala Ramadas
- Subbaraya Shastri
- Venkatamakhi.
- Veena Kuppayyar
- Kshetrajna
- Mysore Sadasiva Rao
- Paidala Guruthy Sastri
- Patnam Subramnya Iyar
- Tyagaraja
- Pallavi Seshayyar

56.4.10. Classification of musical instruments into stringed, wind and percussion group. A general knowledge of the structure of the vina, violin tampuro, gottuvadyam and flute. Tuning of the human voice and the compass of the concert instruments of South India.

56.4.11. Musical sound and voice. Pitch. Intensity and timbre. Sympathetic vibration. Resonance. Echoes, Musical intervals. Modal shift f tonic. (Grahabhedam).

56.5 Carnatic Music (Practical)

The practical work, is to be assessed by the teacher and a Visiting Examiner.

56.5.1 Two padas of Kshetrajan. One Ragamalika. Two Tillanas. Two Javalis and the following compositions:

- Todi — Kaddanna Variki
- Saveri — Sankari Sankuru
- Chakravakam — Etula Brotuvo
- Bhairavi — Neepadamule
- Anandha Bhairvi — Nimadi Challaga
- Karaharapriya — Pakkala Nilabadi
- Sri Ranjani — Marublka
- Harikambhoji — Entharanidays
- Natakuranji — Manasuvishaya nata
- Shana — Rama Ikananu
- Kambhoji — Koniyadina napai
- Sankarabharana — Saroja dala netri
- Hamsadhwani — Vatapi ganapatim
- Begada — Nadopasana
- Atana — Ilalo pranatharthi hara
- Purvi Kalyani — Ninnu Vina gamari
- Shanmukhapriya — Mariveredikkevaraiya rama
- Kalyani — Ninnu Vina gati
- Saranga — Neevada negana

56.5. 2. Alapana of the following ragas.

1. Todi
2. Saveri
3. Bhairavi
4. Anandha Bhairavi
5. Mohana
6. Kedaragoula
7. Kambhoji
8. Yadukula Kambhoji
9. Sankarabharana
10. Begada
11. Kalyani

56.6 Teaching of Music

The above abstracts of culled from the courses prescribed by the council for the Indian School Certificate Examinations for Secondary and Senior Secondary stages have been presented only as illustrations.

This presentation is likely to be helpful in discussing steps and strategies of curriculum transaction which is being attempted here under.

The basic understanding which should underline the local process is that it is the quality of performance that is important in music. In prerequisite therefore is a thorough background of theory in its various ramifications.

The teaching and learning and finally demonstration of musical compulsories however, follow some basic steps which are being explained below:

56.6.1. *Explanation of Theoretical Tenets*: Such a familiarization though it may look directionless in the beginning is but necessary. The student himself/herself realizes while moving on the road to learning.

The teacher has to demonstrate great balance move at a slow pace, progressing with the help of practical examples for making the desired dents on the minds f the learn ness. The practical examples help in capturing and realigning pupils attention and in generalizing the needed motivation to learn. They also genet a desire for attaining excellence and perfection in performance.

56.6.2. *Demonstration will Explanations*: On the completion of each fact theoretically the teacher will need to demonstrated the application of the theoretically principles both in local and instrumental music. The teacher will need to appealed that his demonstration is not a recital but a strategy for Teaching where the presentation will need to be liberally punctuated by explanations.

56.6.3. *Pupils Preliminary Practice*: The next natural step will be to make the students copy the teacher. These exercises will on micro elements of learning. This will need the critical individual attention of the teacher for correcting the mistakes the students are bound to commit at that stage.

The entire process at this stage will be diagnostic and corrective. The teacher may need to give repeated demonstrations of a particular teach of learning until the student is put on the right break.

56.6.4 *Trial Demonstrations by the Students*: When the learning of bits has taken place the students should be required to put that in a coherent form. These presentations by the students need not be interrupted for corrections. After the competition of the demonstration the shortfalls in performance may be pointed out to him and discussed will him for correction. The students should be asked at this stage through personal practice. However the corrected hard spots would still need to be validated through sect oral demonstrations in the presence of the teacher.

56.6.5 *Drill or Practice* is a must for attaining accuracy in performance in all fields and music is no exception. It is the liquor of drill that help a student in self evaluation of his competences, and proficiencies.

It also yields to the student a scene of personal satisfaction.

56.6.6 *Recitals*: Public recitals are a great challenge for a students of music. He has fresh to practice this recital as bash as he earn. It is desirable that he rehearses in front of the mirror perfecting his body language for the recital. So that his memory doest not fail him midway, it is describable that he keeps the ready reckoning notes in front of him. Breathing practice particularly in vocal music stands the performer in good stead as he has to present complete recitals It may also be said that while confidence is a pre-requisites of public recilates. They also yield confidence for better public performances.

56.7 Instrumental Music

The basic theoretical knowledge of music in both vocal and instrumental music are basically the scene. Instead of this voice, the musical instruments are required to produce the desired sounds.

In is therefore, necessaries for the students to get acquainted with various musical instruments and the part they earn play in producing music.

Musical instruments are basically played in three main selections (a) as an accompaniment for supporting vocal music (b) as parts of orchestra and (c) in solo performances. For preparing participants for any these situations the earner teaching learning strategies are required. It is only when the basic skills have been acquired that working in consonance with the vocal musician or the that instruments of the orchestra has to be practiced.

56.7.1 ***Steps in Teaching Instrumental Music***

The basic steps of teaching and learning instrumental music have some similarities and some differences with vocal music. Those related to instrumental music are explained below.

- *Acquiring knowledge about the instruments, one desires* to learn to play on. Particular reference in this regard has to set it to a working situation for producing the desired music. The student has also to be told about the common faults that develop in the instruments and the method of rectifying them. The testing of the instrument, about its operational fitness is another competency that a student needs to acquire.

  The above may appear in under he but is nevertheless important.
- *Assuming the Correct Posture for Handling the Instruments*: The students has try to be optimal in his performance and for this appropriate posture is necessary. As such postures have to be maintained for long durations adequate preparation and practice is necessary which the student may undertake to acquire.
- *Appropriate handling of the instruments* for obtaining optimum output of optimum quality is necessary. The teacher will guide the students in this regard. Musical instruments have also to be often transported and needed precautions about their packing and handling

in transit are also required to be taken so as to save them from damage.

- *Learning to produce the desired musical sounds* through the instrument has to be learnt next. In this teaching and learning assume alternate sequence. The teacher demonstrates first and the student then tries to perform. Learning is bit by bit in an unrelated manner in the beginning. The process follows the "easy to difficult" policy.
- *Strides by the Student in Copying the Teacher and Corrections by the Teacher*: will go on, side by side, when the teacher is satisfied that the students has learned something he should asks the students to demonstrate his skills.
- *Presentation of Micro Skills by the Students*: The student should be allowed to make a full presentation of the skill acquired. He should not be stopped mid-way for making a correction. The shortfalls should be discussed with the student when the presentation is over. The student may than be a asked to correct the shortfall, through personal practice and present himself to the teacher for gathering a validation of his harming acquired the needed skill.
- *Demonstration of a Cluster of Competences*: When the teacher is satisfied that the student has acquired, some micro level competences he could ask the students to make a *demonstration of a meaningful cluster of competences* in one go. This will give practice to the students in making longer presentations establishing unity and coherence in his presentation which may consist of a number of smarter elements.
- *Observation of full recitals*: This is a desirable learning experience and the students could be taken to watch them. The quality of the recitals by masters will impart motivation to the students to attain excellence themselves.
- *Full Scale Presentation by the Student*. This should be done by the students after through preparation and should be watched by others teacher who should give their own observations about the quality of presentation. The teacher could discuss the presentation with the students for helping him improve further.

56.8 Conclusion

All performing arts cannot be learnt from books alone. A one to one interaction with the teacher is necessary pre-requisite for learning. Practice is also a key to perfection.

57

Methods of Teaching at the Senior Secondary Stage

The Methods of Teaching in Senior Secondary classes by and large follow the same instructional strategies as in Secondary classes. The conventional and the unconventional methods described earlier hold good here as well. The differences occur only because of the more technical nature of content.

The Senior Secondary Stage consists of classes XI and XII, but the more important thing about it is the age group of 16+ to 18+ that it caters to. This age group is marked by some distinct personality characteristics like an urge for emotional independence, an aspiration for economic independence, a motivation for assuming a responsible social and civic role and a value based and an ethical interpretation of facts, phenomenon and behaviour of self and others besides a desire for a status in the adult world. They thus start thinking more about the future than about the present.

Educational programmes even otherwise are always future oriented and future for this stage of life being the world of work, they tend to be tailored to being informal vocational preparation for laying down an academic foundation for it.

It is in this context that the curriculum at the Senior Secondary Stage marks the beginning of the subjects of study more or less as 'disciplines'. This is a major departure from the integrative approach in the content of courses pursued until the secondary stage to a more or less disciplinary one. However, the relationship of the subjects of study with other subjects of the curriculum and with life gets further strengthened and the applications of the subjects emerge more strongly than before.

The Two Distinct Streams

At the senior secondary stage two distinct streams are envisaged.

The Academic Stream

The Vocational Stream

Both the stream would have foundation and elective courses in the proportion of 40 per cent and 60 per cent of the total time provided to them respectively. As one of the measures for tackling the problem of unemployment at least to some extent the target is to attract at least 25 per cent of the students to the vocational stream. There could, however, be variations in these proportions, but the genesis still remains.

Vocational courses are also proposed to be increasingly offered through the open schooling system to cater to the needs of the fully employed and the semi-employed, to the semi-skilled workers as also for reaching out to the rural areas.

57.1 National Curriculum Framework 2000

The Academic Stream

The structure of courses at the Academic stream as per the National Curriculum Framework 2000 is conceived as under:

Foundation Courses

- Language and Literature
- Work Education
- Health Physical Education, Games and Sports

Elective Courses

Three of the available courses have to be offered. Apart from the traditional courses some new courses with emergent potentials are proposed to be added like:

- Computer Science
- Bio technology
- Genomics

The courses in new specialisations will be evolved in collaboration with the professionals in the respective fields.

The Vocational Stream

The courses of the vocational stream will be diversified and skill oriented for being effective stepping stones for entering specialised vocational courses or for entering the world of work.

The courses of the Vocational Stream will consists of

- Language
- General Foundation Courses
- Health and Physical Education
- Vocational Electives

The language course could consist of elements of language (functional grammar, usages and operational vocabulary) with focus on two way communication.

The general foundation course in the vocational stream could besides general studies, consist of items like entrepreneurship development environmental issues, rural development and information and communication technology.

Health and Physical Education Programmes are envisaged to consist of 'keeping fit' programmes matching the strenuous physical activities of the different vocations. They will focus on containing physical strain, maintenance of proper postures for effective execution of work, offering relaxation etc. etc.

Vocational Electives

These will be identified and developed in collaboration with the experts in the respective fields. A large variety of the courses are proposed to be offered to cater to:

- local needs;
- wage employment and self-employment opportunities;
- geographical location; and
- interests of students.

A practical and functional orientation to these courses could be given by not only identifying them but also developing them in collaboration with the experts in the given fields.

57.2 National Curriculum Framework 2005

Higher Secondary School

The status of the academic and vocational streams at the higher secondary stage needs to be reviewed in view of the continued preoccupation with and influence of the board and entrance examinations, and in view of the continued privilege given to the so-called academic stream and the failure of the vocational stream to take off. During this period of two years students make choices based on their interests, aptitudes and needs regarding their future life.

The possibilities of choosing optional courses of study for exploring and understanding different areas of knowledge, both in relation to one's interest and one's future career, is integral to this stage. Exploring disciplines and approaching problems and issues from rich interdisciplinary perspectives are possible at this stage. There is a need to allow for such investigations to take place between and outside the 'subjects' chosen for study.

Most boards of study offer a variety of subject areas in addition to the compulsory language courses. There is a concern about the formal or informal restrictions that operate to narrow the choice of subjects or study for students. Several boards restrict the combinations in the form of 'the science stream', 'the arts stream' and 'the commerce stream'. The CBSE does not restrict the possibility of combinations that students can choose, but in view of the increasing popularity of some combinations of subjects of study, and also because of a perception of status of subjects in relation to each other, many such options are now foreclosed to students. Further, universities also need to review their admission criteria as they currently restrict admission based on the kinds and combinations of courses studied at the +2 stage. As a consequence, many significant and meaningful combinations of study, such as, for example, Physics, Mathematics and Philosophy, or Literature, Biology and History, are closed to students.

Recent trends of schools tailoring their classes to medical and engineering courses have led to an artificial restriction on the courses they offer in school, arguably on grounds of popularity and timetabling. In many parts of the country, students who want to study the arts and liberal subjects are left with very few options. Schools also discourage students from opting for unconventional combinations, often on account of timetabling considerations. We believe it is essential to keep all options open for students. In case there are not enough students in a school opting for a particular subject, schools could consider working out arrangements with other schools in the neighbourhood so that they could employ a resource teacher together. Such resource teachers could also be employed at the block level to teach such special subjects that would not otherwise be available in a school. School boards may also consider a more active role in promoting subjects and streams of study.

The courses offered at the +2 stage need to be alive to recent and current developments in the disciplines, as new knowledge areas are carved out, disciplinary boundaries shift and multidisciplinary studies develop. To allow students to engage with areas of study that are growing in importance within the disciplines and fields, courses could also be designed to offer optional modules, rather than trying to cover everything and packing courses with too much information. For example, History could have an optional module to study either Archaeology or World History; similarly, Physics could offer the options of Astronomy, Space Science and Rocketry etc.

Under pressure to 'cover' vast syllabi, many important aspects of learning such as practicals and field trips, and ways of learning such as reference work, project work and presentations, are not fully utilised, to the detriment of overall learning. Well-equipped laboratories and libraries, and access to computers, are essential, and all efforts must be made to ensure that schools and junior colleges are well equipped with such resources.

The vocational stream originally was meant to address the needs of those who would enter the work force earlier than those who would enter the professions via the traditional academic streams, or those who would pursue study and research. We recommend infusing productive work as a pedagogic medium for knowledge acquisition, developing values and multiple skill formation at all stages of education, including the +2 stage.

Given the developmental nature of this stage, guidance and counselling by trained professionals must be made available to children. Interventions to enhance self/career awareness, career exploration and planning are also essential. Besides, this stage coincides with adolescence, a period in an individual's life that is marked by personal, social and emotional crises created due to the demands of adjustment required in family, peer group and school situations. The provision of these services in schools would help create the support system required to cope with increasing academic and social pressures.

57.3 Instructional Strategies at the Senior Secondary Stage

The teaching learning strategies at the senior secondary stage will witness a variety of departures from the practices followed in the past. Some of the significant ones among these will be:

- From teacher dispensed knowledge to self-acquired one through exploration/experimentation and self-learning.
- From textbooks to reference books, library research and surveys.
- From theory to practice.
- From facts and principles to their application.
- From classroom/laboratory oriented learning to environment-based learning.
- From passive learning to activity based learning.
- From acceptance of conclusions drawn by others to self-derived and validated inferences.
- From knowledge-based to skill and vocation-based learning.
- From course completion as the end, to course completion as the beginning of reinforcement through apprenticeship.
- From Individual learning to participatory group team learning.

These, in effect, are very far reaching changes with far reaching implications likely to influence philosophical and attitudinal modifications imparting new meaning to education.

So far as the techniques and methods of teaching are concerned, a judicious choice from among the conventional and the unconventional ones described earlier could be made. In this choice not just the teachers but the students could play an active role.

References

Sources Tapped for Ideas and Extracts

B. Ghosh and Others-Handbook for Primary School Teachers of Social Studies, National Council of Educational Research and Training, New Delhi, 1966 (Methods of Teaching, Social Studies).

B.F. Skinner-The Science of Learning and the Art of Teaching, D. Van Nostraned Company, New York, 1962 (Methods of Teaching and Programmed Learning).

Ball, S. (1985). 'Participant observation with pupils'. In R. Burgess (ed.) *Strategies of Educational Research: Qualitative Methods,* Lewes: Falmer Press.

Barnes, D. (1976). *From Communication to Curriculum,* Harmondsworth: Penguin.

Berliner, D.C. (1987). 'Ways of thinking about students and classrooms by more and less experienced teachers'. In J. Calderhead (ed.) *Exploring Teachers' Thinking,* London: Cassell.

Biggs, J. (1987). 'Student approaches to learning and studying', *British Journal of Educational Psychology,* 63, 1-19.

Bloom, B.S. (1977). *Human Characteristics and School Learning,* New York: McGraw-Hill.

Brophy, J. and Good, T. (1986). 'Teacher behaviour and pupil achievement'. In M. Wittrock (ed.) *Handbook of Research on Teaching,* 3rd edn., London: Macmillan.

Brown, S. and McIntyre, D. (1993). *Making Sense of Teaching,* Buckingham: Open University Press.

Carter, K. (1990). 'Tachers' knowledge and learning to teach'. In W.R. Houston (ed.) *Handbook of Research on Teacher Education,* New York: Macmillan.

Charles E. Skinner-Educational Psychology, Prentice Hall of India Pvt. Ltd., New Delhi, 1970 (Passage to Learning).

Charles E. Skinner-Essentials of Educational Psychology, Asia Publishing House, Bombay, 1960 (Passage to Learning).

Clandinin, J. (1986). *Classroom Practice: Teachers' Images in Action,* London: Falmer Press.

Collicott, S. (1990). 'Who is the national history curriculum for?'. *Teaching History,* October, 8-12.

Cooper, P. (1993c). 'Learning from the pupil perspective', *British Journal of Special Education,* 20, 4.

Cooper, P. and McIntyre, D. (1993). 'Commonality in teachers' and pupils' perceptions of effective classroom learning', *British Journal of Educational Psychology,* 63, 381-99.

Cooper, P. and McIntyre, D. (1995). 'The importance of power sharing in classrooms'. In M. Hughes (ed.) *Teaching and Learning in Changing Times,* Oxford: Blackwell.

E.A. Pires and Others-Handbook of Educational Excursions, Alumni Association, Central Institute of Education, Delhi, 1958 (Techniques of Teaching).

E.L. Thorndike-The Psychology of Learning, Bureau of Publications, Teachers, College Columbia University, New York, 1913 (Passage to Learning).

Edgar Dale-Audio Visual Methods in Teaching, Dryden Press, Holt Rinehart and Winston Inc., New York, 1969. (Conventional methods of Teaching).

Elbaz, F. (1981). 'Teachers' practical knowledge, report of a case study', *Curriculum Inquiry,* 11(1), 73-7.

H.S. Singha and Others-Preparation, Production and Evaluation of Textbooks in Mathematics, National Council of Educational Research and Training, New Delhi, 1973 (Methods of Teaching Mathematics).

H.S. Srivastava and Others-An Approach to Evaluation in Environmental Studies, National Council of Educational Research and Training, New Delhi, 1980 (Methods of Teaching Environmental Studies).

H.S. Srivastava-Challenges in Educational Evaluation, Vikas Publishing House, New Delhi, 1999.

H.S. Srivastava-Instructional Objectives of School Subjects, National Council of Educational Research and Training, New Delhi, 1989 (Methods of Teaching different subjects).

H.S. Srivastava-Manual for Schools, S. Chand & Company, New Delhi, 2002.

J.P. Guilford-General Psychology, D. Van Nostrand Company Inc., Princeton, New Jersey, 1960 (Passage to Learning).

James R. Killian Jr. and Others-Physics, Physical Science Study Committee, USA, Reprinted by National Council of Educational Research and Training, New Delhi (Third Indian Edition), 1967 (Concept and Content of Physics).

K.G. Rastogi and Others-Preparation and Evaluation of Textbooks in Mother Tongue, National Council of Educational Research and Training, New Delhi, 1970 (Methods of Teaching Mother Tongue).

K.G. Saiyidain and Others-The Committee on Improvement of Art Education in our schools, National Council of Education Research and Training, New Delhi, 1967 (Methods of Teaching Art).

K.P. Surendranath and Others-Nation and the School, National Council of Educational Research and Training, New Delhi, 1980 (Curriculum construction).

Kamala Menon-A Handbook of Evaluation in Geography, National Council of Educational Research and Training, New Delhi, 1990 (Methods of Teaching Geography).

Logan, T. (1984). 'Learning through interviewing'. In J. Schostak and T. Logan (eds.) *Pupil Experience*, London: Croom Helm.

M. Pia and M. Waples-Values (Personal, Neighbourly and Community)-All India Association of Catholic Schools, New Delhi, 1978 (Unconventional Approachs to Teaching and Learning).

M.C. Wittrock (ed.) *Handbook of Research on Teaching*, 3rd edn., London: Macmillan.

McArthur, T. (1993). 'Language used as a loaded gun', *Guardian Education*, 20 April, 3.

N.L. Bossing-Progressive Methods of Teaching in Secondary Schools, Houghton Miffin Co., New York, 1964 (Conventional and Unconventional methods of Teaching).

National Curriculum Frameworks-National Council of Educational Research and Training, New Delhi (1965, 1988, 2000 and 2005).

Nisbett, R. and Wilson, T. (1977). 'Telling more than we can know: verbal reports as data', *Psychological Review*, 84(3), 231-59.

Prabhakar Singh and Others-Preparation and Evaluation of Textbooks in Geography, National Council of Educational Research and Training, New Delhi, 1972 (Methods of Teaching Geography).

Pritam Singh and Others-Preparation and Evaluation of Textbooks in Biology, National Council of Educational Research and Training, New Delhi, 1972 (Methods of Teaching Biology).

Pritam Singh and Others-Preparation and Evaluation of Textbooks in General Science, National Council of Educational Research and Training, New Delhi, 1973 (Methods of Teaching Science Subjects).

R.N. Rai and Others-Teachers Handbook of Activities in General Science (Vols. I, II & III) National Council of Educational Research and Training, New Delhi, 1969 (Methods of Teaching Environmental Studies).

Rajammal P. Devadas-Methods of Teaching Home Science, National Council of Educational Research and Training, New Delhi, 1970 (The Passage to Learning and Teaching-Learning Techniques).

Rajammal P. Devadas-Teaching Home Science in Secondary Schools, All India Council for Secondary Education, New Delhi, 1958 (Methods of Teaching Home Science).

Robert J. Havighurst-Human Development and Education, Longmans, Greens, New York, 1953 (Dynamics of Student Groups).

Robert L. Ebel (Ed.)-Encyclopaedia of Educational Research, The MacMillan, London, (1969) (Curriculum the Rationale of Teaching).

Robert W. Richey-Planning for Teaching. McGraw Hill Book Co. Inc., New York, 1958 (Objective-based Teaching).

Rogers, C. (1980). *A Way of Being*, Boston: Houghton Mifflin.

S.H. Khan and Others-Preparation and Evaluation of Textbooks in History, National Council of Educational Research and Training, New Delhi, 1972 (Methods of Teaching History).

S.N. Saha and Others-Preparation and Evaluation of Textbooks in English, National Council of Educational Research and Training, New Delhi, 1970 (Methods of Teaching English/Second Language).

Schon, D.A. (1983). *The Reflective Practitioner*, London: Temple Smith.

Shavelson, R., Webb, N. and Burstein, L. (1986). 'Measurement of teaching'. In M. Wittrock (ed.) *Handbook of Research on Teaching*, London: Macmillan.

Simpson, M. (1989). *A Study of Differentiation and Learning in Schools*, Aberdeen: Northern College.

Slavin, R.E. (1983). *Co-operative Learning*, New York: Longman.

T.S. Mehta and Others-Teaching of History in Secondary Schools, National Council of Educational Research and Training, New Delhi, 1970 (Methods of Teaching Social Studies).

T.S. Mehta and Others-Teaching Social Studies, National Council of Educational Research and Training, New Delhi, 1969 (Methods of Teaching Social Studies).

Theodore Edgar-Creative Thinking, John Wiley and Sons, New York, 1956 (Conventional and unconventional Teaching Techniques).

Thomas E. Clayton-Teaching and Learning-A Psychological Perspective, Prentice Hall Inc., Englewood Cliffs, N.J., 1965 (Passage to Learning).

Thomas N. Risk-Principles and Practices of Teaching in Secondary Schools, American Book Company, 1965 (Methods of Teaching different subjects).

Wang, M. and Walberg, H. (1983). 'Evaluating educational programmes', *Educational Evaluation and Policy Analysis*, 5, 347-66.

Wang, M.C. and Palincsar, A.S. (1989). 'Teaching students to assume an active role in their learning'. In M.G. Reynolds (ed.) *Knowledge Base for the Beginning Teacher*, Oxford: Pergamon.

Weinstein, R. (1986). 'Students' perceptions of schooling', *Elementary School Journal*, 83(4), 297-312.

William Heard Kilpatrick-Philosophy of Education, The MacMillan, New York, 1957 (Some conventional Teaching Techniques).

Wittrock, M.C. (1986). 'Students thought processes'. In M.C. Wittrock (ed.) *Handbook of Research on Teaching*, 3rd edn., London: Macmillan.

Woods, P. (1990). *The Happiest Days? How Pupils Cope with School*, London: Falmer Press.

Index